RESEARCH IN

# READING
# RECOVERY

VOLUME TWO

# RESEARCH IN

# READING RECOVERY

## VOLUME TWO

EDITED BY

### Salli Forbes & Connie Briggs

FOREWORD BY

#### P. David Pearson

AFTERWORD BY

#### Marie Clay

Reading Recovery®

**HEINEMANN**
Portsmouth, NH

Heinemann
A division of Reed Elsevier Inc.
361 Hanover Street
Portsmouth, NH 03801-3912
www.heinemann.com

*Offices and agents throughout the world*

This book includes articles originally published in *Literacy Teaching and Learning: An International Journal of Early Reading and Writing*™ (1998–2003), the journal of the Reading Recovery Council of North America, and reprinted with permission.

The editors and publisher wish to thank those who have generously given permission to reprint borrowed material:

"It Gets Dark" by Laura Ranger is reprinted by permission of the poet, care of Random House New Zealand Ltd.

**Library of Congress Cataloging-in-Publication Data**
Research in reading recovery / edited by Salli Forbes and Connie Briggs ; foreword by P. David Pearson.
    Includes bibliographical references.

    ISBN 0-325-00553-2 (alk. paper)—Volume 2
    1. Reading disability. 2. Reading (Primary). 3. Language arts (Primary).
4. Learning disabled children—Education.  I. Forbes, Salli. II. Briggs, Connie.
LB1050.5.R473 1997                                                          97–139899

Editor:  *Leigh Peake*
Production:  *Lynne Reed*
Cover design:  *Darci Mehall, Aureo Design*
Typesetter:  *Drawing Board Studios*
Manufacturing:  *Steve Bernier*

Printed in the United States of America on acid-free paper
07   06   05   04   03   VP   1   2   3   4   5

*The proceeds of the sale of this book are dedicated to RRCNA so that the Council can continue to support the important work of Reading Recovery professionals throughout North America.*

—Connie Briggs
—Salli Forbes

# Contents

# Foreword

P. David Pearson

When Salli Forbes and Connie Briggs invited me to write a foreword for volume 2 of *Research in Reading Recovery*, I gladly accepted. I did so because I have been a longtime supporter of Reading Recovery. I like its philosophy of championing prevention over remediation. I agree with the consistently reflective stance it takes toward teacher preparation. I appreciate its attention to hard-nosed, rigorous evaluation. And I think it has had a significant influence on how we teach reading in North America.

Salli Forbes and Connie Briggs have assembled a wide-ranging volume of research related to Reading Recovery, all of it drawn from the annals of Reading Recovery's auspicious journal, *Literacy Teaching and Learning*. The articles run from hard-nosed experimental-control evaluations of Reading Recovery (the pieces by Ashdown and Simic, Askew et al., Escamilla et al., Neal and Kelley, and Quay et al.) to a rich case study of a single child and teacher (Fullerton) to explorations of writing (Askew and Fraser, Boocock et al.) to Lyons's overarching review of a "decade of data" to Lyons's (again) fascinating foray into the vortex of emotion and cognition to an examination of the impact of Reading Recovery on home literacy practices (Marvin and Gaffney) to a think piece on how Reading Recovery might affect student aspirations (Kline and Quaglia) to an elaborate analysis of the role of teacher leaders in Reading Recovery (Bussell) and finally to an analysis of one of Reading Recovery's serendipitous side benefits, the incidental acquisition of phonemic awareness (Stahl et al.). The range of pieces is a story in its own right; it says to us that Reading Recovery has become a mature curricular phenomenon. It is attracting spin-offs, connections with other literatures and research traditions, and nuanced internal analyses of its nature and consequences. A trio of pieces—the Lyons piece on emotion, the Stahl et al. piece on phonemic awareness, and the Kline and Quaglia piece on aspirations—are the clearest examples of what might be labeled "creeping constructs"—the application of constructs from other fields to Reading Recovery. When a field of inquiry is in its infancy, scholars ask basic questions: what is it? does it work? how does it work? As a field matures, the questions take on more and more qualifications and contextual nuance. The range of studies represented in this volume suggests that contextual nuance is beginning to infiltrate the research on Reading Recovery.

I cannot preview all of the pieces in the volume, but I can highlight a few that are either representative of a broader collection or so unique that they deserve special mention. First, the "decade of data" piece by Lyons is a must-read because it takes on the most fundamental questions about Reading Recovery as a policy tool head on— does it work? do kids who get it really keep up with their age mates? is it cost effective? do training and professional development have to be so extensive and intensive? Carol answers all of these questions in the affirmative and is able to marshal substantial evidence for each of those yeses. Second, at the other extreme, I would recommend Susan Fullerton's case study of Edward, a particularly truculent student in one of her cohorts. Fullerton's piece is a testament to patience, persistence, and above all flexibility in conducting the situated inquiry one needs in order to find a way to reach even the most fractious of clients. In the end, it was as much motivation as cognition that pointed the way for Fullerton to a pathway that enabled Edward to convince himself that he really could read. Third, I found Jean Bussell's ambitious analysis of the infrastructure of the job of being a teacher leader and the resulting models of adapting to the change and innovation that becoming a teacher leader requires to be informative, fascinating, and in the end absolutely daunting. All I could think of is a hypothetical advertisement: "Wanted. Reading Recovery Teacher Leader. Only superheroes need apply!" I should think that other trainers of teacher leaders would find this piece especially helpful.

Let me also mention the experimental pieces in this volume (the pieces by Ashdown and Simic, Askew et al., Escamilla et al., Neal and Kelley, and Quay et al.). What has emerged over time in the experimental and quasi-experimental research on Reading Recovery is the dual comparison group model; the pattern is to compare students who have been randomly assigned to Reading Recovery with two groups: (a) those who could have been in the Reading Recovery group but were not able to get in due to a lack of resources and (b) to a second group of garden variety first graders who represent what we can expect first graders to do when left to the devices of everyday classroom instruction. The first comparison group helps to answer the question, does Reading Recovery help those students who need it most? The second comparison group provides a basis for answering the question, can Reading Recovery graduates really keep up with their normally progressing peers once they have been through the entire intervention? By the way, the consistent answer to both of these questions, both in the studies reported in this volume and in the broader body of research summarized by Lyons, is yes! And the answer is yes for everyday English speakers, for English language learners who speak English well enough to participate in Reading Recovery in English, and for ELLs who are learning to read in Spanish (in the DLL or Descubriendo la Lectura). The question not answered using the dual comparison group model but addressed by Wasik and Slavin (1994) and Pinnell et al. (1994) is, does Reading Recovery work better than other approaches to early intervention?

I also want to make a couple of other points about Reading Recovery that are not addressed in the volume. These points clearly reflect my own "reading" of the impact of Reading Recovery over its nearly two-decade existence in North America. When I compare the practices that Reading Recovery employs in working with youngsters most at risk for failure to learn to read with practices that have been adopted as a part of the "conventional wisdom" in teaching reading, I see lots of crossover. I mention a few of the more salient:

*Reading Recovery has helped us adopt a completely different model of compensatory education.* Before Reading Recovery came on the scene in 1984, remediation was our dominant model of compensatory education. In fact, by law, we often had to wait until third grade to begin remedial programs because students had to be at least two years behind grade-level expectations. But Reading Recovery ushered in a wave of preventative intervention in the form of tutoring and small-group programs designed to provide the extra scaffolding and feedback that allows students to succeed when, left to cope in large classes on their own, they would otherwise fail. In fact, some of the programs that rode in on the coattails of Reading Recovery criticize it as too expensive in training or delivery or too soft in skill delivery, but few of them would have achieved their current status had not Reading Recovery convinced the education profession that spending resources on prevention was preferable to spending them on expensive and ineffective remedial programs. As a nation we now invest much more heavily in a range of early interventions, including, but by no means limited to, Reading Recovery.

*Reading Recovery portrayed an apprenticeship model of instruction more vividly than anything else we have witnessed.* Reading is a complex task, and we help students deal with complex tasks in one of two ways—either by breaking them down into constituent parts and then mastering each part *or* by providing guided assistance (scaffolding) as we ask students to do something that is just a little too hard for them to do alone. We used the componential approach for several decades, perhaps centuries. In the 1970s we discovered Vygotsky and the zone of proximal development, and now we are much more inclined to view our role as teachers as providing scaffolding to apprentices who are working their way toward expertise. But until Reading Recovery came along, we had only the vaguest sense of what it meant to work in this zone of proximal development and how scaffolding would play itself out in interaction with real students. Reading Recovery unpacked this construct and portrayed it so concretely that teachers could "see" what it looked like. I am not claiming that Marie Clay used Vygotsky as any sort of guiding theoretical light (my own reading of her work is that it is much more grounded in the Piagetian tradition of child development, along with the views of literacy development emanating from Australia and New Zealand in the 1970s), but I do think that Reading Recovery gave us a clear model of what a reading apprenticeship could look like. This essence of the model is captured in the term coined by Marie Clay to characterize the earliest stages of reading development— emergent literacy: literacy is not something you "get ready" for, it is something that "happens" when you, with a little help from your friends, set eye and pen to paper.

*Reading Recovery has provided us with a new model of professional development.* The reading apprenticeship so vividly enacted in the teacher-student dyad also plays out in the professional training model of Reading Recovery, except that it is the "community of scholars," not the dyad, that forms the basis of the apprenticeship in Reading Recovery training. Reading Recovery takes teaching out of the closet (or if you prefer another metaphor, Reading Recovery opens the doors to classrooms closed for too many decades) and makes it a collegial enterprise in which teachers learn to share publicly their practices—warts, blemishes, and all—en route to professional improvement. The dread "behind the glass" activity in which peers hold an ongoing, dynamic discussion of a teaching encounter with a student, coupled with the subsequent debriefing with the teacher in the spotlight, forms the basis of the most powerful approach to improving teaching that I know of. When teachers come together and make their teaching—and their thinking about their teaching—a matter of public discourse, powerful things can happen. This training model shows us that the apprenticeship model works as well for adults as it does for children. It demonstrates just how much we have to learn from one another, and it makes the construct of a community of learners very palpable.

*Reading Recovery helped us rediscover fluency.* Once an explicit goal of instruction, at least until the 1970s or 1980s, fluency vanished for a couple of decades. It has now clearly reemerged as a central goal of early reading instruction. And Reading Recovery, by insisting on regular running records to track fluency and by encouraging daily reading, helped us rediscover the importance of encouraging students regularly to read texts that are well within their comfort range. The regular reading of comfortable (what we call independent-level) texts provides students with an all-important opportunity—to consolidate the learning that we have promoted in our teaching. One important caveat: fluency in Reading Recovery is not about achieving a certain words-correct-per-minute rate (a current goal in so many reading programs developed in the wake of the Reading Excellence Act or Reading First[1]), but about gaining enough control over text to be able to read it with some expression and personal comfort.

*Reading Recovery helped us embrace monitoring for sense-making.* A core concept in Reading Recovery is that what students read should make sense to them. A core feedback strategy for teachers is to encourage students to ask themselves if what they have read makes sense—and if it doesn't, to go back and reconsider what was read. That principle that sense-making is the hallmark of good reading is a strong part of today's classroom enactments of shared and guided reading. Shared and guided reading are the backbone of a host of programs, both commercial and homegrown. I doubt that the principle of monitoring for meaning would be so widespread had not Reading Recovery made it a household word.

There are others, almost as important, that I could add to the list, but I will stop there lest I violate all the conventions of writing a foreword. Let me just say that Connie Briggs and Salli Forbes have assembled an informative array of readings for you and that there is much to learn from a careful examination of these important additions to the Reading Recovery literature. As I suggested at the outset, the range depicted in this volume reveals the maturity of this body of work—the depth, the nuance, the intersection with other literatures. May you enjoy all three of these attributes as you acquire some very important knowledge about one of our field's most important professional contributions—Reading Recovery.

---

[1] The Reading Excellence Act was the brainchild of the Clinton Administration (second term), and Reading First is the reading portion of Bush's reauthorization of Title I, dubbed the No Child Left Behind Act.

# Acknowledgments

This book is a collection of reprints of research articles about Reading Recovery from past issues of *Literacy Teaching and Learning,* the journal of the Reading Recovery Council of North America (RRNCA). It includes articles from the 1998–2002 issues of the journal. It is a sequel to the first volume of *Research in Reading Recovery* edited by Stanley L. Swartz and Adria E. Klein.

The research collected in this volume represents varied issues that are of importance to Reading Recovery and public school professionals as they look at program effectiveness and benefits to children who have difficulty with literacy learning. We would like to thank all of the contributing authors for their dedication in conducting scholarly research that focuses on early literacy intervention and discusses both theory and practice.

It is important to recognize colleagues who contribute to *Literacy Teaching and Learning* in the form of editorial support. Their diligence reflects the high quality of the journal. We want to thank Emily Rodgers, who currently serves as managing editor, and Maribeth Cassidy Schmitt, who served as managing editor from 1998–2001. We also want to acknowledge the current contributing editors: Nancy Anderson, Jane Ashdown, Billie Askew, Kathryn Au, James F. Baumann, Connie Bridge, Janet Bufalino, Jeanne H. Chaney, James W. Cunningham, Maria Luiza Dantas, Diane Deford, Zhihiu Fang, Irene Fountas, Dianne Frasier, Penny Freppon, Susan K. Fullerton, Linda Gambrell, Sharan Gibson, Marjorie Y. Lipson, Carol Lyons, Sarah Mahurt, Michael Meioth, Sam Miller, Paula Moore, Judith Neal, Susan L. Nierstheimer, Joanne Noble, John O'Flahavan, Lynn Paarmann, Gay Su Pinnell, Victoria Purcell-Gates, Taffy E. Raphael, Adrian Rodgers, Laura Roehler, Barbara Schubert, Robert Schwartz, Christopher Gordon, Francisco X. Gomez, Angela Hobsbaum, Carol J. Hopkins, Mary Jett, Peter Johnston, Noel K. Jones, George Kamberelis, Michael Kamil, Elizabeth L. Kaye, Patricia R. Kelly, Blair Koefoed, Diane Lapp, Lawrence Sipe, Lee Skandalaris, M. Trika Smith-Burke, Katherine Dougherty Stahl, Steven Stahl, Susan Stoya, Dorothy S. Strickland, B. Joyce Wiencek, Peter Winograd, Garreth Zalud, and Dorothy Zielke.

We appreciate the support of Leigh Peake, the Heinemann Editorial Director, for the publication of the book. She streamlined the process and made this a pleasurable project on which to work. Her willingness to publish this volume is a great contribution to Reading Recovery professionals worldwide.

Special thanks goes to P. David Pearson for writing the Foreword and to Marie M. Clay for writing the Afterword. Their contributions help us to see what research territory we have traversed and where we need to journey next.

We also want to thank the members of our families and friends for their support and understanding when our work far exceeds the time allotted. The understanding they have shown for the importance of this publication is very much appreciated.

Finally, we want to acknowledge the continued support for this project from Jean Bussell, Executive Director of RRCNA, and Marsha Studebaker, Director of Communications. The expertise and professionalism they contribute are always appreciated. In addition, the RRCNA Publications Committee provided the vision for this second volume of research on Reading Recovery. The members of the committee are

| | |
|---|---|
| Connie Briggs, Chair | Diane Grant |
| Doreen Blackburn | Geraldine Haggard |
| Susan Burroughs-Lange | Eva Konstantellou |
| Diane DeFord | Mary K. Lose |
| Mary Anne Doyle | Judith Neal |
| Rose Mary Estice | Betty Newkirk |
| Salli Forbes | Emily M. Rodgers |
| Dianne Frasier | Maribeth Schmitt |
| Susan Fullerton | James R. Schnug |
| Diana L. Geiser | Robert M. Schwartz |

Special recognition must be given to Maribeth Cassidy Schmidt who served as managing editor of the journal *Literacy Teaching and Learning* during the time that most of the articles in this volume were published. We also recognize the contributions made by Emily Rodgers, the current managing editor.

# RESEARCH IN

# READING

# RECOVERY

## VOLUME TWO

# Early Writing:
# An Exploration of Literacy Opportunities

Billie J. Askew, *Texas Woman's University*
Dianne Frasier, *Harris County Department of Education* and
*Texas Woman's University*

## ABSTRACT

*Early writing experiences provide children with instances in which they may learn the processes and concepts involved in getting meaningful messages into print. This study examined the opportunities low-progress first-grade children had in learning to use strategies while writing a brief message in daily interaction with a Reading Recovery teacher. Specifically, three strategies for writing words were investigated: (a) writing known words, (b) analyzing new words by hearing and recording sounds in words, and (c) analyzing new words through analogy with known words. Eighty-two Reading Recovery children from eight states were the subjects for this study. Data were collected from the children's writing books, writing vocabulary charts, records of text reading, and the teachers' daily lesson records. Analyses demonstrated that low-progress children acquire a considerable amount of knowledge about words, about letters/letter clusters and their sounds, and about the orthography of the language in a relatively short period of time. Limitations and implications of this study are discussed.*

Writing involves a complex series of actions. Children have to think of a message and hold it in the mind. Then they have to think of the first word and how to start it, remember each letter form and its features, and manually reproduce the word letter by letter. Having written that first word (or an approximation), the child must go back to the whole message, retrieve it, and think of the next word. Through writing, children are manipulating and using symbols, and in the process learning how written language works. (Fountas & Pinnell, 1996, p. 14–15)

Few would challenge the importance of writing in early literacy development (Clay, 1975, 1982, 1991, 1993, 1998; Dyson, 1982, 1984; Ferreiro & Teberosky, 1982; Harste, Woodward, & Burke, 1984; Read, 1986; Teale & Sulzby, 1986; Treiman, 1993). The reciprocity between reading and writing is also acknowledged in the literature (Clay, 1982, 1998; DeFord, 1994; Irwin & Doyle, 1992; Morrow, 1997;

Shanahan & Lomax, 1986; Teale & Sulzby, 1986; Tierney & Pearson, 1983; Tierney & Shanahan, 1991).

Young children approach the task of writing a message with communicative intent. The central process that underlies all aspects of writing is meaning. Yet to communicate a message requires development in the conventions of writing (Hiebert & Raphael, 1998). Children already compose messages in conversation. Teachers, then, can help children to compose and write stories by going from ideas to spoken words to printed messages (Clay, 1998).

While the essence of writing is the construction of meaningful messages, in early writing experiences children also learn a host of things about the processes and concepts involved in getting these messages on paper. For example, the daily writing of a story produces a wealth of opportunities to explore the printed form of the written language. Gibson and Levin (1975) listed eight graphic or design characteristics of writing. These design characteristics describe what children learn about the graphic display of the spoken language:

1. Language is formed by tracings on a surface.
2. Writing is rectilinear.
3. Writing is unidirectional.
4. Writing has a fixed orientation.
5. Writing is patterned.
6. Writing has gaps (or spaces) in the graphic display.
7. Written units are roughly equal in size.
8. Writing has various forms that are not usually mixed. (pp. 165–167)

Through their daily writing experiences, children not only have frequent opportunities to explore these design characteristics of our written language, they also are required to engage in many complex processes related to print. For example, Clay (1998) asserts that while creating a story in print, a child must do some of the following:

- attend closely to the features of letters
- learn about letters, distinguishing one from another
- access this letter knowledge in several different ways
- work with letter clusters, as sequences or chunks
- work with words, constructing them from letters, letter clusters, or patterns
- work with syntactic knowledge of what is likely to occur in the language and what does not happen
- use their knowledge of the world to compose the message and anticipate upcoming content
- direct attention to page placement of text, directional rules, serial order, and spaces
- work with some sense of the sequence rules and probability status of any part of the print
- break down the task to its smallest segments while at the same time synthesizing it into words and sentences (pp. 130–131)

Within the task of writing continuous text, children have opportunities to learn about the many concepts that dictate the way in which language is written down (i.e., conventions of print). Children use a variety of strategies as they produce written texts, and three strategies for writing words are the focus for this study: (a) writing known words, (b) analyzing new words by hearing and recording sounds in words (phonology and orthography), and (c) analyzing new words through analogy with known words (Bissex, 1980; Clay & Watson, 1982; Ehri, 1979; Elkonin, 1973; Goswami, 1986; Goswami & Bryant, 1990; Henderson, 1982; Henderson, 1986; Juel, Griffith, & Gough, 1986; Read, 1971, 1975, 1986; Teale & Sulzby, 1986; Treiman, 1993). Reading Recovery teachers engage first-grade children in opportunities to gain control of these three strategies for writing words in daily writing interactions as part of this early intervention literacy program.

The purpose of this study was to explore the opportunities low-progress first graders have for learning to use these strategies while writing a brief message in a daily interaction with a teacher, in this case a Reading Recovery teacher. The following questions guided the study:

- What opportunities for acquiring and using a writing vocabulary of known words are evident in the writing activities of low-progress first-graders in a Reading Recovery setting?
- What opportunities for learning about and using phonological and orthographic principles are evident in the writing samples of low-progress first graders in a Reading Recovery setting?

## Writing in Reading Recovery

Reading Recovery (Clay, 1991, 1993) is an early intervention program for first-graders, delivered by one teacher to one child, that provides a cognitive apprenticeship setting for children who are the lowest performing in their classrooms on literacy tasks. In each Reading Recovery lesson, following a brief conversation with the teacher, the child constructs a short story, usually one or two sentences, based on personal experience or on a book recently read. The writing of the child's orally composed messages is initially shared by the teacher and child. The child writes all that he or she can independently, but the teacher provides assistance as needed until the child takes more control of the task and little teacher help is required.

An unlined book is used for writing these stories. The child's story is written on the bottom page while the top page has working space for problem-solving with the teacher's guidance. The work space is used for the child to engage in strategic processing behaviors such as hearing and recording sounds in words, rehearsing known and almost known frequently used words, and attending to possible analogous relationships.

In Reading Recovery lessons, the interactive framework is a process of scaffolded learning (Clay & Cazden, 1990; Hobsbaum, Peters, & Sylva, 1996). During the writing portion of the lesson, the teacher provides enough support to help the child accomplish tasks that will lead to new learning. The teacher structures the situations so that the child grows into increasingly more complex actions and becomes independent in using these actions in future situations. The highly scaffolded interactions in Reading Recovery, then, help to facilitate a child's learning of "how to learn" in new settings (Lyons, Pinnell, & DeFord, 1993).

The data presented in this study were gleaned from Reading Recovery lessons because this setting allowed for examination of daily writing samples across a series of lessons. The study is not about Reading Recovery itself, but rather about opportunities for young children to learn about printed language during a brief daily interaction with a teacher. Implications for classrooms follow from the impact of engaging young children in the written construction of the language. Following are explanations of the three strategies comprising the focus of this study: writing known words, hearing and recording sounds in words, and analyzing new words through analogy.

## Writing Known Words

Children need to know that sometimes you simply have to know how to write or spell a particular word. There are at least two important reasons for children to acquire a core of words that they know how to write in every detail.

First, as the frequently used words of the language become known, they require less attention and free the writer to attend to other challenges of producing written text. Learning to write frequently used words fluently "helps the child to practise producing the sequence of letters needed for that word and to do this with a minimum of attention . . . like having a little movement programme for producing that word" (Clay, 1993, p. 30). Furthermore, children seem to make sense of the hierarchical relationship of letters to words as they begin to acquire a writing vocabulary.

The frequency principle which applies to all features of all languages must influence opportunities to learn in both reading and writing (Clay, 1998; Clay & Watson, 1982; Gibson & Levin,1975; Treiman, 1992). Frequency "usually ensures repeated exposure and thus repeated encounters. . . . Usage continues to be confirmed until mastered, or known in every respect, or until the response is (almost) automatic. Such (almost) automatic learning supports and provides context for new learning" (Clay, 1998, p. 154).

Wilde (1989) argued that beginning at a relative early age, ownership (such as writing words without having to stop and think about them) is probably the most common spelling strategy. She suggested that this spelling strategy involves knowing how to spell a word and knowing that one knows.

The second reason for acquiring a writing vocabulary is that known words can be used to analyze new words through analogy. Children can see similarities in words, and the "ways words work" become more obvious as children construct words in writing (Clay, 1991; 1993). The importance of analogy is discussed later in this section.

In Reading Recovery, teacher assistance for building a writing vocabulary involves opportunities for children to practice writing newly acquired frequently used words fast, fluently, and flexibly. Additional opportunities over several days bring the word to a point of writing it with a minimum of attention. The teacher then expects the child to initiate the writing of known words in stories independently. The learner not only comes to control more and more high-frequency words, but also shifts from laborious writing of those known words to fluent production (Clay, 1993).

## Hearing and Recording the Sounds in Words

Writing is more potent than reading in forcing children to come to grips with the alphabetic principle (Treiman, 1993). Goswami and Bryant (1990) concluded that although it is difficult to find a connection between phonological awareness and children's reading, there is a strong connection between phonological awareness and children's spelling in writing. They argued that there is abundant evidence that children depend on a phonological code when they are working out how to spell words. Ferreiro and Teberosky (1982) and Harste, Woodward, and Burke (1984) have also shown that writing provides opportunities for children to develop their understandings about how the sounds of language are mapped onto written letters. Treiman (1993) offered support for writing's contribution to sound-letter relationships:

> For first graders, the many benefits of independent writing outweigh the costs. Writing requires children to think about the sounds and meanings of spoken words, to observe the characteristics of printed words, and to form hypotheses about the relations between sounds and letters. All of these activities are of great value in helping children grasp the alphabetic nature of the English writing system. (p. 289)

When writing new words, a useful strategy is to say the word slowly, hearing its sound sequence and attempting to record the appropriate letters for the sounds. Elkonin (1973) wrote that ". . . it is very important to use a method from the beginning that will provide the child with a correct orientation to the role of the sounds in language and acquaint him with the correct sound form and structure of words" (p. 556). He defined sound analysis as ". . . the operation of arranging the succession of sounds in a spoken word. In the process of accomplishing such an operation, the child discovers the basic principle of constructing the sound form of words" (p. 559).

Clay (1977) called for a close look at Elkonin's goals. "He uses the word's **sound form.** He says that sound analysis is **the operation of arranging the succession of sounds in a spoken word.** This is not the same as determining the separate sounds contained in a word" (p. 11). Sounds of a word are altered by surrounding sounds and have different qualities from the same sounds spoken in isolation. The "attributes of each phoneme spill over into that which precedes and that which follows" (Adams, 1990, p. 69). In speech, information about two or more successive phoneme segments is carried on the same piece of sound (Liberman, 1974).

Goswami and Bryant (1990) suggested that "phonological awareness" is a blanket term, representing different ways in which words and syllables can be divided into smaller units of sound. They cited syllables, phonemes, and intra-syllabic units such as onset and rime as types of phonological awareness.

Writing supports phonological awareness, but it also forces children to experiment with the orthography of the language. In addition to learning the graphemic representations of sounds, children learn to cope with English irregularities, the morphological basis of the English writing system, the use of digraphs, and the consonant clusters in the spoken language (Treiman, 1993). Both the phonology and the orthography of English are related to constructing written text from the beginning of writing experiences.

Gibson and Levin (1975) suggested that in writing, orthographic rules govern what sequence of letters and groups of letters may be put together to form words. They reported that in English orthography, there are two separable issues that are often confused: the orthographic rule system (legal letter sequences) and the relationships between these written sequences and the spoken language. The early English writing system abandoned regular letter/sound correspondences to reflect linguistic functions such as word origins, inflectional and morphological units, and differences in word meanings.

Because English has only 26 letters that map on to more than 36 phonemes, the orthographic cipher of English is very complex (Gough, Juel, & Griffith, 1992). Byrne (1992) described the orthographic stage of reading as reached "when the child uses letter groups to identify words, ideally by correspondence to morphemic units, and when the route from print to the lexicon is not necessarily via phonology" (p. 5). Similarly, Gentry (1977) argued that English orthography is a complex, abstract system representing deeper levels of language than the surface sound continuum.

It appears impossible to separate the phonology and the orthography of the language for young readers and writers. Orthographic classification schemes are not sufficient to explain first graders' spellings; Treiman (1993) suggested that it is also important to consider the words' sounds:

> Even first graders seem to have a fairly sophisticated knowledge of the relations between phonemes and graphemes in English. They know that many phonemes have more than one possible spelling. They know that some spellings of a particular phoneme are more common than others. Moreover, children know that the spelling of a phoneme may depend on the phoneme's context. (p. 279)

In Reading Recovery, teacher assistance for hearing and recording sounds in words is based on an adaptation of Elkonin's (1973) work. Elkonin suggested a five-step teaching sequence based on Russian pedagogy: establishing the concept of the task; mastering the operation with objects; mastering the operation at the level of overt speech; mastering the operation with objects; transferring the operation to the mental level; and operating entirely at the mental level. Clay's (1993) procedures for hearing and recording sounds in words are modified from Elkonin, with the sequence determined by finding the problem and searching for a solution. Procedural choices include articulating and, if necessary, using a mirror in order to hear the sounds; using boxes for each sound to be written; attending to spelling using boxes for letters; and working without boxes.

## Analyzing New Words Through Analogy

In addition to an awareness of the phonology of the spoken language and the orthography that controls the written form, children also need to understand that they can use their knowledge about phonology and orthography to get to new words by analogy (Bruck & Treiman, 1992; Ehri & Robbins, 1992; Goswami & Bryant, 1990). While some children tend to use analogy easily in writing, others seem to benefit from explicit attention to phonological and orthographic links.

"As the core of known words builds in writing, and the high-frequency words become known, these provide a series from which other words can be composed taking familiar bits from known words and getting to new words by analogy" (Clay, 1991, p. 244). In addition, she said:

> Knowing forty to fifty words will cover almost all the letters, many high frequency words, many common-letter clusters, and some orthographic or spelling patterns useful for getting to other words by analogy, in either reading or writing. This small writing vocabulary plays host to almost all letter knowledge and quite a variety of the letter-cluster knowledge. The words can be constructed or remembered, or taken apart and used in analogies. (Clay, 1998, p. 149)

Children can use their known words to solve new words. For example, the known word *sock* can be used to analyze new words such as *block,* and the known word *and* can be used to analyze new words such as *landed.* The knowledge of the word *going* may help children in analyzing other words that end with *ing.*

When children understand that words that have sounds in common also frequently share spelling sequences as well, they have a powerful way to figure out how to read and write new words. "They can use the spelling pattern in one word to work out the sound of another word with the same spelling sequence, and to decide how to spell a word which rhymes with a word that they know how to spell already" (Goswami & Bryant, 1990, p. 78).

Although some may argue that analogy is a sophisticated strategy used by older children, Goswami and Bryant (1992) suggested that younger children "may be perfectly capable of using analogies in reading if they know the words on which analogies are meant to be based" (p. 57). Baron (1977) suggested that analogy is a strategy used naturally even by kindergartners. It is a general cognitive strategy used by young children in much categorizing behavior.

A study by Ehri and Robbins (1992) supported Goswami's (1986) claim that reading unfamiliar words by making analogies to known words is easier for beginners than reading unfamiliar words by phonologically recoding the words. However, their findings also indicated that in order for beginners to read words by analogy, they must have phonological recoding skills. The acquisition of the orthographic cipher gives children the ability to generate spellings—when they have been seen the word before and when they have not.

Reading Recovery teachers assist children in generating from what they know to what is new. They point out similarities in words and letter sequences as children construct words in written text. They make explicit links to phonological and orthographic knowledge that the child already controls. Observed changes across time generally reveal that children first use what they know in response to the teacher's prompt; then they see relationships between something they need to write and something they know; finally they initiate the use of what they know about letters and words to get to a new word (Clay, 1993). Selected recorded examples of links made by a teacher or child during Reading Recovery writing lessons are shown in Table 1.

Teachers also explicitly demonstrate that there are alternative ways of getting to new words by providing children with many opportunities to apply alternatives flexibly. These opportunities include problem-solving new words through sound analysis and through multiple experiences with the use of analogy in applying orthographic features and patterns. Adams (1990) commended the Reading Recovery program for explicitly recognizing the importance of phonological and linguistic awareness.

In summary, in the writing of continuous text, children have opportunities to engage in these strategies (writing known words, hearing and recording sounds in words, and analyzing new words through analogy) and it was the purpose of this study to explore them.

## Method

### Subjects

Children served in Reading Recovery are first graders who are identified as the lowest achieving in the class on literacy measures. They work with a specially trained teacher in a one-to-one setting for 30 minutes daily in reading and writing texts. The goal of this short-term early intervention is to enable these children to use reading and writing strategies effectively and independently so that they can function successfully in average settings within the regular classroom.

Subjects for this study were 82 Reading Recovery children from eight states (Arizona, Illinois, Louisiana, Massachusetts, Nebraska, Ohio, Texas, and West Virginia). Of the 82 children, 56 were male and 26 were female. Forty-one children were Anglo, 19 were African-American, 6 were Hispanic, and two were Asian. No ethnicity was recorded for 14 children.

The Reading Recovery teachers of these children represented 37 different training sites and had a wide range of experience in the program: 18 were in their training year, 36 had one to three years of experience, and 21 had more than three years in Reading Recovery.

### Data Sources

Major sources of data included each child's writing book, writing vocabulary chart, record of text reading, and the teacher's daily lesson record. A Reading Recovery child's writing book includes the stories written daily as well as all work completed on a practice page, indicating how the teacher supported the writing. Daily lesson records include information about teacher decisions during the writing portion of the lesson and about the child's contributions to the production of the text. The writing vocabulary chart is a weekly record of each child's known writing vocabulary as it is acquired across the program. The record of text reading level is a weekly account of the texts that were read, including accuracy and self-correction indicators. These records are routinely completed by Reading Recovery teachers during daily lessons or weekly charting of progress.

**Table 1.** Selected Examples of Links Made During Writing in Reading Recovery Lessons

| LESSON NUMBER | WORD TO BE WRITTEN | LINKS TO KNOWN |
|---|---|---|
| 3 | dog | Teacher linked beginning to known word *dad.* "It starts like *dad.*" |
| | my | Teacher linked beginning to known word *mom.* "It starts like *mom.*" |
| 18 | spooky | Teacher linked to known word *too.* |
| 20 | carnival | Child wrote known word *car* then moved on to analyze the rest. |
| 21 | win | Teacher linked to known word *in.* |
| 25 | farm | Teacher asked, "What do you know that starts like that?" Child wrote *far* then added the *m.* |
| 26 | flying | Teacher linked known word *my* to get to *fly.* |
| 27 | his | Child linked known word *is* to get to *his.* |
| 29 | candy | Child linked to known word *can* and teacher linked to *baby.* |
| 43 | stay | After writing *stay,* child says, "Look, it's like *day* and *play!*" |

## Procedures and Analyses

All Reading Recovery observational records for 100 Reading Recovery children were collected from across 8 states representing 37 districts/sites. Training sites were asked to send complete folders for children who began Reading Recovery service at the beginning of their first-grade school year and who successfully completed the program. These two criteria were established in order to maintain a common standard for describing the sample population: children who began first grade among the lowest in a class cohort and whose accelerated progress returned them to an average setting in their classrooms. Complete records were available for 82 children.

In order to limit redundancy, procedures and analyses are described concurrently with specific findings in the following section.

## Findings

### Writing Vocabulary

Three interesting findings emerged from the analysis of children's writing vocabulary opportunities and were related to frequency, change over time, and the relationship between words children were writing and those appearing in books they were reading.

First, all of the words used in all daily stories written by 82 children were listed and analyzed for frequency distribution. There was no natural break in the frequency ranking, so an arbitrary decision was made to consider 24 words for further analysis as the most frequently written words. There was a dramatic range in frequencies across these 24 words—from 1944 occurrences for the most frequently written word *I* to 167 for the word *you.* There were 10 words that appeared 300 or more times and 14 words that appeared between 167 and 299 times. Collectively, these 24 high frequency words alone afforded children multiple opportunities to write all of the vowels (*a, e, i, o, u,* and *y*) and the following consonants: *c, d, f, g, h, k, l, m, n, r, s, t, w, y.*

Of the 82 children, most demonstrated that they could write their own names in every detail before beginning the Reading Recovery intervention. This high frequency word of a very personal nature offered the child unique opportunities for exploring features of printed language. Names frequently introduce orthographic challenges as illustrated by some of the subjects' names in the study: Kimberly, Joshua, Patrick, Ashley, Jonathan, Heather, Anthony, Natasha, Andrew, Shataqua, Shawn, Nicole, and Christopher.

Children demonstrated different profiles in their personal "control" of these frequently written words, as shown by the patterns of two children in Table 2. Frequently written words from the aggregated data are shown in bold. The placement of a word in the "weeks" columns indicates *when* that child first demonstrated knowledge of that word by writing it independently and accurately. Each child demonstrated control of most of the 24 identified high frequency writing words as well as a unique set of known words emanating from the child's messages.

In addition to an aggregated list of 24 frequently written words, children acquired many other words that they could produce in every detail. Additionally, many more words were written with a minimum of teacher assistance. In a timed testing situation at the end of their programs, children also wrote many words not previously used in their Reading Recovery stories in every detail.

Secondly, to determine change across time in children's use of known writing vocabulary words, the researchers calculated the number of words contributed by the child, without teacher interaction or assistance, to the writing of the story at five points in time: at the beginning of their program and at four equal intervals until the end of program. Children were contributing fewer than 30 percent of the words independently and accurately at the beginning of their programs and more than 70 percent at the end. This finding is impressive when it is noted that sentence length, language, and complexity also increased across time as shown in Table 3.

Clear changes were evident in the writing vocabulary controlled by individual children between the time of entry to program and the time of discontinuing from program. Table 4 includes one child's writing vocabulary that serves to illustrate this point. This child acquired a wide variety of known writing words to serve in making analogies and in linking to known words and features of words.

"Known" words, as sources of information, became *opportunities* for a child to solve new words through analogy, beginning with teacher support and shifting to child initiation of the links needed to go from known words to new ones. For example, the child represented in Table 4 controlled the word *like* early in his program, providing an *opportunity* for him to use this known word to get to new words such as *bike* in week 9. Later in the child's program, he had the opportunity to discover exception words with the silent "e" ending such as *give* and *have.*

And finally, although the main goal of this study was the exploration of writing, a comparison was made between words appearing frequently in children's writing and words frequently used in texts these children were reading. The identification of high frequency words in reading was accomplished by analyzing reading texts used by 20

Table 2. The Order in Which Additions to Writing Vocabulary Were Demonstrated by Two Children

**CHILD #1**

WEEKS IN PROGRAM

| 1 | 2 | 3 | 4 | 5 | 6 | 7 | 8 | 9 | 10 | 11 | 12 | 13 | 14 | 15 | 16 | 17 | 18 |
|---|---|---|---|---|---|---|---|---|----|----|----|----|----|----|----|----|----|
| Angelo | to | in | dog | eat | it | down | and | Cook | love | stop | big | cartoons | sun | six | tree | book | love |
| cat | go | my | book | | got | red | | egg | bird | feel | gun | TV | not | fix | but | bag | she |
| mom | I | up | can | | on | the | | bike | cut | off | you | | they | had | took | bus | hop |
| like | a | go | zoo | | hat | | | | he | we | give | | did | | bath | yes | ride |
| | | | see | | | | | | pig | ten | | | today | | | Anthony | tooth |
| | | | do | | | | | | is | into | | | bed | | | play | ball |
| | | | so | | | | | | | at | | | day | | | plays | bat |
| | | | | | | | | | | | | | | | | | good |
| | | | | | | | | | | | | | | | | | have |
| | | | | | | | | | | | | | | | | | pup |

**CHILD #2**

WEEKS IN PROGRAM

| 1 | 2 | 3 | 4 | 5 | 6 | 7 | 8 | 9 | 10 | 11 | 12 | 13 | 14 | 15 | 16 | 17 | 18 |
|---|---|---|---|---|---|---|---|---|----|----|----|----|----|----|----|----|----|
| Ryan | Kyle | I | in | got | we | He | his | sun | that | frog | river | with | room | pine | | | |
| | | a | is | to | mom | The | log | do | going | Sam | mad | like | bed | wood | | | |
| | | cat | | hot | he | It | dog | doing | sat | | frogs | under | box | | | | |
| | | go | | | at | Up | am | | us | | did | came | for | | | | |
| | | | | | | | and | | had | | home | came | for | | | | |
| | | | | | | | my | | can | | last | this | silver | | | | |
| | | | | | | | | | cook | | | outside | bike | | | | |
| | | | | | | | | | just | | | that | him | | | | |
| | | | | | | | | | | | | cold | | | | | |
| | | | | | | | | | | | | toy | | | | | |
| | | | | | | | | | | | | present | | | | | |
| | | | | | | | | | | | | plant | | | | | |
| | | | | | | | | | | | | ice | | | | | |
| | | | | | | | | | | | | went | | | | | |

randomly selected children. Weekly records of text reading were used to select the texts. One book per week was analyzed. All of the words from all of the texts were analyzed for frequency of occurrence.

Of the 24 most frequently occurring words in reading texts and the 24 most frequently occurring words in the children's writing, 15 words appeared on both lists. The words children wrote were often of a personal nature, including ones such as *I, my, me, we,* and *mom,* along with verbs accompanying personal actions such as *like, got, went, can, was, said,* and *going.* High frequency reading words not appearing on the writing list included pronouns such as *he, they,* and *she,* and story-specific words such as *little,* and *old.*

## Evidence of Opportunities to Explore Phonological and Orthographic Principles

Children's writing books, teachers' lesson records, and writing vocabulary charts were used to explore linguistic opportunities in the writing samples. The first analysis involved an examination of all words that children had an *opportunity* to write (the total corpus of words used) for linguistic features including initial consonants, initial consonant blends, consonant clusters, vowel combinations, rimes, inflectional and derivational endings, etc.

Three explanations are needed. First, no one child experienced all of the opportunities described; data were aggregated across all subjects. However, the aggregated data indicate the breadth of possibilities. Second, because all stories were comprised of words children *wanted* to write, there was no predetermined sequence. Opportunities were possible because no control was placed on what the children could explore while recording their messages. Third, all of the stories were written with the support of a teacher who was able to provide scaffolds for the child to learn about a multitude of conventions of written messages.

**Table 3.** Sample Stories from One Child During First Quartile and Fourth Quartile of the Reading Recovery Program

| | |
|---|---|
| First Quartile | • I like the panda bear. |
| | • I put up a toy train. |
| | • A turtle can swim. |
| | • Dad was at work all night. |
| Fourth Quartile | • The giant roared at the people to get some food. The giant was going to hit the people with his bommyknocker. |
| | • The little critter didn't want to clean his room but he did. |
| | • What has an eye but can't see? What goes up when the rain comes down? |
| | • It's my brother's birthday today and a lot of people will come. |

**Table 4.** Changes in Control of Writing Vocabulary for One Child Across Time

| ENTRY WORDS WRITTEN CORRECTLY BEFORE ENTRY INTO READING RECOVERY: WRITING VOCABULARY TEST | END OF PROGRAM WORDS WRITTEN CORRECTLY AND INDEPENDENTLY DURING BRIEF DAILY WRITING EXPERIENCES ACROSS READING RECOVERY LESSONS | | | |
|---|---|---|---|---|
| a | about | did | like | thing |
| go | Alex | digging | look | this |
| Ian | all | do | man | to |
| me | am | door | mess | Travis |
| mom | and | eat | milk | tree |
| no | are | eye | Mr. | two |
| on | as | fall | Mrs. | turning |
| | ask | fast | my | uncle |
| | at | fire | not | until |
| | ate | for | of | up |
| | be | fun | off | us |
| | bee | funny | old | wash |
| | bell | get | one | we |
| | big | going | or | Wesley |
| | boo | good | pan | wet |
| | book | got | people | what |
| | boy | gramma | pig | will |
| | but | he | red | win |
| | by | here | sad | wind |
| | can | hi | see | with |
| | can't | him | she | wonder |
| | car | horse | so | work |
| | come | I | ten | yes |
| | cow | I'll | the | yesterday |
| | cut | is | them | you |
| | dad | it | then | your |
| | date | joy | they | zoo |
| | | | | zoom |

Analyses of opportunities revealed multiple exposures to consonants. For example, the letter *m* appeared in the children's writing an average of 27 times per child in the initial position alone. As shown in Table 4, the child had *known* words to serve as exemplars for most initial consonants (all consonants except *k, q, v,* and *x*).

Collectively, children's writing showed opportunities to write more than 25 different initial consonant blends, as well as numerous consonant digraphs and clusters (see Table 5). Children used at least 25 different vowel combinations in their writing, representing multiple sounds (see Table 6). Most inflectional endings were represented, as well as more than 25 different morphological derivational endings (see Table 7). More than 200 different rimes were represented in the combined writing samples of these low-progress children. In addition, writing samples included abbreviations, compound words, contractions, possessives, silent letters (*e, b, k, gh,* etc.), and more than 4,764 multi-syllable words.

**Table 5.** Consonant Blends, Digraphs, and Clusters Represented in Children's Writing

| INITIAL CONSONANT BLENDS | | | | CONSONANT DIGRAPHS AND CLUSTERS (INITIAL AND FINAL) | | |
|---|---|---|---|---|---|---|
| bl | gl | sk | squ | ch (chick) | ph (f) | th (hard) |
| br | gr | sl | st | chr (Chris) | ng | th (soft) |
| cl | pl | sm | str | ck | qu | thr |
| cr | pr | sn | sw | gh (ghost) | sh | wh |
| dl | sc | sp | tr | gh (silent) | ch | |
| fl | scr | spr | tw | ght | | |
| fr | | | | (double consonants as *ss*, *ll*, etc.) | | |
| N = 82 | | | | | | |

**Table 6.** Vowel Combinations Represented in Children's Writing

| | | | |
|---|---|---|---|
| ai | ei | oo (book) | ow (brown) |
| ar | eigh | oo (door) | ow (grow) |
| au | er | oo (food) | oy |
| aw | ew | or (motor) | ue |
| ay | ey (alley) | or (for) | ui (build) |
| ea (bear) | ey (Breyers) | ou (could) | ui (juice) |
| ea (ear) | ey (they) | ou (country) | ur |
| ea (earth) | ie | ou (coupon) | |
| ea (spread) | ir | ou (course) | |
| eau (beauty) | oa | ou (house) | |
| ee | oi | ou (ought) | |
| N = 82 | | | |

**Table 7.** Endings Represented in Children's Writing

| INFLECTIONAL MORPHEMES | | | DERIVATIONAL MORPHEMES | | | |
|---|---|---|---|---|---|---|
| -d | ed, | ied | -able | -ence | -ful | -ly |
| -ing | | | -al | -ent | -ible | -ment |
| -s, | -es, | -ies | -ate | -er | -ie | -or |
| (third person singular verb) | | -ator | -ery | -ier | -ous | |
| -s, | -es | -ies | -el | -ess | -ious | -tion |
| (plural) | | | | | | |
| | | | -en | -est | -le | -y |
| N = 82 | | | | | | |

As with the acquisition of a writing vocabulary, opportunities for acquiring linguistic understandings differed among individual children. Unique individual profiles revealed no sequence for acquisition of patterns across all children. Each had laid a personal foundation for more understanding of linguistic features. Opportunities provided by this simple teaching interaction were rich, as shown in Figure 1 which illustrates two examples of one child's opportunities to explore linguistic aspects of the language.

In example one, the child was working in sound boxes (one box for each sound). Teaching interactions provided the child opportunities to explore sounds and the letter(s) representing those sounds. Particular opportunities to explore sound analysis are shown in the sound boxes on the practice page: *ow* in the word *down, sh* in the word *shot,* and *er* in the word *Joker.*

In example two, the child was working in letter boxes (one box for each letter). This framework assisted the child to attend to the mismatch between the sounds of the language and the way in which we spell words. In this single writing episode, the child had an opportunity to deal with spelling patterns in *tooth* (*oo* and *th*), *ee* in *sleep, wh* in *when,* and the silent *e* in *gave.* In addition, the child had to attend to the double letter in *dollar* in writing his story.

A final analysis focused on changes in children's independent use of letter-sound relationships in their writing. There was evidence of increased control of phoneme-grapheme correspondence within continuous text across time. At the beginning of the intervention, 38 percent of the phonemes in the children's stories were represented by the correct grapheme without teacher assistance. By the end of the intervention, more than 80 percent of the phonemes were correctly and independently represented by the children.

## Discussion

The children in this study were in classrooms representing a variety of environments for writing opportunities. It is acknowledged that the classroom literacy experiences of these children were not controlled nor are they reported here. However, this study does provide compelling evidence that a brief negotiation of a written sentence or two each day between a teacher and a low-progress first grader yields numerous opportunities for the child to learn many things about how their language is written down.

This study was about *opportunities.* Within the task of writing continuous text, with teacher assistance, a child has opportunities: (a) to learn about the conventional features of written language; (b) to explore the phonology and orthography of the English language; (c) to acquire a writing vocabulary representing words known in every detail; and (d) to use this core of known words representing a wide range of linguistic features and patterns to generate new learning through analogy. Based on data gathered in this study and the current knowledge about early writing behaviors, we can support the importance of early writing in developing these strategies that were the focus of the study and substantiate that control can shift from teacher-assisted performance to self-regulated performance across time even with low-progress first graders. In the following sections each of these strategies is discussed briefly.

## Acquiring and Using a Writing Vocabulary

Findings in this study revealed that in both writing and reading, very few words are high frequency words when viewed as aggregated data. At this early stage, "known words" involve a unique set of words known to the individual learner. While much attention was given in this study to the most frequently written words across the programs of 82 children, it is important to note that all children had control of *many* words other than those identified as high frequency words. This finding is consistent with Ehri's (1992) suggestion that "sight" words in reading are not limited to high frequency words and irregularly spelled words, but include all words read often enough to initiate the formation of connections into memory. For reading and writing, then, it could be said that a frequency principle operates uniquely for individual learners.

It is important to remember that the teachers did not set out to "teach" these particular words to children. Children composed messages and in the process of writing these messages gained control over high frequency words in situations in which *they* initiated the task. Teachers then supported the child in rehearsing the words so that they became (almost) automatic.

It would be unfortunate if the list of high frequency words identified in this study were used as a teaching list for classrooms or were thought of as a suggested sequence for teaching. "The important insight . . . is that a frequency principle operates in these

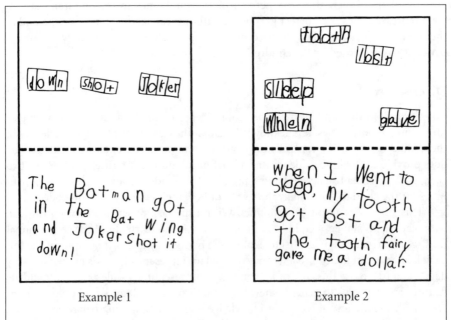

Example 1                                        Example 2

**Figure 1.** Examples of One Child's Opportunities to Explore Linguistic Aspects of the Language

early attempts to write and that easy words are controlled early and provide (a) opportunities to practise these words [and] (b) opportunities to attend to new words" (Clay & Watson, 1982, p. 20).

These data also support the notion that children demonstrate individual profiles in acquisition of writing vocabulary. Children acquired different words at different rates across their programs, providing a compelling argument for including opportunities for children to write their own messages with assistance from a supportive teacher. There appears to be a unique power when children learn from the construction of their own messages.

## Learning About and Using the Phonology and Orthography of English

The present study offers evidence that daily writing experiences provide children with multiple opportunities to explore the code that governs the sounds of the language and their graphic representations. When writing, children have multiple opportunities to learn about letters and the sounds they make, including even the production of letters. In this study, the 24 high frequency writing words alone provided massive practice in producing 19 of the 26 letters: *a, c, d, e, f, g, h, i, k, l, m, n, o, r, s, t, u, w, y*.

In the writing component of Reading Recovery, children are encouraged to hear and record sounds as they analyze new words. They progressively move through a series of procedures adapted from the work of Elkonin (1973). Therefore, the opportunities in this setting that served as the context for the study included both the writing activity itself and the teacher support in doing a phonemic analysis. Massive opportunities were provided through the daily writing of sentences for children to hear and record sounds including vowels and vowel combinations representing multiple sounds, to learn about consonant frameworks, and to gain understandings about the spelling processes involved in representing these sounds. The teacher support included sharing the writing of the difficult parts specific to each child.

To demonstrate such opportunities, the words analyzed on the practice page by one child with the teacher's support were recorded. Samples of words analyzed in sound boxes (i.e., a box for each sound) across this child's program included the following: like, nice, sand, stand, top, him, bike, cross, got, boy, drove, can, miss, pool, broke, down, she's, home, her, bed, cold, head, call, and, crashed, wing, joker, shot, drove, jump, climbed, hill, with, him, flew, space, landed, will, old, want, threw, gang, out, his, gun, apples, hugs, then, took, floor, teacher, when, and fell. This child also had the opportunity to analyze words in letter boxes (i.e., a box for each letter) such as the following: tooth, lost, sleep, when, gave, dollar, show, moon, will, wash, mud, wish, just, house, drove, penguin, second, first, little, would, most, made, spell, turned, boat, water, them, start, had, goalie, kept, pucks, always, stuff, and throw.

When writing words, as in reading them, there are regular words, exception words, and ambiguous words (Goswami & Bryant, 1990). Regular words are those that are sounded and spelled the same way (e.g., *dish*). Exception words violate the predictable spelling of the rime (e.g., *said* would be expected to end with *ed*). Ambiguous words are those for which there are several possible ways to spell the sounds (e.g., *beef*).

The present study demonstrates how children in a daily writing activity have opportunities to explore all three categories. For example, the child represented earlier in Table 4 worked with multiple examples of regular words (e.g., *fast, big*), exception words (e.g., *come, to*), and ambiguous words (e.g., *be, bee, eat*). Writing opportunities present "the vagaries of written language to the child in a more valid form than most sequenced reading and writing curricula, and yet it is an approach in which the poorest performers of the age group succeeded" (Clay & Watson, 1982, p. 30). The child develops a sense of the possibilities that exist in language in a context that is not distorted by an over-emphasis on the regularities.

The 24 most frequently written words from this study alone provided exposure to alternative sounds of vowels within words, introducing children to the flexibility needed in handling letter-sound relationships in English. For example, alternative sounds for the letter o were represented in the frequently written words *to, on, got, for, you,* and *going*.

Irregularity of the English writing system is a source of difficulty for children learning to spell in English, but it is not the only problem. Other difficulties include the morphological basis of the English writing system, the use of digraphs, the consonant clusters in the spoken language, and the reality that English letter names are not always a helpful guide to spelling (Treiman, 1993). In this study, children had multiple opportunities (see Tables 5–7) to deal with all of these challenges in a supportive instructional environment.

Writing provides children with multiple opportunities to use a variety of linguistic features and patterns. Their writing also affords opportunities to experiment with abbreviations, compound words, contractions, possessives, silent letters, and multisyllable words. Table 8 illustrates the opportunities experienced by one Reading Recovery child in his written stories.

## Developing the Potential for Using Analogy to Write New Words

As young children acquire a writing vocabulary and have opportunities for learning about the phonological and orthographic principles of written language, they also have the opportunity to apply these understandings to the generation of new words by analogy. With this knowledge, some children will solve new problems by analogy easily in writing, while others may require a teacher's explicit attention to phonological and orthographic links.

Sources of data for this study were restricted to written records. There was no consistent account of verbal interactions between children and teachers, making it difficult to document the use of analogy. Daily lesson records often revealed evidence that attention was given to the process of using what was known to get to something new, but these notations could not be considered all-inclusive. It was also difficult to determine who initiated the link from the known to the unknown.

What we do know is that when a child has an independent strategy for working out new words by using knowledge he already possesses, he has the power to push his own knowledge further and to gain more independence in the writing task. The child is then learning how to analyze words and how to become an observer of how words work in his language (Clay & Watson, 1982).

Knowing many different words enhances a child's opportunities for getting to new words he needs to write. Writing opportunities in which children compose their own messages encourage them to attempt to construct a wide range of words, allowing them to begin to sense something about the rules and the vagaries of the way English is written down (Clay, 1998). The words (exemplars) controlled by children in this study included both the regularities and the irregularities of the language. The wide range of exemplars should contribute to flexibility and fluency in using analogy to solve new problems when writing continuous text.

## Some Final Observations

Findings from this study reveal that low-progress children can acquire considerable knowledge about words, about letters/letter clusters and their sounds, and about the orthography of the language in a relatively short period of time. In addition to classroom writing opportunities, children composed and wrote a message with a Reading Recovery teacher for approximately 10 minutes daily for an average of 17 weeks during the first half of first grade.

This study also contributes to the growing evidence that children take unique, individual paths in their acquisition of written language. There is clearly no identified sequence emerging with implications for instruction.

"When teaching supports self-initiated writing, more child-generated learning results. Like children learning to speak, writers who wish to be understood learn to put messages on the page in ways that comply with the adult reader's assumptions about written messages" (Clay, 1998, p. 133). Therefore, opportunities for individual exploration permit learning opportunities that will lead children by different paths to common outcomes.

Another implication arising from this study relates to the role of teacher assistance. The type and amount of teacher assistance was not readily available in analyzing the data for this study. However, in the context of Reading Recovery, children's opportunities and actions were combined with supportive teacher interactions.

**Table 8.** Additional Opportunities Within One Child's Written Stories

| EXEMPLARS FROM *KNOWN* WORDS | OPPORTUNITIES FROM ALL STORIES WRITTEN |
| --- | --- |
| • 4 proper names | • 7 contractions |
| • 15 multisyllable words | • 5 possessives |
| • 2 abbreviations | • 7 compound sentences |
| • 2 contractions | • 7 complex sentences |
| • 10 vowel combinations representing different sounds | • 30 inflectional endings |
| • 3 different r-controlled vowels | • 97 multisyllable words |
| | • 17 proper names |
| | • punctuation (period, question mark, exclamation mark, apostrophe, hyphen) |

There is support for such assistance in the literature. For example, Cazden (1992) suggested there are three points on a continuum of social assistance between teachers and children: discovery without a teacher's help, revealing, and telling. She cited Reading Recovery's writing component as one that helps children attend to sounds in their own speech. She used the Reading Recovery procedure adapted from Elkonin's (1973) work to illustrate the concept of "revealing":

> For learners, the activity of having to slow pronunciation in order to match the finger action makes possible a new kind of attention to the sounds of their own speech. The teacher's language is directed to involving the child in the activity, in which the child will come to attend in a new way. Thus a teaching technique has been developed that successfully teaches phonemic awareness by revealing the sound structure to the child without explicitly telling the child linguistic labels or orthographic rules. (Cazden, 1992, p. 307)

Cazden suggested there are at least two reasons that revealing can be more helpful than telling for young learners. First, information gained from telling is often not available for later use. Second, telling about how written language works may risk oversimplifying complex reality.

Gibson and Levin (1975) also cited the importance of teacher assistance. They argued that while the learner himself must search for and discover patterns for transfer of a high level of abstraction to occur, specific help is also a crucial element:

> But it was clearly better to have attention directed to search for invariant features in the stimulus array, and finding them seemed to lead to repetition of the successful strategy and thus to consistently accelerated performance. This is perceptual learning, not just remembering something. Learning to abstract spelling patterns involves active participation by the scholar, not memorizing a verbal rule or simply being shown. (p. 301)

Clay (1998) offers the following teaching moves that could be used to support children's writing:

- bringing the topic into the conversation
- maintaining interactive ease
- prompting constructive activity
- accepting partially correct responses
- playing with anticipation
- asking the child to "learn" something
- lifting the difficulty level
- increasing accessibility of the ideas
- supporting performance
- asking the child to work with new knowledge
- accepting child involvement

- developing attention . . .
- praising strategic behavior
- revisiting the familiar (p. 155)

This study also demonstrates that opportunities to learn when writing have some relationship to opportunities for learning when reading. While the relationship between reading and spelling is not perfect, the store of knowledge that children use for spelling words is similar to the store of knowledge they use for reading (Treiman, 1993). For example, writing requires the child to deal with the distinctive features of letters, to learn about words and how they work, to acknowledge the importance of letter order and spatial concepts, and to learn about conventions such as punctuation and capitalization. Therefore, much learning and many operations needed in early reading are practiced in another form in writing.

Clay (1991) suggests that the processes of reading and writing provide opportunities for children to learn important concepts: (a) links between messages in oral language and messages in printed language; (b) aspects of print to which they must attend; (c) strategies for maintaining fluency, exploring detail, increasing understanding, and correcting errors; (d) feedback mechanisms that keep productions on track; (e) feed-forward mechanisms that keep processing behaviors efficient; and (f) strategies for relating new information to what is already known. While writing knowledge serves as a resource that can help the reader, the reciprocity does not occur spontaneously (Clay, 1993). Again, the teacher's role is important in directing the child to use what he knows in reading when he is writing and vice versa.

While many questions remain, this study of opportunities makes a case for the importance of writing for first graders who are taking their first steps into literacy learning. There is evidence that the lowest-achieving children at the beginning of first grade benefit from opportunities to construct and produce a short story with the supporting guidance of a teacher. Children move toward self-regulated behaviors in writing stories independently, incorporating strategic processes that include hearing and recording sounds in words, acquiring a core of known words, and having opportunities to use known words and features of words to generate new learnings through analogy.

## References

Adams, M. J.(1990). *Beginning to read: Thinking and learning about print.* Cambridge, MA: The MIT Press.

Baron, J. (1977). Mechanisms for pronouncing printed words: Use and acquisition. In D. LaBerge & S. J. Samuels (Eds.), *Basic processes in reading: Perception and comprehension* (pp. 176–216). Hillsdale, NJ: Lawrence Erlbaum Associates.

Bissex, G. (1980). *Gyns at Work: A child learns to write and read.* Cambridge, MA: Harvard University Press.

Bruck, M., & Treiman, R. (1992). Learning to pronounce words: The limitations of analogies. *Reading Research Quarterly, 27,* 374–388.

Byrne, B. (1992). Studies in the acquisition procedure for reading: Rationale, hypotheses, and data. In P. B. Gough, L. C. Ehri, & R. Treiman (Eds.), *Reading acquisition* (pp. 1–34). Hillsdale, NJ: Lawrence Erlbaum Associates.

Cazden, C. B. (1992). Revealing and telling: The socialization of attention in learning to read and write. *Educational Psychology, 12,* 305–313.

Clay, M. M. (1975). *What did I write?* Portsmouth, NH: Heinemann.

Clay, M. M. (1977). *Write now, read later: An evaluation.* Auckland, NZ: Auckland Council of the International Reading Association.

Clay, M. M. (1982). *Observing young readers.* Portsmouth, NH: Heinemann.

Clay, M. M. (1991). *Becoming literate: The construction of inner control.* Portsmouth, NH: Heinemann.

Clay, M. M. (1993). *Reading Recovery: A guidebook for teachers in training.* Portsmouth, NH: Heinemann.

Clay, M. M. (1998). *By different paths to common outcomes.* York, ME: Stenhouse Publishers.

Clay, M. M., & Cazden, C. B. (1990). A Vygotskian interpretation of Reading Recovery. In L. C. Moll (Ed.), *Vygotsky and education: Instructional implications and applications of socio-historical psychology* (pp. 206–222). Cambridge: Cambridge University Press.

Clay, M. M., & Watson, B. (1982). *The success of Maori children in the Reading Recovery programme: Part II.* Wellington, New Zealand: Report to the Director of Research, Ministry of Education.

DeFord, D. E. (1994). Early writing: Teachers and children in Reading Recovery. *Literacy Teaching and Learning: An International Journal of Early Literacy, 1,* 31–56.

Dyson, A. H. (1982). Reading, writing, and language: Young children solving the written language puzzle. *Language Arts, 59,* 820–839.

Dyson, A. H. (1984). Learning to write/learning to do school: Emergent writers' interpretations of school literacy tasks. *Research in the Teaching of English, 18,* 233–264.

Ehri, L. C. (1979). Linguistic insight: Threshold of reading acquisition. In T. G. Waller & G. E. Mackinnon (Eds.), *Reading Research: Advances in theory and practice* (Vol. 1, pp. 63–114). New York: Academic.

Ehri, L. C. (1992). Reconceptualizing the development of sight word reading and its relationship to recoding. In P. B. Gough, L. C. Ehri, & R. Treiman (Eds.), *Reading acquisition* (pp. 107–143). Hillsdale, NJ: Lawrence Erlbaum Associates.

Ehri, L. C., & Robbins, C. (1992). Beginners need some decoding skill to read words by analogy. *Reading Research Quarterly, 27,* 12–26.

Elkonin, D. B. (1973) USSR. In Downing, J. (Ed.), *Comparative reading* (pp. 551–580). New York: Macmillan.

Ferreiro, E., & Teberosky, A. (1982). *Literacy before schooling.* Portsmouth, NH: Heinemann.

Fountas, I. C., & Pinnell, G. S. (1996). *Guided reading: Good first teaching for all children.* Portsmouth, NH: Heinemann.

Gentry, J. R. (1977). A study of the orthographic strategies of beginning readers. Unpublished doctoral dissertation, University of Virginia, Charlottesville.

Gibson, E. J. & Levin, H. (1975). *The psychology of reading.* Cambridge, MA: MIT Press.

Goswami, U. (1986). Children's use of analogy in learning to read: A developmental study. *Journal of Experimental Child Psychology, 42,* 73–83.

Goswami, U., & Bryant, P. E. (1990). *Phonological skills and learning to read.* Hillsdale, NJ: Lawrence Erlbaum Associates.

Goswami, U., & Bryant, P. (1992). Rhyme, analogy, and children's reading. In P. B. Gough, L. C. Ehri, & R. Treiman (Eds.), *Reading acquisition* (pp. 49–63). Hillsdale, NJ: Lawrence Erlbaum Associates.

Gough, P. B., Juel, C., Griffith, P. L. (1992). Reading, spelling, and the orthographic cipher. In P. B. Gough, L. C. Ehri, and R. Treiman (Eds.), *Reading acquisition.* (pp. 35–48). Hillsdale, NJ: Lawrence Erlbaum Associates.

Harste, J., Woodward, V. A., & Burke, C. L. (1984). *Language stories and literacy lessons.* Portsmouth, NH: Heinemann.

Henderson, L. (1982). *Orthography and word recognition in reading.* San Diego, CA: Academic Press.

Henderson, E. H. (1986). *Teaching spelling.* Boston, MA: Houghton Mifflin.

Hiebert, E. H., & Raphael, T. E. (1998). *Early literacy instruction.* Fort Worth: Harcourt Brace College Publishers.

Hobsbaum, A., Peters, S., & Sylva, K. (1996). Scaffolding in Reading Recovery. *Oxford Review of Education, 22,* 17–35.

Irwin, J. W., & Doyle, M. A. (1992). *Reading/Writing connections: Learning from research.* Newark, DE: International Reading Association.

Juel, C., Griffith, P. L., & Gough, P. B. (1986). Acquisition of literacy: A longitudinal study of children in first and second grade. *Journal of Educational Psychology, 78,* 243–255.

Liberman, A. M. (1974). The speech code. In G. A. Miller (Ed.), *Psychology and communication,* Voice of America, Forum Series, 145–158.

Lyons, C. A., Pinnell, G. S., & DeFord, D. E. (1993). *Partners in learning.* Portsmouth, NH: Heinemann.

Morrow, L. (1997). *Literacy development in the early years,* 3rd edition. Boston: Allyn & Bacon.

Read, C. (1971). Preschool children's knowledge of English phonology. *Harvard Educational Review, 41,* 1–34.

Read, C. (1975). Children's categorization of speech sounds in English. (*Research Report No. 17.*) Urbana, IL: National Council of Teachers of English.

Read, C. (1986). *Children's creative spelling.* London: Routledge & Kegan Paul.

Shanahan, T., & Lomax, R. G. (1986). An analysis and comparison of theoretical models of the reading-writing relationship. *Journal of Educational Psychology, 78,* 116–123.

Teale, W. H., & Sulzby, E. (1986). *Emergent literacy: Writing and reading.* Norwood, NH: Ablex.

Tierney, R. J., & Pearson, P. D. (1983). Toward a composing model of reading. *Language Arts, 60,* 568–680.

Tierney, R., & Shanahan, T. (1991). Research on the reading-writing relationship: Interactions, transactions, and outcomes. In P. D. Pearson, R. Barr, M. Kamil, & P. Mosenthal (Eds.), *The handbook of reading research: Vol. II* (pp. 246–280). New York: Longman.

Treiman, R. (1992). The role of intrasyllabic units in learning to read and spell. In P. B. Gough, L. C. Ehri, & R. Treiman (Eds.), *Reading acquisition* (pp. 65–106). Hillsdale, NJ: Lawrence Erlbaum Associates.

Treiman, R. (1993). *Beginning to spell: A study of first-grade children.* New York: Oxford University Press.

Wilde, S. (1989). Understanding spelling strategies: A kidwatcher's guide to spelling, part 2. In K. S. Goodman, Y. M. Goodman, and W. J. Hood (Eds.), *The whole language evaluation book* (pp. 227–236). Portsmouth, NH: Heinemann.

# The Early Development of a Self-Extending System in Writing

Christine Boocock, *Reading Recovery Centre in Auckland*
Stuart McNaughton, Judy M. Parr, *University of Auckland*

## ABSTRACT

*The purpose of this study was to explore how children's writing development changes over time when interpreted from a cognitive processing position. As few methods were available for capturing such a complex behaviour as writing, it was necessary to design a suitable tool to record and then to analyse some of the features of children's behaviour when they were asked to write in the classroom. Target children (N=120) in the first four years of school were observed while writing and their behaviour was recorded and categorised using the generated procedure. Analysis of observations indicated the development of a system of writing strategies through effective monitoring and searching that allows children to take their own learning further. The major change occurred in children's word writing ability between the second and third years at school. Changes were also noted in the use of rereading, editing, resources, and of oral language while writing. Thus, this study demonstrated there is some validity to the notion of a self-extending system in writing and explored some of the behaviours and strategies that may be involved in the operation of such a system.*

Integral to her theory of how children become literate, Clay (1991) describes what she terms a "self-extending system" which incorporates the processes of strategic action, knowledge of the goals, functions and expressions of the skill, and self regulation. The interactive set of strategies which readers develop in this system are said to enable them to detect that an error has been made and to search for ways to correct it, or to use existing knowledge to solve novel problems. This system of strategies ensures that the more readers read, the more skilled they become and the less they need teacher intervention. Over time the system becomes more effective in controlling components of performance that become more fluid and automatic.

However, reading research does not provide a direct model of how such a strategic processing system might operate in writing and little systematic attention has been paid to such development empirically. It is likely that beginning *readers* may achieve a reasonable level of accuracy as they rely on strategies focused on meaning. But beginning *writers* must have additional strategies available from various sources to deliver their message in written form, as writing demands that the writer pay attention to all

25

the levels of language at once. One example of potential differences in the operating characteristics of reading and writing systems is illustrated in the process of self-correction. While reading continuous text, the reader can confirm attempts through searching and monitoring processes that use a variety of sources of information including meaning, structure, phonology, and orthography. When the reader's monitoring efforts indicate an error has occurred and revision processes are mobilised, the internal strategy of self-correction becomes a visible behaviour. Clay (1991) has suggested that such strategic processing is closely related to progress. In writing, however, the strategies of self-checking and self-correcting might operate differently because the early writer is not able to confirm attempts as conclusively as in reading or because the writer is using his or her own output as input (Bereiter & Scardamalia, 1987).

Applying the concept of a self-extending system to writing suggests that it could, in part, operate through increased competency over some of the components of writing, such as motor skills and letter and word knowledge. As these require less conscious attention allocated to them, cognitive resources would become available for more difficult aspects of the task such as spelling multisyllabic words, attending to stylistic features, or linking ideas. Clay (1987) suggests that, for example, "invented spelling can lead to a control over writing that frees the child to write the messages he wants to write" (p. 59). As in reading, if the child solves these more complex aspects using strategies that strengthen each time, slightly more difficult novel problems are able to be solved and new learning occurs. Clearly, the acquisition of this knowledge depends upon the child's developing a system of generative strategies available for use on novel or more complex problems.

If one considers that the developmental functions of a self-extending system include the principle of reciprocal causation described by Stanovich (1986), the overall process may involve what he refers to as the "bootstrapping effect." For example, knowing how to articulate words slowly in writing in order to hear and record the sounds not only provides children with a strategy for dealing with new words, but also affords them the opportunity to confirm and extend the strategy as each new word is successfully solved. Another example would include the existence of a known writing vocabulary, which would allow for the possibility of extending general knowledge about the orthographic regularities of the English language, the chunks of words that can be used, and the morphemic units that occur across words. A self-extending system in writing would generate the power to go beyond itself when tackling problems as it would be constantly attending to things that had not been noticed before, then incorporating them into the existing strategies of the system.

In a discussion of the self-regulatory processes in writing, Zimmerman and Risemberg (1997) describe the behavioural processes of self-monitoring and self-verbalisation. Evidence of an effective processing system at work in writing could be provided by behavioural indicators that suggest the child may be operating a range of searching and checking strategies. For example, slow articulation of words to guide the writing of an unknown word, or using knowledge of one word to write another by analogy are indicators of *searching* processes, as is that of accessing external resources available in the ambient environment to assist with problems. Although the source of this latter assistance is external, using it indicates the child knows that this help is available and how to access it. Indications of *checking* or self-monitoring would be visible when children reread text and/or revise their writing. With increasing expertise, there should be a shift towards personal control over instructional resources (Clay, 1991; McNaughton, 1995).

The way in which the instructional setting is organised may promote or constrain development of a self-extending system in writing. For beginning readers, developmental sequences reflect the organisational procedures and curriculum goals operating in programmes such that different developmental features are associated with different programmes (Clay, 1991). Similarly, in writing, instructional practices and opportunities may operate to affect development. For example, the teacher-child interaction that occurs in conferencing can provide differential opportunities for independence and control (Glasswell, Parr, & McNaughton, 1996).

Research suggests children develop strategic behaviour in writing both outside school (e.g., Chomsky, 1970, 1971; Ferreiro & Teberosky, 1982; Read, 1971, 1975) and in the school classroom (Calkins, 1980; Dyson, 1985; Y. Goodman & Wilde, 1985; Graves, 1973, 1983, 1984; ). For example, Graves (1983) talks of the production of drafts by eight- and nine-year-olds as evidence of "control of the writing process" (p. 4) and, using anecdotal evidence, describes a developmental sequence in the types of changes made. Similarly, for spelling, Gentry (1982) identified changes children go through on their way to becoming competent spellers and Radebaugh (1985) examined the spelling strategies that third- and fourth-graders used to write a word. Indeed, the notion of strategic control is central to literacy learning (Cambourne, 1988, 1995; Clay, 1991). An assumption is made, certainly in New Zealand curriculum materials (e.g., Dancing with the Pen, 1992), that, as in early reading, learners develop strategic control over their writing. But, compelling as this concept is, there has been limited detailed examination of changes in writing behaviour across age or class levels and over time. Assumptions about the developmental shift towards greater strategic control over performance have not been examined systematically and empirically.

This study was designed to examine likely indicators of a self-extending system for writing. To reiterate, such indicators may include observable strategies for: (a) *word solving*, such as using vocalisation to break the word into parts or to make the phoneme-grapheme link; (b) *monitoring* and *editing*, such as rereading to check what has been written, to confirm the intended message, or to provide a cue for what may come next; and (c) *searching*, such as using analogies or classroom resources. The study further aimed to examine developmental shifts with respect to these indicators over the first four years of instruction. The focus of the study centered on answering descriptive questions, namely: What changes can be observed in written language produced by children? What changes occur in the way children check and alter their writing? What changes occur in the way children transcribe their writing, using searching strategies to problem solve?

## Method

### Participants

A total of 120 children, 62 boys and 58 girls, were chosen randomly from the class rolls in three schools. The children were in the first four years of school and there were 30 children at each level. The mean age in each group was: Year 1, five years nine months;

Year 2, six years nine months; Year 3, seven years nine months; and Year 4, eight years eight months.

The three schools were selected on the recommendation of a school language consultant as having assistant principals, in charge of the first three years, who were knowledgeable about the teaching of writing. The 13 teachers had teaching experience ranging from less than one year to 28 years. All schools taught children from beginning instruction to Year 6 (ages 5–11). Two of the schools were in the urban area of South Auckland and one was in what might be described as the "inner city." The enrollments were 533, 305, and 263, respectively, with two schools having single classrooms and one an open plan design. The schools consisted of Anglo/European populations from 49 percent to 80 percent, and of Maori children from 5 percent to 29 percent, with other Pacific Island and Asian groups represented. One of the schools qualified for additional funding from the Ministry of Education to assist them in coping with pressures resulting from the diverse ethnic composition of the school and the proportion of unskilled and unemployed parents in the school community.

## Procedure

A cross-sectional descriptive design was employed. The behaviours of individual children, as they attempted to write meaningful text during classroom writing sessions, were observed and recorded. Informal observations were made of organisational variables operating in the classrooms. Classroom writing programmes were usually of half-an-hour's duration with the younger children using only a part of that time to compose their story. The researcher observed the class from the beginning of the writing period and, when the children had begun to work, observed each of the target children individually for a period of five minutes. All writing behaviour, oral language behaviour, and other behaviours were recorded on a grid using a predetermined coding system (explained below). The concentration was on the transcription aspects of the process, particularly at the word level as this is critical to a developing process. Copies of the total piece of text being written were analysed and ratings of these included considerations of text level features and whether the writing carried a message.

## Coding and Classification of Data

The observational categories initially encompassed six areas which, in pilot observations, were determined to be behaviours occurring whilst the children were writing. These six include: oral behaviours, word writing, rereading, editing, resource use, and interruptions. Subsequently these six were grouped under four categories: (a) oral behaviour, (b) words written, (c) monitoring (rereading and editing), and (d) resource use. In addition, a holistic analysis of the overall quality of the written piece was conducted. Each will be discussed.

**Oral responses.** To determine changes in the quantity of oral responses before or during writing, each child received a rating based on the amount of this activity as follows:

- *Zero points* were given when the child made no oral utterances or lip movements.
- *One point* was given when there were some oral utterances or lip movements (i.e., less than 50% of the words written had some indication of this behaviour associated with their production).
- *Two points* were given when many oral utterances or lip movements were observed (i.e., more than 50% of the words had some indication of this behaviour associated with their production).

**Word writing.** Two sub-categories of written words were used. The first was the number of total words written. All spaced letter groups were counted as words except for place names or children's names. Compound words were counted as one word however they were written. For example, *Faua bale*, to represent *fireball*, was counted as one word. Capitalisation was ignored. The category of *total words written* was used to indicate the competency of children in writing words, regardless of accuracy or assistance. The other sub-category was *total words written correctly for spelling without assistance*. To be counted in this category, no assistance from any source had been observed, including all the categories included in resource use. A word was counted if correctly written for spelling but not necessarily syntactically correct, for example, *of* for *off*. A word was counted as incorrect if a letter, written incorrectly, could be confused with another. For example, *doat* for *boat* was not counted. Apostrophes to denote possession did not have to be present for a word to be counted as correct. Colloquial words were counted as correct if written regularly (e.g., *oh*), as were common abbreviations, (e.g., *M.P.*).

**Monitoring.** This category includes the sub-categories of rereading and editing. Rereading of already composed text was recorded when there was a clear indication through pointing and/or oral reading, or eye or head movement, to identify the starting point of the rereading.

Changes over time in the type and quantity of editing made to text were computed from analysis of observation records. Editing was said to have occurred when the child, without assistance, changed the text already written in a way that altered the form of the text. Sometimes this change was at the letter level, for example changing *i* to *I* or *an tree* to *a tree*. Other changes were at a phrase level and included rejecting the opening to a sentence and beginning with a different form of words. These changes resulted in both correct and incorrect text.

**Resource use.** Resources were classified as human (teacher and peer assistance) and material resources. Information on assistance given to children, whether child- or teacher-initiated, was drawn from the records. A count was made of the frequency with which children received help per word written, regardless of the number of consultations at the letter level, if there were no breaks in the consultation.

Material resources were categorised as one of four types, namely: (a) the child's own text whether a current or previous story; (b) a dictionary—this included alphabet and teacher-produced word lists, notebook dictionaries, or published dictionaries;

(c) general resources—any resource such as a list, display or book that was in the class-room but had not been generated for the writing session; and (d) a specific resource—any resource that had been generated for that specific task, for example, the story written on the board prior to the writing time or the brainstormed list of useful words.

To be included in the analysis, the sequence of behaviour had to have been completed. In a few cases the child had just begun to consult the resource when the observation period finished. If it was unclear to the researcher the reason the child was searching a resource, she asked the child after the observation period to confirm the reason for the search. This most often occurred when the children turned back and searched through their own text.

**Holistic analysis of written pieces.** To obtain an independent measure of the overall quality of the writing, four experienced raters were used. The instructions directed the raters to assess the overall quality of the writing and to assign a rating on a five-point scale. The scale, which is included in the appendix, attempted to capture the overall quality of the child's writing while taking into consideration component aspects of the process (Boocock, 1991). Similar scales were used by Kroll (1983) and by Juel, Griffith, and Gough (1986). The description of the criteria to be assessed on the scale included word writing ability, phonemic analysis, structural considerations, and the extent to which the writing carried a message. As an example, writing samples were rated in category 1 if "The child's writing does not carry the message" and in category 4 if the child's writing consisted of "two or more paragraphs organised around a theme." Raters were also given five rated stories taken from the samples to illustrate the steps of the scale.

## Inter-Observer Reliability

To establish reliability in the coding of data, care was taken to determine inter-observer perceptions. For the on-site observations, an independent observer watched 30 children (25% of the sample, from six of the classrooms) concurrently with the researcher. Inter-observer reliability was calculated overall and for specific categories. Agreement level was calculated on the sequential behavioural record and expressed as a percentage. Agreement was judged to have been achieved when the two observers recorded behaviour as occurring in a particular sequence and in a particular category. Oral responses were not included in this reliability calculation because of the difficulty experienced in arranging for two persons to be in a position to capture oral responses as they occurred. Non-agreement was indicated if only one observer had recorded behaviour as occurring. If a word writing sequence was interrupted by behaviour that only one observer recorded, non-agreement was judged to have been reached for this behaviour, but not necessarily for the word as a whole. Calculated in this way, there was 89.15 percent agreement overall.

To check agreement on specific categories of observation, Pearson product-moment correlations for monitoring behaviours were calculated. The resulting coefficients were 0.94 for *editing* and 0.87 for *rereading of written text*. These results indicate that the behaviour could be captured reliably using these procedures.

With respect to ratings of the quality of writing, four educators independently rated the samples of writing collected at the various observation points. Inter-rater agreement was high (>85%) and the scores assigned were mean ratings.

## Results

To answer questions in the present study concerning change across class level groups, raw scores were computed and group means, percentages or ratios, were calculated for data in the four main category groups. The effect of class level was investigated using two one-way analyses of variance (ANOVA) for the categories of *total words written* and *total words written correctly and unassisted*. Post-hoc tests (Tukey) were used to determine if there were significant differences between class levels.

### Qualitative Ratings of Writing Samples

The mean ratings for overall quality of writing produced were: Year 1, 2.00; Year 2, 2.54; Year 3, 3.17; and Year 4, 3.39. These ratings indicate an increase in writing quality for each class level. To illustrate this qualitative comparison, a category 2 rating was a "simple sentence, clearly delineated, with a clear message" (e.g., "When I went to my nanas hoes/ house to stae/stay the night I fale/fell out of bed."). Although 2.0 was the mean score for Y1 writing, the range was considerable, from samples such as "IFeHPYAyHeCWTJSeEtOVrW" to writing which was rated in category three, involving more extended writing using several sentences. In Y2, the best writing samples received a rating of category 4. Apart from being two or more paragraphs, each consisting of several connected sentences around a theme, such category pieces illustrated mastery of conventions such as spelling and dialogue. The total mean increase between Y3 and Y4 was lower than between other class levels, suggesting an increase in quality was slowing between these levels. Also, the requisite competencies for the quality of writing at the top of the rating scale had not been achieved by most children in the class range of this study.

### Oral Language Behaviour Before and During Writing

The difficulties of capturing oral language behaviours necessitated the use of broad categories. Oral behaviour declined in total across class levels. The percentages of records that contained no oral behaviour were: Y1, 17 percent; Y2, 23 percent; Y3, 43 percent; and Y4, 50 percent. Those records with oral behaviour were divided into two groups according to the proportion of oral behaviour per words written. Those texts with greater than or equal to half the words written involving oral behaviour were: Y1, 60 percent; Y2, 40 percent; Y3, 17 percent; and Y4, 10 percent.

Change across class levels was evident in the type of oral articulation that occurred. It should be noted that some children at Y1 level did not say anything as they wrote whilst some Y4 children responded orally while writing half or more of the words. The three children in Y4 who fell into this category, however, were producing indistinct lip movements or murmurings compared to more overt articulation in the younger children. More of the latter rated in the category of greater than or equal to half the words written involving oral behaviour.

## Words Written

Table 1 presents data on the mean number and range of words written in the five-minute period at each class level. The words written information is expressed in two categories: (a) total words written and (b) total words written correctly and unassisted. Children increased their writing in both categories as they got older. Whilst there were increases in means between Y1 and Y2, and between Y3 and Y4, a major increase occurred on both types of words written between Y2 and Y3. Consideration of the written products suggests that for some children, the increase in the total words written was partly accounted for by the use of approximations or invented spellings (e.g., "my tay gun that shats plsdc sdcs that are savin ainchs laing" <my toy gun that shoots plastic sticks that are seven inches long>). These data are presented in Figure 1.

It is important to note that the range in both categories of words written was considerable at all class levels, with the less expert writers in each class producing very little. The top of the range continued to increase with age. The percentage of total words written correctly without assistance was: Y1, 70.2 percent; Y2, 75.5 percent; Y3, 87.2 percent; and Y4, 90 percent. The mean percentage of correct unassisted different words written of three letters or more was: Y1, 26.5 percent; Y2, 28.14 percent; Y3, 41.8 percent; and Y4, 46.6 percent.

To examine these differences, one-way analyses of variance (ANOVA) were conducted on the two categories, that is, total words written and total words written without assistance. The main effect of class level was significant on both variables: total words

**Table 1** Mean Number and Range of Total Words and Total Unassisted Correct Words Written in Five Minutes for Class Years

| WORDS WRITTEN | CLASS YEARS[a] | | | |
| --- | --- | --- | --- | --- |
| | Y1 | Y2 | Y3 | Y4 |
| | Mean (SD) | Mean (SD) | Mean (SD) | Mean (SD) |
| Words Total | 9.73 (0.37) | 13.47 (2.49) | 28.43 (1.69) | 32.10 (4.73) |
| Total Unassisted Correct Words | .6.87 (0.31) | 10.13 (1.30) | 24.77 (0.66) | 28.87 (2.66) |

[a]n = 30 for each class level

written, $F(3, 116) = 16.70$, p < .01 and total unassisted correct words written, $F(3, 116) =$ 19.09, p < .01. Post hoc comparisons were made using Tukey (HSD) tests to establish significant differences between means. For total words written, these differences were between Y1 and both Y3 and Y4, and between Y2 and both Y3 and Y4, $q(116) = 11.30$, p < .01. For the category of total unassisted correct words these differences were similarly between Y1 and Y3 and Y4, and between Y2 and Y3 and Y4, $q(116) = 10.37$, p < .01.

## Monitoring

**Rereading.** Two types of behaviour were used to illustrate children's monitoring as they wrote. One source of data was the rereading of text that had been previously written and the other was changes made to the text as it was being written.

The proportion of writing samples containing rereading behaviour was Y1, 63%; Y2, 77%; Y3, 70%; and Y4, 50%. The percentage of children who reread fluctuated across the class levels with the lowest level occurring in Y4. The mean amount of children's rereading behaviour was adjusted for ten words written. These data are presented in Figure 2. It can be seen that the children in Y1 and Y2 reread a greater proportion of what they had written than those in Y3 and Y4.

**Editing.** The percentage of writing samples containing edits was: Y1, 27%; Y2, 67%; Y3, 73%; and Y4, 83%. The edits included changes to punctuation, whole words, and letters within words. The mean number of edits adjusted for ten words written per child was calculated and the results are presented in Figure 3. The graph indicates the direction of change from low levels of editing in Y1 to an increase in Y2 and a levelling off at Y3 and Y4.

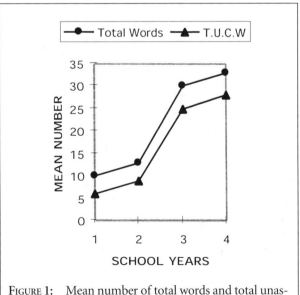

FIGURE 1:   Mean number of total words and total unassisted correct words

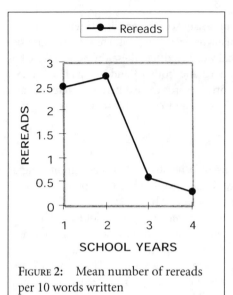

**FIGURE 2:** Mean number of rereads per 10 words written

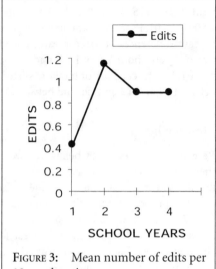

**FIGURE 3:** Mean number of edits per 10 words written

## Resources Used

The nature of teacher and peer interaction occurring during writing and the physical resources provided in the classroom were recorded. Constraints on the use of human and material sources of assistance were also noted. These constraints mainly involved the apparent emphasis placed on children's getting down their own messages by attempting problem words, which were to be checked later for spelling and meaning. As a result, in most Y3 and Y4 classes, children were discouraged from seeking out dictionary resources while they were writing.

Some comments can be made about patterns of assistance and availability that occurred. All teachers were available to children in some manner. They roved around the classroom, sat at their table, or sat at children's writing tables. All children sat in groups, often with individual desks for the older children or at larger tables that could seat four to six children. Peer interaction was encouraged to some degree although teachers often requested quieter noise levels while the children were working. In only one Y4 class did the teacher insist on absolute quiet when children were writing. Data from observations of teacher assistance, peer assistance, as well as that of materials as resource assistance are discussed below.

**Teacher assistance.** Instances of this type of interaction were obtained from observations of teacher-initiated behaviour with respect to the target children. Quantitative analysis of this category was restricted to a count of the number of words that included some consultation with a teacher and whether that assistance was utilised in the text subsequently written. Teacher help given to target children while they were being observed was restricted to the Y1, Y2, and Y4 levels because all Y3 target children wrote without teacher assistance during the observation time. It had been anticipated that more intensive teacher interaction might occur at the early levels, particularly whenever the child did not fully control the task and this proved to be the case. Eight of the target children received teacher assistance while being observed at the Y1 level, one child received assistance at Y2, and two at Y4. Even with the small number of teacher-child interactions observed, it is possible to comment on a pattern of interaction that emerged. Most of the teacher interactions occurred in one Y1 classroom, although teacher interactions occurred in three other classrooms. The teachers drew the children's attention to many aspects of language in brief exchanges as the children wrote; these included: (a) the meaning of their message, (b) the structure of their sentences, (c) the relationship between letters and sounds, and (d) the correct spelling of a word. The teachers also drew children's attention to external resources that were available. In only one instance did a teacher tell the child a spelling without prior or subsequent discussion. A pattern emerged from the data where the teacher was working with children who did not control many aspects of writing. The teacher worked with the child and did what she deemed to be necessary for the task to be completed successfully, whilst also trying to take the child's learning further.

**Peer assistance.** Children's interactions with peers were obtained and analysed in the same manner as those of teacher-child ones. All interaction with peers around particular problems resulted in the sample child simply being told letters or words, except for one child in Y1 who prompted the target child to articulate slowly the word requested. Of the two class levels where peer help was recorded, the information used by the target child was correct three times in Y1 and incorrect twice, and in Y4, correct eight times and incorrect once. The support of peers was given high priority in most classrooms. In some classes more competent children were observed to give considerable help to less competent writers, sometimes limiting their own writing efforts.

**Assistance from material resources.** The writing problems for which the children sought external help, other than from teachers and peers, predominantly involved the writing of words and letters. The categories of resources that children sought for help were their own text, a published dictionary, any teacher-written list, a general classroom resource, or specific teacher-written resources. Children across the class levels used their own text to refer to the spellings of words most frequently (Y1, 8 times; Y2, 1 time; Y3, 10 times; and Y4, 7 times). Use of other resources occurred infrequently.

## Discussion

### Change Over Time in Writing: Text Quality and Word Use

**Across-group differences.** The two measures used to detect change over time in children's writing yielded quite different results. The global rating of texts indicated the children, on average, did improve the quality of their writing. This was particularly marked at the early levels and there was some variability across schools. On the word writing measure, in contrast, some startling shifts in behaviour occurred between the Y2 and Y3 class levels. A possible explanation for this sudden increase in the number of words written correctly without assistance relates to our initial discussion of the development of skilled behaviour and the possible existence of a self-extending system in writing. Such an increase would appear to confirm the existence of processing mechanisms that enable children, who previously may have established control of only a small number of words, to develop ways of expanding their vocabularies. This would account for the sharp increase between the Y2 and Y3 level.

During the task of writing continuous text, the children's attention was focused on words they wanted to write and it seems that, through continued correct use of the most common ones, learning was taking place. These high frequency words became progressively easier to write fluently resulting in a threefold increase in the mean number of words written per five-minute period from Y1 to Y4. At the same time, the number of total words written correctly without assistance increased fourfold. These findings are consistent with the position that in learning how to write a few words accurately, they have also developed important generative strategies. They have learnt how to learn words independently in order to write novel ones. As this happens, other processing capacity becomes available for strategies to be extended and for attention to be given to other words and to other aspects of the process.

The data from this study support the movement towards control over longer, less frequently used words. The development of these generative strategies would enable this element of the processing system to become self-extending. The levelling off of mean number of total words that were written correctly without assistance that occurred between Y3 and Y4 may indicate that once children are able to write a core of frequently used words, their attention turns to other aspects of the writing process. However, this may reflect a programme effect. If children are choosing topics to write about, as they were in many classrooms, they themselves may be limiting their exposure to less frequently used unknown words by writing about familiar subjects. Therefore, the opportunities to extend the set of strategies available to them would be restricted.

**Individual differences.** By Y4 the gap had increased between the most competent and the least competent writers in both word writing categories. At this level the difference between the highest and lowest number words written for both categories had doubled in comparison to the first year of school. Croft (1987) reported increases in the variability of achievement in accurate spelling and the quantity of writing from Y3 to Y8. This research supports the finding of variability increasing with age in these two areas and also shows such variability occurring at an earlier age.

Evidence suggests that whilst the competent children are improving in writing, the children at the bottom end of the achievement range are not. These lower-achieving children may perceive the task as too frustrating, resulting in a sense of failure, less engagement in the task, and lower achievement. Stanovich (1986) has described this phenomenon in relation to progress in reading, in which the rich get richer and the poor poorer, as the "Matthew Effect." Essentially, the more children read, the better they become at it. Those who do not read well, and consequently do not have the opportunity to practice competent reading, do not improve. This study confirms the potential for this effect to be operating in writing. Such an outcome would be consistent with current theories of development (Vygotsky, 1978; Wood, Bruner, & Ross, 1976) which suggest that intensive individual instruction from experienced teachers who scaffold the task based on the elements of the writing process the child could control, would be beneficial in attempting to close the gap in achievement. Observations of teachers revealed that in most Y1 and Y2 classes, more individual teaching time was given to all children while writing than was the case in Y3 and Y4 classes.

This study also provides support for the notion that the lowest-achieving readers and writers would benefit from individual instruction at the point when most children are getting underway in reading and writing in order to prevent the cycle of non-achievement. Many children in New Zealand have that opportunity in a Reading Recovery programme (Clay, 1993). This programme includes a writing component in which the child writes a simple sentence with the aid of the teacher. In this study, the researchers noted that the least competent writers at Y3 and Y4 were children who had not had the opportunity to participate in the Reading Recovery programme, or who were new settlers from non-English speaking countries.

## Change Over Time in Writing: Monitoring and Searching Behaviour

According to Clay's theory of children becoming literate (1991), monitoring strategies that are observable, such as rereading and editing text, and internal and external searching strategies would be important to the creation and increasing power of a self-extending system as they would generate, in a cumulative way, new knowledge and understandings about language. With respect to the areas investigated in this study, some comments can be made regarding strategy use.

The rereading behaviour that was evident suggested shifts in the amount of text children had to monitor overtly to keep control of the task. At Y3 and Y4 the children were able to write more words in the same amount of time and to maintain control over what they were producing before rereading their text. It is plausible to assume they were monitoring more internally as they wrote their stories, since their edits increased over time, while their overt rereading did not. This would suggest there was more processing capacity available for attending to other aspects of the process so they have the potential to notice more and learn more by themselves.

In the present study, another indicator of strategy use in writing was the child's use of resources to aid problem solving. We found there was limited use of other people and external material resources provided by the environment. Children were relying primarily on their own resources when writing, either through knowing how to write the word or attempting a spelling, often through an analysis of sounds. Factors in the environment appeared to contribute to this emphasis. For example, in some classes the children were encouraged to attempt to write the word themselves and check their spelling after the end of the writing period or when they finished the story. If the aim is developing active problem solving through a flexible system of strategies, the learner needs the opportunity to engage with the whole process in order to learn how to orchestrate the many components. Those classrooms that do not provide the children with knowledge of how to access a variety of resources to solve their problems are limiting learning opportunities.

If there were a self-extending system operating, what would be the role of the teacher? It would seem that the influence of the teacher, as well as the programme, would be most critical at the time when the children are developing a processing system, leading eventually to the children's being able to extend their learning further on their own. The nature of the teacher's assistance should be consistent with the notion of scaffolding within the children's zone of proximal development (Vygotsky, 1978; Wood, Bruner, & Ross, 1976) and be focused on developing a flexible system of strategies for operating effectively using both internal and external assistance.

Teacher observations in this study yielded examples of graduated responses of teachers to children at lower achievement levels that fitted the scaffolding model. In time, the role of the teacher might shift to extending the range of opportunities to use this processing system to solve novel problems in text writing. Therefore, exposure to the special properties of different types of writing may be appropriate. In the present study, most writing was of a personal narrative type, however, some teachers said they interspersed this type of writing with other genres during the year. Indeed there was evidence on the walls of the classrooms that children were engaged in a variety of writing opportunities. This writing conformed to the qualities of transactional writing and indicated children were being exposed to other genres.

An important part of building the use of material resources into a child's repertoire of strategies would be providing a range of resources and showing how to access them to search for new information or how to check with attempts already made. Such instruction could begin in the initial classes with resources appropriate to the children's progress in writing.

It seems a balance would need to be struck, on the one hand, between children having access to and knowing how to use all the resources available to them in a way that enabled practising what they knew and, on the other hand, pushing their own learning further by encountering new problems to solve. An imbalance in the use of a range of strategies, such as occurred when children copied whole texts from the teacher's writing, provided fewer opportunities for learning.

Some comments can be made regarding possible ways of increasing access to resources. For example, in a large class where access to a teacher is difficult, it may be possible to increase the number of adults in the room, particularly when children are forming their processing system. In this study only two classes had some assistance from other teachers and parents. Special considerations are needed when incorporating peer assistance into the classroom environment. In terms of Vygotsky's theory (1978), the peer must be a more competent one to affect the course of development. In the few examples available in this study, peer assistance was not always helpful at the Y1 level, as the children were of similar expertise. At the Y4 level, peers offering help were invariably more competent and could assist children to solve their problems. To be an effective resource, children of diverse ability levels need to be available in the instructional setting.

## Changes to Oral Language Use

This study confirmed a trend towards the development of direct processing from thought to written language without the intermediary of sound. It demonstrated the relative importance of oral behaviour, both phoneme analysis and the oral composition of text, when children first begin to write, but supported the notion that this behaviour is internalised over time. The analysis of data showed that silent writing occurred at all class levels. From a processing position, the children may not have acquired phonemic knowledge. Alternatively, they may have possessed other more efficient strategies to access words. Also, those children who did not orally compose text in advance may not have developed the strategy or may have moved beyond needing to use it.

## Conclusion and Limitations of the Study

Three limitations should be kept in mind when considering the findings of this study. The first is that the small-scale nature of this study meant the cross-section of children sampled at each class level was only 30. This number limits the generalisability of the data in describing inter-individual change. Second, the research view changes across class levels, but to investigate this question further, we would need a longitudinal study of specific children to capture intra-individual change over time. The study pointed to environmental features that may constrain or increase the behaviour, but could not confirm their effect. Finally, it may be that five minutes per child for observation was insufficient to capture the use of material resources by the children. From the high percentages of words written without assistance, it would seem that occasions when external help was needed were not themselves high in number and, therefore, a study of these would require longer observation periods.

The purpose of this study was to explore how children's writing development changes over time when interpreted from a cognitive processing position. As few methods were available for capturing such a complex behaviour as writing, it was necessary to design a suitable tool to record and then to analyse some of the features of children's behaviour when they were asked to write in the classroom. It has been possible to suggest tentatively how children become more skilled at writing to the point where they are able to assume responsibility for their own learning. Further, this study demonstrated that there is some validity to the notion of a self-extending system in writing and explored some of the behaviours and strategies that may be involved in the operation of such a system. Additional research is needed to investigate the mechanisms of its operation. Another question to be explored is the nature of the reciprocity between the processing systems of reading and writing.

## References

Bereiter, C., & Scardamalia, M. (1987). *The psychology of written composition.* Hillsdale, NJ: Lawrence Erlbaum.

Boocock, C. *Observing children write in the first four years of school.* Unpublished masters thesis, University of Auckland.

Calkins, L. (1983). *Lessons from a child.* Portsmouth, NJ: Heinemann.

Cambourne, B. (1988). *The whole story: Natural learning and the acquisition of literacy in the classroom.* Gosford, New South Wales: Ashton Scholastic.

Cambourne, B. (1995). Toward an educationally relevant theory of literacy learning: Twenty years of enquiry. *The Reading Teacher, 49,* 182–190.

Chomsky, C. (1970). Reading, writing, and phonology. *Harvard Educational Review, 40,* 287–309.

Chomsky, C. (1971). Write first: Read later. *Childhood Education, 47,* 396–399.

Clay, M. M. (1966). *Emergent reading behaviour.* Unpublished doctoral thesis, University of Auckland.

Clay, M. M. (1969). Reading errors and self-correction behaviour. *British Journal of Educational Psychology, 39,* 47–56.

Clay, M. M. (1987). *Writing begins at home.* Auckland, NZ: Heinemann.

Clay, M. M. (1991). *Becoming literate: The construction of inner control.* Auckland, NZ: Heinemann.

Clay, M. M. (1993). *Reading Recovery: A guidebook for teachers in training.* Auckland, NZ: Heinemann.

Croft, C. (1983). Teacher's manual for Spell-Write. Wellington, NZ: New Zealand Council for Educational Research.

Croft, C. (1987). Word use and spelling mistakes in a national sample of primary writing. *New Zealand Journal of Educational Studies, 22,* 215–220.

Dyson, A. H. (1985). Three emergent writers and the school curriculum: Copying and other myths. *The Elementary School Journal, 4,* 497–511.

Ferreiro, E., & Teberosky, A. (1982). *Literacy before schooling.* Exeter, NH: Heinemann.

Gentry, R. (1982). Spelling genius at work. *The Reading Teacher, 36,* 192–199.

Glasswell, K., Parr, J., & McNaughton, S. (1996). *Developmental pathways in the construction of writing expertise.* Paper presented to the New Zealand Association for Research in Education, Nelson, NZ.

Goodman, K. S. (1970). Using children's reading miscues for new teaching strategies. *The Reading Teacher, 23,* 455–459.

Goodman, Y., & Wilde, S. J. (1985). *Writing development: Third and fourth grade O'Odham (Papago) students* (Research Report No.14). The University of Arizona.

Graves, D. (1973*). Children's writing: Research directions and hypotheses based upon an examination of the writing processes of seven-year-old children.* Unpublished doctoral thesis, University of Buffalo.

Graves, D. (1983). *Teachers and children at work.* Exeter, NH: Heinemann.

Graves, D. (1984). *A researcher learns to write.* Exeter, NH: Heinemann.

Holdaway, D. (1979). *The foundations of literacy.* Sydney, NZ: Ashton Scholastic.

Juel, C., Griffith, P. L., & Gough, P. G. (1986). Acquisition of literacy: A longitudinal study of children in first and second grade. *Journal of Educational Psychology, 78,* 234–255.

Kroll, B. (1983). Antecedents of individual differences in children's writing attainment. In B. Kroll & G. Wells (Eds.). *Explorations in the development of writing.* Chichester, NY: John Wiley & Sons.

Luria, A. R. (1970, March). The functional organisation of the brain. *Scientific American, 222,* 66–78.

McNaughton, S. (1987). *Being skilled: The socializations of learning to read.* London: Methuen.

McNaughton, S. (1995). *Patterns of emergent literacy.* Auckland, NZ: Oxford University Press.

Ministry of Education. (1992). *Dancing with the pen: The learner as a writer.* Wellington, NZ: Learning Media.

Radebaugh, M. (1985). Children's perceptions of their spelling strategies. *The Reading Teacher, 38,* 532–536.

Read, C. (1971). Pre-school children's knowledge of English phonology. *Harvard Educational Review, 41,* 1–34.

Read, C. (1975). *Children's categorisation of speech sounds in English.* Urbana, IL: National Council of Teachers of English.

Scardamalia, M. (1981). How children cope with the cognitive demands of writing. In C. Frederiksen & J. Dominic (Vol. Eds.). *Writing: The nature, development and teaching of written communication.* Writing: Process development and communication (Vol. 2, pp. 81–103). Hillsdale, NJ: Lawrence Erlbaum.

Stanovich, K. E. (1986). Matthew effects in reading: Some consequences of individual differences in the acquisition of literacy. *Reading Research Quarterly, 21,* 360–406.

Vygotsky, L. S. (1978). *Mind in society.* Cambridge, MA: Harvard University Press.

Wood, D., Bruner, J. S., & Ross, G. (1976). The role of tutoring in problem-solving. *Journal of Child Psychology and Psychiatry, 17,* 89–100.

Zimmerman, B., & Risemberg, R. (1997). Becoming a self-regulated writer: A social cognitive perspective. *Contemporary Educational Psychology, 22,* 73–101.

# Appendix

## Holistic Analysis of Writing

**Instructions to Raters.** Please read these copies of draft writing. Where it is part of an ongoing story, this is included with the last date shown giving an indication of the amount of writing completed in one day. Allocate for the writing a rating according to the accompanying rating sheet. These categories are aimed at capturing the quality of the message the children are able to compose with the assistance available in their classroom. If assigning a rating of 3 or 4 according to the categories on the rating sheet, please indicate whether the writing fits A or B.

## Rating Categories

CATEGORY 1
The child's writing doesn't carry the message
- Letters used predominately
- May include a few high frequency words

CATEGORY 2
One simple sentence with words clearly delineated and a clear message
- A few high frequency words written correctly.
- Dominant sounds recorded in other words

CATEGORY 3
One paragraph using 2–6 sentences
- Many small high frequency words written correctly
- Either A) Many sounds correct in other words
  Or B) Gaps left for proofreading

CATEGORY 4
Two or more paragraphs using 6+ sentences around a theme
- Most high frequency words written correctly
- Either A) Few words written incorrectly
  Or B) Gaps left for proofreading

CATEGORY 5
More than two paragraphs possibly written over many days
- Most words written correctly
- More sophisticated sentence structures vocabulary and/or more literacy composition

# Achieving Motivation:
# Guiding Edward's Journey to Literacy

Susan King Fullerton, *The Ohio State University*

## ABSTRACT

*This article is a retrospective account of a teacher working with a child learning to read and write in Reading Recovery. Looking back provides further opportunity for analysis and recognition of changes or important moments in time with an awareness that may not typically occur in the throes of working with a challenging, at-risk child. This account builds upon observational records, a case study, and examples of the child's work, intersecting with a theoretical view that focuses on the complex relationship of emotions, motivation, and cognition in learning, providing insights into ways a teacher may scaffold for changes in motivational and cognitive processing.*

**Susan:** "What's the next word you need to write?"
**Edward:** "I don't know how to write it!"
**Susan:** "Say it slowly. What can you hear?"
**Edward:** "But I don't know that word!"
*Little black dots scattered across the page as Edward rapidly tapped the pen on the paper.*
**Susan:** "Edward, you try it. Say it slowly. That will help you write the word."
*When Edward still said nothing, I slowly said the word. He then responded with the first letter.*
**Susan:** "Good! What else do you hear?"
*A long black line snaked its way across the page as Edward lightly trailed the pen across the paper. He looked at me sideways to see how I would react. I took the pen from his hand and again prompted him to say the word slowly.*

Variations on this scene played out more times than I would like to admit in my work with Edward. As he became more resistant, I would become anxious, wondering what he might do next. Would he get so frustrated that he would bite me, as he had his classroom teacher? My thoughts would become confused and disorganized in trying to focus on my teaching goals while attempting to keep him on task, not to mention how frustrated I was with my ineffectiveness. I felt so incapable that I wanted to quit! I soon became aware of how anxiety and frustration affected my teaching, but it took longer for me to realize that these feelings were also present in Edward. He too felt anxious and incapable—and he too wanted to quit!

43

The complexity of cognitive, motivational, and emotional factors that influenced Edward's behavior also influenced mine—and made it more difficult for me to make on-the-spot decisions and to teach with the clarity of thought and observation that was required. However, working with Edward each day challenged me to reflect more intensely, to think and teach differently, to put aside my own familiar patterns of responding, and to stay more attuned to Edward's ways of responding. I have reflected on how my work with this child influenced my own emotions, motivation, and cognition. It would be difficult to capture the complexity of this teaching-learning interaction without such consideration.

Unfortunately, my initial perspective was much more simplistic. I felt he was just unwilling to try. When I encouraged him to make attempts, he diverted his attention (and mine) by focusing on some other object, topic, or event (such as the black marks on the paper). As his emotional levels became elevated, so did the level of avoidance and anger. As I observed these cycles occur, I came to realize that each instantiation of such an event further bound these negative emotions and learning together, reinforcing the likelihood that the most inappropriate responses would bring about the desired effect—avoidance. He would not have to display his perceived inabilities or failure. Avoidance, at any cost, became the motivating force. The note that I jotted down when I first began to work with him—"I need to avoid giving him the opportunity to say, 'I don't know'"—was much more revealing than I initially recognized. My work with Edward became the impetus for my thinking more deeply about the functioning of the brain; the relationship of emotion, motivation, and cognition; and most importantly, about the view that children come to school with different ways of knowing and responding (Clay, 1998). These reflections became the driving forces behind my renewed interest in theories of motivation.

In the last decade, there has been increasing awareness of the importance of motivation in relation to literacy, but theory and research in motivation has had fewer connections to the study of emotions and emotional development. For children such as Edward, and arguably for all learners, a knowledge base that combines these two areas may contribute to increasing understandings of teaching and learning. In the first section of this article, I provide a brief explanation of the role of emotions in learning. The second section provides an overview of the theoretical constructs of achievement motivation and attribution theory and their relationship to emotions and cognition, followed by a discussion of the stance toward learning characterized as learned helplessness. In counterpoint to the discussion of learned helplessness, the relationship of motivation and self-regulation will be addressed. Throughout, I will provide vignettes of my work with Edward, describing how these theoretical constructs relate to work we do with at-risk learners. Edward's story serves as one exemplar of the complexity of emotions, motivation, and cognition and provides insights into the ways that interactions and scaffolding within literacy events influence changes in motivational and cognitive processing.

## The Roles of Emotion and Motivation in Learning

Since the 18th century, psychologists have recognized a division of the mind as having three parts: cognition (or thought), affect (including emotion), and motivation (Salovey & Sluyter, 1997). Yet, of these three, cognition alone has received primary attention in theory and research related to learning, and as a result, "we've never incorporated emotion comfortably into the curriculum and classroom" (Sylwester, 1995, p. 72). The relationship of cognition and affect has been an important area of study in psychology for more than 15 years (Salovey & Sluyter, 1997), but until recently there was little connection between the two in education.

While affect or motivation was included in a few models of reading processes, their role in reading achievement and reading behavior has received little attention "beyond appearing as a 'box' in the figure depicting the model" (Athey, 1985, p. 527). When Wigfield and Asher (1984) provided a review of achievement motivation theories in the first edition of the *Handbook of Reading Research*, they noted the few early studies relating reading and motivation. Only since the early 1990s has there been sustained research in motivation (Guthrie & Wigfield, 2000), primarily through the work of researchers at the National Reading Research Center who have developed a body of research relating reading, motivation, and engagement. Still, for the most part, the role of emotions is seldom incorporated into the discussion. This is beginning to change. Cross-pollination of theory and research—particularly in fields such as neuroscience, psychology, and education—has begun to offer new insights into the relationship of cognition, emotion, and motivation, which in turn can inform reading research and instruction. In this paper, I present an example of the complex nature of emotion, motivation, and cognition in early literacy learning through the story of Edward's literacy journey.

## The Role of Emotion

Lyons (1999) provided an explanation of the neurophysiological and cognitive relationships of emotions to learning. Understanding the interrelatedness of emotions, motivation, and cognition serves to clarify their role in learning. While the workings of the brain are not the focus for this article, some key points will highlight the relationships that exist among emotions, motivation, and cognition.

**Emotional Development.** It is important to consider that biologically, some aspects of emotional development precede cognitive development. Research in neurobiology indicates that the emotional (limbic) system develops prior to brain networks devoted to cognition, for example, the neocortex (Greenberg & Snell, 1997; see also Davidson, 1984). The frontal lobe serves as the command center of the brain and plays an important role in mediating and regulating emotions and behavior from infancy through each stage of development. More specifically, the frontal lobe is responsible for acts related to programming, regulation, and verification, actions that are coordinated with the help of speech (Luria, 1973). Throughout childhood, interconnections increase and become differentiated between the limbic system and the neocortex, which makes language possible, allowing for both emotional experiences to be processed and linked with other areas of the brain and for "qualitative changes in emotional development" (Greenberg & Snell, 1997, p. 107).

Greenberg and Snell (1997) posit that "neural templates are being laid down for the management of emotion through connections formed as a result of critical learning experiences during childhood" (p. 108). From a neurological perspective, the frontal lobe works in conjunction with the reticular activating system (RAS), which is located in the upper portion of the brain stem. The RAS's role is to direct consciousness and attention. Working in conjunction with the frontal lobes and the limbic system, which regulates emotions, it provides a mechanism for selecting and directing attention, as well as feedback mechanisms to monitor behavior. Thus, as Greenspan (1997) explains, "each sensation, as it is registered . . . gives rise to an affect or emotion" (p. 18). He provides an example: A mother's laugh has not only particular auditory or sensory signals but emotional ones as well, and these responses are coded together in the brain. They might be coded as sounds-laughter and humor-fun with mom. "It is this *dual coding* of experience that is the key to understanding how emotions organize intellectual capacities and indeed create the sense of self" (p. 18).

Yet, every sensation does not produce the same response in individuals. Any parent who has nurtured more than one child can attest to Greenspan's (1997) assertion that there are "inborn differences in sensory makeup" (p. 19) that produce different emotional responses in different human beings. This distinctive emotional and sensory makeup accounts for unique individuals or learners, with the dual coding providing a cross-referencing of memories, experiences, and feelings, resulting in a sort of mental cataloguing of related sensory input (Greenspan, 1997). Thus, emotion and cognition function as partners in the mind (LeDoux, 1996). In support of cognition, emotion's most critical role is to "create, organize, and orchestrate many of the mind's most important functions" (Greenspan, 1997, p. 7). Emotion affects cognitive mental functions such as memory, attention, and perception (Lane, Nadel, Allen, & Kaszniak, 2000). Greenberg and Snell (1997) more strongly stress the role of emotion. They assert that "emotion . . . drives attention, which drives learning and memory" (p.103). Rather than a "dichotomy" (Greenspan, 1997) of mind and body, these researchers suggest there is a complex and integrated body-mind (brain) system with our emotions "as the glue that bonds the body/brain integration" (Sylwester, 1995, p. 73). In Edward's case, it seemed that the glue that began to bind his thoughts and feelings together was very negatively charged, fueling his anxiety, embarrassment, and eventual distrust of peers and adults in the school setting, resulting in unacceptable behaviors.

**Edward's Cognitive and Emotional Development.** For some children the partnership of emotion and cognition can serve as an impetus to propel learning, but in body-mind systems gone awry, behaviors that result may not be compatible with factors that ensure learning. As early as first grade, some children do not see themselves as capable learners. Edward was one of those children.

When I think of Edward, the word fragile comes to mind. He, as well as his world, seemed fragile. He was small for a first grader. He seemed lost in the shoes that were too big and that he could never keep tied. His voice was even fragile—babyish, shaky, and high pitched. In the beginning, his voice often faltered. His language sometimes came in phrases that did not make sense, and sometimes he could not get out the words. The harder he tried, the more he repeated words or phrases, stuttering and stammering, and sometimes he just gave up, not expressing his ideas.

According to Greenspan (1997), capacities for learning language require an emotional base. Without mastery of

> the capacity for reciprocal emotional and social signaling, [language ability may develop in a] fragmented manner. . . . Words lack meaning, pronouns are confused, and scraps of rote learning dominate . . . speech. Social interests remain focused on [the child's] body or inanimate objects. (p. 32)

When I first began to work with Edward, he hardly spoke. If I asked a question or did anything that seemed to make him feel uncomfortable, he sometimes made repetitive movements with his hands, or he rocked in his chair. If he had a marker in his hand, he would make random marks on the page. Sometimes he would grab objects from my desk or knock things over.

I wondered if he was trying to distract me or shut me out and remove himself from the current situation. Throughout the time I worked with him, this type of responding escalated based on what I came to infer as a heightened stress level.

Here again is an example of how the body and mind are mutually influential. In response to certain kinds of stress, the body creates the hormone cortisol. Chronic stress is associated with high levels of this hormone. "In humans and animals alike, these hormones abound when we find ourselves in situations where other individuals or events control us and we feel helpless" (Caine & Caine, 1991, p. 66). Consequently, our capacity to think, solve problems, and make connections is impeded because of the "inseparability of body, emotion, and intellect" (p. 66). *Downshifting* (Hart, 1983) is the brain's response to negative stress or distress. In Hart's theory, the brain actually shifts from operation within the region of the neocortex to the more automatic limbic system and the triune brain's reptilian complex. This conceptualization of the brain comes from MacLean, the former head of the Laboratory of Brain Evolution and Behavior at the National Institute of Mental Health, and provides a model of how the brain evolved (see Wellman, in Costa & Garmston, 1997). This model suggests that the reticular activation system, referred to earlier, is located at the bottom of the reptilian complex. It is the receptor of information and attention. The cerebellum, which receives sensory input from muscle receptors and sense organs, integrates information and coordinates skilled movement. Actions such as movement and speaking are controlled as the cerebellum receives commands from the cerebral cortex. If downshifting has occurred, there is a shift of operation from the newer, more rational neocortex down to the reptilian brain. It is here that autoreflex systems are controlled, governing several basic body systems as well as inner drives, such as our sense of territorial boundaries and our fight, flight, or freeze instincts (see Caine & Caine, 1991; Wellman in Costa & Garmston, 1997).

Edward's responses seemed to be representative of this model of brain functioning, and as I became more understanding of the underlying reasons for these responses, I attempted to adjust my teaching based on signs of this downshifting. It became clear that for Edward, the neural linkage of negative emotional responses to school was strong. His emotions were driving his attention, and when presented with academic tasks, particularly literacy activities, his behavior seemed to represent fight or flight instincts. When initial responses of avoidance or distraction failed, he sometimes resorted to physical acts of resistance such as kicking me under the table. My only consolation was that these problems were much less severe in the tutoring context than in his classroom, where he was often relegated to time-out, sent to an in-school suspension classroom, and on a few occasions, suspended. His parents were deeply concerned about his difficulties but expressed confusion, frustration, and even anger in response to Edward's behavior and their inability to help him function appropriately and successfully at home and school.

I could understand and relate to their frustration. When I began to work with Edward in Reading Recovery, he had completed one year of schooling. He was characterized as bright by the professionals working with him; yet, based on scores from *An Observation Survey of Early Literacy Achievement* (Clay, 1993a) and his teacher's referral, Edward was one of the lowest first graders in a multi-age classroom of kindergartners and first graders. Edward was also characterized by his teacher as being extremely difficult.

When I observed him within his classroom, during center times, he frequently chose non-literacy tasks such as playing with blocks or working at the sand table. I would watch him, almost in parallel play, doing what classmates were doing, but not interacting. Perhaps he had come to realize that inevitably, contact with peers seemed to cause difficulty and result in his being sent to time-out or more serious punishment. Prior to kindergarten, he had had limited interactions with other children or adults beyond his parents and grandparents. Unaccustomed to schooling, Edward lacked the social skills many of the children displayed, and his interests were not typical of most children. One day while he was discussing an anatomy book from home, detailing particular parts of the body and how they functioned, it became clear that he lacked a common register of language and had different interests than most kindergartners and first graders. When Edward was a part of whole class literacy activities, as children sat around the teacher, he always sat on the outer perimeters of the circle, near the back. He seemed uninterested in much of the first-grade curriculum and appeared frustrated that he could not quickly master the beginning literacy tasks so that he could more independently engage in reading texts that really interested him.

What was occurring within Edward over and over again was the dual coding of responses (Greenspan, 1997), connecting a variety of negative sensory input with literacy tasks. Environmental influences, through his interactions with teachers and parents, however unintentional, negatively affected the way that he viewed learning to read and write, as well as his view of himself as a learner. His early associations with learning to read resulted in difficulty or lack of interest. In turn, these negative events were registered with corresponding emotions, organizing and influencing his cognition, creating a poor sense of self and making it difficult to attend—he lacked the motivation to learn.

## The Role of Motivation

Motivation has an important, multidimensional role in the complex and integrated mind-body system. It modulates and influences behavior and, in turn, learning, in complex and varied ways. Once thought to be centered around drives, current theorists recognize that goals, beliefs, self-efficacy, values, and social comparisons are all factors related to motivation.

**Achievement Motivation.** Achievement motivation refers to a willingness to achieve competency through effortful activity (Elliot & Church, 1997). While there are many different views of achievement motivation, attribution theory, self-efficacy theory, self-worth theory, and expectancy-value theory, all focus on perceptions that influence a learner's achievement-oriented behavior (see for example, Atkinson, 1957; Bandura, 1986; Covington, 1992; Eccles et al., 1983; Nicholls, 1984; Schunk 1984; Weiner, 1992). In order to understand what factors influence a child's willingness to learn and achieve competence, the child's own perceptions of his or her abilities and achievements must be considered. Achievement motivation theory focuses on the relationship of motivation to learning and hypothesizes that the causes that are attributed to success or failure influence future achievement-oriented behavior (Covington & Omelich, 1979), such as willingness to demonstrate effort (Weiner, 1992).

The notion of perception is critical in understanding this theory; each learner's own "interpretation of reality" (Blumenfeld, Pintrich, Meece, & Wessels, 1982, p. 402) must be considered in regard to success or failure, for it is perceptions that mediate achievement behavior (Blumenfeld et al., 1982). Perceptions affect each person's reactions or motives to succeed and to avoid failure, thus impacting achievement-oriented behavior (Weiner, 1992). Whatever a person attributes success or failure to is key.

Attribution theory, primarily based on Heider's (1958) seminal work, was developed to explain people's perceptions and causal beliefs. Attributions, or the causes that an individual perceives as affecting success or failure, are primary motivational factors (Heider, 1958). While not intended as all-inclusive, early achievement motivation research proposed four primary factors that explained learner's attributions for success or failure: ability, effort, task difficulty, and luck (see Weiner, 1979). More recent research has suggested overlapping dimensions of causality: locus, stability, and controllability (Weiner & Graham, 1984). For example, luck is external to the individual (locus), unstable, and uncontrollable. In contrast, effort is internal to the individual, not stable (i.e., an individual does not necessarily apply the same degree of effort at all times), and controllable (see Weiner, 1979, 1986).

In differentiating causality as internal or external (Weiner, 1979, 1986), the constructs of *contingency* (Peterson, Maier, & Seligman, 1993) and *locus of control* (Rotter, 1966) are important to consider. Contingency refers to the relationship between actions and outcomes. "The most important contingency here is uncontrollability: a random relationship between an individual's actions and outcomes. The opposite contingency, controllability, obviously occurs when the individual's actions reliably produce outcomes" (Peterson et al., 1993, p. 8). The notion of random outcomes (signifying uncontrollability) as contrasted with reliable outcomes (controllability) is linked to the locus of control: a cause can be perceived as an outcome of a person's actions (internal) or from some other factor such as luck (external). Perception of the cause—the way a person explains the contingency—influences cognition. According to Peterson and his colleagues, several steps are involved. First, the person must perceive the contingency. "His perception of it may be accurate, or he may see it as something it was not. So, for example, a controllable event may be perceived as uncontrollable, or vice versa" (p. 8). Next, an explanation for the failure, such as bad luck or stupidity, is formed. The result is that the person uses this perception and explanation "to form an expectation about the future. If he experiences a failure that he believes was caused by his own stupidity, then he will expect to fail again when he finds himself in situations requiring intelligence" (Peterson et al., 1993, p. 8). Thus, whether accurate or not, a learner's repeated perceptions of either incapability or lack of success, or both, may begin a cycle of future expectations of failure.

A number of studies have identified the types of attributions that learners use to explain success or failure along with their relationship to external or internal controllability. While the "number of perceived causes is virtually infinite" (Weiner & Graham, 1984, p. 168), researchers have identified study participants' most common attributions, or causes, for success or failure: intelligence, ability, memory, effort, work and study habits, mood, prior experience, interest, task difficulty, luck, attitude, and ability to concentrate or attend. (For further discussion of these attributions, see Weiner & Graham, 1984; Weiner, 1986. For examples of free-response investigations, see Anderson, 1983; Burger, Cooper, & Good, 1982; Elig & Frieze, 1979; Frieze & Snyder, 1980.) Often success or failure is attributed to effort and ability, which is usually considered internal, within the control of the individual.

Such factors are related to ability beliefs (Wigfield, 1997)—a learner's perceived competency in a particular area (see Frieze & Snyder, 1980; Nicholls, 1984; Stipek & MacIver, 1989). While viewed as controllable, factors such as the nature of the task or task difficulty, directions, and instruction are not within the control of the learner. Other factors such as luck, illness, teacher bias, or negativity are external and are viewed as more likely to be unstable and uncontrollable, although they are within the teacher's control. According to Minton (1979 in Blumenfeld et al., 1982), factors that elementary-age students used to judge ability included speed of work completion, effort, and teacher evaluation and satisfaction.

A study that has particular significance in explaining young children's attributions and sources of control is Stipek's (1981) research with kindergartners and first graders. In this study, high effort was linked with high ability. The quality of efforts was not taken into account. These young students believed that if learners worked hard and finished their work, they were capable. In other words, they tended not to make differentiations between ability, effort, and outcome (Nicholls, 1978) in terms of task difficulty or quality of performance (Blumenfeld et al., 1982). Moreover, for these young children, ability was judged as dependent on effort, and effort was often equated with good conduct. Therefore, conduct became a factor when explaining outcome (Blumenfeld et al., 1982).

An individual's beliefs about his or her capabilities to learn or behave in a particular way has been termed *self-efficacy* (see Bandura, 1986, 1997; Schunk, 1990). As discussed previously, beliefs, perceptions, and behaviors are linked and influenced by environmental or contextual factors. The influence of home and school factors on self-efficacy has been noted by researchers (see Dweck & Bempechat, 1983; Johnston & Winograd, 1985; Pressley et al., 1995), so teachers' and parents' attributions and their views of intelligence and abilities send strong messages to learners. Research shows self-efficacy to be a good predictor of motivation, affecting behaviors such as task choice, effort, perseverance, and achievement and other self-regulatory behaviors (See Schunk, 1990, 1996; Bandura, 1986). However, the learner must believe that it is possible to improve and further develop abilities. "Students who feel efficacious about reading or writing well are apt to concentrate on the task, use proper procedures, manage time effectively, seek assistance as necessary, monitor performance, and adjust strategies as needed" (Schunk & Zimmerman, 1997, p. 37). Moreover, if a learner feels in control of his learning, he can usually overcome temporary setbacks or difficulties. In fact, students who have strong self-efficacy in the face of fears or doubts about performance may increase effort and attempt to be even more strategic as compared to learners who are overconfident and may actually decrease their efforts (Salomon, 1984).

**Edward's Motivation.** The linkage of ability, effort, and conduct in a young learner's perceptions may help to explain Edward's dilemma. In the classroom, Edward seemed to have no confidence in his ability to perform literacy tasks, and his teachers were dissatisfied with his unwillingness to attempt or demonstrate effort. His behavior suggested that he did not see himself as capable of success—that he viewed success as outside of his control. His teachers had become concerned about his unpredictable behavior, and at the onset of a problem, he was isolated. If good conduct was in fact an attribution that he connected with success (Stipek, 1981), he must have perceived himself as a terrible failure. Furthermore, if ability was perceived as dependent on effort, he and his peers may have felt that he demonstrated low capability. When I began to work with Edward in late September, it appeared that many outside forces influenced him to respond in increasingly unproductive ways, either passively or aggressively, depending on how out of control he felt. In response, I felt dismay at seeing him spend so much time outside the learning environment. Clearly, school personnel attributed the causes of his academic and behavioral difficulties to problems within the child rather than the instructional environment.

Ability, effort, and outcome are not necessarily distinguishable in children's perceptions. They do not engage in the "ego-protective strategy of attributing failure to external causes" as much as adults do (Wigfield, 1988, p. 79). Therefore, factors such as poor instruction, teacher bias, or negativity have the potential to seriously impact self-efficacy and be even more devastating for learners who fail.

Students like Edward, who are most at risk, may not be able to reliably gauge their own progress and may look to teachers or parents to provide feedback on performance (Schunk & Zimmerman, 1997). What happens when the feedback the child is given is primarily negative or responses to the child's difficulties are punitive? School personnel seemed to feel that Edward was incapable of behaving and learning. The anxiety of his parents was palpable, and they expressed their frustrations in trying to cope with Edward and the school's response toward him. They felt they had no control over Edward or what was happening in school. As a person placed for training (as a Reading Recovery university trainer) within the school rather than working as a district employee, I had good rapport with the parents and faculty, but little power (i.e., control) to influence decisions about Edward. Thus, all of us, along with Edward, were experiencing feelings of low self-efficacy. In cases such as Edward's, the emotional and motivational ramifications, and the resulting impact on literacy learning, are quite serious.

## Influences on Learning to Read: The Interconnectedness of Emotion, Motivation, and Cognition

In the early grades, one of the most emphasized and valued abilities that young learners develop is reading. Yet, until recently, there has been limited information about motivation in reading, particularly in regard to the early stages of reading acquisition (see Baker, Afflerbach, & Reinking, 1996; Guthrie & Wigfield, 2000; Wigfield, 1997). Guthrie and Wigfield (2000) define reading motivation as *"the individual's personal goals, values, and beliefs with regard to the topics, processes, and outcomes of reading"* (p. 405). This definition emphasizes how motivation affects cognition or the strategic processes a learner invokes or chooses not to invoke. In this section, the link between emotion, motivation, and cognition, particularly beliefs about self and ability, will be further clarified in relation to learning to read. Implicit in motivation is the idea of setting goals and taking action, which is oppositional to behaviors represented in learned helplessness (Seligman & Maier, 1967). The construct of learned helplessness will be juxtaposed with its antithesis, the active and self-regulated learner.

### Learned Helplessness or Active Engagement

Reading ability is a strong determinant of school success and children's perceptions of their skills in other areas. As students progress through the grades, their actual ability becomes intertwined with their attitudes and beliefs regarding success or failure. In other words, it becomes increasingly more difficult to divorce skill and will (Paris & Cross, 1983; Paris, Lipson, & Wixson, 1983/1994). Learning involves both skill (ability) and will (the desire, effort, and persistence to perform cognitive tasks), so the role that motivation and attributions play in relation to skill and will are quite critical to learning.

Strategies are employed to achieve goals. If a goal is deemed unreachable or if a learner does not feel in control of the learning process, then the learner sees no reason to make the necessary effort to use a strategy. Furthermore, if there has been a prolonged series of unsuccessful events, the learner is caught in a cycle of failure, finding it less stressful for poor outcomes to be attributed to lack of effort. For whatever reason, learners with these attributions may become inactive or act in a *passive failure* mode (Johnston & Winograd, 1985). This inactivity is often the result of an individual's perceptions, with a view toward unstable and uncontrollable outcomes. Past outcomes can only be reliable predictors of future outcomes if they are caused by stable factors (Abramson, Garber, & Seligman, 1980). For example, if an individual perceives ability as a stable trait and has not performed well in the past, he has no reason to believe that this will change. Also, if an individual believes that he is not in control of his own learning, as when attributing outcomes to luck or teacher control, the motivation for attempting or persevering with difficult tasks may not be present. Characteristically, these individuals adopt an attitude of "expected failure [and] lack the perseverance [to complete tasks; often they] give up before they begin a task" (Mark, 1983, p. 1). These individuals have been labeled learned helpless (Seligman & Maier, 1967).

For over three decades, Seligman and his colleagues (see for example, Abramson et al., 1980; Abramson, Seligman, & Teasdale, 1978; Peterson et al., 1993; Seligman &

Maier, 1967; Seligman et al., 1984), and shortly afterward, Dweck with her colleagues (see for example, Diener & Dweck, 1978, 1980; Dweck, 1975, 1983, 1998), have studied the phenomenon of learned helplessness. In spite of strong performances on previous tasks, students characterized as learned helpless expressed a lack of belief in their ability with ascriptions such as "I never did have a good rememory" or "I'm not smart enough" (Diener & Dweck, 1978, p. 458). Attempts at other kinds of strategies or increased or sustained effort were not present in their actions. Their behavior contrasts the group of students who were characterized as mastery oriented. These learners might also be described as active and engaged. Such students increased their efforts when difficulties occurred or attempted to find other methods of problem solving. These non-helpless students were characterized as *consistently persisting* until they accomplished a task. Examples of their comments included "I need to concentrate" or "I should slow down and try to figure this out" (Diener & Dweck, 1978, p. 459). In fact, the researchers noted that oftentimes, these mastery-oriented learners did not even make attributions when faced with difficulties. Instead, they focused on self-monitoring with verbalizations such as those just mentioned (Diener & Dweck, 1978).

During the months that I worked with Edward in Reading Recovery, I also worked with Molly, an average student from Edward's classroom. (These case studies were a part of my training in Reading Recovery.) Molly viewed herself as a successful reader and learner. She confidently initiated conversations about herself, her environment, and her learning. She exhibited confidence and enthusiasm during all literacy tasks. From our first interactions, Molly demonstrated a willingness to be an active participant in her own learning. She expressed her ideas, took over new learning quickly, and worked independently whenever possible. Molly resembled mastery-oriented learners, a descriptor coined by Diener and Dweck (1978). Unlike Edward, she maintained a consistently positive view of her abilities. Based on her own statements, she liked school, worked hard, and was a "good reader" and a "pretty good" writer. She indicated many times that she was "really good at lots of things in school." In fact, her view of herself and her ability seemed to be higher than her teacher characterized. This may explain how she maintained her self-confidence even though her teacher viewed her rate of progress as slowing since the beginning of the year.

As pointed out earlier, young children do not make distinctions between effort, ability, and outcome; rather, they consider children who try harder as smarter than those who make less effort (Nicholls, 1978). In addition, students typically equate success with factors such as speed, how quickly work was completed; effort, how hard one tried; and teacher evaluation, how pleased and well-behaved one is from the teacher's viewpoint (Minton, 1979, in Blumenfeld et al., 1982). Therefore, it is not surprising that within his classroom, Edward was having little success in the view of his peers and teachers. According to his teacher, Edward appealed to her constantly for help and did very few tasks without constant supervision. In her opinion, Edward was incapable of independent functioning, either socially or academically. He spent much of his time isolated from his peers and from the work of the classroom.

Edward puzzled me. Even when I joked or teased him, or praised him for effort, success, or good behavior, I noted how bright yet unresponsive and passive he was. In early research, clinical psychologists were intrigued because learned helplessness looked so much like depression. Observing them in the lab, Seligman (1995) characterized helpless animals and people as "passive, slow, sad" (p. 3). Even now, reading this, I recall Edward's shuffling feet, his slouched shoulders, his unresponsive face, and I hear his stammering voice.

My hypotheses for the causes of Edward's behavior and responses are tentative, but I suggest that Edward felt he had little control within his environment, and because of his fairly isolated early childhood experiences, he had had little guidance in sorting out appropriate ways of responding and interacting. Often his response was to isolate himself and attempt no interaction. The difficulties that he had had in school further exacerbated his difficulties and subsequent withdrawal, whether imposed by him or others. When he was placed in situations requiring interactions, he lacked the social skills to respond appropriately, so his passive responses of "I can't" or "I don't know" or his aggressive responses resulted in time-outs or in-school suspensions, reinforcing the view (from himself and others) that isolation or passivity was the answer. Edward preferred to withdraw but responded with aggression when his peers or teachers (including me) insisted on his participation. His response further reinforced the need for withdrawal, in this case, physical withdrawal from the environment.

Edward had been unable to figure out how to control his environment, so inevitably, he found ways to escape. From his point of view, those inappropriate responses may have signified glimmers of hope that he could still attempt some type of action or control, albeit inappropriate.

## Connecting Emotions, Motivation, and Cognition

What influences these two stances (active versus passive) toward learning? What do researchers theorize is taking place in the mind? In relation to motivation, the result of procedural knowledge (how to behave or do something) is represented by products—the results of goal attainment. To explain how an active or passive stance occurs, Winne and Marx (1989) hypothesize that cognitive processing principles also serve to explain motivational processing: "Motivational content is coded in the same form as other information—namely, as primitive concepts, propositions, and schemata" (p. 244). These primitive motivational concepts are emotions (Weiner, 1986, 1992) and account directly for individuals' affect: "The etymology of 'emotion' reaches into the Latin *ex* (from) and *movere* (to move), combining in *exmovere* (to move away). Hence, emotions are the source of 'motive force'" (Winne & Marx, 1989, p. 245), and it is emotions that move students to take action or to become passive. Experiences, instruction, and participation in learning bring about the linking of motivational concepts and information that are stored in working memory. Motivational constructs or propositions are the results of this "emotion-information processing connection" (p. 245). These propositions (i.e., constructs, schemata) connect motivational content (emotions, attributions, and expectancies for success or failure) with cognitive operations, thus impacting an individual's willingness to demonstrate effort and establish future goals (Winne & Marx, 1989).

The result of Winne and Marx's hypotheses parallels Greenspan's (1997) explanation of the dual coding of emotions and cognition. When procedures are maintained that allow the learner to control the task and move toward goal attainment, there is the stimulation of positive motivational content or affect (feelings of success). This motivational content (i.e., emotions) is stored. Thus, positive feelings such as pride, happiness, and a sense of well-being and control are maintained in working memory. If however, as students work through a task, monitor their progress, and deem the product to be insufficient or deficient, "negative motivational content can be stimulated" (Winne & Marx, 1989, p. 247). With repeated occurrences, "emotional states of anxiety and helplessness are established" (p. 247) with the script or representative schema for behavior characterized by a state of learned helplessness.

The behavior most representative of learned helplessness is passivity. When individuals perceive an inevitable lack of control, they fail to initiate and monitor their actions. What may help to decrease learned helplessness is to somehow replace the script for passive responses with active procedures. An essential question, however, is how this script might be replaced. Corno and Rohrkemper (1985) suggest that the process of self-regulated learning might be a tool "through which students gain academic competence as well as a strong sense of personal responsibility" (p. 60). They define self-regulated learning "as the highest form of cognitive engagement a student can use to learn in classrooms" (p. 60). But what serves as a catalyst for this transformation? For children such as Edward, it is unlikely that the script will be replaced and self-regulation will occur without intervention and strong support from others.

## The Development of a Self-Regulated Learner

Social mediation is an area that has just begun to receive attention in research on motivation. In the development of motivation, recent studies have focused on the role of others such as peers, parents, and teachers (see Baker et al., 1996; Gambrell & Morrow, 1996; Oldfather, 1992, 1994; Sonnenschein, Brody, & Munsterman, 1996). In my work with Edward, the script of passivity was transformed by the cognitive and emotional changes that occurred through social mediation. As mentioned previously, the learning context can potentially enhance or deter motivation. Gambrell and Morrow (1996) suggest three dimensions of learning that intersected with my role as mediator in Edward's literacy journey: challenge, collaboration, and choice. While there are additional factors that contributed to changes in motivational and strategic processes, these interrelated factors promoted positive responses to learning and enabled Edward to take control of his learning process, shifting from a stance of passivity and helplessness to an active, self-regulated learner.

### Challenge

In the previous section, an explanation was provided for the connection of motivational content (i.e., emotions and expectancies for success or failure) with cognitive operations. Feelings of success occur when learners feel in control of tasks and are moving toward goals. Therefore, decisions about whether to be effortful and strategic are related to task demands (Anderson & Armbruster, 1984).

> Learners of any age are more likely to take active control of their own cognitive endeavors when they are faced with tasks of intermediate difficulty (since if the task is too easy, they need not bother; if the task is too hard, they may give up). (Baker & Brown, 1984, p. 354)

What keeps the learner active is this just-right level of challenge. For students who have taken a passive stance toward learning, the role of responsive meaning maker comes less easily, and the child must be shown and guided in ways that will promote the "active construction of a network of strategies" (Clay, 1991a, p. 327). Demonstrating, guiding, and adjusting the level of challenges are all component parts of the teacher's role in scaffolding within Reading Recovery lessons.

Yet, the management of challenge was the most difficult dimension in my attempts to support Edward's motivation. In fact, early on, I contributed to Edward's feelings of anxiousness and poor self-perception. While one of the lowest students in first grade, Edward's entry scores on the *Observation Survey of Early Literacy Achievement* (Clay, 1993a) were much higher than the other three children I tutored. All his stanines were above 1, except for text reading and hearing sounds in words; letter identification and the word test were the highest at stanine 4. I was seduced by his test scores into developing preconceived ideas about what he should be able to do. I made assumptions based on his scores rather than being guided by my observations and Edward's responding. As later lessons would indicate, Edward had a foundation of literacy knowledge to build on, and he could learn quickly, but he did not know this. In his view, reading was about knowing words, and he did not know enough of them. Early on, both of us would become frustrated as he competently read and then gave up when he made an error. With one error, the task had become too hard! It took too many days for me to finally realize that I had to eliminate this unproductive response and ensure that he perceived himself as successful.

To improve my work with Edward, I regularly reviewed records and notes from previous sessions. As I began to look back at the first sessions during Roaming Around the Known, I noted some points that I had previously taken for granted. The primary reason for using the first two weeks of the child's tutoring program to Roam Around the Known is that "it requires the teacher to stop teaching from her preconceived ideas. She has to work from the child's responses" (Clay, 1993b, p.13). Working within this framework, I had collaborated with Edward on each task. As I reread my notes, I recognized that I had set him up for success. In hindsight, I also realized that having choices gave him a sense of control. During Roaming Around the Known sessions, he chose the books that he wanted to reread. I encouraged him to choose the topics for the books I would make and to dictate some of the stories. At first, because the language was more complex in the dictated texts, I read the books with him to ensure that he would feel competent. In the more patterned published texts, I supported his recall of the events as well as the language pattern before he started reading with statements such as, "Here's the book where the cat sat on the mat, and then those other animals sat on the mat . . ."

Such scaffolding, with the level of challenge gauged for Edward alone, positively influenced the ways he responded. In fact, new behaviors and responses emerged. For example, it was clear that rapport had developed and things were changing when Edward, typically unresponsive, offered an unsolicited comment: "They're doing show and tell in my class today. I could bring in a lizard, if I had a lizard." My response that we could make a book about that resulted in his idea for a story that was written with my assistance: "I like (both of which Edward wrote) Lizard (he wrote the *L*). I want A Lizards." He wrote the *i, w, a, l,* and *s*. Clay states that "the struggling reader has stopped using many strategies because he could not make them work [but when supported in] using the things he can do you will find that he begins to try again some of those discarded strategies" (Clay, 1993b, p. 14). Clearly, under the right conditions, there was already much that Edward knew and could draw upon, but at times he needed me to be the "rememberer" and "the organizer," assisting him in linking his existing but unrecognized knowledge to new learning. Thus, Edward's knowledge and his oral language became the tools that we used as I worked alongside him.

Unfortunately, after less than two weeks, the momentum was interrupted when Edward was suspended. Looking back, I now recognize that this suspension eroded the rapport that had been established. Upon his return, Edward was even more apprehensive about interacting, but I did not let that concern hinder me from pushing my agenda forward. We had to make up for lost time! Not surprisingly, the result was a lack of cooperation and collaboration across many lessons.

Edward's accelerated progress during Roaming Around the Known sessions had heightened my awareness of his vast background knowledge and sophisticated interests along with his capacity to learn. Yet, in the first weeks of lessons, I found myself constantly struggling with Edward as if we were in a tug-of-war while I attempted to reconcile his passive behaviors with the knowledge he held. Finally, I realized that I had taken away much of the collaboration and the choices that were hallmarks of our work together during Roaming Around the Known sessions. With this recognition, the successful interactions of Roaming Around the Known served as a compass to help me "find points of contact in . . . [Edward's] prior learning," to situate learning within the things that Edward *could* do (Clay, 1998, p. 3).

Such endeavors paid off in several unexpected ways. Very slowly, I began to see Edward increase his willingness to take risks. Short and Burke (1991) suggest that a primary factor related to risk taking is operating within what is known.

> Exploration of new ideas always operates on the edge of the known. Just past the boundaries of our currently comfortable beliefs is an area where we have some expectations but few certainties. . . . Our learning needs to both connect with and go beyond what is already known to us. (p. 18)

But moving too far away from the known can hamper learning because it results in a

> loss of context within which to organize and interpret. . . . We cannot find the connections between the new findings and what we already know. . . . The new

insights remain floating out there somewhere, unconnected and therefore difficult to learn and easy to forget. (p. 18)

Yet, when guided by a more knowledgeable other, the learner can be supported in taking risks and can develop new learning in the area known as the zone of proximal development (Vygotsky, 1978).

## Collaboration

By working in the realm of the known, keeping new learning at the right level of challenge, and using my language to guide Edward's behavior, I served as the connector, the organizer, and the rememberer. Even for a time, my language, or words, served as a mechanism of self-control, gradually guiding Edward in changing ineffective patterns of responding. Initially, because of negative emotions and the limited self-efficacy that colored his responses, Edward was quite skeptical of my words, particularly the praise and encouragement.

For example, as I listened to him read the text *Catch That Frog,* I was pleased by his good approximation (i.e., *after* and then *across* were substituted for the word *around*). Edward then monitored his error. Realizing he was not right but not knowing how to fix it, Edward reacted with frustration. However, at the end of the book, my response served to adjust strategic as well as motivational processes to encourage further risk taking and to show him I valued his processing. I said, "That was some good work! When you tried this, you were thinking about what made sense, sounded right, and looked right at the beginning of this word. Then, you did something else that was great! You kept working! And you noticed that something still didn't look right, but you weren't sure how to fix it. Next time, when you give it another try—read it again and use the beginning and other parts of the word, like the end, to help you figure it out. Let's try that again and I'll help you."

Of course, this did not bring about an immediate change in behavior and self-perception; but after many instantiations, there was a gradual shift in motivational and cognitive processing enabling Edward to regulate his behavior more independently. Greenspan (1997) points out that "when adults help children master a skill in steps that match their own strengths and tendencies, youngsters experience the exhilaration of doing something well that is intrinsic in the human nervous system" (p. 223). Such powerful feelings influence the motivational processes that encourage a learner to continue to endeavor. When learners learn, when they take control, "they go on to extend their own learning. Even at a low level of simple performance, a sense of control and a sense of being effective will generate attention, interest, and motivation" (Clay, 1998, p. 4). This was the key for Edward. He was learning so much, and yet he seemed unaware of his knowledge. My job was to help him discover it!

In the earlier example of Edward's reading of *Catch That Frog,* my teaching focused on what was appropriate and most productive for this child. In Edward's case, he almost always knew when he was not right and deeply felt the impact, although he was also afraid to try to fix it for fear of being wrong again. In discussing learned helpless children, Dweck (1975) offers this advice:

An instructional program for children who have difficulty dealing with failure would do well not to skirt the issue by trying to ensure success or by glossing over failure. Instead, it should include procedures for dealing with this problem directly. This is not to suggest that failure should be included in great amounts or that failure per se is desirable, but rather, that errors should be capitalized upon as vehicles for teaching the child how to handle failure. (p. 684)

Edward's frustration began with noting the error because he was unsure of how to fix it. By praising his efforts and then saying, "Next time, give it another try. Read it again and use the beginning and end of the word to help you figure it out," I valued the work he had done while providing additional choices or options for how he might respond. In other words, my scaffolding provided reinforcement for Edward's self-monitoring, perhaps the most important foundational behavior for other self-regulatory processes (Zimmerman, 1998), allowing me to then support Edward in developing additional ways of problem-solving text difficulties. Gradually, through demonstration, working with him, and eventually prompting him to work independently, I helped Edward become, and perceive himself as an engaged, active problem-solver.

Initially, this engagement occurred only during reading. Edward resisted my encouragement during writing. Perhaps the nature of the process contributed to his discomfort. During writing, the child's processing is slowed down, and the links that are made in relation to sounds and letters are more easily discerned (Clay, 1982; DeFord, 1994), but so are the errors! To Edward, it was too risky to make such attempts. In reading, errors did not seem quite so glaring, but marks on the paper produced evidence of things that Edward did not know—that he was not able to control confidently. With time, I came to recognize that I was expecting him to take on too much of the task too soon, and I began to increase my support and decrease the number of sounds that I expected him to hear and record. I also realized that by insisting that Edward take on so much of the task so quickly, I had contributed to his feelings of a lack of control and capability.

## Choice

The opportunity to make choices gives learners a sense of control (Gambrell & Morrow, 1996). In retrospect, I have greater awareness of the potential and necessity of choice in Edward's learning. Earlier, I discussed how choices were provided and supported in reading and writing selections, but Edward's strategic decision making, his choices regarding how to respond, were even more important. In reading, my language or prompts provided Edward with strategic options or choices. Unfortunately, in our early lessons I did not make these choices as clear in writing—that he had control over what he chose to write and how he might use the Elkonin boxes as a scaffold.

## Altering Edward's Path of Progress

Clay and Cazden (1990) have suggested that the Reading Recovery program serves as a scaffold. My understanding of this became much clearer because of Edward. For him, the lesson framework provided support in two ways. First, the framework gave him a sense of control. The components were something that he could predict, and thereby control. Edward came to understand and anticipate what would happen next, which seemed to have a calming effect—"Now we're going to make some words" or "Now we get to read the new book." He came to realize that there was variability through the freedom of choice and decision making within each component, but always, certain aspects were known. Again, working within the known promoted a sense of control, which promoted risk taking.

The second way in which the lesson provides a scaffold relates to the recursive nature of learning established through this framework. Each experience within each day's lesson provides opportunities for increased fluency and flexibility with things that are known. For example, rereading his favorite books with increasing fluency gave Edward a heightened sense of control and capability. Over time, this provided momentum, and he eventually began to show willingness to take risks in writing, which came later in the lesson. The first instance of this occurred when I encouraged him to read his story he had written the day before: "Lucy is my dog. Lucy is brown and black and white." Edward and I began to talk about Lucy and his two cats, which ultimately resulted in his decision to write more about Lucy and to add something about one of the cats: "Lucy is small. Lucy can chase the cat." I wrote *Lucy* and waited. He then quickly wrote *is*. When I encouraged him to say *small* slowly, the Elkonin boxes provided the structure for him to confidently push the counters into the boxes, hearing and recording the *s* and *l* in *small,* supported by the Elkonin boxes. He also was able to correctly write *can*, he heard the *s* at the end of *chase,* and then he wrote *the* and *cat.* The conversation, based on Edward's interests and supported by his knowledge, provided choices for his writing. The conversation and the Elkonin boxes provided ways for Edward to become increasingly independent in guiding his learning. As his teacher, I monitored and regulated my own behavior in order to offer appropriate levels of support and expectation, empowering him to work at a level of just-right challenge without calling up the scripts for passivity. Our work together and Edward's new ways of responding provides an illustration of Clay's (1998) words:

> Learner-centered instruction is…starting where the learner already is and helping that learner to move toward a new degree of control over novel tasks, teaching so that learners are successful and are able to say, "I am in control of this." From there they go on to extend their own learning (pp. 3–4).

For Edward, his script of passivity was replaced as he gained competence and a sense of self-efficacy.

One memorable event gave me hope that Edward's self-perceptions were changing. As I walked down the hall, I saw Edward sitting outside the art room in time-out. This scene had played out many times in the past. Typically when I would speak, he would not, or he would mumble hello if I waited for his response. But this day it was different! For the first time, he called to me before I even approached him. "Hi, Susan. When are you going to pick me up today? I brought my books back.…" These and many more words came pouring out of him, quickly and excitedly, before I had even said a word. I talked with him for a few moments, and as I walked away, I was struck by how his words had come spilling out, as if they had been bottled up and were suddenly freed. Clearly, Edward had much to share, and he seemed to know it.

Placement in Reading Recovery halted an unproductive literacy path for Edward. His lack of progress and his patterns of responding represented a path towards learned helplessness (Seligman & Maier, 1967) or passive failure (Johnston & Winograd, 1985). Clay (1991b) states that "it stands to reason that if children have difficulties and if we take…all who are low achievers, they are likely to have different problems, one from another" (p. 63). For a child such as Edward, instruction that was individually designed to meet his needs and to capitalize on his strengths empowered him to progress.

As I learned to work with Edward each day in Reading Recovery, I became increasingly aware of the dimensions of challenge, collaboration, and choice. By working within Edward's zone of proximal development (Vygotsky, 1978), he was provided with just enough challenge, enabling him to learn, resulting in "self-perceived competence" (Gambrell & Morrow, 1996, p. 11). Within each of the components, he was given choices, promoting "self-perceived control" (p. 11). Our collaboration grew and became more productive because of careful observations, decision making, and scaffolding based on Edward's strengths and attention to the next few things he needed to learn—first through my guidance, and gradually through expectations that he would take control of tasks. Such "collaboration facilitates goal attainment and increases task engagement" (Gambrell & Morrow, p. 11). These factors of self-perceived competence and control, goal attainment, and engagement all relate to learners' self-efficacy and motivations and are critical considerations in relation to self-regulation. In these learning contexts, demonstrations and carefully designed experiences help students to understand that "competent functioning is often a result of using appropriate strategies rather than superior innate ability or just trying hard" (Pressley et al., 1995, p. 9). As success occurs, learners are motivated to continue to make efforts toward competency. Self-regulated learning occurs through this "fusion of *skill* and *will*" (Garcia, 1995, p. 29).

By the end of our time together, Edward was reading at a level typical of the end of the year in first grade, rather than the middle of the year when his time in Reading Recovery ended. He had surpassed most of the average students in his class, including Molly. The work that Edward and I did across many months is one representation of the dynamic role of emotions, motivation, and cognition, and it provides insights into the ways interactions and scaffolding influence changes in motivational and cognitive processing. Hopefully, throughout all teachers' careers, there will be children who force them to put aside ways of teaching and responding that have become almost automatic, forcing them to examine their beliefs and their teaching with fresh eyes. Edward did this for me. My interactions with Edward reminded me of a quote that I had forgotten but eventually came to know again. Pearson (1996) reminds us that we must expect every child to achieve and acknowledge what they bring to the context:

> A teacher's job . . . is always to bridge from the known to the new. There really is no other choice. Children are who they are. They know what they know. They bring what they bring. Our job is not to wish that students knew more

or knew differently. Our job is to turn students' knowledge and the diversity of knowledge we encounter into a curricular strength rather than an instructional inconvenience. We can do that only if we hold high expectations for all students, convey great respect for the knowledge and culture they bring to the classroom, and offer lots of support in helping them achieve those expectations. (p. 272)

# References

Abramson, L. Y., Garber, J., & Seligman, M. E. P. (1980). Learned helplessness in humans: An attributional analysis. In J. Garber & M. E. P. Seligman (Eds.), *Human helplessness: Theory and applications* (pp. 3–34). New York: Academic Press.

Abramson, L. Y., Seligman, M. E. P., & Teasdale, J. D. (1978). Learned helplessness in humans: Critique and reformulation. *Journal of Abnormal Psychology, 87,* 49–74.

Anderson, C. A. (1983). The causal structure of situations: The generation of plausible causal attributions as a function of the type of event situation. *Journal of Experimental Social Psychology, 19,* 185–203.

Anderson, T. H., & Armbruster, B. B. (1984). Studying. In P. D. Pearson, R. Barr, M. L. Kamil, & P. Mosenthal (Eds.), *Handbook of reading research* (Vol. 1, pp. 657–679). New York: Longman.

Athey, I. (1985). Language models and reading. In H. Singer & R. B. Ruddell (Eds.), *Theoretical models and processes of reading* (3rd ed., pp. 35–62). Newark, DE: International Reading Association.

Atkinson, J. W. (1957). Motivational determinants of risk taking behavior. *Psychological Review, 64,* 359–372.

Baker, L., Afflerbach, P., & Reinking, D. (1996). Developing engaged readers in school and home communities: An overview. In L. Baker, P. Afflerbach, & D. Reinking (Eds.), *Developing engaged readers in school and home communities* (pp. xiii–xxvii). Mahwah, NJ: Erlbaum.

Baker, L., Allen, J., Shockley, B., Pellegrini, A. D., Galda, L., & Stahl, S. (1996). Connecting school and home: Constructing partnerships to foster reading development. In L. Baker, P. Afflerbach, & D. Reinking (Eds.), *Developing engaged readers in school and home communities* (pp. 21–41). Mahwah, NJ: Erlbaum.

Baker, L., & Brown, A. L. (1984). Metacognitive skills and reading. In P. D. Pearson, R. Barr, M. L. Kamil, & P. Mosenthal (Eds.), *Handbook of reading research* (Vol. 1, pp. 353–394). New York: Longman.

Bandura, A. (1986). *Social foundations of thought and action: A social cognitive theory.* Englewood Cliffs, NJ: Prentice-Hall.

Bandura, A. (1997). *Self-efficacy: The exercise of control.* New York: W. H. Freeman.

Blumenfeld, P. C., Pintrich, P. R., Meece, J., & Wessels, K. (1982). The formation and role of self-perceptions of ability in elementary classrooms. *The Elementary School Journal, 82,* 401–420.

Burger, J. M., Cooper, H. M., & Good, T. L. (1982). Teacher attribution of student performance: Effects of outcome. *Personality and Social Psychology Bulletin, 4,* 685–690.

Caine, R. N., & Caine, G. (1991). *Making connections: Teaching and the human brain.* Alexandria, VA: Association for Supervision and Curriculum Development.

Clay, M. M. (1982). *Observing young children.* Portsmouth, NH: Heinemann.

Clay, M. M. (1991a). *Becoming literate: The construction of inner control.* Portsmouth, NH: Heinemann.

Clay, M. M. (1991b). Reading Recovery surprises. In D. E. DeFord, C. A. Lyons, & G. S. Pinnell (Eds.), *Bridges to literacy: Learning from Reading Recovery* (pp. 55–74). Portsmouth, NH: Heinemann.

Clay, M. M. (1993a). *An observation survey of early literacy achievement.* Portsmouth, NH: Heinemann.

Clay, M. M. (1993b). *Reading Recovery: A guidebook for teachers in training.* Portsmouth, NH: Heinemann.

Clay, M. M. (1998). *By different paths to common outcomes.* York, ME: Stenhouse.

Clay, M. M., & Cazden, C. B. (1990). A Vygotskian interpretation of Reading Recovery. In. L. C. Moll (Ed.), *Vygotsky and education: Instructional implications and applications of sociohistorical psychology* (pp. 206–222). New York: Cambridge University Press.

Corno, L., & Rohrkemper, M. M. (1985). The intrinsic motivation to learn in classrooms. In C. Ames & R. Ames (Eds.), *Research in motivation in education: Vol. 2. The classroom milieu* (pp. 53–90). New York: Academic Press.

Costa, A. L., & Garmston, R. J. (1997). *The art of cognitive coaching: Foundation seminar.* Berkeley, CA: The Institute for Intelligent Behavior.

Covington, M. V. (1992). *Making the grade: A self-worth perspective on motivation and school reform.* Cambridge, England: Cambridge University Press.

Covington, M. V., & Omelich, C. L. (1979). It's best to be able and virtuous too: Student and teacher evaluative responses to successful effort. *Journal of Educational Psychology, 71,* 688–700.

Davidson, R. J. (1984). Affect, cognition, and hemispheric specialization. In C. E. Izard, J. Kagan, & R. B. Zajonc (Eds.), *Emotions, cognition, and behavior* (pp. 320–365). New York: Cambridge University Press.

DeFord, D. E. (1994). Early writing: Teachers and children in Reading Recovery. *Literacy Teaching and Learning: An International Journal of Early Reading and Writing, 1,* 31–56.

Diener, C. I., & Dweck, C. S. (1978). An analysis of learned helplessness: Continuous changes in performance, strategy, and achievement cognitions following failure. *Journal of Personality and Social Psychology, 36,* 451–462.

Diener, C. I., & Dweck, C. S. (1980). An analysis of learned helplessness: II. The processing of success. *Journal of Personality and Social Psychology, 39,* 940–952.

Dweck, C. S. (1975). The role of expectations and attributions in the alleviation of learned helplessness. *Journal of Personality and Social Psychology, 31,* 674–685.

Dweck, C. S. (1983). Children's theories of intelligence: Consequences for learning. In S. G. Paris, G. M. Olson, & H. W. Stevenson (Eds.), *Learning and motivation in the classroom* (pp. 239–256). Hillsdale, NJ: Erlbaum.

Dweck, C. S. (1998). The development of early self-conceptions: Their relevance for motivational processes. In J. Heckhausen & C. S. Dweck (Eds.), *Motivation and self-regulation across the life span* (pp. 257–280). New York: Cambridge University Press.

Dweck, C. S., & Bempechat, J. (1983). Children's theories of intelligence: Consequences for learning. In S. G. Paris, G. M. Olson, & H. W. Stevenson (Eds.), *Learning and motivation in the classroom* (pp. 239–256). Hillsdale, NJ: Erlbaum.

Eccles, J. S., Adler, T. F., Futterman, R., Goff, S. B., Kaczala, C. M., Meece, J., & Midgley, C. (1983). Expectancies, values and academic behaviors. In J. T. Spence (Ed.), *Achievement and achievement motives* (pp. 75–146). San Francisco: W. H. Freeman.

Elig, T. W., & Frieze, I. H. (1979). Measuring causal attributions for success and failure. *Journal of Personality and Social Psychology, 37,* 621–634.

Elliot, A. J., & Church, M. A. (1997). A hierarchical model of approach and avoidance achievement motivation. *Journal of Personality and Social Psychology, 72,* 218–232.

Frieze, I. H., & Snyder, H. N. (1980). Children's beliefs about the causes of success and failure in school settings. *Journal of Educational Psychology, 72,* 186–196.

Gambrell, L. B., & Morrow, L. M. (1996). Creating motivating contexts for literacy learning. In L. Baker, P. Afflerbach, & D. Reinking (Eds.), *Developing engaged readers in school and home communities* (pp. 115–136). Mahwah, NJ: Erlbaum.

Garcia, T. (1995). The role of motivational strategies in self-regulated learning. In P. Pintrich (Ed.), *New directions for teaching and learning: Understanding self-regulated learning* (pp. 29–42). San Francisco: Jossey-Bass.

Greenberg, M. T., & Snell, J. L. (1997). Brain development and emotional development: The role of teaching in organizing the frontal lobe. In P. Salovey & D. J. Sluyter (Eds.), *Emotional development and emotional intelligence* (pp. 93–119). New York: HarperCollins.

Greenspan, S. I. (1997). *The growth of the mind and the endangered origins of intelligence.* Reading, MA: Addison-Wesley.

Guthrie, J. T., & Wigfield, A. (2000). Engagement and motivation in reading. In M. L. Kamil, P. B. Mosenthal, P. D. Pearson, & R. Barr (Eds.), *Handbook of reading research* (Vol. 3, pp. 403–422). Mahwah, NJ: Erlbaum.

Hart, L. A. (1983). *Human brain and human learning.* New Rochelle, NY: Brain Age Publications.

Heider, F. (1958). *The psychology of interpersonal relations.* New York: Wiley.

Johnston, P. H., & Winograd, P. N. (1985). Passive failure in reading. *Journal of Reading Behavior, 27,* 279–301.

Lane, R. D., Nadel, L., Allen, J. J. B., & Kaszniak, A. W. (2000). The study of emotion from the perspective of cognitive neuroscience. In R. D. Lane & L. Nadel (Eds.), *Cognitive neuroscience of emotion.* New York: Oxford University Press.

LeDoux, J. (1996). *The emotional brain: The mysterious underpinnings of emotional life.* New York: Simon & Schuster.

Lyons, C. A. (1999). Emotions, cognition, and becoming a reader: A message to teachers of struggling learners. *Literacy Teaching and Learning: An International Journal of Early Reading and Writing, 4,* 67–87.

Luria, A. R. (1973). *The working brain: An introduction to neuropsychology.* New York: Basic Books.

Mark, S. F. (1983). To succeed or not to succeed: A critical review of issues in learned helplessness. *Contemporary Educational Psychology, 8,* 1–19.

Nicholls, J. G. (1978). The development of the concepts of effort and ability, perception of academic attainment, and the understanding that difficult tasks require more ability. *Child Development, 49,* 800–814.

Nicholls, J. G. (1984). Conception of ability and achievement motivation. In R. Ames & C. Ames (Eds.), *Research on motivation in education: Student motivation* (Vol. 1, pp. 39–73). Orlando, FL: Academic Press.

Oldfather, P. (1992, December). Sharing the ownership of knowing: A constructivist concept of motivation for literacy learning. Paper presented at the annual meeting of the National Reading Conference, San Antonio, TX.

Oldfather, P. (1994). When students do not feel motivated for literacy learning: How a responsive classroom culture helps. *(Reading Research Rep. No. 8).* Athens, GA: National Reading Research Center.

Paris, S. G., & Cross, D. R. (1983). Ordinary learning: Pragmatic connections among children's beliefs, motives, and actions. In J. Bisanz, G. L. Bisanz, & R. Kail (Eds.), *Learning in children: Progress in cognitive development research* (pp. 137–169). New York: Springer-Verlag.

Paris, S. G., Lipson, M. Y., & Wixson, K. K. (1983/1994). Becoming a strategic reader. In R. R. Ruddell, M. R. Ruddell, & H. Singer (Eds.), *Theoretical models and processes of reading* (4th ed., pp. 788–810). Newark, DE: International Reading Association.

Pearson, P. D. (1996). Reclaiming the center. In M. F. Graves, P. van den Broek, and B. M. Taylor (Eds.), *The first R: Every child's right to read* (pp. 259–274). Newark, DE: International Reading Association.

Peterson, C., Maier, S. F., & Seligman, M. E. P. (1993). *Learned helplessness: A theory for the age of personal control.* New York: Oxford University Press.

Pressley, M., Woloshyn, V., Burkell, J., Cariglia-Bull, T., Lysynchuk, L., McGoldrick, J. A., Schneider, B., Snyder, B. L., & Symons, S. (1995). *Cognitive strategy instruction that really improves children's academic performance* (2nd ed.). Cambridge, MA: Brookline Books.

Rotter, J. B. (1966). Generalized expectancies for internal versus external control of reinforcement. *Psychological Monographs, 80,* 1–28.

Salomon, G. (1984). Television is "easy" and print is "tough:" The differential investment of mental effort in learning as a function of perceptions and attributions. *Journal of Educational Psychology, 76,* 647–658.

Salovey, P., & Sluyter, D. J. (Eds.). (1997). *Emotional development and emotional intelligence.* New York: HarperCollins.

Schunk, D. H. (1984). Self-efficacy perspective on achievement behavior. *Educational Psychologist, 19,* 48–58.

Schunk, D. H. (1990). Goal setting and self-efficacy during self-regulated learning. *Educational Psychologist, 25,* 71–86.

Schunk, D. H. (1996). Goal and self-evaluative influences during children's cognitive skill learning. *American Educational Research Journal, 33,* 359–382.

Schunk, D. H., & Zimmerman, B. J. (1997). Developing self-efficacious readers and writers: The role of social and self-regulatory processes. In J. T. Guthrie & A. Wigfield (Eds.), *Reading engagement: Motivating readers through integrated instruction* (pp. 34–50). Newark, DE: International Reading Association.

Seligman, M. E. P. (1995). *The optimistic child.* Boston, MA: Houghton-Mifflin.

Seligman, M. E. P., & Maier, S. F. (1967). Failure to escape traumatic shock. *Journal of Experimental Psychology, 74,* 1–9.

Seligman, M. E. P., Peterson, C., Kaslow, N. J., Tanenbaum, R. J., Alloy, L. B., & Abramson, L. Y. (1984). Attributional style and depressive symptoms among children. *Journal of Abnormal Psychology, 83,* 235–238.

Short, K. G., & Burke, C. (1991). *Creating curriculum: Teachers and students as a community of learners.* Portsmouth, NH: Heinemann.

Sonnenschein, S., Brody, G., & Munsterman, K. (1996). The influence of family beliefs and practice on children's early reading development. In L. Baker, P. Afflerbach, & D. Reinking (Eds.), *Developing engaged readers in school and home communities* (pp. 3–20). Mahwah, NJ: Erlbaum.

Stipek, D. (1981). Children's perceptions of their own and their classmates' ability. *Journal of Educational Psychology, 73,* 404–410.

Stipek, D. J., & MacIver, D. (1989). Developmental change in children's assessment of intellectual competence. *Child Development, 60,* 521–538.

Sylwester, R. (1995). *A celebration of neurons: An educator's guide to the human brain.* Alexandria, VA: Association for Supervision and Curriculum Development.

Vygotsky, L. S. (1978). *Mind in society: The development of higher psychological processes.* Cambridge, MA: Harvard University Press.

Weiner, B. (1979). A theory of motivation for some classroom experiences. *Journal of Educational Psychology, 71,* 3–25.

Weiner, B. (1986). *An attributional theory of motivation and emotion.* New York: Springer-Verlag.

Weiner, B. (1992). *Human motivation: Metaphors, theories, and research.* Newbury Park, CA: Sage.

Weiner, B., & Graham, S. (1984). An attributional approach to emotional development. In C. E. Izard, J. Kagan, & R. B. Zajonc (Eds.), *Emotions, cognition, and behavior* (pp. 167–191). New York: Cambridge University Press.

Wigfield, A. (1988). Children's attributions for success and failure: Effects of age and attentional focus. *Journal of Educational Psychology, 80,* 76–81.

Wigfield, A. (1997). Children's motivations for reading and reading engagement. In J. T. Guthrie & A. Wigfield (Eds.), *Reading engagement: Motivating readers through integrated instruction* (pp. 14–33). Newark, DE: International Reading Association.

Wigfield, A., & Asher, S. R. (1984). Social and motivational influences on reading. In P. D. Pearson, R. Barr, M. L. Kamil, & P. Mosenthal (Eds.), *Handbook of reading research*, (Vol. 1, pp. 423–452). New York: Longman.

Winne, P. H., & Marx, R. W. (1989). A cognitive-processing analysis of motivation within classroom tasks. In C. Ames & R. Ames (Eds.), *Research on motivation in education: Vol. 3. Goals and cognitions*. San Diego: Academic Press.

Zimmerman, B. J. (1998). Developing self-fulfilling cycles of academic regulation: An analysis of exemplary instructional models. In D. H. Schunk & B. J. Zimmerman (Eds.), *Self-regulated learning: From teaching to self-reflective practice* (pp. 1–19). New York: The Guilford Press.

# Emotions, Cognition, and Becoming a Reader: A Message to Teachers of Struggling Learners

Carol A. Lyons, *The Ohio State University*

## ABSTRACT

*This paper considers the emotional nature of learning and the critical role emotions play in the making of the mind. It reflects an effort to connect recent theoretical perspectives with the teaching of struggling learners. Perspectives explored include: the recent neurological research on the interaction between cognition (reason) and emotion (feelings) in the development of plans of action and decision making, the role of language in the development of the mind, and the development of higher-order functions arising from social interaction. Implications of these theories for practice are also examined.*

Historically, a dichotomy has existed between cognition or intellectual behavior and emotion or affective behavior. This dichotomy is apparent in our schools, classrooms, and curricula. For example, it is not uncommon for school counselors to offer emotional support for children who have experienced a traumatic event such as a fire or death of a classmate. In most schools, when children are experiencing a personal crisis, there is an attempt to meet individual emotional needs. However, school personnel generally hold an impersonal, cognitive view when it comes to addressing children's individual *learning* needs. This view holds that one approach to instruction will fit all children. Thus, making it the child's responsibility for learning the material as it is presented. For children who do not effectively engage in these types of learning activities, medication often becomes the answer.

Generally speaking, schools operate on the principle that cognitive growth will result in academic achievement. If educators can identify the one best way to teach reading, deliver that program to all children, test scores will improve. Although school mission statements may include concern for improving self-esteem and cultural awareness, the graded course of study and curriculum is nearly always based on learning specific content, developing specific skills, demonstrating specific competencies, and testing to determine if children have acquired a specific body of knowledge.

It is time for educators to erase the dichotomy by considering the wealth of information that has become available substantiating the role that both intellectual and affective behavior play in learning. It is as Dr. Stanley Greenspan (1997) suggests in his book, *The Growth of the Mind,* our educational system's failure to educate the masses

69

of children who are cognitively capable of learning is due to reliance on a model that ignores the emotional nature of learning and the critical role emotions play in the making of mind.

## Processes That Build the Mind

Clinical studies of infants and children conducted by neurologists, pediatricians, and psychiatrists have revealed that cognition (i.e., reason) and emotion (i.e., feelings) begin to interact from birth and continue for a lifetime. Emotions were found to be an integral and inseparable part of the learning process (Damasio, 1994; Konner, 1991). After two decades of clinical research and experience in infant and child development Greenspan (1997) concluded that "emotions, not cognitive stimulation, serve as the mind's primary architect" (p. 1) and "babies' emotional exchanges with their caregivers, rather than their ability to fit pegs into holes or find beads under cups, should become the primary measuring rod of developmental and intellectual competence" (p. 9).

Over a period of about twenty-six years, thirteen of which have been spent working as a Reading Recovery teacher and university trainer, I have found support for the position that emotions play a primary and critical role in learning through four kinds of personal experiences. These experiences include: (a) interactions and conversations with my son, Ken, from birth through college, medical school, and pediatric residency; (b) the teaching of Reading Recovery (RR) children, many of whom were identified as learning disabled or developmentally handicapped; (c) twelve years of research examining teacher/child interactions of effective Reading Recovery teachers; and (d) clinical studies of learning disabled and RR children using the electroencephalogram (EEG) and brain electrical activity mapping (BEAM) tools to track brain activity during problem solving while reading.

These first hand experiences have lead me to believe there are certain kinds of nurturing that propel children's intellectual and emotional development and that affective experience facilitates children's ability to engage successfully in the variety of problem-solving tasks needed to become a proficient reader and writer.

In my view, research conducted by Greenspan (1997) has much to say to researchers and educators interested in how individuals become literate. His work describes and explains how new capacities emerge at different stages of a child's development. These include a "progression of abilities, such as attention and self-regulation, engagement, intentionality, and complex pattern making, that underlie the sense of self, consciousness, and moral awareness" (p. 125). Two personal experiences involving my son Ken provide insight into the development of reason and its inseparable dependence on emotion: The Button Jar and the Calendar Trick.

### The Button Jar

My Grandma Mueller loved to sew. As the first born and only grandchild for five years, I received many of Grandma's homemade creations. I would go to the store to help Grandma select the "perfect buttons" for each of my homemade outfits. I generally chose unusual buttons in a variety of colors, shapes, sizes, and what I called "fancy buttons" which were animals, flowers, clowns, and holiday figures. When she died in 1970, Grandma willed me her sewing machine, a sewing box, and a large glass pickle jar filled with buttons. The sewing machine was placed in our spare bedroom and on top of the sewing machine I placed the large glass button jar.

When Kenny was five months old, he started to crawl. Once on the floor, the first place he always went was to the spare bedroom where he would immediately point to the button jar. I think he was fascinated with the many colors, sizes, and shapes of the hundreds of buttons that filled the jar.

I would put the button jar on the floor so that he could take a closer look at it. But looking was not enough; he wanted to touch the buttons. I would open the jar and dump a few buttons on the hardwood floor. I showed him how to push the buttons one-by-one into a pile. Then the two of us would pick up each button and return it to the button jar. I watched him very closely so that he would not put the buttons in his mouth, which of course is what he usually tried to do. After repeatedly telling him not to put the buttons in his mouth because he might swallow them and get sick, I had to tell him that the next time he tried to put the buttons in his mouth, I would put the button jar away. The day after that warning, he learned that I meant what I said. The button jar was put away for several days until he promised that he would not put any buttons in his mouth again.

After about three weeks of pushing the buttons into piles, I showed him how to sort the buttons by color. While demonstrating the process, I would say, "Let's put all the white buttons in this pile." With my help, Ken learned how to make a pile of red, white, and black buttons. We would have a conversation about the color of each group, with my doing all the talking, and Ken making babbling sounds. He would look at me with that proud look mothers come to understand when a child feels good about what he has accomplished. We both had fun and I believe he knew he was pleasing me.

When Ken was eight months old, he started to associate a color word to each pile of different colored buttons. When I asked him to show me the red pile of buttons, he could point to the red pile. He could group the buttons according to a specific color, but could not yet produce the word to associate with each color. Once he could sort by color, I showed him how to count the buttons in each pile. He started to learn the number concepts of one, two, and three and say a word to represent each button he counted.

One day he pointed out that some of the buttons had holes and others had no holes. So we sorted buttons into piles of "holes" and "no holes." Ken, not I, had discovered another classification system. From that activity, we sorted buttons by the number of holes; that is, two holes, four holes, six holes, etc. He also noticed that some buttons were smooth, others were rough, some were square, and others were round. He had not acquired a word to label the concepts, but he noticed differences and similarities among buttons, thus completing the task visually. By the time he was one, Ken had developed a classification system and specific words (e.g., color, shapes, number of holes) to describe this classification system.

Every day we played the button game. I would push all the white buttons together and ask him to tell me how I grouped the buttons. He would look at the piles and say "white pile, no holes, two holes," etc. Then our roles reversed. Ken would sort the buttons into specific groups and I would tell him how he had classified them. We took great delight in this activity, talking and laughing trying to trick each other. Sometimes I would put a red button into the white pile and he would squeal and tell me, "No!" and push it into the correct pile. Then I would watch him place a button in the wrong pile and he would watch me to see if I discovered his error. In his baby book I wrote that at 12 months of age, Ken's favorite pastime was playing with the button jar.

What did Ken learn playing with the buttons? What may have been going on inside his brain? Distinguished Soviet psychologist Alexander Luria's description of the functional organization of the brain (1973) provides a plausible explanation.

## The Neuropsychology of Learning

Luria (1973) believed that human mental processes involve complex functional systems that work together and make their own particular contribution to the organization of the overall system. He proposed three principal functional units of the brain whose participation is necessary for any type of cognitive activity (see Figure 1).

Unit I, located in the brain stem, is responsible for regulating tone or waking. The most important part of the first functional unit is the reticular activating system (RAS), a small structure located near the top of the brain stem. The RAS serves as a

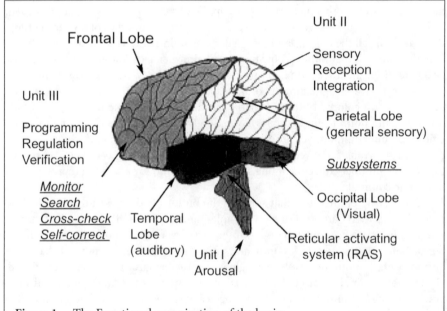

**Figure 1.** The Functional organization of the brain
*Note:* Adapted from *The Working Brain* by A. Luria, 1973, New York: Basic Books.

trap door or gatekeeper, allowing stimuli to enter the brain and be relayed through the limbic system to the appropriate cortical areas. This interaction helps with attention, thinking, balance, and coordinated movement. As children grow, they learn to send messages from the cortex to focus their attention. In this way, the RAS plays an integral role in directing consciousness and attention. On the other hand, without the reticular formation's alerting signals, the brain grows sleepy and disengages.

The RAS was responsible for focusing and sustaining Ken's attention while we played the button jar game. From the first moment the button jar was placed on the floor, he was focused, interested, and engaged in what I was doing and saying. He was able to sustain and focus his attention, even as the activities became more challenging.

The second functional unit (Unit II) is primarily responsible for the reception, analysis, integration, and storage of information. This unit occupies the posterior region of the cerebral hemispheres and incorporates the visual (occipital), auditory (temporal), and general sensory (parietal) regions. The temporal lobe located near our ears is an area believed to be responsible for hearing, listening, language, and memory storage. The occipital lobe processes our vision. The parietal lobe deals with the reception of sensory information that involves movement.

Each of these lobes processes the same information in different ways and in different parts of the brain. There is much overlap in the functions of each of these lobes. These three areas of the brain appear to be involved with types of memory. The parietal, upper temporal and occipital lobes seem to serve as short-term memory banks for auditory, visual, and kinesthetic (motion, perception) impulses (Luria, 1973). Discussion of actions described as subsystems in Bruner's (1973) and Clay's (1991) work are similar to behaviors associated with Unit II.

The sensing, receiving, and integrating unit is involved in specific interactions that involve cortical processing in the temporal, occipital and parietal lobes of the brain. Through the button jar game, Ken learned how to integrate and coordinate actions while involving these three lobes of the brain. He learned to:

- Coordinate and control arm, hand, and eye movements while placing buttons into discrete groups.
- Integrate and connect gesture, touch, sounds, and words with feelings.

The third functional unit is the frontal lobe, which is located in the area around the forehead. It is involved in purposeful acts, which Luria termed programming, regulation, and verification. The frontal lobe plays an essential role in regulating the state of the activity, organizing and changing it in accordance with complex intentions and plans formulated with the aid of speech (Luria, 1973). As the frontal lobes mature, they team up with the RAS, which directs arousal and alertness, and with the limbic system, which regulates hormones and emotions, forming a loop that works to select and direct attention. An important function of this loop is regulation of the child's ability to use "feedback" as an ongoing check on behavior. This feedback system helps the child monitor and catch errors and remember what he or she is supposed to do to resolve problems. Problem solving actions such as monitoring, searching, cross-checking, and self-correcting involve the frontal lobes. Varied experiences with the button jar provided opportunities for Ken to program, regulate, and verify his actions. He learned how to:

- Associate a specific word (number or color word) with an object.
- Categorize objects into discrete groups according to a plan of action.
- Develop a flexible classification system.
- Recognize similar and different patterns.
- Develop a feedback system to monitor his behavior.
- Reorganize or reclassify individual buttons in a variety of ways.
- Find solutions or rationale for Mom's plan for organizing and developing a category.
- Use language to regulate his behavior to develop his own plan for organizing information.
- Correct his behavior when necessary.

Understanding the role of the three functional units of the brain and the important ways in which each unit participates in the organization of human behavior may contribute to an explanation of the nature of Ken's reasoning as we played with the buttons.

## The Relationship Between Cognitive and Emotional Development

Recent neurological research (Damasio, 1994) may help us better understand how cognition (reason) and emotion (feelings) interact to support problem-solving and our ability to make decisions and generate plans of action. Three major principles that support the links between infants' emotional and cognitive development are discussed by Greenspan (1997).

First, the foundations of learning are the infant's own natural intentions. This principle suggests that it is the *child* not the parent or caretaker who determines and controls where attention will be focused and subsequently what is learned. The child's reticular activating system (RAS) located in Unit I arouses and focuses the brain's processing. It is responsible for arousal and consciousness and is critical to focusing our attentional system. So attempting to develop Ken's ability to learn color words or number concepts by manipulating buttons would probably not have worked if it had been my idea.

Greenspan's (1997) research indicates that when an infant is confused, senses disapproval, or feels anxious, there is a psychological and physiological reaction in the brain that inhibits processing. The child's RAS shuts down and he will look away. However, if the parent follows the child's interest, many learning opportunities will arise because the infant has voluntarily attended and engaged.

Secondly, each sensation, as it is registered by a child, gives rise to an affect or emotion. This process is called "dual coding" of experience and is the key to understanding how emotions organize intellectual capacities and create the sense of self and well-being. According to Greenspan (1997):

Emotions and intellect are NOT two separate parts of a person. Emotions are the organizer or the "supersense," helping to organize all the sensory information coming our way. Experience is stored and organized in the brain with a dual code. The dual code consists of the sensory experience and the emotional or affective reaction to the experience, both of which will be coded together in the brain. This double coding allows the child to cross-reference each memory or experience in a mental catalog and feeling and to reconstruct it when needed. (p. 21)

The dual coding phenomenon may help to explain the relationship between Ken's cognitive and emotional development. I believe that his capacity to reason (e.g., sort buttons in discrete categories) was followed by mechanisms of emotions, which occurred as he began experiencing feelings of affirmation and support from me. Once this occurred, systematic connections between categories of objects and situations, on the one hand, and emotions, on the other were formed in his mind. He labeled and coded the buttons as bright, smooth, red, etc. and also by emotional qualities connected with feelings he exhibited while playing with the buttons. This double coding allowed him to cross-reference the category system with a positive memory.

Third, parts of the brain and nervous system that deal with emotional regulation play a crucial role in planning, discriminating and choosing between alternatives, monitoring, self-correcting, and regulating one's behavior. Recent neurological research (Damasio, 1994) demonstrates that neuronal development in the prefrontal cortex (Unit III) regulates emotions. Furthermore, damage to the prefrontal cortex seriously impairs a child's judgment and regulation of behavior. When the regulatory system is working well, infants between three and eight months can register the appropriate sense perceptions when presented with sights and sounds, attend and discriminate among them, and comprehend sensations that they see, touch, and hear (Greenspan, 1997).

Each sensation that Ken registered gave rise to an affect or emotion. He squealed with delight while touching and pushing the buttons on the floor. He also came to understand that if he tried to put a button in his mouth, the button jar would disappear and the game would end. He responded to the button jar game in terms of the emotional as well as the physical effect on him. From an emotional perspective, he learned how to regulate his behavior by not doing what he wanted to do, which was to eat the buttons.

In one study, Greenspan (1997) found that measurements of emotional regulatory function, taken at eight months of age, correlated with children's mental capabilities indicated on standardized IQ tests at age four.

In developing the mind, intellectual learning shared common origins with emotional learning. Both stem from early affective interactions. Both are influenced by individuals, and both must proceed in a step-wise fashion, from one developmental level to another. The sort of learning a child acquires in kindergarten and primary grades is not the true foundation of his or her education. In fact, early school work cannot proceed without previous mastery of various mental tasks. The three R's and all that follows, symbolic and increasing abstract academic knowledge, cannot be understood by a person who has not grasped the skills that make learning possible. (p. 210)

Greenspan's view of the developing mind provides a plausible explanation for how Ken created the calendar trick.

## The Calendar Trick

Every year I buy a linen calendar towel that depicts the days of the week for each month over the course of that year. I have a collection of towels that spans over forty years. When Ken was two, one of his favorite pastimes was going to the kitchen drawer and throwing the calendar towels out on the floor. Instead of sleeping during naptime, he would take five to ten towels to his room, and carefully line them up according to years on the floor. I never understood why he did this, but as long as he was quiet, I did not care.

When he was two and one-half years old, Ken would ask my husband and me to give him a date and he would tell us on which day of the week the date fell. For example, we would say, "August 7," and he would reply, "Thursday." He was invariably right. We could ask him random dates in different months and years and he always would tell us the correct day of the week. What was particularly amazing was how fast he could do this trick. When asked how he did it, he said he did not know. What we did learn, however, was that he recognized similarities and differences among dates for each month depicted on the towel and he recognized recurring patterns of numbers among the days of the week and months of the year.

The neighbors and relatives soon learned about Ken's calendar trick. He could tell people on which day of the week their birthday would fall two or three years later, or on which day Christmas fell four years ago. He could tell us the day of the week for specific dates in the past, present, and future years, even accounting for a leap year. We did receive an invitation to take Ken to appear on the *Tonight Show* with Johnny Carson, which we turned down. (However, my husband did consider taking Ken to the local bar to make some money.)

When he was three and one-half years old, he finally told us how he did the calendar trick. He said that if you know on which day of the week the first of the month falls, you can figure out the rest of days for every month in the year. Because the same day of the week has the same numbers all the time. If the first day of January falls on a Thursday, then the other Thursdays in January will be on 8, 15, 22, and 29. If the first day of March falls on Sunday, then the remaining Sundays in March will be 8, 15, 22, and 29. What Ken had discovered was patterns among and across the dates of each day of the week and in each month of a specific year. He had developed a more complex and intricate skill beyond what he had learned while playing with buttons. He had generalized properties and skills learned in one context and applied them to a new context.

Recent neurological research (Damasio, 1994; Greenspan, 1997) provides some explanation for how he acquired the ability to go from concrete thinking and categorizing developed through various activities involving the button jar, to abstract thought developed independently and evident in the calendar trick. The research shows that our minds can instantly retrieve similarly coded information relevant in one situation and use it in a similar way for a new situation. Such neurobiological clinical research has indicated that the brain is a natural pattern seeker and synthesizer that actively searches for patterns to categorize, organize, synthesize, code information into memory, and then retrieve it.

Ken was able to retrieve this stored information rapidly and reliably because his affective capacity organized information in an especially functional and meaningful manner. Because the information was dual coded according to its affective, sensory, and cognitive qualities, he had the structure and circuitry established in his brain to enable him to retrieve it easily. He probably was also intrinsically motivated to share the calendar trick with us because he had received such positive reinforcement in the button jar game. The pleasure he experienced was not simply one of mastery, but one of feeling good and seeing the pleasure of others. But the important question is how did he teach himself to do this? An examination of the neuronal development systems of the brain, electrical and chemical, provides some insights.

## Neuronal Development of the Electrical Brain

Babies are born with over 100 billion neurons or nerve cells designed to communicate electrochemically with one another. Each neuron has three main parts: cell body, axon, and dendrites. The cell body is the nucleus of the neuron. An axon is a long, slim, "tree-trunk" fiber that transmits signals from the cell body to other cells via junctions called synapses. Dendrites are networks of short fibers that branch out from an axon, receive signals from the ends of axons from other neurons, and bring the signals to their neuron's own cell body (Lambert, Bramwell, & Lawther, 1982). This complex electrical and chemical processing system regulates communication and action (see Figure 2).

Each neuron communicates to other neurons by firing an electrical impulse or message along the input axon. The input axon sends impulses or messages to the cell body. The cell body receives the electrical impulses and sends them to the output axon. The output axon carries the electrical impulses to other neurons over a gap called a synapse.

Each neuron has many dendrites, each of which picks up electrical impulses and sends chemical messages to another neuron cell, starting the process over again. Dendritic spines develop and shift in response to the need to connect assemblies of neurons into memories. They can deteriorate or lose strength from lack of use and gain strength from frequent use. The dendrite spines allow for short periods of continuous attention to develop a permanent record or memory. Cells which become stimulated by picking up and relaying messages develop new dendrite spines and more complex neural networks (Healy, 1994).

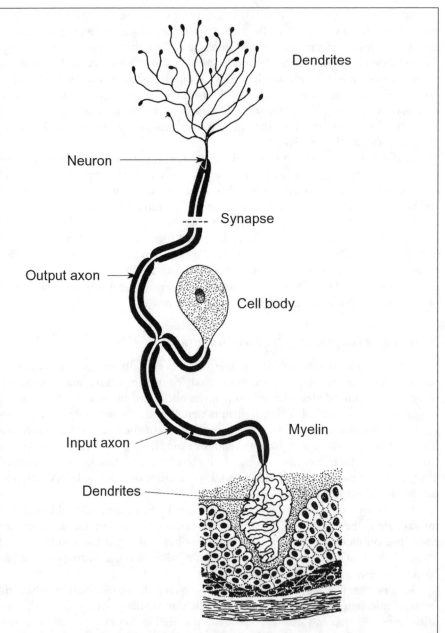

**Figure 2.** One neuron consisting of a cell body, tail-like axon, and dendrites. *Note:* Adapted from *The Brain: A User's Manual* by D. Lambert, M. Bramwell, and G. Lawther, 1982, New York, G. P. Putnam.

As electrical messages are processed over and over again the axons develop a fatty, white/light gray cellular insulation called myelin. Myelin facilitates rapid conduction of the electrical impulses. It makes the axons more efficient, enabling electrical impulses to travel up to 12 times faster. The more myelin there is coating the axons, the more automatic the processing (Lambert et al, 1982).

For years, scientists have had tools that allowed them to observe and study the electrical communication system of the brain. Only recently, however, have tools been developed that allow researchers to understand better the *chemical* communication system of the brain.

## The Chemical Brain

The axon of one neuron releases a chemical agent called a neurotransmitter to stimulate the dendrites of another cell. This reaction occurs at a synapse. The neurotransmitters bind to receptors on other neurons, causing an electrical charge that redirects the neural pathways. The effect on an individual is a change in physical activity, including behavior, mood, and emotion. The adult human has trillions of synapses that connect to the network of our brains. If they are not connected, they disappear (Pert, 1997).

Neuroscientists believe that there are 70 to 80 different kinds of neurotransmitters. Seratonin, for example, is a mood-controlling neurotransmitter. When released in an individual, it is associated with feeling good about oneself and having a positive attitude. High seratonin levels are associated with attention and memory. When individuals feel successful, happy, and proud that they have overcome a difficult task, seratonin levels increase. When they experience failure and feel dejected about not being able to learn, seratonin levels decrease. Neurotransmitters either enhance or inhibit further transmission of impulse to dendrites (Damasio, 1994).

From the first hour of birth, our brains are getting wired, developing tracks that will last us for a lifetime. Early brain stimulation is critical to learning and emotions play a major role in developing cognitive abilities. The critical time to build neural networks is during the first three years of life. By the time a child is three years old, his or her brain has already reached two-thirds to three-quarters of its adult size. By age five, when a child enters kindergarten, so much of the brain is developed that a child who has not acquired the necessary skills of attention, communication, and the ability to participate actively in relationships (give and take with others) is at a disadvantage. The earlier the child is provided opportunities to build this complex electrical and chemical neural network that becomes the mind, the easier it will be for the child to learn (Greenspan, 1997).

Thus, emotions (feelings) are part and parcel of what we call cognition (reasoning); they play a critical role in forming ideas and generalizing information (i.e., seeing the forest through the trees). They orchestrate many of the mind's most important functions, such as classifying and organizing information, problem solving and evaluating the consequence of our actions (Greenspan, 1997).

Neurologists believe that when a child reaches puberty the brain has stopped growing. This does not mean that one cannot continue to learn; certainly our experiences after adolescence demonstrate this. However, it is the case that the most opportune time for building the neural network that is the foundation for learning *how to learn* has come to an end. It stands to reason then, that the more opportunities or experiences a child has had during the first three years of life, preschool, and early elementary school, the more neural pathways he or she has developed. The process is self-perpetuating. That is, the more neural pathways developed, the more dendritic branches appear. The more dendritic branches appearing, the more connections can be made among neurons. The more connections among neurons being made, the more complex reasoning and myelin building can occur. The more myelin is accumulating, the faster and more automatic the child can process information.

I believe the button jar game was the foundation for the calendar trick. Ken had rich and varied opportunities to develop a complex electrical and chemical neural network that mylinated during those early years. But what about those children who enter school having had limited early childhood opportunities to set the circuitry of their brains? What can be done today to overcome their inadequate beginnings and to help them learn how to learn to read and write?

## Emotions, Cognitive Development, and Reading Recovery

Three bodies of research provide insights regarding instructional contexts that may help primary level teachers become more efficient and effective. They include the role of emotions, the role of language, and the role of social interaction in the making of the mind. To illustrate these points, following is an example of how Reading Recovery (RR) teachers support children in ways that are based on these theoretical principles. (Reading Recovery is an early intervention literacy program that serves first-grade children who are at risk of failure in learning to read and write. Children receive individual tutoring daily from a specially trained teacher.)

### The Role of Emotions

The first body of research discusses the critical role emotions play in developing the brain structure required for attending, organizing, categorizing, storing, and retrieving information. Research (Damasio, 1994; Greenspan, 1997) has demonstrated that feeling successful is critical to keeping the RAS open. The RAS must be opened and aroused in order for the child to attend; without attention, the child will not learn. Having a positive, non-threatening, non-stressful experience while learning enhances the child's opportunities for success.

Effective RR teachers create an instructional environment that includes two major features to help the child feel positive and successful, both of which support and sustain attention. First, they teach the child the task. Second, they keep the task easy so that the child will feel successful and will attend to the process. An example to describe how this is accomplished follows.

Reading Recovery teachers must teach children "how words work" so they can use what they know about a word to problem solve words in reading or writing. The teacher begins by having the child make a familiar word that has a few letters that he or she is sure the child knows. The teacher may use the known word 'cat,' for example. The teacher gives the child the exact number of magnetic letters and either demonstrates how to put the three letters together to make the word 'cat' or asks the child to make the word by himself. The teacher and/or child make and break apart the known word several times. Starting with a known word frees the child to focus on how individual letters make up words, and how words can be taken apart letter by letter.

The child begins to understand how words are constructed and a process for constructing them. The teacher has organized the experience so that the child is successful, assuring he or she will voluntarily and easily engage in the activity. In teaching the task and the process of constructing a word by using a word the child knows, the teacher has made it easy for a child to learn how words work. But this activity teaches the child much more. It teaches him or her how to:

- Focus and sustain attention.
- Associate letters to a sound and sounds to letters.
- Discriminate between and among features of letters.
- Categorize letters into groups that are similar and different to make a word.
- Reorganize and reclassify letters into different words.

The list of processing behaviors should sound familiar because those are the skills Ken developed while playing with the buttons. He learned to discriminate features of objects (buttons) which he then used to discriminate among features of letters. Perhaps that is why he was reading at age three and one-half without formalized schooling. Children who engage in the process of making and breaking words apart and constructing new words from known ones develop the capacity to plan, guide, and monitor behavior. These are the problem solving skills that are used every time they read and write.

## The Role of Language

The second body of research that has implications for RR teachers involves the role of language in the development of the mind. Four principles regarding the role of language are critical to teachers' work in Reading Recovery.

First, in order to learn language, children must come to understand that language has a purpose and function and that they must learn how to use it to communicate their needs and desires. Neurological research has demonstrated that every child is born with billions of neurons and thus has the potential to learn language. But as Greenspan's research (1997) indicates, unless the child masters the ability for reciprocal emotional and social signaling, his or her ability to use language functionally develops poorly, often in a fragmented manner. Words lack meaning, pronouns are confused, scraps of rote learning, such as repeating illogical phrases that are not connected to what he is doing in a meaningful way, will dominate speech. Marie Clay (1993) writes:

> Some children have particular difficulty in calling up an association or label for a word, or a name for a letter. This low recall means that the earliest, easiest, and most basic links of oral language with print are very difficult for the child to establish. (p. 25)

While sorting buttons during infancy, Ken learned to associate a word (red) to a specific color and a number word (three) to a specific number of buttons. He was developing strategies for remembering color and number words. Just think of how many opportunities his neural network had to mylinate prior to former schooling. He could see similarities and differences among features of letter (e.g., noticing where to put the stick to make a lower case b or d), just as he saw similarities and differences among buttons and number patterns on calendar towels.

Secondly, the origins of language are found in the parent's verbal commands and directives and this language or speech usually plays a regulatory function in everyday life. Luria (1982) contends that the real birth of regulatory speech is when the child responds to a parent's directive. When I asked Ken to group all the white buttons with two holes together in a pile, he complied with my verbal request and regulated his behavior to accomplish the task.

The same process occurs many times throughout a RR lesson. Reading Recovery teachers organize and regulate a child's behavior through language. For example, in *Reading Recovery: A Guidebook for Teachers in Training* (Clay, 1993), there is a section devoted to helping a child who enters RR with very low letter knowledge (i.e., Learning to Look at Print, pp. 24–28). Clay suggests the following procedure to help the child orchestrate three ways of remembering:

1. Movement—The teacher holds the child's hand and guides him, eventually calling for the child to do so independently.
2. Words—The teacher verbally describes the movement while she is making the letter or word and asks the child to do so independently.
3. Visual Form—The teacher writes the letter, providing a visual model and asks the child to do so independently.

The child's behavior is regulated through the teacher's verbal directives. The teacher must be careful to use language specific enough to match the action the child must perform. For example, while writing a lower case b, the teacher must guide the child's hand to form the letter while saying the words, "Down, up, and around." Words and movement must be coordinated.

Third, when young children learn to use language effectively to make sense of their experiences, they begin to plan and regulate their actions. Infant research (Luria, 1982) demonstrates that regulation of behavior by speech is attained slowly over time. It appears first in interaction with others, and later, children can be heard directing their own behavior or problem solving out loud.

While playing the button jar game, Ken would talk to himself and give his plan away. While listening carefully to what he said to himself, I knew when he was going to put one red button into the white pile. He made his thoughts explicit. Sometimes RR children do the same thing. They will say, "That didn't make sense." or "That didn't match." The words provide an oral feedback system that acts as a call for action.

Finally, language guides the behavior according to a verbalized plan and modulates arousal of the brain through motor activity to meet the demands of the task (Luria, 1982). This principle is supported often in Reading Recovery, especially in early lessons. RR teachers' oral language in the form of prompts guides the children to think about something to do. For example, when children notice that what they read did not match the words on the page, they might say, "That didn't match;" "There were too many words;" "There were not enough words;" or "I better try that again and read it with my finger to make it match." They learned those words to regulate their actions by listening and reacting to the teacher's prompts. Eventually teachers will not have to use prompts because the children's internal verbalized plan will be functionally successfully.

## The Role of Social Interaction

The third body of research that contributes to our understanding of the making of mind, the making of a reader and writer is Vygotsky's theory that higher-order functions (such as problem solving, reasoning, planning, remembering, and communicating) develop out of social interaction. Vygotsky (1978) argued that:

> Every function in the child's cultural development appears twice; first, on the social level, and later, on the individual level; first, between people (interpsychologically), and then inside the child (intrapsychologically). This applies equally to voluntary attention, to local memory, and to the formation of concepts. All the higher functions originate as actual relations between human individuals. (p. 57)

This growth occurs in the zone of proximal development, which is the "distance between the actual development level as determined by independent problem solving and the level of potential development as determined through problem solving under adult guidance or in collaboration with more capable peers" (Vygotsky, 1978. p. 86).

Following are examples of two children, my son Ken and Trevor, a Reading Recovery child, which illustrate shifts that occur in learning as children progress through the zone of proximal development (ZPD) as illustrated in Figure 3.

**Zone of actual development.** The zone of actual development refers to what the child can do independently. Through close observation, RR teachers determine concepts the child has already acquired. For example, Trevor could write the first letter of his name independently, which meant that he had full, mature control of the functions for forming that letter. The RR program is built upon a firm foundation rooted in what the child knows and can do independently. The information gained from both *An Observation Survey of Early Literacy Achievement* (Clay, 1993) and from the first 10 sessions of the Reading Recovery program, called "Roaming Around the Known," serves to uncover what the child knows and can do without assistance. The teacher can determine the aspects of the child's problem solving that have already matured, that is, those that are the end products of development.

**The zone of proximal development (ZPD).** The ZPD defines those functions that are in the process of maturation, functions that will mature tomorrow or next week. The ZPD has three overlapping phases: (a) assistance provided by a more capable other; (b) transition from other-assistance to self-assistance; and (c) assistance provided by the self.

The stage of *assistance provided by a more capable other* refers to a situation where parents, caregivers, teachers, etc., may organize activities and facilitate learning by regulating the difficulty of the tasks and modeling mature performance through joint

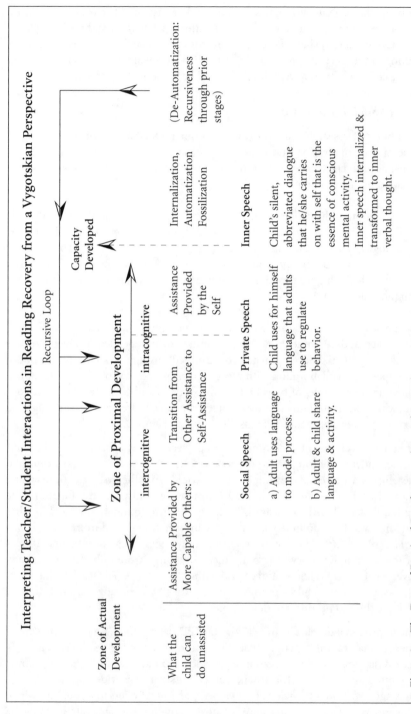

**Interpreting Teacher/Student Interactions in Reading Recovery from a Vygotskian Perspective**

Recursive Loop

**Zone of Proximal Development**

| Zone of Actual Development | | | Capacity Developed |
| --- | --- | --- | --- |
| | intercognitive | intracognitive | |
| What the child can do unassisted | Assistance Provided by More Capable Others: | Transition from Other Assistance to Self-Assistance | Assistance Provided by the Self | Internalization, Automatization Fossilization | (De-Automatization: Recursiveness through prior stages) |
| | **Social Speech** | **Private Speech** | | **Inner Speech** | |
| | a) Adult uses language to model process.<br><br>b) Adult & child share language & activity. | Child uses for himself language that adults use to regulate behavior. | | Child's silent, abbreviated dialogue that he/she carries on with self that is the essence of conscious mental activity.<br><br>Inner speech internalized & transformed to inner verbal thought. | |

**Figure 3.** The Zone of Proximal Development (Vygotsky, 1978)

*Note:* Adapted from *Rousing Minds to Life*, by R. Tharp and R. Gallimore, 1988, New York: Cambridge University Press.

participation of the adult and child in those activities. For example, when Ken and I had our first interactions with the button jar, I spilled the buttons on the floor, took his hand, and showed him how to push each button into a pile according to specific color. I was deliberate in my actions, but did not intentionally create a "lesson;" that is, I did not explicitly and intentionally focus on instruction or set out to teach him color words, etc. However, in our joint interactions a tacit lesson was learned.

This is not the case in a Reading Recovery lesson. The teacher consciously and intentionally creates an activity that engages children in such a way that they have opportunities to use what they know and can do to solve a problem. The teacher structures children's participation so they handle manageable, but comfortably challenging, portions of the activity that increase in complexity with their developing understanding and skill. For example, teachers explicitly teach children how to visually scan a line of text from the left to the right by holding the "pointing finger" to demonstrate how to match what they say to what they see as the teacher reads the text with them on an individual basis. Through routine and often tacit guided participation, children gain control of directionality and learn how to match words seen on the printed page with words spoken (i.e., achieve a one-to-one match).

Vygotsky (1978) emphasized language as the most powerful tool for thinking and communicating between individuals. Two types of social speech were evident during the interactions described above. Initially the adult uses language to model the process. For example, through conversation while sorting buttons by color, I believe Ken developed an understanding of how to classify objects by color and the concept of "word" to correspond to each pile of buttons. While engaged in the "sorting buttons by color" activity, my language was very specific. I would say, "Push all the red buttons here." As he became more involved in the activity, he assumed my role and started using my words to regulate what he was doing. For example, he would say, "Push all the red buttons over here" as he found red buttons scattered on the floor and pushed them into the "red" pile.

During RR lessons, the teacher assumes a role similar to the one I had while playing with Ken. However, RR teachers explicitly teach children using specific language to model a process. They routinely adjust their interactions and structure lessons, tasks, and social speech in ways consistent with providing increasingly more challenging activities as children develop additional competencies.

In Figure 3, the dotted line separating *assistance provided by more capable others* and *transition from other-assistance to self-assistance* is designed to show the fluid and flexible adjusting of teacher and child roles and responsibilities as they progress through the program. This transition involves the teacher in a process of assisting children in posing and solving problems through the creation and arrangement of children's activities and responsibilities. For example, in the button jar game, as Ken become more capable of sorting the buttons by color, shape, holes, etc., my role become less directive and our social speech shifted to meet this adjustment. In Reading Recovery, when the child's eyes routinely complete a left to right visual scan of words in a sentence, the RR teacher might ask the child to "Read it with your finger," to support his or her processing.

The dotted line separating *transition from other-assistance to self-assistance* and eventually to *assistance provided by the self* completes the zone of proximal development. The dotted line represents teachers' challenging and supporting children in a process of posing and solving increasingly complex problems that the teacher, and eventually the child, have created as activities. As this process occurs the child's thinking and problem solving are his or hers alone; that is, they occur within the child's mind (intracognitive). During this process the child uses private speech, which is likely the language the teacher used to regulate his or her behavior.

Private speech is self-directing and self-guiding (Vygotsky, 1978). As an example, Ken revealed his plan for sorting buttons out loud through private speech. Once this stage occurs, the child has developed the capacity to initiate and successfully complete a task.

*Internalization, automatization,* and *fossilization* occur when the child has emerged from the ZPD into the developmental stage for the activity or process learned. For example, in the case where a RR child has developed the ability to read fluently and flexibly in a left to right direction, executing this directional reading in a smooth and integrated way, the process (left-to-right serial order) would be considered as internalized and automatized. Vygotsky (1978) described it as the "fruits" of the development, but he also discussed it as "fossilized" which suggests the fixity of the process.

During this period of development there is a transition from private speech to inner speech. Inner speech is the child's silent, abbreviated self-dialogue that is the essence of conscious mental activity. Vygotsky (1978) postulated that "language arises initially as a means of communication between the child and period in his environment. Only subsequently, upon conversion to internal speech, does it come to organize the child's thought, that is, become an internal mental function" (p. 89). When this occurs, assistance from the adult is no longer needed. The following example illustrates a child who, by evidence of his inner speech, has reached this phase of development. He has emerged from the zone of proximal development.

Trevor had been in the Reading Recovery program for seven weeks and this was his first attempt to read the level 6 book Willy the Helper.

> **The text:** On Monday, Willy helped me fold the clothes.
> **Student talk:** *On Monday, Willy helped me fix, there's no 'x' (hesitates), find, f-i-n-d, there's no 'o', fold, yea, that looks right. On Monday, Willy helped me fold the clothes.*

It is obvious that Trevor had developed a plan to guide and monitor his behavior independently. Fortunately, he revealed his thinking through verbalized inner speech. Eventually Trevor's inner speech would be internalized and transformed to inner verbal thought. His overt behaviors did, however, suggest shifts in problem solving. For example, Trevor's first plan was to think of a word that began with 'f' that would make sense in the sentence—'fix' was a meaningful prediction. However, when he said the word aloud, he did not hear or see an 'x'. His next move was to think of a word that made sense, started with an 'f' and ended with a 'd'. He tried 'find'. Once again, 'find' was a good choice because it began with an 'f' and ended with a 'd' and made sense, but after saying the word slowly he did not hear an 'o', the second letter he saw of the unknown word. He had to think of a word that started with an 'f' and was followed by an 'o'. He tried 'fold' and listened to the sounds of each letter in the word, checked them against what he saw in print, and he then pronounced that "The word looked right." He was now ready to read the entire sentence accurately and fluently.

Trevor's behaviors suggested a smooth integration of several task components, each of which was taught several times three to four weeks prior to this lesson. He had developed a flexible strategy system for problem solving that enabled him to predict and confirm words that would make sense, look right, and sound right in a particular sentence. Trevor had developed the ability to regulate his own behavior.

According to Diaz, Neal, and Amaya-Williams (1990), self-regulation is "the child's capacity to plan, guide, and monitor his or her behavior from within and flexibly according to changing circumstances" (p. 130). The word "capacity" combines two separate but interrelated concepts, that of will and skill. If the child does not have the will to learn, there is no interest, no motivation, no focused attention, and few opportunities for the child to develop higher order reasoning. The research of Damasio (1994) and Greenspan (1997) supports the links between feelings and reason; that is, emotion and cognition.

Developing specific skills is equally important. The child must have learned and developed some fundamental cognitive skills in order to make continuous progress. For example, the child must develop the skill to distinguish the features of specific letters (lines, circles, squiggles), to recognize similarities and differences among letters, to determine features of a letter that other letters have in common, and to provide a label (letter name) for specific letters in order to organize them into a specific sequence to make up a word.

For some children, these skills are not going to emerge as easily as they did for Ken. Not because they do not have enough neurons, but because connections between neurons and dendrites have not been established or routinely used enough to become mylinated. This is true because some children have had fewer opportunities to engage in reading and writing activities prior to formal schooling. But time has not run out for such children. Reading Recovery teachers know that it is possible, with expert teaching, to provide learning opportunities that enable children who enter school with a low repertoire of literacy skills to become proficient readers and writers in a relatively short period of time.

Neurological studies (Greenspan, 1997) have also demonstrated how experience, organized and directed through specific speech and language patterns, develops the growth of brain structures and minds in such a way that one can see connections among neurons and dendrites. Through repetition and mylination, these neurons and dendrites can become stronger, speedier, and more flexible.

*De-automatization of performance* represents the final stage of the described process. Life-long learning by all individuals involves the same regulated ZPD sequences—from other assistance to self-assistance—recurring over and over again for the development of new capacities. However, for every individual there is a point in time when he or she needs assistance while learning a new skill. When this occurs, recursiveness through prior stages takes place. In some cases the individual can provide assistance for himself. Other times, however, he or she may need expert help from another individual.

Prior to reading *Willy the Helper,* Trevor's lessons were a mix of other-regulation and self-regulation sometimes occurring in one sentence in the text. Each strategy used (check first letter, last letter, middle of the word) to analyze and read the word 'find' was taught many times while reading and writing texts and sorting letters within words using magnetic letters. A fundamental principle that underpins Vygotsky's (1978) theory of learning is that the instructional activity of teaching and learning is effective only when it proceeds ahead of development. This theoretical principle becomes evident in an analysis of multiple interactions between Trevor and his RR teacher as they progressed through the RR program.

My experiences in the examination of teacher/child interactions while observing and analyzing hundreds of Reading Recovery lessons and interviewing many teachers have led me to discern five characteristics of effective RR teachers (Lyons, Pinnell, & DeFord, 1993). First, they know how to create opportunities for children to learn *how to learn* as they progress from other-assistance to self-assistance within the ZPD. Second, they understand and are able to discuss the learning and teaching processes at both theoretical and practical levels. Third, they can recognize specific behaviors that indicate shifts in children's learning and conceptual development.

Fourth, they know how to create opportunities (through arrangement of materials and conversations) to accommodate specific child needs and to shift instruction when behaviors suggest a task is too easy or too difficult. Finally, they listen carefully to the child's language as he or she transitions from stage to stage through to self-regulation: (a) from social speech between the teacher and child, (b) to private speech, where the child uses the language of the teacher to control reading and writing behaviors, (c) to inner speech where the child's abbreviated self-dialogue controls his actions, and finally, (d) to inner verbal thought.

## Implications for Teachers

The theories discussed in this article serve to present a challenge to teachers of struggling learners. The practical implications of these theories that explain the making of the mind suggest three important things teachers may do to facilitate joyful and accelerative learning:

- Provide emotional support and encouragement for children's imperfect attempts and partially right responses.
- Expect all children to make accelerated progress such that they can benefit from classroom instruction.
- Remember it is the quality of experience and instruction, not the child's cognition, that determines success or failure.

Melvin Konner (1991), a physician and anthropologist who has studied the emotional and cognitive development of children, writes:

Consistently losing does not promote self-esteem, no matter how impervious to reality you may be. So every educational program needs to make a choice. You can get short-term gains in self-esteem and continue to lose ground; or you try this theory: that self-esteem can come from making great effort, from facing uncertainty and overcoming obstacles that we are not sure we can meet, from doing our level best. (p. 231)

I believe effective teachers function in such a way as to support this point of view.

Teachers of at-risk learners may have to struggle with children from time to time to get them to overcome doubts about themselves, to dig in, and to make strong attempts. It is a challenge, but only by accepting it will teachers get to see the excitement in a child's face when he or she closes the cover on a new book just read and says in a thrilled, surprised voice, "I did it!"

True self-esteem grows from mastery of genuine challenges. Recent neurological research (Damasio, 1994; Greenspan, 1997) suggests that no human being can learn material presented in a form that his or her nervous system cannot handle. Children given tasks beyond their capacity lose confidence, the will to learn, and self-respect. They become defeated. As educators, we should take seriously Greenspan's (1997) challenge set forth in the opening of this article, that is, to consider the emotional nature of learning and the critical role emotions play in the making of the mind. To ignore that is to fail children.

## References

Bruner, J. S. (1973). Organization of early skilled action. *Child Development, 44,* 1–11.

Clay, M. M. (1991). *Becoming literate: The construction of inner control.* Portsmouth, NH: Heinemann.

Clay, M. M. (1993). *Reading Recovery: A guidebook for teachers in training.* Portsmouth, NH: Heinemann.

Damasio, A. R. (1994). *Descartes' error: Emotion, reason, and the human brain.* New York: Avon Books.

Diaz, R. M., Neal, C .J., Amaya-Williams, M. (1990). The social origins of self-regulation. In L. C. Moll (Ed.), *Vygotsky and education: Instructional implications and applications of sociohistorical psychology.* New York: Cambridge University Press.

Greenspan, S. I. (1997). *The growth of the mind.* Reading, MA: Addison Wesley.

Healy, J. M. (1994). *Your child's growing mind.* New York: Doubleday.

Konner, M. (1991). *Childhood.* Boston: Little Brown.

Lambert, D., Bramwell, M., & Lawther, G. (Eds.). (1982). *The brain: A user's manual.* New York: G. P. Putnam.

Lyons, C. A., Pinnell, G. S., & DeFord, D. E. (1993). *Partners in learning: Teachers and children in Reading Recovery.* New York: Teachers College Press.

Luria, A. R. (1973). *The working brain: An introduction to neuropsychology.* New York: Basic Books.

Luria, A. R. (1976). *Cognitive development: Its cultural and social formations*. Cambridge, MA: Harvard University Press.

Pert, C. B. (1997). *Molecules of emotion*. New York: Scribner.

Tharp, R., & Gallimore, R. (1988). *Rousing minds to life*. New York: Cambridge University Press.

Vygotsky, L. S. (1978). *Mind in society: The development of higher psychological processes*. Cambridge MA: Harvard University Press.

# Student Aspirations: Reading Recovery May Influence More Than Literacy Development

Anne K. Rhodes-Kline, *U.S. General Accounting Office*
Russell J. Quaglia, *University of Maine*

## ABSTRACT

*The effects of the Reading Recovery (RR) program on at-risk children's literacy development have been well documented. However, the effects of the Reading Recovery program, which combines one-on-one attention with an individualized approach, may go beyond the realm of reading and writing to affect students' aspirations. This paper represents an effort to connect practices of the RR program with known conditions for student aspirations. The implications of this work suggest that investing effort in RR may affect not only children's literacy development, but also their aspirations, which are generalizable to other areas of the children's lives.*

The Reading Recovery (RR) program has been evaluated extensively with regard to its impact on children's literacy development. The original studies were conducted by Clay (1985), the founder of the program, but her results have been replicated around the world (e.g., Pinnell, Lyons, & DeFord, 1996). The program has been studied in terms of its cost effectiveness (Dyer, 1992) and how it compares to other early literacy programs (Pinnell, Lyons, DeFord, Bryk, & Seltzer, 1994). In this paper we argue that its effects may be even more far-reaching, to the aspirations of the students who participate.

RR is an early intervention program for first graders who are at risk for literacy failure. Children are selected for the program based on both the recommendations of the kindergarten teacher and their performance on a series of literacy-related tasks (Clay, 1993a). The program involves intensive, daily, one-on-one sessions between the at-risk child and the RR teacher for 30 minutes. One of the defining characteristics of the program is its individualized nature. The RR teacher gathers detailed information regarding each child's strengths and weaknesses each day, and uses such information in planning the next day's lesson. Experienced teachers go through a year of intensive additional training to become RR teachers. Reading Recovery training includes the study of theories of literacy acquisition and detailed methods of data collection. Careful observation allows a RR teacher to notice and to build upon the cognitive operations a child already possesses, but which may not be evident in a classroom setting.

Such one-on-one instruction, targeted to each child's specific needs, allows at-risk children to accelerate their learning, catching up to their peers. The extra instruction is short-term; students are released from the program when they have achieved the average literacy level of the other first graders in the class and have demonstrated they are capable of continuing to develop their reading and writing competencies without special tutoring (Clay, 1991, 1993a, 1993b).

Aspirations are an individual's ability to identify and set goals for the future, while being inspired in the present to work toward those goals (Quaglia & Cobb, 1996). Although not dealt with directly by Clay, it seems plausible that children's aspirations may be affected by their experience in Reading Recovery. In what follows, we will attempt to link the RR program characteristics and outcomes with what is known about student aspirations. After relevant research on student aspirations has been described, theoretical explanations for our contention that RR may be expected to affect the aspirations of children will be delineated, and qualitative evidence to support this supposition will be provided.

## Research on Student Aspirations

The National Center for Student Aspirations (NCSA) has studied the effects of various factors on student aspirations. While much of the research has focused on older children and adolescents, there is no reason not to expect parallel processes in younger children.

Through research and practical application in schools, conditions that impact the development of student aspirations in schools have been identified. Specifically, the NCSA (1995) has identified eight conditions that positively affect student aspirations, including, as described below: *achievement, belonging, curiosity, empowerment, excitement, mentoring, risk-taking,* and *self-confidence.*

*Achievement* includes effort, accomplishment, citizenship, and perseverance.

*Belonging* involves a relationship between two or more individuals, characterized by a sense of connection, support, and community.

*Curiosity* is characterized as inquisitiveness, an eagerness and strong desire to satisfy the mind with new discoveries.

*Empowerment* means allowing students to take control and to assume responsibility for their academic, social, and personal actions.

*Excitement* refers to being "worked up" about something, being emotionally involved, and having an intense experience in the learning process.

*Mentoring* involves ensuring students have someone they can talk to and confide in during both pleasant and difficult times.

*Risk-taking* involves a deliberate and thoughtful activity which includes choosing healthy and sensible options.

*Self-confidence* is characterized by belief in oneself to be successful.

Primary functions of the NCSA involve survey development along with program delivery and dissemination. Most of the survey development has been conducted with middle level and high school students. The current survey includes two scales that represent aspirations (ambition, inspiration), two scales for student self-description (achievement motivation, general enjoyment of life), and eight scales related to school climate conditions (achievement, belonging, curiosity, empowerment, excitement, mentoring, risk-taking, and self-confidence). The middle-level survey includes items such as:

"During class time, the things I learn are important to my future."
"My teacher makes class fun."
"My teacher makes me feel comfortable when I ask for help."

The survey is intended for group administration, and the results of the survey are used by schools to assess their students' level of aspirations, allowing research based interventions to be targeted appropriately on the aspirations relevant to aspects of school climate that students traditionally perceive in a relatively negative light (Plucker, 1996).

## Reading Recovery and Student Aspirations

Although Clay, the founder of the RR program, does not discuss student aspirations in her work, a strong argument can be made that participation in RR likely will affect the conditions for student aspirations, either directly or indirectly. Following is a discussion of how each condition for aspiration relates to Reading Recovery tutoring.

The primary expected outcome of participation in the RR program is increased literacy achievement, and it is expected to occur at an accelerated rate compared with other children in the classroom. Clay (1993) writes, "the child . . . has been making very slow progress and has been dropping further and further behind his classmates. In order to become an average-progress child, he would have to make fast progress, faster than his classmates, to catch up to them" (p. 8). Throughout the program, children are encouraged to make efforts and praised for their perseverance. The goal is for them to become independent learners, capable of continuing to learn on their own. These aspects of achievement are especially similar to those necessary for aspirations. Because, according to the NCSA, achievement is one of the preconditions for aspirations, RR would be expected to affect student aspirations positively, through increased achievement, as well as student awareness of success.

Secondly, the relationship between the RR teacher and the student is one of mentoring. The RR teacher shares the student's successes as well as challenges. It is imperative that a positive relationship be established between the child and the RR teacher. Regarding the first two weeks of the RR program where such a relationship is built, Clay (1993b) writes:

Hold his interest, bolster his confidence, make him your co-worker. Get the responding fluent and habituated but even at this stage encourage flexibility, using the same knowledge in different ways. Confidence, ease, flexibility and, with luck, discovery are the keynotes of this period which I have called "roaming around the known." Do not move too soon; be sure the foundation is firm and the child confident. (p. 13)

During the initial two weeks of RR, in establishing a relationship characterized by mentoring, the RR teacher is expected, according to Clay, to affect the child's self-confidence and sense of curiosity, two more of the NCSA's eight conditions for aspirations. RR, therefore, would likely affect student aspirations directly through these channels as well.

The self-confidence Marie Clay described would follow naturally from increased achievement. That is, a child who can achieve more, and who can recognize his or her achievements, may become more confident as a result. False praise from teachers will be recognized and not valued, but children whose literacy skills are truly improving will know, and this will be reinforced by teachers and parents who also see the improvement. Actual achievement, coupled with praise, will raise a child's self-confidence.

Before a child is discontinued from the program, he or she needs to have established a "self-extending system", a phrase Clay (1993b) uses to describe children's ability to continue to add to their repertoires of literacy strategies on their own in the classroom. She explains when a child has a self-extending system, he or she can be thought of as empowered:

> Acceleration is achieved as the child takes over the learning process and works independently, discovering new things for himself inside and outside the lessons. He comes to push the boundaries of his own knowledge, and not only during his lessons. The teacher must watch for and use this personal searching on the part of the child. . . . The teacher will foster and support acceleration as she moves the child quickly through his programme . . . but the teacher cannot produce or induce it. . . . It is the learner who accelerates because some things which no longer need his attention are done more easily, freeing him to attend to new things. When this happens at an ever-increasing rate acceleration of learning occurs. (p. 9)

Thus, empowerment is an additional route through which RR may affect student aspirations.

Risk-taking is essential to the development of empowerment. The RR teacher provides a supportive, trusting environment that allows children to feel safe enough to attempt difficult tasks, while risking being wrong. Learning to take risks is fundamental to all children's success, according to Clay (1993b). She writes,

> the programme sets the highest value on independent responding, and this must involve risks of being wrong. . . . The goal of the teaching is to assist the child to produce effective strategies for working on text, not to accumulate items of knowledge. A teacher who allowed only for correct responding would not be allowing the child to learn self-correcting behaviors! . . . Any theoretical position which includes self-monitoring and self-correcting as significant behavior in reading or in writing implies the existence of near misses, uncorrected responses and sometimes corrected responses. The important thing about the self-corrections is that the child initiates them be-

cause he sees that something is wrong and calls up his own resources for working on a solution. (p. 15)

Concomitantly, RR may positively impact children's excitement about school and learning. Tutoring sessions are conducted in such a way that children are challenged, while at the same time are capable of meeting those challenges. While students may struggle with literacy learning in the classroom in the early stages of their program, they are able to enjoy the time in RR because they can be successful from the beginning. This, of course, changes over time as children's progress is accelerated and they can derive excitement from their classroom environment. Such success in RR and then in the classroom likely affects children's sense of belonging, as well.

## Qualitative Evidence

As part of program evaluation for the RR program in one northern New England state, parents, classroom teachers, administrators, and RR teachers responded to open-ended survey questions, and they rated the program along dimensions of quality. The survey was distributed to 1429 parents, 535 classroom teachers, 250 administrators, and 250 RR teachers, and was returned with a response rate of 82%. Respondents from all categories rated the program favorably, with a number commenting that it had affected children's attitudes and aspirations as well as their literacy skills.

Parents' reactions to the program were almost singular in their support. Many expressed appreciation for the changes in their children's skills, such as: "The program is the best thing that could have been done for our son and I am very pleased that the school cares enough about its children to have this program."

Some parents noted the accomplishments of their children after the RR program, such as: "My son certainly has learned new ways of figuring out the words that he doesn't know and is more willing to try to do things on his own."

Other parents noted improvements in their children's attitudes about school and their self-esteem after the RR program. Examples include: "She enjoys school more and feels that she can help the teacher with the younger children." "My son has become more confident in participating in class. His self-esteem has definitely been boosted." "[Child] went from feeling 'stupid' to having a lot of confidence in her reading abilities. She is very proud of her skills and is always looking for someone to read to."

Many classroom teachers' comments reflected positively on their own children's progress. One teacher wrote: "RR has made teaching reading much smoother in my class. Children who need extra help receive it and many of them are able to move quickly enough to become independent readers and writers."

Some comments from classroom teachers also indicated that RR may have affected students' attitudes and self-esteem. For example, two teachers wrote: "New confidence and self-esteem has helped in all classroom areas not just in reading" and "Increased self-esteem about learning to read; attitude shift from 'I can't' to 'I can'; increased independence in the classroom."

In addition to supporting the program's effects on early literacy, some administrators also noted changes in children's self-esteem after taking part in RR. For example:

"The children with whom [RR Teacher] has worked have made significant gains in self-confidence and in other subjects, not to mention impressive gains in reading."

Although far from being scientifically collected, we believe these comments are significant because they were unsolicited. Respondents were asked to give their reactions to the RR program and its impact on children's literacy development, but were not asked to comment on self-esteem, aspirations, or attitudes. Yet many noted gains in the very areas we know to be critical to the development of aspirations as discussed here. Seemingly, RR is affecting the conditions necessary for aspirations in a positive way, as evidenced by the comments collected through these surveys.

## Future Directions in Research

We suggest that Reading Recovery and other early interventions for at-risk children be evaluated for their effects on the whole child, as well as on specific areas of scholastic development. We are currently working to develop an instrument that would measure the eight preconditions for aspirations in K–2 children. The conditions described earlier in this paper have been validated with older children and adolescents. These may or may not be the preconditions for aspirations among young (i.e., K–2) children, but it nonetheless represents a starting point. Once established, such an instrument would allow quantitative research in this area to move forward.

There are a number of hurdles to measuring any attitudinal construct in the early elementary school population. First, because children in the early elementary grades may have shorter memories and shorter attention spans than older children (Hughes, 1984), surveys for this age group must be shorter in length than those for other age groups.

Secondly, the cognitive abilities and language development of young children constrain the use of potential items as well as overall survey length. Many words and phrases which would be appropriate in surveys for adults or even adolescents, cannot be used because the young respondents would not understand them.

Finally, the construct of "social desirability" is a problem when measuring attitudes of young children. Social desirability refers to a tendency to give answers that make oneself look good (Robinson, Shaver, & Wrightsman, 1991). In a research context, this can translate into answers that reflect how the respondent wants to be viewed, rather than how the respondent feels most of the time. Gilberts (1983) suggests this is a difficulty when measuring self-esteem in children, but that it is most problematic in children below age four.

McKenna and Kear's Elementary Reading Attitude Survey (1990) notably appears to have overcome some of these hurdles. Their twenty-item scale measures children's attitudes about reading. All items begin with the phrase, "How do you feel . . ." For example, one item asks, "How do you feel when it's time for reading class?" To make the response categories more accessible to young children, the scale features the comic strip character Garfield in four poses, roughly equivalent to the responses, "Very Happy," "Happy," "Unhappy," and "Very Unhappy." The survey was field tested with over eighteen thousand first through sixth grade children, and it demonstrated both internal consistency and known-groups validity. The "attitudes about reading" construct is quite different from aspirations, however, the characteristics of a successful instrument are often generalizable across constructs and this work may apply to the assessment of aspirations.

Although the eight conditions for aspirations have not been measured in early elementary school aged children, at least one study attempted to measure a related construct in this population. Traynelis-Yurek & Hansell (1993) measured the self-esteem of first graders at risk for reading failure following participation in a program designed to help them learn to read and write (the program may have been Reading Recovery, but the authors did not specify). Although the methodology used in the study does not allow strong conclusions to be drawn regarding either the validity or the reliability of their proposed instrument, Traynelis-Yurek and Hansell made a notable attempt at creating an instrument suitable for young children. Their most important finding was that the children discriminated between and among items. That is, all the items showed variance. Although far from a developed instrument, their results suggest distinct possibilities for measuring young children's aspirations.

In a time of scarce resources and an abundance of programs to implement, it is important to recognize those programs that may have a positive impact on the whole child. RR may be such a program. Its successes as an early intervention program for children with minimal literacy skills are well documented. However, by design or not, we see a program that operationalizes the conditions which influence the development of student aspirations.

## References

Clay, M.M. (1985). *The early detection of reading difficulties. (3rd ed.)*. Portsmouth, NH: Heinemann.

Clay, M.M. (1991). *Becoming literate: The construction of inner control*. Auckland, NZ: Heinemann.

Clay, M.M. (1993a). *An observation survey of early literacy achievement*. Portsmouth, NH: Heinemann.

Clay, M.M. (1993b). *Reading Recovery: A guidebook for teachers in training*. Portsmouth, NH: Heinemann.

Dyer, P. C. (1992). Reading Recovery: A cost-effectiveness and educational-outcomes analysis. *ERS Spectrum, 10*, 10–19.

Gilberts, R. (1983). The evaluation of self-esteem. *Family and Community Health, 6*, 29–49.

Hughes, H. M. (1984). Measures of self-concept and self-esteem for children ages 3–12 years: A review and recommendations. *Clinical Psychology Review, 4*, 657–692.

McKenna, M. C., & Kear, D. J. (1990). Measuring attitude toward reading: A new tool for teachers. *The Reading Teacher, 43*, 626–639.

National Center for Student Aspirations (1995). *Student aspirations: A decade of inquiry*. Orono, ME: University of Maine Center for Research and Evaluation.

Pinnell, G. S., Lyons, C. A., DeFord, D. E., Bryk, A. S., & Seltzer, M. (1994). Comparing instructional models for the literacy education of high-risk first graders. *Reading Research Quarterly, 29*, 8–39.

Pinnell, G. S., Lyons, C. A., DeFord, D. E. (1996). *Reading Recovery executive summary.* Columbus, OH: Reading Recovery Council of North America.

Plucker, J. A. (1996). Construct validity of the Student Aspirations Survey. *Journal of Research in Rural Education, 12,* 127–132.

Quaglia, R., & Cobb, C. (1996). A theoretical construct for studying student aspirations. *Journal of Research in Rural Education, 12,* 161–171.

Robinson, J. P., Shaver, P. R., & Wrightsman, L. S. (Eds.). (1991). *Measures of personality and social psychological attitudes.* New York: Harcourt Brace Jovanovich.

Traynelis-Yurek, E., & Hansell, T. S. (1993). Self-esteem of low achieving first grade readers following instructional intervention. *Reading Improvement, 30,* 140–146.

# The Development of Phonological Awareness and Orthographic Processing in Reading Recovery

Katherine Anne Dougherty Stahl, *Clarke County (GA) Public Schools*
Steven A. Stahl, *The University of Georgia*
Michael C. McKenna, *Georgia Southern University*

## ABSTRACT

*Success in Reading Recovery has traditionally been measured by text reading, concordant with its meaning-driven theoretical base. Yet Reading Recovery lessons include a considerable amount of attention to the visual or orthographic patterns in words and phonological awareness instruction as well. In this study, children in Reading Recovery were found to perform significantly better than a control group not only on Reading Recovery measures, but also on measures of phonological awareness. Children successfully discontinued from Reading Recovery were also found to perform as well as a group of average achieving first graders on a measure of orthographic processing. This suggests that Reading Recovery has effects beyond those ordinarily claimed.*

Reading Recovery is a program intended to accelerate the progress of the lowest-achieving 20% of first-grade children so that they are able to perform as well as the average children in their classrooms (Klein, Kelly, & Pinnell, 1997). Reading Recovery has demonstrated impressive rates of success and a number of evaluations have supported the program's effectiveness (e.g., Center, Wheldall, Freeman, Outhred, & McNaught, 1995; Shanahan & Barr, 1995; Wasik & Slavin, 1993). For example, in their conservative analysis, Center et al. (1995) found that Reading Recovery was able to accelerate the reading progress of 35% of the children who would not, under other programs, reach the level of their successful peers. In addition, group programs that are based on similar theoretical perspectives have been successful in increasing children's reading achievement (e.g., Fountas & Pinnell, 1996; Hiebert, 1994; Taylor, Short, & Shearer, 1990).

Because Reading Recovery educators view the program as a meaning-oriented approach, and consider one of its major goals to be the improvement of students' ability to read and comprehend connected text, evaluations of Reading Recovery have stressed text reading as an outcome measure. However, there are aspects of the program that seem to be especially conducive to growth in other aspects of beginning reading, such as phonemic awareness and orthographic knowledge. Those studies that have used isolated word measures have found that Reading Recovery does seem to improve students' word identification. For example, Center et al. (1995) found that Reading Recovery students performed significantly better than a control group on measures of isolated word reading and word attack, but not on a measure of phoneme awareness (see Askew, Fountas, Lyons, Pinnell, & Schmitt, 1998, for review).

Although Reading Recovery teachers generally work within the context of reading and writing connected text, they also pay considerable attention to word and sub-word level information (e.g., letter, clusters) during lessons. In fact, Adams (1990) and J. S. Chall (personal communication, 1998) have both cited Reading Recovery as an exemplar of high quality phonics instruction. Attending to both spelling-sound relationships and phonological awareness is integral to the lesson framework.

## How Orthographic Knowledge and Phonological Awareness Develop in Reading Recovery Instruction

The goal of Reading Recovery is for the child to develop a "self-extending" system in reading and writing (Clay, 1991; Clay, 1993b) so that he or she can function independently and benefit from classroom instruction. This self-extending system comprises strategies that enable the child to grow and learn from his or her own attempts to read and write. The successful child demonstrates reading behaviors that signal the underlying strategies used, including the integration of cueing systems, self-monitoring, and self-correction. Such strategy use involves the orchestration of orthographic knowledge (including phonological awareness) with semantic and syntactic knowledge to aid in word recognition.

The development of orthographic knowledge in both word recognition and spelling is well-documented. The basic tenet is that children move through a series of stages, becoming increasingly sophisticated at using letter-sound knowledge to identify words (Ehri, 1998; Stahl & Murray, 1998). As children learn to recognize words, they first recognize them holistically, as a single logograph. For example, children at this stage may recognize words such as "look" through the two "eyes" in the middle or the word "monkey" by its "tail." This is considered a pre-alphabetic stage (Ehri, 1995), since children are not using letters and sounds, but rather are using the visual representation of each word.

As children develop phonological awareness, they may begin to use some partial sound information in the word, such as an initial or final sound (see Stahl & Murray, 1998). Ehri called this stage *phonetic cue reading or partial alphabetic reading*. In this stage, a child might substitute a word that begins with the same letter, such as "bird" for "bear," when reading words either in text or in lists. As children learn more words, phonetic cue reading becomes less efficient and children analyze the word more deeply.

In the *cipher* or *full alphabetic* phase (Ehri, 1995), children use all the letters and sounds to identify words. Children's reading may still appear labored as they rely on sounding out the word (i.e., using a letter-to-sound analysis) or on other, less efficient strategies. At this stage, they are engaging in either this letter-to-sound analysis or in the use of analogies to identify the whole word.

Following this stage, children move to automatic word recognition, what Ehri calls the *consolidated* phase. It is within this stage that children seemingly are able to identify the word as a whole or through rapid recognition of chunks within the word. At this point, children are free to allocate all of their attention to comprehension, for word recognition has become fluent and transparent. With greater practice, children develop such automatic word recognition that they can concentrate fully on the meaning (Chall, 1996; Ehri, 1995).

Stahl and Murray (1998) suggest that children in the first stage lack rudimentary phonological awareness. To reach the second stage, children need to possess not only knowledge of the alphabet, but also the insight that words can be broken into onsets and rimes. Accordingly, the third stage depends on both more sophisticated phonological and orthographic insights. As children learn more about the spellings of words, they can use that knowledge to perform more sophisticated phonological tasks.

Reading Recovery lessons proceed in a manner consistent with the development of orthographic knowledge and phonological awareness. Three features of the lesson improve children's knowledge of words—the use of gradient texts, the use of Elkonin boxes in writing practice, and planned word analysis activities.

## Gradient Texts

Students are immersed in easy-to-read books in which the orchestration of the reading process can take place at an appropriate level. The use of gradient, predictable materials provides for a gradual move from an excessive reliance on meaning (context) and structural (syntactic) cueing systems to an increased integration of visual (graphemic or letter-sound) cues.

Even children who have little knowledge of orthography have many language skills that enable them to read without phonological awareness or letter knowledge (Perfetti, Beck, Bell, & Hughes, 1987). In the beginning of a student's work in Reading Recovery, highly predictable books may be used to develop concepts of print. These would include directionality, word-to-word matching, and so on. As students gain greater control over print concepts, the teacher, in a supportive text reading environment, introduces books that are gradually less predictable. This requires that the children use increasing amounts of visual information to recognize words, thereby increasing their reliance on orthography as they progress through the program.

Children who have a self-extending system in reading and writing understand how words work and how they can use what they know to problem-solve difficult words they encounter (Clay, 1993b). To solve novel words one has developed "the cipher"—the analogical mechanism that has been internalized by the process called "cryptanalysis" (Ehri & Wilce, 1985; Gough & Juel, 1991). "Cryptanalytic intent" is the realization by the reader that there is a system to be mastered.

When the cipher has been discovered, children begin to see reading and words in a new way, although actual reading measurements may not register any immediate change (Chall, 1983; Gough & Juel, 1991). Both Clay (1991) and Chall (1996) concur that a major breakthrough in reading occurs when a child can let go of excessive attachment to meaning and syntactic substitution and see reading as a problem-solving process.

## Phonological Awareness and Writing

Current theorists no longer believe that letter knowledge and phonological awareness cause reading success to proceed in a linear fashion. Recent research has uncovered a reciprocal causation (Adams, 1990; Clay, 1991; Juel, 1988; Perfetti et al., 1987; Stahl & Murray, 1998; Stanovich, 1986; Stanovich & West, 1989) between children's increasing phonological insights and their knowledge of the alphabetic system. Stahl and Murray (1998) suggest that a certain amount of phonological insight—the ability to segment an onset and a rime—combined with letter knowledge, leads to the insight that letters in words have relationships with speech sounds. This recognition is reflected in both children's initial reading attempts (Ehri, 1991) and their invented spellings (Bear & Barone, 1989). Children's ability to relate sounds and letters increases as they have opportunities both to analyze spoken words further and to tie them to elements of orthography.

In Reading Recovery, phonological awareness is developed largely through activities that support writing. When a child has reached an appropriate level of understanding, the child will be taught to analyze a word using a phonological awareness technique adapted from Elkonin (1973). The technique progresses through stages from simply saying a word slowly in order to hear the sounds, to writing the letters that represent the sounds. Teacher involvement gradually changes over time to allow for independence in processing at each stage.

Initially, to learn the task of analyzing a word into its component sounds, the teacher and the child articulate a word slowly. When the child can do this independently, the teacher helps him or her slide a marker into a box representing each phoneme. When the child can perform this task independently, the teacher selects a word from the child's dictated sentence for the purpose of helping him or her hear and record the sounds of that word. The teacher draws a series of boxes, one for each phoneme in the word. The child then slowly articulates the word, sliding a marker into a box as each phoneme is spoken, and then records the letter or letters that represent that sound. Essentially, this is a shift in the task from a phonological activity to a spelling strategy.

Gradually, the child eliminates the use of the marker and eventually does not require the boxes to hear and record the sounds.

The use of Elkonin boxes is based on a theory of mental process learning, which moves from the establishment of the task, to operating with objects, verbalizing the operation, and finally, operating mentally. Impressive experimental evidence supports the effectiveness of using Elkonin boxes (e.g., Ball & Blachman, 1991; DeFord, 1994; Elkonin, 1973). In DeFord's (1994) study relating writing and Reading Recovery student achievement, more frequent use of boxes for hearing sounds in words was consistently associated with well above average scores on tasks on *An Observation Survey of Early Literacy Achievement* (Clay, 1993).

## Planned Word Analysis

Another feature of Reading Recovery lessons that influences the development of phonological awareness and orthographic knowledge is a teaching activity referred to as "making and breaking," a planned word analysis activity from the procedures intended to help children in "Linking Sound Sequence with Letter Sequence" (Clay, 1993b, p. 43). This activity was given greater emphasis in Reading Recovery lessons in Clay's revised book as a response "to recent research on phonological awareness, onset and rime, and analogy" (Clay, 1993b, p. 44).

During the "making and breaking" activity, the child uses magnetic letters to construct words and take words apart. These activities may include, but are not limited to, manipulations of onset and rimes. Stahl and Murray (1994, 1998) concluded that the ability to manipulate onsets and rimes within syllables relates strongly to reading progress, once an adequate level of letter recognition is achieved.

When teachers use gradient texts for reading, Elkonin boxes for hearing sounds in words, and "making and breaking" activities for linking sound sequence with letter sequence, the lesson's emphasis is on the system, or the process, not on an item (Clay, 1993b). When the teacher emphasizes the visual cueing system, it is used as one tool, or strategy, in an effort to help students understand text, rather than as an end in itself. It is this goal that distinguishes Reading Recovery lessons from traditional phonics lessons.

## Previous Research on Reading Recovery and Metalinguistic Development

Previous research evidence shows strong support for the effectiveness of Reading Recovery (Center et al., 1995; Clay, 1993b, Iversen & Tunmer, 1993; Wasik & Slavin, 1993). However, some of these studies had some methodological concerns about Reading Recovery-based research reports. One concern is Reading Recovery's research emphasis on discontinuants (Center et al., 1995; Iversen & Tunmer, 1993). These studies addressed an additional concern over the absence of a phonological recoding instrument in Reading Recovery assessments. Center et al. (1995) and Wasik and Slavin (1993) investigated limitations of the *An Observation Survey of Early Literacy Achievement* (Clay,1993a). It is the only battery of tests used to determine selection of children receiving and discontinuing from Reading Recovery service.

Children who are pre-tested, tutored in the Reading Recovery format, and then re-tested in the same format, may have an advantage over children not required to perform similar tasks on a daily basis. There may be a bias in favor of skills taught in low levels of text reading, where assessment tends to measure concepts about print and the utilization of syntax and context (Wasik & Slavin, 1993).

Based on these concerns, Center et al. (1995) included a more detailed testing procedure on first graders in Reading Recovery. The researchers found no marked pretest differences between students who could be successfully discontinued and those who could not be, except in metalinguistic areas (phoneme awareness and phonological recoding). Center et al. suggest that children with poor metalinguistic skills are less likely to be successfully discontinued.

Hatcher, Hulme, and Ellis (1994) compared three individual intervention methods: phonological training, reading and phonology (based on a Reading Recovery model but incorporating 10 minutes of phonological activities) and a reading only intervention (similar to Reading Recovery). The reading and phonology group made the greatest progress in contextual reading achievement and comprehension. Although the phonological training group had the highest scores in phonological skills, they were unable to use the skills in contextual reading.

Iversen and Tunmer (1993) had similar positive results with greater attention to phonological processing within a Reading Recovery lesson. They modified a Reading Recovery lesson by adding daily activities specifically focused on word analysis. They found that students in the modified program discontinued with fewer lessons, but that there was no overall difference in the achievement of the two groups of students. Iversen and Tunmer theorized that the additional emphasis on the visual cueing system within their study caused a greater overall promotion of word analysis and less reliance on context. Results of a path analysis suggested that instruction and manipulation of phonograms promotes the development of orthographic processing, allowing children to analyze words at a deeper level.

The aim of early reading instruction is to enable children to develop a self-extending system. This involves the development of orthographic processing, among other abilities. Both phonological processing abilities and exposure to print are prerequisites and facilitators of this aim (Clay, 1991; Cunningham, 1990; Perfetti et al., 1987; Stanovich, 1986). Reading Recovery has been effective in promoting reading success for "at-risk" first graders through the use of a metalevel instructional model (Clay, 1991; Clay, 1993b; Iversen & Tunmer, 1993; Wasik & Slavin, 1993). Despite the wide range of measures used to assess emergent reading in *An Observation Survey of Early Literacy Achievement* (Clay, 1993a), more refined measures of phonological processing may be needed to give an accurate portrayal of children's metalinguistic abilities (Iversen & Tunmer, 1993; Stahl & Murray, 1994; Yopp, 1988).

The purpose of this study was to use refined measures of phonological and orthographic processing in conjunction with *An Observation Survey of Early Literacy Achievement* (Clay, 1993a) to determine whether techniques utilized in Reading Recovery lessons are effective in promoting progress in the metalinguistic areas of phonological awareness and phonological recoding.

## Method

### Participants

The participants in this study were first-grade students in a public elementary school in a small city in south Georgia. Students receiving Reading Recovery were the treatment group (n = 12). The control group (n = 19) was comprised of students who qualified for Reading Recovery service, but who were not accepted into one of the available first-round slots (i.e., they were on a "waiting list" to be served) because of the selection criteria (i.e., serving the lowest children first).

Originally, there were five girls and seven boys in the Reading Recovery group. One of the girls moved at the end of her program, before testing could be completed. There were six girls and thirteen boys in the control group. All students were six or seven years old and were in first grade for the first time. The majority of the students came from middle to low socioeconomic families. The Reading Recovery group consisted of 64% African-American participants and 36% European-American participants. The control group included 63% African-American participants and 37% European-American participants.

All participants were "at-risk" students who were given *An Observation Survey of Early Literacy Achievement* (Clay, 1993a) as part of the school Reading Recovery selection process. This selection process began at the end of the students' kindergarten year when the teachers ranked students in their classes from those needing the most help to those needing the least help in reading and writing activities. At the beginning of the next school year, first-grade teachers followed the same ranking procedure for their students. Based on a comparison and compilation of both sets of rankings, Reading Recovery teachers formulated a list of students who were achieving in the lowest 25% of the ranked lists (n = 31).

The six survey tasks were administered to those children by the three Reading Recovery teachers (including the first author). The children were then priority ranked based on the results of the survey and Reading Recovery teachers' observations of the students. In this particular county, the selection process for Reading Recovery gave weight to the results of the following survey subtests in descending order: Text Reading, Concepts About Print, Writing Vocabulary, Hearing Sounds in Words (Dictation Task), Ohio Word Test, and Letter Identification. The authors acknowledge this is a variance from the procedures recommended by Reading Recovery standards.

The 12 available Reading Recovery slots were filled by selecting the children with the lowest scores on the survey tasks. At this stage, students who were among the lowest-achieving group were placed on the "waiting list" only if their oral language was extremely developmentally delayed or if the student support team process recommendation for a long-term program was close to completion. (The authors acknowledge this is another variance from standards.)

Both Reading Recovery and control group students were from five first-grade classrooms receiving approximately two hours of language arts instruction daily. All of the classrooms incorporated instruction in literacy groups, which are designed to provide a small group setting where children can participate in literacy activities at their ability level. The control group did not receive any support beyond what was offered within their classroom. There was little consistency in methods of literacy instruction among the first-grade classrooms in this school.

## Measures

Pretest and posttest scores were compared to determine achievement on two subtests of *An Observation Survey of Early Literacy Achievement* (Clay, 1993a). The subtests that were relevant to this study were Letter Identification and Hearing and Recording Sounds in Words (Dictation Task). In addition to Clay's instruments, the Yopp-Singer Test of Phoneme Segmentation (Yopp, 1988) was given as a more refined measure of phonological processing. In addition, a pseudoword reading measure developed for this study (see Appendix) was used to measure children's knowledge of orthographic patterns. By utilizing instruments not affiliated with Reading Recovery, we hoped to have measures in which the instructional format of Reading Recovery did not provide a treatment group advantage. Behaviors demonstrated on these tasks reflect children's phonological processing abilities as well as the early orthographic connections they are making.

The Letter Identification task is an assessment of letter recognition of the fifty-four capital and lower case letters, plus conventional print forms of a and g, arranged in a random manner. Children may identify the letters by name, sound, or by identifying a word that begins with the letter. Reliability measures were calculated in 1990 and yielded a Cronbach's alpha coefficient of .95. Concurrent validity was established in 1966 yielding a .85 correlation with the Word Reading subtest (Clay, 1993a).

The Hearing Sounds in Words task requires the child to record one or two dictated sentences. There are 37 possible points with one point scored for each correctly analyzed and recorded phoneme. Points are given if the child uses graphemes that may record the sound even if the spelling is not correct (e.g., "koming" for "coming"). Reliability measures were calculated in 1990 and yielded a Cronbach's alpha coefficient of .96. No validity information is available for this subtest (Clay, 1993a).

The Yopp-Singer Test of Phoneme Segmentation is used to measure each child's ability to hear and articulate sequentially the separate sounds of 22 words (Yopp, 1995). Reliability was calculated at .95 using Cronbach's alpha (Yopp, 1988). Construct validity was determined using a factor analysis (Yopp, 1988). Of the ten measures included in Yopp's (1988) study, it had the highest predictive validity with a reading task. Predictive validity based on a seven-year longitudinal study ranged from .58 to .74 (Yopp, 1995).

We had planned to determine the orthographic stage of word recognition achieved by the discontinued Reading Recovery students by gauging each child's ability to "pronounce" pseudowords. For the purpose of this study, pseudoword decoding was selected because prior research has found it to be the best measure of phonological recoding and one of the best indications of the development of "the cipher" (Gough & Tunmer, 1986). We designed this test (see Appendix) using a constant onset and twenty common rimes (Wylie & Durrell, 1970). The validity of the test was determined by jurying six reading specialists. Pilot testing was conducted among first-term second graders who had been discontinued from Reading Recovery the previous school year and average and above average first grade-readers during the current year.

## Procedures

The total battery of six tasks from *An Observation Survey of Early Literacy Achievement* (Clay, 1993a) was given as a pretest to all subjects by three trained Reading Recovery teachers (including the researcher) during the first two weeks of the school year. The results of the Letter Identification task and the Hearing Sounds in Words task were used as measures of letter familiarity and phonological processing for the purposes of this study. The Yopp-Singer Test of Phoneme Segmentation (Yopp, 1995) was conducted by the researcher during weeks three and four before Reading Recovery lessons were started.

Based on the prioritized survey pretest results, four students were selected for treatment by each of the three Reading Recovery teachers (n = 12). Each member of the treatment group received a daily 30 minute, individualized, prescriptive, tutoring session according to the standard Reading Recovery lesson format (Clay, 1993b).

Posttest procedures occurred between week 12 through week 16 as explained below. In order to be discontinued from Reading Recovery mid-year in this district, children must be able (a) to read text level 10 with at least 90% accuracy and with evidence of a self-extending system, (b) to spell correctly 30 high-frequency words within 10 minutes, and (c) to demonstrate mastery of the Hearing Sounds in Words task (Clay, 1993a). Such criterion levels correspond to the class average in this particular school. Text Reading evaluations were conducted by a Reading Recovery teacher who had not been the child's Reading Recovery instructor. The other discontinuation measures were conducted by the child's Reading Recovery instructor.

Two students in this study were successfully discontinued from the program during week 12. Four students were discontinued during week 15. The student who moved during week 15 was being tested for discontinuation but moved before testing was concluded. Her results are not included in this study. The other five treatment group students were given the Letter Identification and Hearing Sounds in Words tasks (Clay, 1993a) as posttests during week 16 by their Reading Recovery instructor.

Letter Identification and Hearing Sounds in Words posttests (Clay, 1993a) were administered individually to all control group students by one of the three Reading Recovery teachers during weeks 14 to 16. The phoneme segmentation test was given individually to all participants by the first author during weeks 16 and 17. In addition, the first author conducted all pseudoword assessments at the time of discontinuation of individual Reading Recovery students.

## Results and Discussion

Independent t-test analysis of the pretests did not find significant differences between the Reading Recovery and the control group students. Even though the differences were not statistically reliable, as seen in Table 1, the control group performed slightly better on all measures than the experimental group. Such a finding is consistent with the selection process of taking the lowest-achieving children into the program first. Recall that the greatest weight was given to the Text Reading, Concepts About Print, and Writing Vocabulary tests in the screening and selection process, with lesser weight given to the measures of interest in this study. Since little or no weight was given to the Letter Identification or Hearing Sounds in Words tests in the screening process, we did not anticipate that the Reading Recovery group and control group would differ on these measures, nor on the Yopp-Singer measure.

Because the sample size was small, as might be expected in a study of Reading Recovery students, we examined the distribution of the data using Kolmogorov-Smirnov tests to determine the appropriateness of parametric statistical procedures. Of the six pretests and posttests, only the Letter Identification posttest differed significantly from a normal distribution, allowing the use of parametric statistical analysis. Children in both groups approached the ceiling in Letter Identification at posttest, leading to a significantly skewed distribution.

Table 1. Means of Reading Recovery Group and Control Group on Pretest
and Posttest Measures

| VARIABLE | MAXIMUM SCORE | READING RECOVERY | | CONTROL GROUP | |
|---|---|---|---|---|---|
| | | M | SD | M | SD |
| Letter Identification | 54 | | | | |
| Pretest | | 33.36 | 11.34 | 41.21 | 10.43 |
| Posttest | | 50.64 | 2.80 | 48.58 | 6.96 |
| Dictation Task | 37 | | | | |
| Pretest | | 5.36 | 5.26 | 8.42 | 6.35 |
| Posttest | | 31.18 | 2.04 | 23.37 | 8.86 |
| Phoneme Segmentation | 22 | | | | |
| Pretest | | 5.73 | 6.13 | 6.26 | 5.06 |
| Posttest | | 15.55 | 4.01 | 11.21 | 7.15 |

Means for pretests and posttests are shown on Table 1. Analysis of covariance was used to examine treatment effects. For each posttest, we used the corresponding pretest as a covariate. (The data met the assumptions of analysis of covariance.) For all three analyses, there was a significant treatment effect (Hearing Sounds in Words, $F (1,27) = 12.11, p < .002$; Yopp-Singer, $F (1, 27) = 6.72, p < .02$). Respective effect sizes ($\eta^2$) were .30 for Hearing Sounds in Words and .13 for the Yopp-Singer. The Wilcoxin Matched-Pairs Signed Ranks Test, a non-parametric test suitable for examining pretest-posttest differences, found significant gains in letter identification, $Z = -4.75, p < .001$.

In the following sections, we will discuss the findings relative to the focus of the study; that is, measures of phonological and orthographic processing, which were used to determine if Reading Recovery lessons are effective in promoting progress in the metalinguistic areas of phonological awareness and phonological recoding.

## Phonological Processing

The results described above suggest strongly that Reading Recovery students gained in phonological processing, even without additional lesson components. Based on the results of this study, all students in Reading Recovery made significantly greater improvement in phonological processing tasks than students not yet served. The relative magnitude of the effects corresponds to the degree of similarity between Reading Recovery lessons and outcome measures. Dictation is stressed daily during Reading Recovery lessons, so one would expect that the effects from the treatment would be high on this measure. Letter identification is usually stressed only during the beginning lessons. There is explicit instruction in phoneme awareness only through the use of Elkonin boxes during the writing segment. This instruction is brief and of a different form than the Yopp-Singer tasks. Therefore, we expected the effect size to be lower for this measure.

This study supports the findings of Iversen and Tunmer (1993), namely that all "at-risk" students exhibited deficiencies in phonological processing abilities initially.

Yopp (1988) reported average scores of 11.8 on her segmentation test when given to kindergarten students. The pretest mean of all first-grade participants in this study was 6.07. On posttest measures, students with high knowledge of orthography and correct spelling would frequently make the sounds of the letters that spelled the word instead of repeating the phonemes in the given word. This could indicate that phoneme segmentation abilities are reflective of a child's knowledge of how words work in reading and writing. However, a larger sample size would be required to demonstrate that this trend is generalizable to a larger population.

## Pseudoword Reading

Students who were discontinued from Reading Recovery within the time frame of this study were given a pseudoword decoding test. To inform our work, we had previously conducted a pilot study of pseudoword reading that revealed differences in abilities in the areas of accuracy and automaticity among students in the different developmental stages defined in this study. Based on the pilot study, students reading at a second grade level (as measured by teacher observations) read the 20 pseudowords within three minutes and had accuracy rates of 90% and above (Gough & Juel, 1991). We judged these students to be reading at the consolidated processing stage.

Students (n = 8) reading at a first grade level (again, from teacher observation) had scores ranging from 20% to 80%. None of these students was able to read the word cards with automaticity. They scanned each word visually and with their fingers, deleted the initial consonant before saying the whole pseudoword (e.g.,"ump, zump"), made verbal analogies (e.g., "can, zan"), and when necessary used letter-by-letter decoding. These students were judged to be at the full alphabetic phase, according to Ehri's (1995) model described earlier. (See Pseudoword Test in Appendix.)

These procedures took four to ten minutes to perform. Accuracy ranged from 30% to 80% and appeared to correlate negatively with the amount of time it took to attempt the 20 pseudowords.

In the current study, discontinued Reading Recovery students (n = 6) displayed a range of accuracy from 10% to 60%, slightly lower than that of the average first-grade reader but within the full alphabetic stage. Their attempts to associate the given letters of the pseudowords to the sounds were similar to those made by the children reading at the first grade level in the pilot study. This suggests that these discontinued students were using strategies similar to children in the alphabetic stage (Ehri, 1998), a stage reached by normally achieving first graders.

Students who were reading at the second grade instructional level appeared to have arrived at the consolidated phase based on the automaticity and accuracy of their responses. However, most children in the sixteenth week of first grade may not yet have had enough exposure to print and be fluent enough with words for orthographic processing to be fully developed (Adams, 1990; Chall, 1983). The average ability first-grade readers were still operating in various levels of the alphabetic stage. The children at the lowest level appeared to be engaging in tedious, letter-by-letter reading. Those in the level immediately preceding the automaticity of the orthographic stage appeared to be noticing the familiar rime and adding the onset, without verbalizing the analogy.

## Limitations of the Study

There are several limitations to this study to consider. First, we used a small sample size. This study's lack of power is of concern only if we failed to reject a null hypothesis. The lack of power would increase the probability of a Type II error. But since all analyses produced statistically significant findings, this is not an issue. The fact that we found statistical significance with such a small sample size suggests that the effects are robust. Second, the students were evaluated by other Reading Recovery teachers in the same school, who were aware of these children from ongoing discussions. It is possible that these discussions may have biased the examiners. Because Reading Recovery teachers receive extensive training in coding running records, it is unlikely that any other group of individuals would be as reliable in administering or coding. However, it would have been preferable to tape record the final evaluations and have them checked by a neutral party. Third, some Reading Recovery teachers may have given different emphasis to the activities discussed earlier in this paper, in spite of the extensive training designed to create uniformity of instruction. These results may not generalize to other Reading Recovery teachers.

Finally, we should have administered the pseudoword measure to both groups. As a result, we cannot conclude that Reading Recovery instruction produces better word recognition skills than a control intervention would have. However, the results do support the idea that many discontinuants reach the alphabetic phase of word recognition, and process words in ways similar to average first graders. This is useful information.

## Concluding Remarks

Reading Recovery is intended to be a supplemental program, given only to children who have difficulties in learning to read. To improve the reading instruction of all children in first grade, students need high quality classroom reading instruction, with programs such as Reading Recovery available for children who do not yet benefit from that instruction.

Although Clay based Reading Recovery on her theory of reading development, we have found that the instruction and the growth of children is consonant with other models of reading development, notably Ehri's (1995) model. Although Ehri's model concentrates on word recognition, rather than reading in general, Reading Recovery lessons seem to have a positive effect on both aspects of reading.

Adams (1990) cites Reading Recovery as an example of a quality beginning reading program, showing a balance between text reading and explicit instruction in decoding, aspects not claimed by advocates (e.g., Clay, 1993b; Klein et al., 1997). Gains achieved by Reading Recovery students on phonological processing tasks in this study provide strong support for the program's effectiveness in promoting these abilities. The inclusion of all Reading Recovery participants and the utilization of measures other than Clay's *Observation Survey of Early Literacy Achievement* (1993a) should dispel some of the methodological concerns stated in other reports (Center et al., 1995; Wasik & Slavin, 1993). This study also reinforced the value of pseudowords as a measure of recoding abilities and as an aid in determining a student's developmental reading stage.

# References

Adams, M. J. (1990). *Beginning to read: Thinking and learning about print.* Cambridge, MA: MIT Press.

Askew, B .J., Fountas, I. C., Lyons, C. A., Pinnell, G. S., & Schmitt, M. C. (1998). *Reading Recovery review: Understandings, outcomes, and implications.* Columbus, OH: Reading Recovery Council of North America.

Ball, E. W., & Blachman, B. A. (1991). Does phoneme awareness training in kindergarten make a difference in early word recognition and developmental spelling? *Reading Research Quarterly, 26,* 49–66.

Bear, D. R., & Barone, D. (1989). Using children's spellings to group for word study and directed reading in the primary classroom. *Reading Psychology, 10,* 275–292.

Center, Y., Wheldall, K., Freeman, L., Outhred, L., & McNaught, M. (1995). An evaluation of Reading Recovery. *Reading Research Quarterly, 30* (2), 240–263.

Chall, J. S. (1996). *Stages of reading development.* (reprinted with a new foreword). New York: McGraw-Hill.

Chall, J. S. (1996). *Stages of reading development.* (2nd ed.). Fort Worth, TX: Harcourt-Brace.

Clay, M. M. (1991). *Becoming literate: The construction of inner control.* Portsmouth, NH.: Heinemann.

Clay, M. M. (1993a). *An observation survey of early literacy achievement.* Portsmouth, NH.: Heinemann.

Clay, M. M. (1993b). *Reading Recovery: A guidebook for teachers in training.* Portsmouth, NH.: Heinemann.

Clay, M. M. (1995). *Reading Recovery: A guidebook for teachers in training.* Portsmouth, NH: Heinemann.

Cunningham, A. E. (1990). Explicit versus implicit instruction in phonemic awareness. *Journal of Experimental Child Psychology, 50,* 429-444.

DeFord, D. (1994). Early writing: Teachers and children in Reading Recovery. *Literacy, Teaching and Learning: An International Journal of Early Literacy, 1* (1), 31–56.

Ehri, L. C. (1995). Phases of development in learning to read words by sight. *Journal of Research in Reading, 18,* 116–125.

Ehri, L. C. (1998). Grapheme-phoneme knowledge is necessary for learning to read words in English. In J. Metsala & L. C. Ehri (Eds.), *Word recognition in beginning literacy.* Mahwah, NJ: Lawrence Erlbaum Associates.

Ehri, L. C., & Wilce, L. S. (1985). Movement into reading: Is the first stage of printed word learning visual or phonetic? *Reading Research Quarterly, 20* (2), 163–179.

Elkonin, D. B. (1973). U.S.S.R. In J. Downing (Ed.), *Comparative reading* (pp. 551–579). New York: Macmillan.

Fountas, I. C., & Pinnell, G. S. (1996). *Guided reading: Good first teaching for all children.* Portsmouth, NH: Heinemann.

Gough, P. B., & Juel, C. (1991). The first stages of word recognition. In L. Rieben & C. Perfetti (Eds.), *Learning to read: Basic research and its implications* (pp. 47–56). Hillsdale, NJ: Erlbaum.

Gough, P. B., & Tunmer, W. E. (1986). Decoding, reading, and reading disability. *Remedial and Special Education, 7,* 6–10.

Hatcher, P. J., Hulme, C., & Ellis, A.W. (1994). Ameliorating early reading failure by integrating the teaching of reading and phonological skills: The phonological linkage hypothesis. *Child Development, 65,* 41–57.

Hiebert, E. H. (1994). A small group literacy intervention with Chapter 1 students. In E. H. Hiebert & B. M. Taylor (Eds.), *Getting reading right from the start* (pp. 85–106). Boston: Allyn & Bacon.

Iversen, S., & Tunmer, W. (1993). Phonological processing skills and the Reading Recovery program. *Journal of Educational Psychology, 85* (1), 112–126.

Juel, C. (1988). Learning to read and write: A longitudinal study of 54 children from first through fourth grades. *Journal of Educational Psychology, 80,* 437–447.

Just, M. A., & Carpenter, P. A. (1987). *The psychology of reading and language comprehension.* Boston: Allyn and Bacon.

Klein, A. F., Kelly, P. R., & Pinnell, G. S. (1997). Teaching from theory: Decision making in Reading Recovery. In S. A. Stahl & D. A. Hayes (Eds.), *Instructional Models in Reading* (pp. 161–179). Hillsdale, NJ: Lawrence Erlbaum Associates.

Perfetti, C. A., Beck, I. L., Bell, L., & Hughes, C. (1987). Phonemic knowledge and learning to read are reciprocal: A longitudinal study of first grade children. *Merrill-Palmer Quarterly, 33,* 283–319.

Peterson, B. (1991). Selecting books for beginning readers. In D. E. DeFord, C. A. Lyons, & G. S. Pinnell (Eds.), *Bridges to literacy: Learning from Reading Recovery* (pp. 119–147).

Shanahan, T., & Barr, R. (1995). A synthesis of research on Reading Recovery. *Reading Research Quarterly, 30,* 958–996.

Stahl, S. A. (1992). Saying the "p" word: Nine guidelines for exemplary phonics instruction. *The Reading Teacher, 45* (8), 618–625.

Stahl, S. A., & Murray, B. A. (1994). Defining phonological awareness and its relationship to early reading. *Journal of Educational Psychology, 86,* 221–234.

Stahl, S. A., & Murray, B. A. (1998). Issues involved in defining phonological awareness and its relation to early reading. In J. Metsala & L. C. Ehri (Eds.), *Word Recognition in Beginning Literacy.* Mahwah, NJ: Erlbaum.

Stanovich, K. E. (1980). Toward an interactive-compensatory model of individual differences in the development of reading fluency. *Reading Research Quarterly, 16,* 32–65.

Stanovich, K. E. (1986). Matthew effects in reading: Some consequences of individual differences in the acquisition of literacy. *Reading Research Quarterly, 21,* 360–406.

Stanovich, K. E., & West, R. (1989). Exposure to print and orthographic processing. *Reading Research Quarterly, 26,* 402–429.

Taylor, B. M., Short, R., & Shearer, B. (1990). Early intervention in reading: Prevention of reading failure by first grade classroom teachers. Paper presented at annual meeting, National Reading Conference, Miami, FL.

Wasik, B. A., & Slavin, R. E. (1993). Preventing early reading failure with one-to-one tutoring: A review of five programs. *Reading Research Quarterly, 28,* 179–200.

Wylie, R. E., & Durrell, D. D. (1970). Teaching vowels through phonograms. *Elementary English, 47,* 787–791.

Yopp, H. K. (1988). The validity and reliability of phonemic awareness tests. *Reading Research Quarterly, 23,* 159–177.

Yopp, H. K. (1992). Developing phonemic awareness in young children. *The Reading Teacher, 45,* 696–703.

Yopp, H. K. (1995). A test for assessing phonemic awareness in young children. *The Reading Teacher, 49,* 20–29.

# Appendix

## Pseudoword Learning Test

Child's Name _____

Date _____

| | | | | |
|------|------|------|------|------|
| zack | zain | zake | zale | zall |
| zame | zan | zank | zap | zash |
| zat | zate | zaw | zay | zeat |
| zell | zest | zice | zick | zide |
| zight | zill | zin | zine | zing |
| zink | zip | zit | zock | zoke |
| zop | zot | zore | zuck | zug |
| zump | zunk | | | |

# Is Early Literacy Intervention Effective for English Language Learners? Evidence from Reading Recovery

Jane Ashdown, *New York University*
Ognjen Simic, *New York University*

## ABSTRACT

*The literacy achievement of 25,601 first-grade students who received Reading Recovery tutoring services, from school year 1992–93 to 1997–98, is examined in order to evaluate the performance of children in this group who were English language learners. The children in the Reading Recovery Group were compared with a Random Sample Group of 18,363 first graders drawn from the classroom population of children not identified as needing assistance, and with a Comparison Group of 11,267 first-grade children who were in need of Reading Recovery but did not receive it because of a lack of resources. The results suggest that Reading Recovery is an effective intervention that narrows the reading achievement gap between native and non-native speakers. Because some school administrators and teachers appear to lack confidence in the potential for non-native speaking children to benefit from this literacy intervention, implications of these perceptions are discussed with respect to key principles of Reading Recovery's implementation in schools.*

Educators, parents, and policy makers continue to debate the most effective instructional approaches necessary to provide a meaningful education to English language learners; that is, children who are learning to speak English as an additional language (Collier, 1992; Wilkinson, 1998). In addition, there is continuing concern about educational inequalities in academic achievement between language-minority students and native English speakers (Cummins, 1986) as schools serve increasing numbers of English language learners from diverse language contexts (Hornberger, 1992; Lucas, Henze, & Donato, 1990). The purpose of this study was to evaluate Reading Recovery as a supplemental literacy program for first graders, and to discuss whether this early intervention contributes to English language learners' capacity to reach native speaker norms for academic achievement, specifically in terms of reading. In other words, we were interested in investigating whether Reading Recovery is effective as an instructional intervention for English language learners and, thereby, contributes to reducing inequalities in academic achievement between native and non-native speakers educated in monolingual English classroom contexts.

## Research on Literacy Instruction for English Language Learners

In addressing the question of whether Reading Recovery is effective for children who are learning English as an additional language, we reviewed research studies in the following areas:

- Evaluation studies of the effectiveness of classroom literacy instruction on the reading achievement of children who are English language learners.
- Evaluation studies of the effectiveness of Reading Recovery as an early intervention for all children as well as English language learners.

### Research on Classroom Literacy Instruction

An examination of research addressing the effectiveness of classroom literacy instruction for English language learners reveals that the field is dominated by questions regarding the use of a language other than English for instructional purposes. In particular, researchers have compared the academic achievement of students with English as a second language who have received classroom instruction in a variety of first and second language settings.

Ramirez and colleagues (Ramirez, Yuen, Ramey, & Pasta, 1991), compared outcomes for students in typical bilingual program adopted by schools, that is, "early-exit" instruction involving part-day Spanish instruction in kindergarten through second grade, with two alternative programs. These alternatives were (a) "late-exit" bi-lingual programs with initial instruction in Spanish, followed by balanced (50%/50%) instruction in English and Spanish from kindergarten through sixth grade, and (b) "structured immersion" programs with instruction given only in English. The Ramirez study was a longitudinal evaluation that followed children in each program from grades one to three. There were 319 children in the early-exit program, 233 children in the structured immersion program, and 170 children in the late-exit program. An additional group of 154 students in the late-exit bi-lingual program continued in the study from fourth to sixth grade in order to capture the particular outcomes of this instructional design.

According to Collier (1992) the Ramirez study confirmed evidence from numerous other investigations examining long-term achievement of English language learners. Improved academic achievement in a second language is positively related to the support children receive for education in their first language. For example, in Ramirez et al. (1991) the children in all three programs did equally well at first grade on the Comprehensive Test of Basic Skills in reading and mathematics. However, by fourth grade there were strong differences in academic performance between cohorts. Children in the late-exit bilingual program were making faster progress in both English reading and math than children in the early-exit and structured immersion cohorts.

A meta-analysis of research on literacy achievement for English language learners, included in the report by the National Research Council's Committee on the Prevention of Reading Difficulties (National Research Council, 1998), confirms the potential risks to sustained achievement levels when children experience initial literacy instruction in a second language:

The accumulated wisdom of research in the field of bi-lingualism and literacy tends to converge on the conclusion that initial literacy instruction in a second language can be successful, that it carries with it a higher risk of reading problems and of lower ultimate literacy attainment than initial literacy instruction in a first language, and that this risk may compound the risks associated with poverty, low levels of parental education, poor schooling, and other such factors. (p. 234)

Despite these findings, school systems are often faced with few instructional choices other than immersion in monolingual English classes for English language learners. Schools have to identify instructional approaches that foster effective literacy learning for all children, including English language learners speaking a variety of primary languages, such as Spanish, Chinese, Russian, Arabic and many others. Many investigations in the area of literacy acquisition have examined the instructional contexts that best support such learners.

For example, New Zealand has recently experienced net migration gains of peoples from the Pacific Islands and Asia who speak a variety of languages. Wilkinson (1998) reported on the New Zealand data from an international evaluation of educational achievement in 32 countries. These data revealed that despite the high literacy levels of many nine- and fourteen-year old New Zealand students, those whose home language was different from the language of school (i.e., English) were performing below native English speakers on comprehension and word recognition measures. Frequent assessment of students' reading and regular reading aloud by the teacher were instructional practices correlated with closing the achievement gap on both these measures.

In summary, there is strong evidence of the positive impact on reading achievement of initial literacy instruction being conducted in a child's native language. However, the above research also suggests that where native language literacy instruction is not available, instructional practices that best support the literacy achievement of English language learners must be identified if inequalities in reading achievement are to be reduced.

## Research on Reading Recovery Instruction

Many school systems, wanting to address the needs of "at-risk" literacy learners including those children who speak languages other than English, have implemented Reading Recovery as an early intervention and prevention program (delivered in English) that supplements classroom literacy instruction during first grade. Skilled teachers, specifically trained for the purpose, provide daily, 30-minute lessons to those children identified as having serious literacy learning difficulties and are the lowest performing readers in the cohort. The aim of Reading Recovery is to ensure that children receiving this individual tutoring catch up as quickly as possible with their classmates, usually in 16 to 20 weeks, so they can continue to make progress in reading and writing in a variety of classroom instructional contexts without needing further special assistance.

**Reading Recovery for all students.** There have been many evaluations of Reading Recovery conducted by those implementing the program. Lyons (1998) reviews over ten years of data collected as part of a national design, demonstrating the effectiveness of the program. From 1985 to 1997, a total of 436,249 first grade children entered the program, of which 60% met the criteria for discontinuing; that is, they read at or above the average of their class by the end of first grade and were able to continue to improve in literacy learning without needing further intervention. Most of the remaining children made progress, but did not have enough time in the school year to complete their programs. These are impressive results, considering that all children enrolled in Reading Recovery were the lowest performing readers in their first grade cohort.

Other studies, including those conducted by independent evaluators, have reported similar favorable results. Shanahan and Barr (1995), in their independent evaluation of Reading Recovery, conclude that Reading Recovery attains its stated goal by bringing the children's learning up to that of their average-achieving peers. They report that many children leave the program with well developed reading strategies, including phonemic awareness and spelling knowledge. However, the researchers point to problems in reporting approaches that may inflate the learning gains of Reading Recovery children. Shanahan and Barr call for clearer specifications of success, the documenting of outcomes on all students receiving Reading Recovery, and more rigorous research studies.

Other researchers of Reading Recovery who were seeking to assess the program's effectiveness, have suggested developing predictive models that would identify the characteristics of students most likely to succeed in Reading Recovery. For example, such a model has been proposed by researchers driven by cost-efficiency considerations (Batelle Institute, 1995). Identifying children more likely to succeed, it is argued, would drive down costs. By avoiding children predicted to fail, Reading Recovery could serve more children, more quickly.

Such an approach is dismissed by Reading Recovery professionals for practical and ethical reasons. By admitting the lowest scoring students, it is countered, Reading Recovery is potentially more cost-effective, because a significant number of these children who succeed in Reading Recovery do not later become a burden to the system, in terms of costly supplemental services in higher grades. In addition, children who are not among the most needy are the ones who are more likely to "survive" without costly special services, and benefit from classroom instruction alone.

**Reading Recovery for English language learners.** In our experience, English language learners, as a group, are students vulnerable to cost efficiency considerations and may be regarded as less likely to succeed in Reading Recovery as a monolingual English literacy intervention. Until recently there have been few attempts to disaggregate the impact of Reading Recovery on the performance of children who are learning English as another language. However, a study conducted in England included evidence of success of English language learners in Reading Recovery (Hobsbaum, 1995). More recently, Neal and Kelly (1999) examined reading and writing success for two groups of bi-lingual children receiving either Reading Recovery, where instruction is delivered in English, or Descubriendo La Lectura, a reconstruction of Reading Recovery, where intervention instruction is delivered in Spanish while children are receiving classroom literacy instruction in Spanish. The results indicated that both populations of students made progress and reached average levels of classroom literacy performance.

## Purpose of the Study

Where bi-lingual education is not available, schools are faced with the challenge of how to foster high levels of literacy achievement for English language learners effectively. Evidence of Reading Recovery's effectiveness encourages school districts concerned with improving literacy achievement to adopt this program as a "safety net" for low performing students. We presumed it would be valuable to add to evaluations of Reading Recovery's contribution to the literacy achievement of English language learners, and to examine the extent to which it represents an appropriate educational program for this group of students.

In particular we were interested in whether such a contribution closes the achievement gap typically observed between native and non-native English speakers. To understand the impact of Reading Recovery on the reading achievement of first graders who are English language learners, we sought to answer the following questions:

1. Are there differences in outcomes, rate of completion, and delivery of Reading Recovery as a literacy intervention for children who are English language learners, as compared to native English speakers?
2. Does Reading Recovery narrow the gap in reading achievement between English language learners and native English-speaking children in first grade?

The focus of our attention centered on distinctions in Reading Recovery services and program performance between native and non-native English speakers. This reflects our broad interest in how, as an early literacy intervention, Reading Recovery works for children who have varying levels of competence in the English language.

## Method

### Measures and Criteria for Evaluating Success

The data used in this study were drawn from the *Reading Recovery Data Sheet*, produced by the National Data Evaluation Center at The Ohio State University. This is a national questionnaire used to record reading and writing scores, demographic information, and other data on all children selected for Reading Recovery, as well as on a sample of children randomly drawn from the general first grade classroom population.

Children are selected for Reading Recovery based on their performance on six literacy assessment tasks included in *An Observation Survey of Early Literacy Achievement* (Clay, 1993a), which were administered by Reading Recovery teachers. The children selected for services are the lowest performing first-grade children, deemed most "at-risk" of literacy failure in regular education classrooms. Clay (1993a) reports on the satisfactory measurement characteristics of the observation survey tasks, which assess letter identification (LI), sight reading vocabulary (Ohio Word Test = WT), concepts about print (CAP), writing vocabulary (WV), the capacity to hear and record sounds in words (HRSIW), and performance in reading a graded set of previously unseen texts (Text Reading Level = TRL). These graded texts have been benchmarked for use nationally in Reading Recovery and range in difficulty from pre-primer through sixth grade, leveled from 1 to 30 for use in first grade. For example, successful reading of levels 16 to 18 indicates appropriate grade level performance for the end of first grade to the beginning of second grade. In administering *An Observation Survey of Early Literacy Achievement* (Clay, 1993a) to children who speak English as a second language, there is a minimum requirement that they understand teacher-given directions for the tasks.

Evaluating success in Reading Recovery is based on two sources of information. One source is the combined judgments of the child's Reading Recovery teacher and the classroom teacher that the child is reading at or above the average performance of classroom peers. These judgments are checked against a second source of information, that is, testing at exit from the program using all six tasks on *An Observation Survey of Early Literacy Achievement* (Clay, 1993a). The specific decision to "discontinue" the tutoring of an individual child therefore depends on several sources of information and is evaluated against the following two criteria:

1.  The extent to which the child has developed a self-sustaining learning system so that he or she can benefit from classroom instruction without the need for further intervention.
2.  Results from exit testing by an independent observer (i.e., a teacher other than the child's Reading Recovery teacher) that indicate the child is reading close to his/her average performing peers. Note that the group's average band is based on the observation survey performance of a classroom random sample (mean +/- .5 SD), which is used as an empirical frame of reference to evaluate this achievement at the end of the school year.

Classroom reading achievement varies widely from district to district. "Discontinued from tutoring" as a label, is a relative criterion represented by varying achievement levels in different schools within sites (districts or collections of districts) implementing Reading Recovery. A "self-extending learning system" as a criterion for exiting the program depends on the clinical judgment of a Reading Recovery teacher that the child's observed reading and writing behaviors are evidence of cognitive capacities to make further literacy learning gains without continued individual tutoring (Clay, 1991). This criterion of a self-extending learning system is intended to be universal across all participating districts. A consistent teacher-training model in Reading Recovery, and continued support to teachers, ensures adherence to this criterion.

## Participants

The selection of children into Reading Recovery is a nationally uniform procedure driven by the principles of its original design (Clay, 1993b). The children included in this study were initially identified for Reading Recovery as being among the lowest 20% of their first grade in reading according to their classroom teacher's judgment. Administration of *An Observation Survey of Early Literacy Achievement* (Clay, 1993a) by the Reading Recovery teacher provided further information to select the lowest performing children in need of immediate literacy tutoring. The national evaluation design calls for the testing of Reading Recovery children at the beginning of the school year, at program entry and exit, and at year-end.

The *Reading Recovery Group* included in this study comprised all children served regardless of their program status—successful, appropriately referred for specialist services including special education, having incomplete programs, or moved away from the school. Our choice was to include *all* of these students in the study, even if their exposure to Reading Recovery was minimal (a couple of lessons), in order to avoid any ambiguity in the definition of the intervention, a problem that plagued some previous research on Reading Recovery (see Shanahan & Barr, 1995).

Not all children who are initially identified as needing Reading Recovery eventually receive services. The most needy children are served first. Of the remaining children, some make progress through regular classroom instruction during the year, and thus do not need services. Others remain "at-risk," but do not receive Reading Recovery due to lack of resources. All of these children comprised the Comparison Group for this study. The evaluation design implemented by sites affiliated with New York University expands on the national design by collecting data on this *Comparison Group*, which we treat as an approximate solution for a control group of "at-risk" students.

The remainder of the classroom population, i.e., children generally considered not at-risk, served as a basis from which a random sample was drawn for each Reading Recovery site, again under the uniform procedures. The *Random Sample Group* was drawn from approximately the top 80% of students in Reading Recovery classrooms and was tested at the beginning and end of the school year, using *An Observation Survey of Early Literacy Achievement* (Clay, 1993a), in order to provide a benchmark for reading achievement in a Reading Recovery site.

From the total number of 55,875 students in the groups (Reading Recovery, Random Sample, and Comparison) in NYU-affiliated sites, 644 children for whom information on native language was not available were eliminated from the study. The remaining 55,231 children were identified as English native speakers ("English" = 45,303 children), fluent non-native speakers ("Fluent ESL" = 6,388 children), and non-native speakers with limited English proficiency ("LEP" = 3,540 children) based on the data collected through the national Reading Recovery questionnaire (see Table 1). Children were characterized as such either through the results of a language proficiency test, if such a test was given by a district, or through classroom teacher judgment. All of the children came from monolingual classrooms, where instruction was in English.

Of all English language learners in the study, Spanish was the native language for the majority of the limited English proficient students (54%), with Chinese spoken by 26%, and other languages by 19%. Again Spanish was the dominant native language for language learners who were fluent in English—74% spoke Spanish, 6% spoke Chinese, and 20% spoke other languages.

## Reading Recovery Sites

The database used in this study spans six years of Reading Recovery implementation (school year 1992–93 to school year 1997–98) at 37 Reading Recovery sites affiliated with New York University. These sites, which may be a single school district or a

**Table 1.** Native Language Composition of Study Samples

| | NATIVE LANGUAGE | | | |
| | ENGLISH | FLUENT ESL | LEP | TOTAL |
| SAMPLE | | | | |
|---|---|---|---|---|
| Reading Recovery | | | | |
| Count | 20863 | 2924 | 1814 | 25601 |
| % | 81.5 | 11.4 | 7.1 | 100 |
| Comparison Group | | | | |
| Count | 8845 | 1427 | 995 | 11267 |
| % | 78.5 | 12.7 | 8.8 | 100 |
| Random Sample | | | | |
| Count | 15595 | 2037 | 731 | 18363 |
| % | 84.9 | 11.1 | 4.0 | 100 |

*Note:* LEP = Low English Proficiency

consortium of districts working together to implement Reading Recovery, represent a variety of educational environments, including urban, suburban, and rural settings. Districts also varied in the number of years of Reading Recovery implementation, the number of certified Reading Recovery teachers available relative to need for service in schools (i.e., level of coverage), and the level of their experience in Reading Recovery.

## Data Analyses

The first research question, which concerned the outcomes, completion rates, and delivery of Reading Recovery, was answered by a comparison of the proportion of children of different language backgrounds who were selected to receive Reading Recovery services, who completed full Reading Recovery instruction, and who were deemed successful in Reading Recovery. Pearson's Chi-square tests were used to report on the statistical significance of the differences between two groups of English language learners (LEP and fluent ESL) and native English speakers (English).

To answer our second question, whether Reading Recovery closes the literacy achievement gap between native-speakers and English language learners in first grade, proved a challenging task, considering that our data derive from a field implementation of Reading Recovery in a variety of educational settings. To search for differences we used analysis of variance, with *language* (English, Fluent ESL, and LEP) and *sample group* (Reading Recovery, Random Sample, and Comparison) as fixed factors; *Reading Recovery Site* as a randomly varying factor; and *Text Reading Level* as a dependent variable.

By including *Reading Recovery Site* as a random factor in our model, we took into account the similarity of students within sites, due to shared curriculum, educational policies, geography, and other features. Differences between the groups of students who share educational settings are all the more important when one considers the heterogeneous nature of school systems that implement Reading Recovery in the wider

New York metropolitan area. Including this source of variation explicitly provided us with better estimates of error and, thereby, gave us more confidence in estimates of effects, which were of primary interest to us. Specifically, the interaction of *language* and *sample group* effects represents a direct test of the hypothesis that the differences in reading achievement between language groups are smaller for Reading Recovery students than they are for the other two groups of first-graders (Random Sample Group and Comparison Group).

## Results

### Analysis of Outcomes, Completion Rates, and Delivery of Reading Recovery

The first study question concerned the extent to which there was any evidence of differences in outcomes and completion rates between Reading Recovery children from the three language groups. In addition we questioned whether there was equity in the delivery of Reading Recovery to children regardless of their native language background.

*Program outcomes.* We initially analyzed whether there were differences in outcomes for Reading Recovery children who were English language learners, consisting of fluent and limited English proficient, as compared to native speakers. Table 2 presents program success rates for children in three different language groups (English, Fluent ESL and LEP children) as well as rates of program completion.

The success rates in Table 1 are expressed as a percentage of all students served in Reading Recovery. Of the 25,601 children served in this six-year period, 16,033 (63%) successfully exited the program, while the remaining 9,568 (37%) children were not successful. Since these figures account for all children served in the program, the "not successful" group includes children who moved from the school, those who lacked opportunity to complete a full program before the end of the school year, and those who were recommended for other services, including special education.

Table 2. Reading Recovery Program Success and Program Completion Rates for Three Language Groups

| LANGUAGE | | OUTCOME | | COMPLETION | |
| | | SUCCESSFUL | NOT SUCCESSFUL | COMPLETE | INCOMPLETE |
| --- | --- | --- | --- | --- | --- |
| English | Count | 12975 | 7888 | 15756 | 5107 |
| | % | 62.2 | 37.8 | 75.5 | 24.5 |
| Fluent ESL | Count | 1938 | 986 | 2253 | 671 |
| | % | 66.3 | 33.7 | 77.1 | 22.9 |
| LEP | Count | 1120 | 694 | 1348 | 466 |
| | % | 61.7 | 38.3 | 74.3 | 25.7 |
| Total | Count | 16033 | 9568 | 19357 | 6244 |
| | % | 62.6 | 37.4 | 75.6 | 24.4 |

Statistically significant differences (chi-square = 18.960, $df = 2, p < 0.0001$) in success rates were observed among the language groups. Fluent ESL children have a higher success rate (66.3%) than either native English speakers (62.2%) or LEP students (61.7%). However, it appears that the limited English proficient children were just as successful as their native English-speaking peers.

**Completion of Reading Recovery.** In addition to considering success rates for Reading Recovery children, we also examined the extent to which children from different language groups had an opportunity to receive at least sixty lessons (a "full program" definition established when the program was first implemented in the United States), regardless of whether they successfully exited the program or not. We were interested in whether all Reading Recovery children had an equal opportunity to be successful, by receiving a full Reading Recovery program, regardless of their language background and English proficiency. Analysis of the data demonstrated that language proficiency was not a factor impacting children's opportunities to complete the program. There were no significant differences in program completion rates (see Table 1) between the three language groups (Chi-square = 5.046, $df = 2, p = 0.08$). In addition to student mobility, referral to special services was the most frequent reason for exiting the Reading Recovery program before completion. The analysis of completion rates suggests that these factors (mobility and referral) did not differentially impact Reading Recovery students from these three language groups.

**Program delivery.** In order to examine the selection process for Reading Recovery, we analyzed the language composition of each study sample—Reading Recovery Group, Comparison Group and Random Sample Group. We observed that the Reading Recovery Group contained a disproportionate number of native English speakers with respect to the Comparison Group (81.5% vs. 78.5%). This difference is statistically significant, as indicated by Pearson's Chi-square test (chi-square = 50.3, $df = 2, p < .0001$). Both Fluent ESL students (12.7% vs. 11.4%) and, especially, LEP students (8.8% vs. 7.1%), were less likely to be served in Reading Recovery than their peers who are native English speakers (and, thus, became part of the Comparison Group).

This finding is intriguing, considering that Reading Recovery targets the lowest performing first graders. It was revealed by an analysis of the measures from *An Observation Survey of Early Literacy Achievement* (Clay, 1993a), taken at the beginning of the school year, that LEP students who were selected into Reading Recovery indeed had somewhat higher scores than the LEP students who were not selected. In contrast, between English speaking and Fluent ESL students, it was clear that students with the lowest observation survey scores were the ones selected. This pattern of results indicates that sometimes decision-making may have been influenced by factors other than literacy assessment and this will be discussed later.

## Analysis of Reading Achievement by Group

Consistent with the Reading Recovery evaluation design, four of the tasks from *An Observation Survey of Early Literacy Achievement* (Clay, 1993a), including text reading, writing vocabulary, word recognition, and hearing and recording sounds in words,

**Table 3.** Year-End Observation Survey Scores

| | MEAN SCORE | | | |
| SAMPLE | TRL | WV | OWT | HRSIW |
| --- | --- | --- | --- | --- |
| Reading Recovery | | | | |
| English | 15.73 | 46.33 | 16.74 | 33.77 |
| Fluent ESL | 15.26 | 47.20 | 16.79 | 33.31 |
| LEP | 14.61 | 48.09 | 16.52 | 33.10 |
| Comparison Group | | | | |
| English | 12.21 | 37.55 | 14.95 | 30.68 |
| Fluent ESL | 10.05 | 34.45 | 13.53 | 28.26 |
| LEP | 7.66 | 32.92 | 12.12 | 25.54 |
| Random Sample | | | | |
| English | 19.78 | 47.00 | 17.97 | 34.22 |
| Fluent ESL | 16.16 | 43.43 | 16.90 | 32.25 |
| LEP | 11.72 | 38.19 | 14.94 | 29.34 |

*Note:* TRL = Text Reading Level; WV = Writing Vocabulary; OWT = Ohio Word Test; HRSIW = Hearing and Recording Sounds in Words Test; LEP = Low English Proficiency.

were administered at the end of the school year to all Reading Recovery children, as well as to the Random Sample, and to the children who were initially diagnosed as "at-risk" but were not served in Reading Recovery (i.e., the Comparison Group).

Average year-end scores for these three sample groups (see Table 3) appear to support the hypothesis that Reading Recovery closes the reading achievement gap between native and non-native English speakers. On all four measures, smaller differences in reading and writing achievement associated with native language proficiency were evident for Reading Recovery children.

The Text Reading Level (TRL) task is by far the most comprehensive and clinically meaningful of the tasks. The TRL scores provided in Table 3 represent the difficulty level achieved by students on a series of previously unseen, graded text passages, read with at least 90% accuracy. In the context of classroom instruction these results indicate that LEP children who had received Reading Recovery services were reading texts with a difficulty level equivalent to a Grade 1 basal reader. In contrast, LEP students in the Random Sample, a group that had not been identified as needing supplemental tutoring, were reading at only the Primer level at the end of first grade.

For two of these four observation survey measures, Hearing and Recording Sound in Words (sentence dictation task) and the Ohio Word Test (high-frequency word list), further statistical analysis was not advisable due to strong ceiling effects which resulted in skewed distributions of students' scores. For brevity's sake, we report the analysis of variance for Text Reading Level only, while noting that using Writing Vocabulary as a dependent variable led to exactly the same pattern of results.

An analysis of variance was conducted with *language* and *sample* as fixed factors, *site* as a random factor, and text reading level as the dependent variable. Tests of the main effects and interactions are presented in Table 4. The interaction of *sample* and *language*, which represents a direct test of the hypothesis regarding Reading Recovery's impact on the reading achievement gap, is graphically illustrated in Figure 1. All of the tests were statistically significant, and differences among means were in the expected direction.

It is apparent that the gap between the three language groups varied significantly, but was much smaller for children who received Reading Recovery, than for the children who did not. Non-native English-speaking children, especially LEP children, lagged behind native speakers both in the sample drawn from the lower (Comparison Group) and higher (Random Sample) end of the classroom reading achievement spectrum. Among Reading Recovery children these differences were drastically reduced.

On average, Random Sample children scored higher than those children considered "at-risk." This result inevitably follows from the evaluation design, where one group is sampled from the higher and the other from the lower end of the achievement range. Also, our definition of "Reading Recovery children" was all-inclusive, and did not omit children who were either unsuccessful or had incomplete programs. When the same analysis was conducted using only the children who were successful (63% of the cohort), the difference between Reading Recovery and Random Sample disappeared, as Reading Recovery children scored on the level of their peers. The same pattern of results was evident when Writing Vocabulary (a timed word writing task) was used as a dependent variable, giving additional weight to our claim.

Analysis of variance also revealed a statistically significant three-way interaction, which indicated that "closing the gap" could not be fully generalized across all locations where Reading Recovery is implemented. Although seemingly problematic, such an effect was hardly surprising, given the variety of urban, suburban, and rural school districts, with diverse student populations that are characteristic of Reading Recovery sites in the New York metropolitan region. However, when initial differences among students, as expressed in fall scores on the Concepts About Print task, were taken into account, this interaction was no longer significant. (Note: Full Analysis of Covariance results are not reported here, but are available from the authors.)

**Table 4.** Tests of Between-Subjects Effects: Spring Text Reading Level

| SOURCE | F | DF | SIG. |
|---|---|---|---|
| Language | 34.2 | (2,194.3) | .000 |
| Sample | 65.1 | (2,153.1) | .000 |
| Site | 7.1 | (36,106.6) | .000 |
| Language X Sample | 11.7 | (4,1093.9) | .000 |
| Language X Site | 3.3 | (70,158.7) | .000 |
| Sample X Site | 4.5 | (72,239.7) | .000 |
| Language X Sample X Site | 1.5 | (129,50670) | .001 |

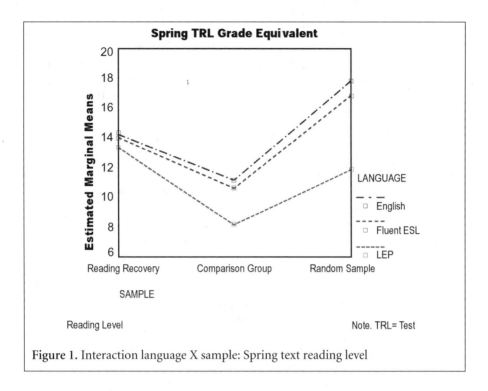

**Figure 1.** Interaction language X sample: Spring text reading level

Such a result, from the analysis of covariance, indicates that individual differences in pre-existing knowledge among students are one possible reason for this site-to-site variation, and not a failed implementation, or an ill fit of Reading Recovery as a literacy intervention in particular sites.

## Discussion

This study has reported results from administrations of *An Observation Survey of Early Literacy Achievement* (Clay, 1993a) on 55,231 children. Of these children, 25,601 received Reading Recovery services in first grade during a six-year period from 1992 to 1998. Results have been used to evaluate whether Reading Recovery, as an early literacy intervention, is effective for students who were learning English as another language. In the following sections, we discuss the findings from this study by exploring several issues: (a) English language proficiency as a possible factor in whether children are selected for Reading Recovery services, (b) the relationship between reading achievement and English language proficiency, and (c) limitations and directions for further investigation.

### English Language Proficiency as a Factor in Selection

The earlier analysis of success rates for children in Reading Recovery suggests that both native speakers and English language learners are equally likely to be successful and to complete the program. If anything, fluent ESL students are more likely to be successful than native speakers. This is an interesting outcome. Similar findings were summarized by Collier (1989), from studies of children who initially learned two languages simultaneously and outperformed monolingual students in the late elementary years on measures that included linguistic and metalinguistic abilities, cognitive flexibility, and concept formation. In part this is attributed to the children's continued cognitive development in both languages.

Reading Recovery tutoring for these fluent ESL students, who initially experienced reading difficulties, may have contributed to language development in English, while other experiences (provided by parents, for example) contributed to continued cognitive development in another language. Such combined cognitive inputs may have allowed these children to begin outperforming their monolingual peers in literacy.

However, our analysis of the scores at the beginning of first grade on *An Observation Survey of Early Literacy Achievement* (Clay, 1993a) suggested that the lowest performing among LEP children were not always selected for Reading Recovery tutoring. In addition, both Fluent ESL, and LEP children are under-represented in Reading Recovery, with respect to other students "at-risk" in the Comparison Group (see Table 2). As indicated earlier, there may be several practices at the school level shaping such a pattern of results. For example, this pattern may reflect some schools' decisions to delay admission into Reading Recovery for children with English as a second language, particularly LEP children, driven by a belief that their English language skills first need to improve to a certain level, before they can be considered for literacy tutoring.

Another practice may be that within a context of limited resources, there is sometimes *pressure* in schools to select students for Reading Recovery for whom progress appears to be more likely, and to exclude those for whom the prognosis appears poor. Anecdotal evidence suggests that both of these practices may reflect a perception among teachers and administrators, that children with limited English proficiency are not suited for Reading Recovery instruction. Whatever the reasons, these practices can lead to decreased opportunities for English language learners to receive the literacy tutoring which would benefit them immediately, according to the data presented in this study. In order to understand these practices more thoroughly, further attention needs to be paid to the effects of other programs and services offered to English language learners, in conjunction with Reading Recovery.

Attempts to predict the reading progress of an individual child initially identified as needing Reading Recovery, suffer from an inherent lack of validity, especially with the low levels of literacy skills that "at-risk" children possess before the first grade. Evidence from Reading Recovery research (Clay, 1993b) demonstrates that it is only after ten weeks in the program that predictions of success can be made with any confidence. Even then predictions still carry a risk of error in at least 30% of cases. Continuous observation and diagnostic teaching (optimally 20 weeks) by a Reading Recovery teacher provides more reliable information on which to make valid and fair assessments on the level of the individual child, particularly when the child's classroom teacher raises questions about the need for referral to special education services.

Since the general pattern of results suggests that Reading Recovery "works" for all students, it is obviously important to ensure that language proficiency does not result in children's inappropriate exclusion from the program. Given the demonstrated effectiveness of the program for all language groups, districts can have confidence that Reading Recovery is an appropriate instructional intervention for these children as well.

## Reading Achievement as it Relates to English Language Proficiency

It is evident from the data that Reading Recovery not only contributed to improving the literacy performance of all three language groups (English, Fluent ESL, and LEP), but also reduced the variability in performance among them. Within the Random Sample and the Comparison Groups, however, differences between language groups persisted. At the end of the year, LEP children in both of these groups significantly lagged behind their fluent non-native and native English-speaking peers.

Without an intensive literacy intervention, such as Reading Recovery, non-native English speakers are likely to fall behind by the end of first grade. The data derived from this study indicate that a reading achievement gap exists, both for children initially thought to be "at-risk," and for all other students in first grade. Quality classroom instruction in the primary grades that is tailored to meet diverse learning needs is clearly called for as the first strategy in the prevention of literacy learning difficulties.

However, given the broader research findings on academic achievement in literacy for second language learners (Ramirez et al., 1991), we believe that it is unrealistic to assume that Reading Recovery, as a first grade intervention, can completely protect against the need for further supplementary help. Reading Recovery as an early intervention is designed to reduce the long-term need for remedial reading programs. In the increasingly demanding literacy environment of monolingual English school learning beyond the early grades, school administrators and teachers need to continue to monitor the language and literacy needs of non-native English speakers, and to provide periodic assistance where needed.

## Limitations and Directions for Further Research

The general conclusion of this study points to the effectiveness of Reading Recovery tutoring in producing similar outcomes for students with different levels of English proficiency, and offers an appropriate solution for first graders initially experiencing problems in reading and writing. The national Reading Recovery evaluation design, which provided the data for this study, places constraints on the interpretation of the results that are even greater than those typically associated with correlational studies. This is especially true with respect to causality. Issues of program implementation in part determined the selection of students into groups for the purpose of the study. As such, the size of the Comparison Group ("at-risk" students who did not receive the program) was influenced by the level of program implementation in a school. Similarly, some of the clinically valuable measures administered under the Reading Recovery design are ill-suited for statistical analysis due to difficulty level and ceiling effects.

Apparent differences in reading achievement between native English speakers and English language learners may be influenced by other factors, such as characteristics of students (other than native language) and characteristics of their educational environments. Our design takes into account variation across sites, which has typically not been included as a factor in previous studies of Reading Recovery's effectiveness, and eliminates this source of bias from estimates of effects.

Future research studies should take a step further, and try to determine the extent of the influence of specific factors at both student and site levels. Other student characteristics, such as ethnicity, race, socio-economic status, cultural background, and the characteristics of students' native language, are likely to be important factors in the performance of students. Characteristics of Reading Recovery sites as educational environments, such as number of years of Reading Recovery implementation, level of coverage, teachers' experience, urban/suburban location, and district demographics, are also potential explanatory factors for the performance of students at-risk. A convincing case can even be made for the interaction of factors from these two levels (students and sites), especially in a metropolitan area that is characterized by considerable diversity of students.

For example, in some school districts, a number of English language learners may come from populations with relatively high socio-economic status, while native English speakers in some urban districts tend to be of low socio-economic status. In-depth consideration of factors such as these would help evaluation research move beyond general conclusions about the program's effectiveness, and make specific recommendations concerning early literacy intervention for diverse groups of at-risk students. Unfortunately, this diversity is extremely difficult to quantify and control for in this sample of students drawn from sites affiliated with NYU. Despite its large size, the sample used in this study lacked adequate distribution of student characteristics over sites, which is more likely to be found in a national-level sample of Reading Recovery sites and students.

At least some of the issues raised by this study, such as decision-making about which students to admit into Reading Recovery, appear to be related to the characteristics of sites, but it is not possible to explore these hypotheses in great detail from the data at hand. However, a modified national Reading Recovery evaluation design, in place from school year 1998–99, does include additional descriptors on the teacher- and school-level (locale, teacher experience, level of implementation, to mention a few), which will enable more detailed analyses in the future.

Finally, how well the effects of this literacy intervention for English language learners transfer into sustained gains beyond first grade is an issue that remains to be explored. This is crucially important in the light of the fact that English language learners are more likely to be found on the wrong side of the gap in reading achievement, a gap that widens in the course of elementary education and beyond.

## Conclusions

Selecting the lowest performing children for Reading Recovery is a key design principle of this program's implementation. We believe that doubts that may exist in some schools about fully adhering to such a principle with respect to English language learners are not supported by the data presented here. The results reported in Table 1 and Figure 1 represent strong evidence that the one-to-one tutoring offered in Reading Recovery constitutes an appropriate setting, in addition to the classroom, to support language and literacy development for children with limited English proficiency.

The substantial database on which we were able to draw allowed us to monitor various aspects of Reading Recovery's implementation and effectiveness. Without such a database across sites, and without the capacity from an external agency to analyze such data (in this case, New York University), identifying potential bias in the delivery of services to English language learners would not have been possible. This speaks in some ways to the value of school-university partnerships in program evaluation.

## References

Batelle Institute. (1995). *Longitudinal study of Reading Recovery: 1990–91 through 1993–94.* Ohio Department of Education.

Clay, M. M. (1991). *Becoming literate: The construction of inner control.* Portsmouth, NH: Heinemann.

Clay, M. M. (1993a). *An observation survey of early literacy achievement.* Portsmouth, NH: Heinemann.

Clay, M. M. (1993b). *Reading Recovery: A guidebook for teachers in training.* Portsmouth, NH: Heinemann.

Collier, V. P. (1989). How long? A synthesis of research on academic achievement in a second language. *TESOL Quarterly, 23*, 509–531.

Collier, V. P. (1992). A synthesis of studies examining long-term language minority student data on academic achievement. *Bilingual Research Journal, 16* (1 & 2), 187–212.

Cummins, J. (1986). Empowering minority students: A framework for intervention. *Harvard Education Review, 56*(1), 18–36.

Hobsbaum, A. (1995). Reading Recovery in England. *Literacy Teaching and Learning: An International Journal of Early Reading and Writing, 1*, 21–39.

Hornberger, N. (1992). Biliteracy contexts, continua and contrasts: Policy and curriculum for Cambodian and Puerto Rican students in Philadelphia. *Education and Urban Society, 24*(2), 196–211.

Lucas, T., Henze, R., & Donato, R. (1990). Promoting the success of Latino language-minority students: An exploratory study of six high schools. *Harvard Education Review, 60*, 315–340.

Lyons, C. A. (1998). Reading Recovery in the United States: More than a decade of data. *Literacy Teaching and Learning: An International Journal of Early Reading and Writing, 3*(1), 77–92.

Neal, J. C., & Kelly, P. R. (1999). The success of Reading Recovery for English language learners and Descubriendo La Lectura for bilingual students in California. *Literacy Teaching and Learning: An International Journal of Early Reading and Writing, 4*(2), 81–108.

Pinnell, G. S., Lyons, C. A., DeFord, D. E., Bryk, A. S., & Seltzer, M. (1994). Comparing instructional models for the literacy education of high risk first graders. *Reading Research Quarterly, 29*(1), 9–39.

Ramirez, J., Yuen, S., Ramey, D., & Pasta, D. (1991). *Final report: Longitudinal study of structured English immersion strategy, early-exit and late-exit bilingual education programs for language minority children, I & II* (U. S. D. E. Publication No. 300-87-0156). San Mateo, CA: Aguirre International.

Shanahan, T., & Barr, R. (1995). Reading Recovery: An independent evaluation of the effects of an early instructional intervention for "at-risk" learners. *Reading Research Quarterly, 30,* 958–996.

Snow, C. E., Burns, S. M., & Griffin, P. (Eds.). (1998). *Preventing reading difficulties in young children.* Washington, D.C.: National Academy Press.

Wilkinson, I. (1998). Dealing with diversity: Achievement gaps in reading literacy among New Zealand students. *Reading Research Quarterly, 33,* 144–167.

# Making a Case for Prevention in Education

Billie J. Askew, *Texas Woman's University*
Elizabeth Kaye, *Texas Woman's University*
Dianne F. Frasier, *Fort Bend ISD, Sugar Land, TX*
Mohsen Mobasher, *Texas Woman's University*
Nancy Anderson, *Texas Woman's University*
Yvonne G. Rodríguez, *Texas Woman's University*

## ABSTRACT

*Typically, students who are experiencing difficulty learning to read in the classroom are referred for long-term assistance to remedial or special education services. We examined what happens when another layer of assistance is added to this typical delivery model, this one provided before referral to long-term special education services is even considered. This model of preventing reading difficulties is informed by the construct of prevention used in the medical field and recasts assistance as a three-tiered process: primary prevention in the form of classroom instruction offered to all students; a secondary prevention offered to those students for whom classroom instruction is not enough; and finally, tertiary prevention provided to students who have not made adequate progress even after primary and secondary prevention measures have been employed.*

*We hypothesized that the inclusion of this secondary prevention measure would dramatically reduce the numbers of children in long-term remediation services.*

*Reading Recovery was used as a case example of a secondary prevention measure to test this hypothesis. Data were gathered on 116 Reading Recovery students and 129 random sample children in first grade and fourth grade in 45 schools. Findings are promising and support the investment of resources in a short-term secondary prevention option for young children having literacy difficulties at the outset of schooling.*

In a poetic parable, Malins (1936) spoke of a community with a dangerous cliff over which many had fallen. Some called for a fence around the edge of the cliff to prevent the falls, while others argued for an ambulance in the valley to rescue the injured. In the poem, the cry for the ambulance carried the day even though a sensible few could hardly bear the nonsense.

Then an old sage remarked: "It's a marvel to me
That people give far more attention
To repairing results than to stopping the cause,
When they'd much better aim at prevention.
Let us stop at its source all this mischief," cried he,
"Come, neighbors and friends, let us rally;
If the cliff we will fence we might almost dispense
With the ambulance down in the valley." (p. 273)

The poem is analogous to the way that schools generally provide assistance to children with learning difficulties: usually providing help after the occurrence of a problem rather than at the first sign of trouble. As a result, by the time help arrives, the problem is often so serious that long-term support is needed, and there is little hope that the problem can ever truly be remedied.

In the early 1960s, for example, children who were not making progress with classroom instruction were either retained in grade level or referred to special services staff for evaluation and possible placement in special education. Now, 40 years later, there are few notable changes in these views toward problem learners. Remedial services through Title I and special education have become today's response to problem learners. Many primary children receive Title I remedial services throughout their elementary years. For others, Title I serves as a waiting area, providing interim services until the students' performance lags far enough behind their peers and they become eligible for special education services (Gaffney, 1998). Implicit in these decisions is the notion of waiting for failure to occur and then providing remediation. The possibility of prevention is overlooked. Ambulances are still being placed in the valley.

In fact, with a few notable exceptions such as Head Start, prevention has rarely been acknowledged as part of educational theory and practice. Perhaps the exploration of preventive moves in education has been slowed by some old ways of thinking, such as the belief that given enough time, children will mature into readers. Prevention has, however, long been a hallmark of the health and sciences field (Zins, Conye, & Ponti, 1988). In the section that follows, we will describe how a health sciences view of prevention can inform a framework for prevention in the field of education.

## A Conceptual Framework for Defining Prevention

Caplan (1961, 1964), credited with providing a conceptual model for later prevention work, identified three levels of prevention: primary, secondary, and tertiary. Pianta (1990) used Caplan's model as a framework for placing special education into a continuum of prevention.

### Primary Prevention

An example of primary prevention in the health field is measles inoculation. Primary prevention is available to everyone even though they have not been identified as having a problem. The prevention is offered because there is widespread agreement that doing so will prevent problems from occurring (Pianta, 1990). In schools, the equivalent to an inoculation is classroom instruction. Classroom instruction provided to everyone serves as the first line of prevention against subsequent problems and reduces their rate of occurrence.

Holdaway (1978) identified the following preventive measures against reading difficulties that are present in classrooms:

- sensitive observation of reading behaviors (using Clay's Observation Tasks as a guide)
- timely intervention as problems arise (day to day, moment by moment, individual when needed)
- growing independence in the learner
- early use of multi-disciplinary teamwork when learners are having difficulty

Few would disagree that effective classroom programs are needed as primary prevention (Snow, Burns, & Griffin, 1998). Good first teaching, however, must be paired with safety nets for children who need something extra (Fountas & Pinnell, 1999) because even with excellent staff development and well-trained teachers, some children will still need a secondary intervention to prevent future problems (Leslie & Allen, 1999).

## Secondary Prevention

Secondary prevention is directed to a select group of the population who have been identified as having a greater chance of developing problems in a specific area. In the health field, for example, it is well accepted that the elderly are more likely to suffer consequences of the flu, so they are targeted to receive flu shots. Secondary prevention is selective and involves early diagnosis and treatment of problems before they develop into potentially handicapping conditions (Keogh, Wilcoxen, & Bernheimer, 1986). While effective primary prevention should reduce the incidence of the disorder and prevalence rates, effective secondary prevention should decrease the duration and severity of individual cases (Lorion, 1983).

Primary prevention, or classroom instruction, alone can not work for each individual child because it does not address the unique differences found among young learners. A secondary prevention allows early identification of potential problems, enabling the school system to intervene appropriately. Clay (1991) articulates this reasoning well:

> If we can detect the process of learning to read 'going wrong' within a year of school entry then it would be folly to wait several years before providing children with extra help. An earlier offer of effective help to the child might reduce the magnitude of reading problems in later schooling. (p. 13)

## Tertiary Prevention

Tertiary prevention becomes necessary after the occurrence of serious and enduring problems. The most common forms of tertiary prevention in public schools are special education, retention in grade level, and long-term remedial services such as Title I. At the tertiary level the focus shifts from preventing problems to remediating them in order to lessen the effect of the problem as much as possible.

Federal funds are often targeted at the tertiary level in the form of special education and remedial programs, but usually there are no mandates or funding from the government for primary and secondary prevention (Pianta, 1990). This means, in effect, that a disproportional amount of resources are directed at the tertiary level of prevention in the education system. By contrast, in the medical field it would be unusual to focus so much attention on tertiary prevention while ignoring the opportunities for primary and secondary prevention. Indeed, if the overriding goal of a prevention perspective is to reduce the need for extensive tertiary services by providing effective primary and secondary services (Keogh et al., 1986), it would seem that money spent on earlier prevention would be a more responsible expenditure of education funds.

## *The Authors' Hypothesis*

While there can be no guaranteed inoculation against future failure, we hypothesize that effective secondary prevention efforts in education can reduce the need for more expensive, long-term tertiary measures that are needed after the occurrence of failure. We view secondary prevention as

> the first action in a chain of interactions (or transactions) between the child (or family) and environment in which each causes the other to evolve along a new path. Children who experience early intervention may follow more preferred paths in all the social systems in which they live—family, school, and economy. (Barnett & Escobar, 1987, p. 396)

We are referring to secondary prevention efforts that include early identification0 of the learning process going wrong, followed by timely, effective, short-term intervening actions. These efforts reside within school contexts and are influenced by many factors within the school, including the quality of primary prevention practices in classrooms.

## Making a Case for Secondary Prevention in Education

One of the earliest and most comprehensive explorations of the impact of secondary preventive educational programs was the Ypsilanti Perry Preschool Project (Schweinhart & Weikart, 1980; Weikart et al., 1978), designed to help economically disadvantaged children at high academic risk cope with school and adult life in mainstream society. A report on the Perry Preschool Project children through age 15 showed greater school achievement up the grades, fewer years in special education services, and greater satisfaction and aspirations by parents about the participating children's schooling than for children in the nonparticipating control group. The Perry Preschool Project also encouraged consideration of the cost benefits of prevention by citing issues such as retention, special education, Title I, drop-out, future delinquency, projected lifetime earnings, incarceration, welfare assistance, use of social services, and increased possibility of participation in the labor force.

In the area of literacy, Juel's (1988) longitudinal study of children from Grade 1 to Grade 4 offers compelling support for the need for secondary prevention in schools. She found that the probability that a poor reader at the end of Grade 1 would remain a poor reader at the end of Grade 4 was very high (.88). If a child was at least an average reader in Grade 1, the probability that that child would become a poor reader in Grade 4 was only .12. Therefore, evidence is strong that poor first-grade readers almost invariably remain poor readers by the end of fourth grade. Conversely, average readers in Grade 1 are likely to be average in Grade 4.

Wasik and Slavin (1993) suggested that because remediation after the primary grades is largely ineffective, it may be easier to prevent learning problems than to remediate them in later grades:

> Considering how much progress the average reader makes in reading between the first and last days of first grade, it is easy to see how students who fail to learn to read during first grade are far behind their peers and will have difficulty catching up. (p. 179)

Waiting creates gaps or deficits, with serious consequences for a child's school achievement, personality, and confidence. When a child has practiced primitive skills and daily habituated the wrong responses, there will be blocks to learning (Clay, 1993a). Juel (1988) argues that it is hard to make up for years of lost experiences, citing the lack of success in comprehension studies with older readers.

Several researchers have argued for secondary prevention from a cost-benefit perspective (Barnett, 1985a, 1985b; Barnett & Escobar, 1987; Gaffney, 1994; Graden et al., 1985; Keogh et al., 1986; Schweinhart & Weikart, 1980; Weikart et al., 1978). Barnett and Escobar argued that intervening early with disadvantaged children can yield an economic return in reductions needed for special education services, reductions in crime and delinquency, increased employment and earnings, and decreased dependence on welfare. They also cited outcomes for which dollar values could not be estimated, such as increased educational attainment and decreased births to teenage mothers.

There is growing evidence that intervening early with secondary preventions does indeed provide promising results (for example, Clay, 1979). In a longitudinal study of children receiving tutoring in first grade (Vellutino et al., 1996; Vellutino, Scanlon, & Tanzman, 1998), 67.1% of poor readers who received daily one-to-one tutoring scored within the average or above average range on standardized tests of reading achievement after one semester of tutoring. Results also confirmed that early, labor-intensive secondary prevention can be reasonably effective in distinguishing between children who are classified as learning disabled and those who need not be so classified when provided adequate intervention.

Several other examples of early secondary prevention have shown some measure of success within the past decade (Hiebert, Colt, Catto, & Gury, 1992; Juel, 1996; Pinnell, Lyons, DeFord, Bryk, & Seltzer, 1994; Slavin, Madden, Karweit, Livermon, & Dolan, 1990; Taylor, Frye, Short, & Shearer, 1992). These quite different interventions—including Success for All, Reading Recovery, a restructured Chapter 1 program, a small-group in-classroom program, and a tutoring program—all demonstrated that children with reading difficulties can benefit from early attention and intensive tutoring (Leslie & Allen, 1999).

Pianta (1990) identified three requirements for implementing prevention programs in schools: (a) identifying and defining the outcomes to be prevented, (b) developing programs for screening and monitoring risk, and (c) discussing the scope of services to be offered by schools. When investing in prevention programs, systems are taking out insurance to protect against future failure. The amount of the investment depends on how much protection the system needs and wants.

In summary, there is evidence of the benefits of prevention from a wide variety of studies. There is also evidence that waiting yields gaps that are difficult to close. In this paper we propose to examine the case for secondary prevention using the example of Reading Recovery, a short-term literacy tutoring program designed for the lowest-achieving students who have fallen behind their peers after one year of classroom instruction.

## Exploring Secondary Prevention: Reading Recovery as a Case Example

Any program that claims to be preventive must be able to demonstrate that the treatment has an effect on the problem (Morris, 1999). Therefore, in our examination of Reading Recovery as an example of secondary prevention, we questioned whether or not Reading Recovery prevented or substantially reduced literacy difficulties among the children served over time. We also questioned how the literacy performance of these children aligned with the average class performance in their school settings. In order to investigate these questions, we used a longitudinal research design. Before we describe the methodology we would like to review some challenges of conducting this type of research.

### Acknowledging the Challenges of Longitudinal Research

Longitudinal intervention research can be classified into three categories: efficacy, effectiveness, and efficiency (Feinstein, 1977). Efficacy studies are used to determine if the intervention works under optimal conditions. While they are informative, they do not address the application in naturalistic settings without external controls. Effectiveness studies, however, assess whether the intervention works in the field and can be integrated into existing systems. Efficiency studies refer to analysis of costs and benefits of the intervention. The study reported here assessed effectiveness, examining whether the intervention worked in schools and if the effectiveness extended beyond the end of the intervention or treatment (Black & Holden, 1995).

Two concerns about the validity of longitudinal studies involve sample selection and attrition (Barnett & Escobar, 1987). Target populations need to be defined so that the population actually represented by the sample is clear. In this study, two target populations were selected: Reading Recovery students and non-Reading Recovery students. The Reading Recovery target population included first-grade children across the state who were tested for Reading Recovery at the beginning of the school year and subsequently met the requirements for successfully discontinuing from Reading Recovery services. The target population for the non-Reading Recovery random sample group (to represent average literacy performance) included all first graders not served by Reading Recovery in the schools selected for the study. Procedures used to select samples from each of the target populations are described later in the methodology section.

To offset problems of attrition in longitudinal studies, caution was taken to produce a sample for analysis that did not differ from the initial sample. Both the magnitude of the attrition and the pattern of the attrition were considered, as suggested by Menard (1991). In this study, analyses included only the subjects remaining three years later, at the end of Grade 4. The remaining sample was compared to the initial sample, and the pattern of attrition was insignificant.

The study presented here met the general definition of longitudinal research (Menard, 1991). First, data were collected for each subject at five distinct time periods. Second, subjects were comparable from one period to the next. And finally, analyses included comparison of data across periods.

This study was designed to describe patterns of change, not to establish causal relationships. Change was explored across two major dimensions: student performance data on a variety of measures and classroom teachers' self-reported perceptions of the children's literacy behaviors in their classrooms.

Inherent problems of longitudinal studies—sampling procedures, attrition of subjects, cohort differences, and testing effects (Nesselroade & Baltes, 1974)—are acknowledged. Because of these and other potential limitations, a field-trial study with a different cohort of subjects was conducted, beginning one year prior to the study reported here. Some changes were made in sampling procedures and data collection procedures based on field-trial data, yet findings in both studies were similar. We acknowledge that, ultimately, only findings that emerge strongly and repeatedly across multiple studies employing different methods can be trusted (Walberg & Reynolds, 1997).

## Reading Recovery as an Example of Secondary Prevention

Children identified and selected for Reading Recovery service have already had one year of classroom instruction in kindergarten and, after exposure to that primary prevention, have emerged from the whole population as children who are beginning to experience reading and writing difficulties. These children receive Reading Recovery lessons from a specially trained teacher for an intensive 30 minutes daily for approximately 12 to 20 weeks. Each child's series of lessons is uniquely designed and individually delivered to suit that child's needs and progressions. The ultimate goal is to enable these young readers and writers to use strategies effectively and independently so that they can function successfully within an average literacy setting in their classrooms without the need of a tertiary or remedial program. In other words, the aim is a return to primary prevention—good classroom programs for all children.

Reading Recovery uses systematic and simultaneous replication studies to document program outcomes for all children served, adhering to duplication of methods, instruments, and time lines across many sites. Replication is important because it allows scientists to verify research results (Frymier, Barber, Gansneder, & Robertson, 1989).

There is also evidence of subsequent gains in follow-up studies in New Zealand (Clay, 1993b), in the United States (Askew & Frasier, 1994; DeFord, Pinnell, Lyons, & Place, 1990; Jaggar & Simic, 1996), and in Australia (Rowe, 1995). The study presented here adds to the exploration of secondary prevention by examining subsequent gains of former Reading Recovery children.

## Rationales for Design Decisions

Given the cautions expressed by authorities in the previous sections, it is important to provide rationales for decisions related to design and methodology of longitudinal studies. Relevant decisions are explained below.

**Conducting multiple studies.** A series of cross-sectional studies of former Reading Recovery children (Askew, Wickstrom, & Frasier, 1996) preceded the longitudinal study presented here. While these cross-sectional studies provide compelling information, longitudinal studies were needed to observe change over time by following intact groups of children (Goldstein, 1979).

Neither a cross-sectional study nor a single longitudinal study can eliminate questions about group membership. Problems can be remedied somewhat through designs in which the recruitment of multiple samples is separated in time (Black & Holden, 1995). Therefore, a field study with different samples began a year prior to the study presented here in order to test methods and to serve as a basis of comparison relative to outcomes.

**Use of average band as a comparative measure of average progress.** There are several ways to assess the stability of program outcomes. In these studies, Reading Recovery students' subsequent literacy progress was compared with progress of children defined as performing within an average band of achievement in the same schools.

In order to test whether former Reading Recovery students continued to demonstrate average levels of achievement after first grade, the design called for a validation of average progress. Using a randomly selected group of non-Reading Recovery children, means for literacy measures were used to create an average band of one standard deviation above and below the mean. The band was used to define average performance and to describe the progress of former discontinued Reading Recovery children relative to that definition of average in Grades 2, 3, and 4. In addition to aggregated data, the number or percentage of individual children attaining successful academic performance is provided whenever appropriate.

**Study of discontinued children.** Reading Recovery is designed to serve the lowest-achieving students in the first-grade cohort in a school and leads to one of two positive outcomes: successful performance within an average literacy setting in the classroom or recommendation for additional assessment and possibly additional services. Children whose programs are discontinued have successfully completed the program as evidenced by scores on the tasks in *An Observation Survey of Early Literacy Achievement* (Clay, 1993a), having a system of strategic reading and writing behaviors in place, and attaining literacy performance that is within the class average. Service is discontinued as soon as it is determined that the child can engage with and profit from classroom instruction.

Students who have been discontinued from Reading Recovery should demonstrate average-band performance with their peers immediately following the intervention in Grade 1. Also, if Reading Recovery fits the definition of a secondary prevention, the reading difficulty should not develop into a handicapping condition over time. We attempted to determine if the students' average range of performance persisted in subsequent years. Limited data were also available on not-discontinued children who had the opportunity for a full Reading Recovery program but did not achieve average-band performance.

**Rationales for selection of measures.** Three measures were considered important to the stakeholders in this study: (a) performance on standardized measures that included assessment of comprehension (Hiebert, 1994; Shanahan & Barr, 1995), (b) performance on a high-stakes state assessment of literacy skills, and (c) classroom teachers' reported perceptions of children's literacy performance. Therefore, measures to explore elimination or reduction of literacy difficulties included the Gates-MacGinitie Reading Test (GMRT; MacGinitie & MacGinitie, 1989), reading and writing scores from a state-mandated assessment instrument, and a classroom teacher questionnaire. In addition, a test of oral text reading was used to provide information about oral reading behaviors and text reading levels.

## Sources of Data and Time Lines

The GMRT was selected as the standardized reading measure because of ease of administration, conservation of time in administration and scoring, general acceptance and wide use in schools, the inclusion of a comprehension measure, and the ability to compare scores across grade levels at equal intervals. Level R, Form K was used in first grade in order to get pre- and post-test scores. For the remaining levels, Form K for the appropriate grade level was administered.

The Texas Assessment of Academic Skills (TAAS) yielded reading and writing scores. This measure was selected because of the importance placed on results by the state, districts, schools, teachers, and community members. The TAAS is not considered a minimum skills test but a more robust measure of literacy performance.

The test of oral text reading comprised a graded series of passages leveled and tested at The Ohio State University. Running records were used to determine the highest level read by a child at 90% accuracy or higher (Clay, 1993b). Passages for Levels 14–16 were taken from end-of-first-grade materials, Levels 18–20 from second-grade texts, Levels 22–24 from third-grade texts, and Level 26 from a fourth-grade reader.

Questionnaires were developed to elicit classroom teachers' reported perceptions of literacy performance of all children in the study (see Appendix A). Questionnaires were also developed to gather information about the participating schools (see Appendix B).

Entry data (Observation Survey and GMRT) were collected for both the Reading Recovery group and non-Reading Recovery random sample group at the beginning of first grade. The GMRT, tests of oral reading, and classroom teacher questionnaires were administered during the last month of each school year. Data for the TAAS were collected at the end of Grades 3 and 4. Data were collected by classroom teachers, Reading Recovery teachers, and Reading Recovery teacher leaders. Reading Recovery teacher leaders submitted scores on the TAAS.

## Procedures

**Selection of schools and subjects.** Two groups of children were identified for the study: a group of Reading Recovery children and a group of children representing average classroom performance. Both groups received primary prevention services (classroom instruction), but the Reading Recovery group also received secondary prevention services.

Subjects were selected in the fall of 1995 in order to collect entry data. Selection was based on a series of sampling procedures. Using a table of random numbers, 50 schools were randomly selected from more than 800 schools with Reading Recovery in one state. Participation was high, with 45 schools taking part in the first year. At the outset of the study, educators from each of the schools completed a form describing the school on a variety of factors (see Appendix B). Table 1 provides descriptive data about the 45 participating schools.

At the beginning of Grade 1, it was impossible to identify all of the children who would be served by Reading Recovery or how they would progress. Therefore, we used the following categories to select a large sample of Reading Recovery children from the 45 participating schools:

- all children served by Reading Recovery at the beginning of the academic year (ranging from 4 to 12 students per school depending on the number of Reading Recovery teachers),
- up to eight children demonstrating need for service by Reading Recovery but not served at the beginning of the year because all slots were taken (to bring the total number of potential Reading Recovery children to 12 per school), and
- six children randomly selected, using a table of random numbers, from the remaining first-grade population.

From this large group of students identified at the beginning of first grade, two groups of students were selected for this study: 218 discontinued Reading Recovery students and 244 random sample students not served by Reading Recovery. Limited data were gathered on a small group of children who had full programs but did not meet discontinuing criteria.

At the end of fourth grade, data were available for 116 of the original 218 Reading Recovery students and 129 of the 244 random sample children. Although attrition rates were higher than expected, the pattern of attrition posed no problems. Differences between the initial sample and the remaining sample were minimal and did not favor either group.

The samples for the Reading Recovery group and random sample group represented similar ethnic diversity (see Table 2). There were more males in the Reading Recovery group (60%) than in the random sample group (52%).

**Table 1.** Description of Participating Schools at Beginning of Study (Shown as Percentage of Schools)

| LEVEL OF READING RECOVERY COVERAGE | | ETHNIC REPRESENTATION | |
|---|---|---|---|
| High | 53% | Majority Anglo | 33% |
| Moderate | 20% | Majority African-American | 2% |
| Low | 27% | Majority Hispanic | 27% |
| | | No Majority | 31% |
| READING RECOVERY TEACHERS | | No Data | 7% |
| All Trained | 44% | | |
| All In Training | 13% | FUNDING SOURCES FOR READING RECOVERY | |
| Some Trained | 42% | Title I | 64% |
| or In Training | | Local | 11% |
| | | State | 11% |
| YEARS OF READING RECOVERY IN THE SCHOOL | | Multiple | 13% |
| 1 | 20% | | |
| 2 | 31% | ELIGIBILITY FOR TITLE I FUNDING | |
| 3 | 16% | Yes | 78% |
| 4 | 7% | No | 22% |
| 5 | 9% | | |
| 6 or more | 17% | DESCRIPTION OF LOCALE | |
| | | Urban | 20% |
| OTHER ROLES OF READING RECOVERY TEACHERS | | Suburban | 40% |
| Title I/Groups | 67% | Rural | 7% |
| Classroom Teacher | 31% | Small Town | 33% |
| Reading Specialist | 9% | | |
| Special Education | 7% | CONSIDERED HIGH-NEED SCHOOL | |
| Part-Time | 4% | Yes | 71% |
| Other | 7% | No | 29% |
| (multiple models in some schools) | | | |

*Note:* All data are described at level of the school and represent responses from all 45 participating schools.

**Table 2.** Race/Ethnicity for Random Sample and Discontinued Reading Recovery Students

| | READING RECOVERY | RANDOM SAMPLE |
|---|---|---|
| White | 51% | 52% |
| Hispanic | 30% | 26% |
| African-American | 18% | 15% |
| Other* | 1% | 7% |

*includes Asian and Native American

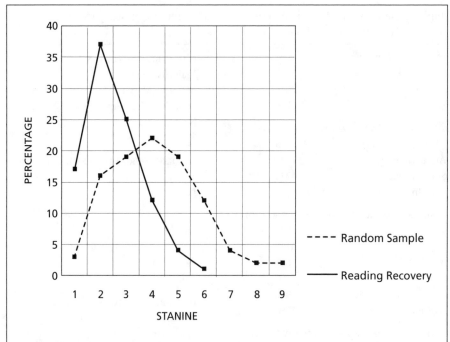

**Figure 1.** Stanine Distribution on Gates-MacGinitie Total at Beginning of Study (Enrty Date)

## Results

There were significant differences (p < .01) between the first-grade entry scores of Reading Recovery children and random sample children. These differences validated the selection of an identified group needing secondary prevention.

Figure 1 shows the Gates stanine distribution for each group upon entry to first grade. The mean GMRT stanine for the random sample group was 4 compared with 2 for the discontinued Reading Recovery group. This finding documents group differences between the Reading Recovery students and the random sample that existed prior to the intervention.

Entry data on Observation Survey measures, as shown in Figure 2, also documented significant performance differences between the two groups at the outset of the study.

Table 3 shows achievement outcomes at the end of Grade 4 as measured by running records (Clay, 1993b), TAAS, and GMRT.

On running records, the test of oral text reading, both groups read above-level materials at 90% accuracy or higher at the end of Grade 4, showing change over time in oral reading of continuous text. The mean text reading level for Reading Recovery children was 32 compared to 33 for the random sample group.

Scores on the reading subtest of the TAAS also provided evidence of continuing gains of Reading Recovery children. At the end of fourth grade, the mean reading

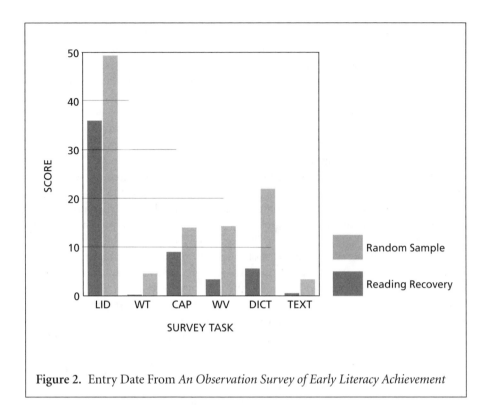

**Figure 2.** Entry Date From *An Observation Survey of Early Literacy Achievement*

**Table 3.** Outcome Data at End of Grade 4

|  | READING RECOVERY | RANDOM SAMPLE |
|---|---|---|
| Mean Oral Text Reading Level | 32 | 33 |
| (Level 26 = Grade 4 materials) | | |
| Children Scoring 90% or Better | 95% | 98% |
| on Text Level 26 or Above | | |
| Mean Vocabulary Stanine (Gates) | 4 | 5 |
| Mean Comprehension Stanine (Gates) | 4 | 5 |
| Mean Total Stanine (Gates) | 4 | 5 |
| Children Scoring Stanine 4 or Better | 63% | 84% |
| on Gates Comprehension | | |
| Mean Reading Score on Texas | 80 | 86 |
| Assessment of Academic Skills (TAAS) | | |
| Children Passing TAAS Reading Test | 85% | 90% |
| Mean Score on TAAS Writing Sample | 2.3 | 2.7 |
| Children Passing TAAS Writing Sample | 90% | 97% |

subtest score on the TAAS for Reading Recovery children was 80 compared with 86 for the random group. (A score of 70 is passing.) Eighty-five percent of the Reading Recovery children passed the reading test; 90% of the random group passed. On the writing sample, 90% of the Reading Recovery group and 97% of the random group had passing scores.

Further evidence of gains for Reading Recovery children was revealed by comparing entry stanine distributions to distributions in Grade 4. The distribution of scores moved to include more average and some high stanine scores as compared with low scores with little variation at the beginning of Grade 1.

One reason for selecting the GMRT was the ability to use extended scale scores (ESS) to examine gains across years of testing. ESS were developed to follow progress over a period of several years on a single, continuous scale. The ESS measures reading achievement in equal units. For example, a difference of 50 units represents the same difference all along the scale. Gains in ESS scores for the Reading Recovery and random sample groups across all four years of the study are shown in Table 4.

Gates vocabulary and comprehension scores were not available in first grade because the form used to compare fall and spring growth yielded only a total score (Level R, Form K). Therefore, total score gains, which included comprehension measures in Grades 2, 3, and 4, were used across the grades. Gains in Grade 1 for Reading Recovery children provided powerful evidence of accelerated progress. As shown in Table 4, Reading Recovery gains surpassed those of their classroom peers between Grades 2 and 3 and closely matched gains between Grades 3 and 4. This finding provided compelling evidence of continuing annual literacy gains for former Reading Recovery children—gains that closely matched those of their classmates.

ESS scores were used to create a path of progress for the random sample group to represent average performance and progress. An average band of one standard devia-

**Table 4.** Gains on Gates-MacGinitie Reading Test Across Four Time Intervals (Reported in Extended Scale Score Gains)

|  | GRADE-LEVEL INTERVALS | | | | |
|  | Pre 1–Post 1 | 1–2 | 2–3 | 3–4 | Total Gains |
| --- | --- | --- | --- | --- | --- |
| VOCABULARY | | | | | |
| Reading Recovery | na | na | 33 | 23 | na |
| Random Sample | na | na | 29 | 24 | na |
| COMPREHENSION | | | | | |
| Reading Recovery | na | na | 40 | 25 | na |
| Random Sample | na | na | 34 | 28 | na |
| TOTAL | | | | | |
| Reading Recovery | 162 | 42 | 37 | 27 | 268 |
| Random Sample | 118 | 47 | 27 | 27 | 219 |

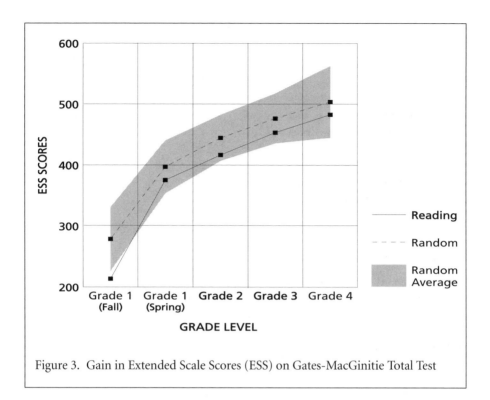

Figure 3. Gain in Extended Scale Scores (ESS) on Gates-MacGinitie Total Test

tion above and below the mean accounted for variability in average classroom performance. In Figure 3, ESS total scores across the five testing administrations were plotted for both groups, and an average band of performance is shown. Reading Recovery children remained within the average band of classroom performance at each testing point after the intervention.

Classroom teachers completed questionnaires about each child in both groups each year. Their reported perceptions of the children, shown in Table 5, validate assessment data indicating that most of the Reading Recovery children were performing within expected ranges of their classrooms at the end of fourth grade. Few of these initially low-performing children were receiving literacy services outside the classroom.

Reading Recovery children who had a full program but did not discontinue were also studied on a limited basis. At the end of Grade 4, 36 of these children remained in the stu dy. On the test of oral text reading, 17% successfully read materials at or above level at the end of Grade 2, 38% at the end of Grade 3, and 50% at the end of Grade 4— evidence of continued growth. Fourth-grade classroom teachers reported that 27% of these children had a strong average-to-high reading ability (3 to 5 on a 5-point Likert scale). Of the children remaining in this group, only one-third were receiving learning disabilities or Title I services for reading. Although data on these children were limited, findings are promising. More investigation of not-discontinued children is called for.

**Table 5.** Reported Data From Classroom Teachers at End of Grade 4

|  | READING RECOVERY | RANDOM SAMPLE |
|---|---|---|
| Placed in Materials At or Above Grade Level | 84% | 91% |
| Not Receiving Title I or LD Literacy Services | 84% | 98% |
| Classroom Teacher Ratings<br>of Reading Ability as Strong Average to High<br>(3–5 on a 5-point Likert scale) | 74% | 86% |
| Classroom Teacher Ratings<br>of Positive Attitudes Toward Reading<br>(3–5 on a 5-point scale) | 76% | 90% |

## Summary and Discussion

It was argued earlier that effective secondary prevention is the first action in a chain of interactions or transactions that lead children to follow more preferred literacy paths in their school settings. Using the case example of Reading Recovery, we argue that secondary prevention has a distinctive and promising role (a) in closing the literacy achievement gap at the outset of schooling, (b) in reducing the need for tertiary prevention and freeing up those services for those who really need them, and (c) in creating a systemic plan for prevention in which all interactions are considered in preventing literacy failure. These arguments call for schools to consider policies and practices for preventing failure that include the full range of prevention—primary, secondary, and tertiary.

### Preferred Paths

Evidence that secondary prevention leads to preferred paths of literacy achievement is shown in subsequent classroom performance. Findings in this study indicate that a secondary prevention program, in this case Reading Recovery, closes or narrows initial achievement gaps in classrooms. Children who are successful in secondary prevention programs are fully assimilated into primary prevention (classroom) programs once more. There is also evidence that a return to primary prevention programs, along with other interactions within the life and schooling of the children, fosters subsequent achievement. At the end of fourth grade, the majority of the discontinued Reading Recovery children had scores considered to be average or meeting passing criteria on standardized and criterion measures—a very satisfactory outcome in their school setting. They were generally perceived by their teachers as performing within average ranges of their classrooms, providing further evidence that the children followed preferred paths as an outcome of this secondary prevention opportunity.

Findings in the Reading Recovery case example match Juel's (1988) finding that children who are average readers in Grade 1 remain average readers in Grade 4. It is imperative, then, that all children have opportunities for secondary prevention in

Grade 1 to realize average performance in later years. Findings also support Shanahan and Barr's (1995) proposition that when secondary prevention options bring children to average and they continue to progress at average rates, there are major implications for the timing of special support and the allocation of resources. Secondary prevention can reduce the incidence and the prevalence of a particular problem—in this case, literacy failure.

Many factors may affect a child's continuing performance on literacy tasks following an intervention, including subsequent instructional experiences (Frater & Staniland, 1994). Shanahan and Barr (1995) suggest that while an intervention may accelerate children's progress, instruction that is responsive to higher achievement is needed for the promise of the intervention to be realized. It is important, then, to institutionalize early secondary prevention as part of the overall system of delivering education, serving as a first step in a process of promoting literacy learning at all levels of schooling.

Relatively few of the Reading Recovery children were placed in tertiary or remedial settings. Approximately 85% of the children were not receiving learning disabilities or Title I reading support in fourth grade. These findings support the argument of Vellutino et al. (1996) that

> to render a diagnosis of specific reading disability in the absence of early and labor-intensive remedial reading that has been tailored to the child's individual needs is, at best, a hazardous and dubious enterprise, given all the stereotypes attached to this diagnosis. (p. 632)

Findings also support Pianta's (1990) notion that prevention does not replace all remedial programs, but it lowers the stress on such programs and reserves them for children with more severe problems.

## Change Over Time

Shanahan and Barr (1995) suggested that children's progress is usually accelerated during the period of support, but they questioned whether the rate of learning continues at an accelerated or average rate or whether it returns to slow progress as shown prior to the intervention. Studies have generally shown diminished levels of learning once support has been removed (Bronfenbrenner, 1974; Page & Grandon, 1981). Yet in the secondary prevention study reported here, a large number of former Reading Recovery children who reached an average range of classroom literacy performance in Grade 1 continued to demonstrate an average range of grade-level expectations in subsequent years.

In fact, findings in this case example indicate a general trend toward higher performance for Reading Recovery children across the grades. For example, state assessment data showed an increase across time in individual performance. The percentage of Reading Recovery children passing the reading subtest in Grade 3 was 72%, while 85% passed the test in Grade 4. Others (Rowe, 1995; Shanahan & Barr, 1995) have documented this trend, offering support for a successful return to good primary prevention: classrooms that continue to prevent problems that could lead to long-term remediation.

Studies point to a tentative hold on reading and writing progress in the year or two after the Reading Recovery experience, but an increasingly firm hold on progress similar to that of their class average by Grade 4. Based on her research, Clay (1993b) recommends that schools adopt a watch-dog role for former Reading Recovery children and monitor their progress sensitively, providing further help if needed. She suggests that "although Reading Recovery children may perform well in their classes they remain at-risk children for two or more years after completion of their program" (p. 96). This suggestion is consistent with the notion of a series of interactions and transactions that lead to sustaining preferred paths in literacy settings in schools.

A large Australian study by Rowe (1995) found that Reading Recovery, as an early action followed by a series of interactions within school programs, distributed Reading Recovery children across the same range as the remainder of the school population but with fewer low scores by Grades 5 and 6. The longitudinal study presented here supports Rowe's findings of changed distributions over time.

All secondary prevention efforts should include examination of implications across time, not only of the intervening actions, but also of the subsequent interactions and opportunities. Therefore, only a system perspective of prevention as part of a chain of interactions enables educators to evaluate the parts of a prevention plan and the relationship of all parts to the conceptual whole.

## Challenges

If secondary prevention is an early action in a chain of interactions between children and their school environment, issues of program implementation within the school are crucial. Outcomes of secondary prevention programs must be interpreted in light of factors such as age of the implementation within the school, capacity for serving all children needing the service, teacher training and expertise, administrative support, understandings and support from school faculty, classroom and other school programs that support continued progress, and a system for monitoring children's progress and solving problems related to implementation.

While the Reading Recovery case example reported here did not address all implementation challenges, some data were available for examination. For example, 51% of the schools were in their first or second year of Reading Recovery implementation, a tenuous time for examining outcomes. More than half the schools were reporting data on teachers in training, limiting analysis of the full potential of the program. Only about half the schools had adequate teacher resources to serve most of the children needing the support, again limiting examination of the full potential of the prevention effort. Therefore, data should be interpreted in light of such factors. Assessing the efficacy of secondary prevention options calls for the examination of implementation factors as well as post-program environments and their effect on long-term outcomes of programs (Wahlberg & Reynolds, 1997).

"What is possible when we change the design and delivery of traditional education for the children that teachers find hard to teach?" (Clay, 1993b, p. 97). This question guided the explorations that validated the impact of Reading Recovery on the literacy possibilities for young children who find learning to read and write difficult. This question can also guide explorations of subsequent achievement trends of children involved in secondary preventions in their schools and the factors that may influence those trends. While this study offers a promising contribution to that exploration, a challenge goes out for multiple studies employing a variety of methods to explore these trends.

The complexities of examining the long-term effectiveness of prevention efforts in schools are clear. Yet studies such as the case example presented here are adding to a growing body of literature that supports the principle of secondary prevention in schooling—prevention that reduces the duration of serious and enduring problems. These children were initially the lowest literacy performers in their classrooms. Yet because of the compelling findings from the study reported here, we can argue for resources to build strong fences in order to dramatically reduce the number of ambulances down in the valley.

> Better guide well the young than reclaim them when old,
> For the voice of true wisdom is calling.
> "To rescue the fallen is good, but 'tis best
> To prevent other people from falling."
> Better close up the source of temptation and crime
> Than deliver from dungeon or galley;
> Better put a strong fence 'round the top of the cliff
> Than an ambulance down in the valley.
>                                     (Malins, 1936, p. 274)

## References

Askew, B. J., & Frasier, D. F. (1994). Sustained effects of Reading Recovery intervention on the cognitive behaviors of second grade children. *Literacy, Teaching and Learning: An International Journal of Early Literacy, 1,* 87–107.

Askew, B. J., Wickstrom, C., & Frasier, D. F. (1996, April). An exploration of literacy behaviors of children following an early intervention program. Paper presented at the American Educational Research Association Conference, New York, NY.

Barnett, W. S. (1985a). Benefit-cost analysis of the Perry Preschool Program and its long-term effects. *Educational Evaluation and Policy Analysis, 7,* 333–342.

Barnett, W. S. (1985b). The Perry Preschool Program and its long-term effects: A benefit cost analysis. (*High/Scope Early Childhood Policy Papers No. 2*). Ypsilanti, MI: High/Scope Educational Research Foundation.

Barnett, W. S., & Escobar, C. M. (1987). The economics of early educational intervention: A review. *Review of Educational Research, 57*(4), 387–414.

Black, M. M., & Holden, E. W. (1995). Longitudinal intervention research in children's health and development. *Journal of Clinical Child Psychology, 24,* 163–172.

Bronfenbrenner, U. (1974). Is early intervention effective? In M. Guttentag & S. Struening (Eds.), *Handbook of evaluation research Vol. 2* (pp. 519–603). Beverly Hills, CA: Sage.

Caplan, G. (Ed.). (1961). *Prevention of mental disorders in children.* New York: Basic Books.

Caplan, G. (1964). *Principles of preventive psychiatry.* New York: Basic Books.

Clay, M. M. (1979). *Reading: The patterning of complex behavior.* Auckland, New Zealand: Heinemann.

Clay, M. M. (1982). *Observing young readers.* Portsmouth, NH: Heinemann.

Clay, M. M. (1991). *Becoming literate: The construction of inner control.* Portsmouth, NH: Heinemann.

Clay, M. M. (1993a). *An observation survey of early literacy achievement.* Portsmouth, NH: Heinemann.

Clay, M. M. (1993b). *Reading Recovery: A guidebook for teachers in training.* Portsmouth, NH: Heinemann.

DeFord, D. E., Pinnell, G. S., Lyons, C. A., & Place, A. W. (1990). *The Reading Recovery follow-up study, Vol. II 1987–89.* Columbus, OH: The Ohio State University.

Feinstein, A. R. (1977). *Clinical biostatistics.* St. Louis, MO: Mosby.

Fountas, I. C., & Pinnell, G. S. (1999). What does good first teaching mean? In J. S. Gaffney & B. J. Askew (Eds.), *Stirring the waters: The influence of Marie Clay* (pp. 165–185). Portsmouth, NH: Heinemann.

Frater, G., & Staniland, A. (1994). Reading Recovery in New Zealand: A report from the Office of Her Majesty's Chief Inspector of Schools. *Literacy, Teaching and Learning: An International Journal of Early Literacy, 1*(1), 143–162.

Frymier, J., Barber, L., Gansneder, B., & Robertson, N. (1989). Simultaneous replication: A technique for large-scale research. *Phi Delta Kappa, 71,* 228–231.

Gaffney, J. S. (1994). Reading Recovery: Widening the scope of prevention for children at risk of reading failure. In K. D. Wood & B. Algozzine (Eds.), *Teaching reading to high-risk learners* (pp. 231–246). Boston, MA: Allyn and Bacon.

Gaffney, J. S. (1998). The prevention of reading failure: Teaching reading and writing. In J. Osborn & F. Lehr (Eds.), *Literacy for all* (pp. 100–110). New York: Guilford Press.

Goldstein, H. (1979). *The design and analysis of longitudinal studies.* New York: Academic Press.

Graden, J. L., Casey, A., & Christenson, S. L. (1985). Implementing a preferral intervention system: Part I. The model. *Exceptional Children, 51*(5), 377–384.

Hiebert, E. H. (1994). Reading Recovery in the United States: What difference does it make to an age cohort? *Educational Researcher, 23,* 15–25.

Hiebert, E. H., Colt, J. M., Catto, S. L., and Gury, E. C. (1992). Reading and writing of first-grade students in a restructured Chapter 1 program. *American Educational Research Journal, 29,* 545–572.

Holdaway, D. (1978). *The foundations of literacy.* Sydney, Australia: Ashton-Scholastic.

Jaggar, A. M., & Simic, O. (1996). *A four-year follow-up study of Reading Recovery children in New York State: Preliminary report.* New York: New York University, School of Education.

Juel, C. (1996). What makes literacy tutoring effective? *Reading Research Quarterly, 31,* 268–288.

Juel, C. (1988). Learning to read and write: A longitudinal study of 54 children from first through fourth grades. *Journal of Educational Psychology, 80*(4), 437–447.

Keogh, B. K., Wilcoxen, A. G., & Bernheimer, L. (1986). Prevention services for at-risk children: Evidence for policy and practice. In D. C. Farran & J. D. McKinney (Eds.), *Risk in intellectual and psychosocial development* (pp. 287–316). Orlando, FL: Academic Press.

Leslie, L., & Allen, L. (1999). Factors that predict success in an early literacy intervention project. *Reading Research Quarterly, 34*(4), 404–424.

Lorion, R. P. (1983). Evaluating preventive interventions: Guidelines for the serious social change agent. In R. D. Felner, L. A. Jason, J. N. Moritsugu, & S. Farber (Eds.), *Preventive psychology: Theory, research and practice* (pp. 251–268). New York: Pergamon Press.

MacGinitie, W. H., & MacGinitie, R. K. (1989). *Gates-MacGinitie Reading Tests.* Chicago, IL: Riverside Publishing.

Malins, J. (1936). A fence or an ambulance. In H. Felleman (Ed.), *The best loved poems of the American people* (pp. 273–274). Garden City, NY: Garden City Books.

Menard, S. (1991). *Longitudinal research.* Newbury Park, CA: Sage.

Morris, D. (1999). Preventing reading failure in the primary grades. In T. Shanahan & F. V. Rodriguez-Brown, (Eds.), *48th Yearbook of the National Reading Conference* (pp.17–38). Chicago, IL: National Reading Conference.

Nesselroade, J. R., & Baltes, P. B. (1974). Sequential strategies and the role of cohort effects in behavioral development: Adolescent personality (1970–1972) as a sample case. In S. A. Mednick, M. Harway, & K. M. Finello (Eds.), *Handbook of longitudinal research* (pp. 55–87). New York: Praeger.

Page, E. B., & Grandon, G. M. (1981). Massive intervention and child intelligence: The Milwaukee Project in critical perspective. *Journal of Special Education, 15,* 239–256.

Pianta, R. C. (1990). Widening the debate on educational reform: Prevention as a viable alternative. *Exceptional Children, 56*(4), 306–313.

Pinnell, G. S., Lyons, C. A., DeFord, D. E., Bryk, A. S., & Seltzer, M. (1994). Comparing instructional models for the literacy education of high-risk first graders. *Reading Research Quarterly, 29,* 8–39.

Rowe, K. J. (1995). Factors affecting students' progress in reading: Key findings from a longitudinal study. *Literacy, Teaching and Learning: An International Journal of Early Literacy, 1,* 57–110.

Schweinhart, L. J., & Weikart, D. P. (1980). *Young children grow up: The effects of the Perry Preschool Program on youths through age 15.* Ypsilanti, MI: High/Scope Educational Research Foundation.

Shanahan, T., & Barr, R. (1995). Reading Recovery: An independent evaluation of the effects of an early instructional intervention for at-risk learners. *Reading Research Quarterly, 30,* 958–996.

Slavin, R. E., Karweit, N. L., & Wasik, B. A. (1992). Preventing early school failure: What works? *Educational Leadership, 50,* 10–19.

Slavin, R. E., Madden, N. A., Karweit, N. L., Livermon, B., & Dolan, L. (1990). Success for all: First-year outcomes of a comprehensive plan for reforming urban education. *American Educational Research Journal, 27,* 255–278.

Snow, C. E., Burns, M. S., & Griffin, P. (1998). *Preventing reading difficulties in young children.* Washington, DC: National Academy Press.

Taylor, B. M., Frye, B., Short, R., & Shearer, B. (1992). Classroom teachers prevent reading failure among low-achieving first grade students. *The Reading Teacher, 45,* 592–598.

Vellutino, F. R., Scanlon, D. M., Sipay, E. R., Small, S. G., Chen, R., Pratt, A., et al. (1996). Cognitive profiles of difficult-to-remediate and readily remediated poor readers: Early intervention as a vehicle for distinguishing between cognitive and experiential deficits as basic causes of specific reading disability. *Journal of Educational Psychology, 88*(4), 601–638.

Vellutino, F. R., Scanlon, D. M., & Tanzman, M. S. (1998). The case for early intervention in diagnosing specific reading disability. *Journal of School Psychology, 30*(4), 367–397.

Walberg, H. J., & Reynolds, A. J. (1997). Longitudinal evaluation of program effectiveness. In B. Spodek & O. N. Saracho (Eds.), *Issues in early childhood educational assessment and evaluation* (pp. 28–47). New York: Teachers College Press.

Wasik, B. A., & Slavin, R. E. (1993). Preventing early reading failure with one-to-one tutoring: A review of five programs. *Reading Research Quarterly, 28,* 179–200.

Weikart, D. P., Bond, J. T., & McNeil, J. T. (1978). *The Ypsilanti Perry Preschool Project: Preschool years and longitudinal results through fourth grade.* Ypsilanti, MI: High/Scope Educational Research Foundation.

Zins, J. E., Conye, R. K., & Ponto, C. R. (1988). Primary prevention: Expanding the impact of psychological services in the schools. *School Psychology Review, 17,* 542–549.

# Appendix A

## Classroom Teacher Questionnaire

To the Classroom Teacher: We are interested in the reading and writing performance of children in your grade level. Would you please help by completing this questionnaire about the child named below and returning it to _____.
All information will remain confidential and will be reported as aggregated data only. No names of children, teachers, schools, or districts will be used.

Child's Name or Number _____

Classroom Teacher _____

Grade Level _____ School District _____

1. Check the appropriate ethnic description:

   _____ Anglo               _____ Hispanic            _____ Native American

   _____ African-American    _____ Asian               _____ Other

2. Is this child _____ male?    _____ female?

3. Is this child currently receiving any of the following services? Check all that apply.

   _____ Title I Readinmg

   _____ ESL
          If yes, for how much time each day? _____

   _____ Speech
          If yes, for what services? _____

   _____ LD Resource for Reading
          If yes, for how much time each day? _____

   _____ LD Resource for Math
          If yes, for how much time each day? _____

   _____ Content Mastery for Reading
   _____ Other (Please describe and be specific)

4. Has this child been retained in previous years? _____

   If so, at what grade level? _____

   Will this child be retained this year? _____

5. How would you categorize this child's overall reading performance? Check one.

_____Excellent _____ Good _____ Average _____ Fair _____ Poor

6. Please give specific reasons why this child's performance is categorized in this way.

_____

_____

_____

7. What grade did this child receive in reading on the last report card? _____

8. Does this child work in on-level reading materials in your classroom? _____

9. Rate the attributes that best describe the child by circling the appropriate numbers.

| | Weak | | | | Strong |
|---|---|---|---|---|---|
| Reading Ability | 1 | 2 | 3 | 4 | 5 |
| Writing Ability | 1 | 2 | 3 | 4 | 5 |
| Attitude Toward Reading | 1 | 2 | 3 | 4 | 5 |
| Attitude Toward Writing | 1 | 2 | 3 | 4 | 5 |
| Chooses to Read When Time Allows | 1 | 2 | 3 | 4 | 5 |
| Selects Books on His/Her Own | 1 | 2 | 3 | 4 | 5 |
| Independent in Class Work | 1 | 2 | 3 | 4 | 5 |
| Tries Hard | 1 | 2 | 3 | 4 | 5 |
| Completes Work | 1 | 2 | 3 | 4 | 5 |
| Attends Well in Class Work | 1 | 2 | 3 | 4 | 5 |
| Responds in Group Discussions | 1 | 2 | 3 | 4 | 5 |

10. Other Comments:

_____

_____

_____

_____

_____

The return of this completed questionnaire constitutes your informed consent to participate in this study of young readers and writers. We appreciate your help!

# Appendix B

## School Information Questionnaire

**Note:** All school data will be reported as aggregated data. Names of schools and districts will not appear in any reports generated from this study. Page 1 is to be completed during the first year of the study (Grade 1) and page 2 during the final year of the study (Grade 4).

Name of School _____

Name of District _____

Name of Person Completing Form _____

*Please answer the following questions to the best of your ability. Make good estimates if data are not available.*

How many first graders (in regular English classrooms) were in the school during the 1995–1996 school year?                    _____

How many Reading Recovery teachers were in the school during the 1995–1996 school year?                    _____

Were the teachers trained or in training during the 1995–1996 school year?

                    _____

How many years had the school been involved in Reading Recovery in the 1995–1996 school year?                    _____

How was Reading Recovery funded in the school during the 1995–1996 school year?

_____

_____

_____

What implementation model(s) were used in the school during the 1995–1996 school year? (shared first grade, shared kindergarten, Title I teacher, etc.)

_____

_____

_____

What was the ethnic representation in the school during the 1995–1996 school year? (give approximate percentages for each of the following)

    Anglo \_\_\_\_\_     Asian \_\_\_\_\_     Hispanic \_\_\_\_\_

    African-American \_\_\_\_\_     Other \_\_\_\_\_

Did the school qualify for Title I funding during the 1995–1996 school year?

          _____

*The following questions refer to the context of the school following the 1998–1999 school year.*

Describe in general terms the general classroom reading/writing program(s) in the school in Grades 2, 3, and 4. Be as comprehensive as possible.

Have there been any general or specific classroom literacy initiatives within the school since the 1995–1996 school year?

_____

_____

_____

_____

Is the overall performance of children in classrooms in Grade 4 in the school, as measured by standardized measures and state assessment measures, considered high, high average, average, low average, or low?

_____

_____

_____

_____

Is the school considered a high-need school within the district? _____

Does the school have Reading Recovery teams? _____

Is the school considered urban, suburban, rural, or small town? _____

# Teacher Leadership: A Key Factor in Reading Recovery's Success

Jean F. Bussell

*Reading Recovery Council of North America*

## ABSTRACT

*The problem of sustaining an innovation is a reality in many schools because of changes in personnel and the multiplicity of options for innovation from internal and external sources. Reading Recovery, an early literacy intervention program, has a record of fifteen years of staying power in school districts across the United States. This study was designed to explore the role of the teacher leader as the central figure in the successful adoption, implementation, and institutionalization of Reading Recovery as an innovation in an educational setting.*

*Both descriptive quantitative and qualitative research approaches were used to gather data from teacher leaders regarding their behaviors, attitudes, and perceptions in implementing their role. These data were analyzed using the theoretical framework of teacher leader as change agent in the innovation process.*

*The data indicate that teacher leaders routinely engage in activities and behaviors that are identified in the literature as supporting the introduction and sustained implementation of an innovation. Teacher leaders participate with the system in (a) developing a sense of need for change, (b) establishing an information-exchange relationship around ways to address that need, (c) diagnosing problems and considering how Reading Recovery could intervene to solve them, (d) creating an intent to change, and (e) translating that intent into action. Teacher leaders work to stabilize and sustain the implementation by developing ongoing support, establishing credibility, collaborating with decision-makers and opinion leaders, demonstrating and evaluating the effectiveness of Reading Recovery, and maintaining the quality of the implementation.*

*The study provides evidence that the role of the teacher leader is complex and requires integration and operationalization of a wide and diverse range of approaches to insure the effective implementation of Reading Recovery. The role of the Reading Recovery teacher leader serves as an exemplar from which others interested in educational reform can learn.*

# Introduction

## *Characteristics of Educational Reform*

Educational reform is essential because of the fundamental change in the American economy from an industrial base to an information-knowledge base. This change creates the need for a different kind of education provided by a different kind of educational system. Nobel laureate Kenneth G. Wilson believes that "Americans, including those now graduating from school, simply are not educated to sustain middle-class incomes in an economy and society based in knowledge, driven by information, and defined by change" (Wilson & Daviss, 1994, pp. 1–2). Other researchers and societal observers amplify Wilson and Daviss' perspective in describing the state of affairs of America's educational system and its challenges in the 21st century (Allington, 1995; Atkinson & Jackson, 1992; Hinds, 1999; National Research Council, 1999) The history of change initiatives to address past and present problems is well-documented (Evans, 1996; Goodlad, 1984).

The key to reform is a change design that works. According to Askew, Fountas, Lyons, Pinnell, and Schmitt (1998), when innovations [reforms] are introduced into an educational system, one of three things is likely to happen:

- Because of the difficulties involved in change, the educational innovation is adopted but is rejected before a true test is made.
- The innovation is adopted in a half-hearted way so that the characteristics that provided the benefit are "watered down" or eliminated altogether.
- The innovation is adopted but after a short time is, itself, changed so that the system is accommodated. (p. 15)

To avoid such results and to achieve institutionalization of an innovation, Clay (1994b) cites Dalin suggesting that innovation requires a "pedagogical plan to support the innovation so that the system learns what is required and how to get it into place" (p.124). Clay also emphasizes that the innovation "must be insistent, persistent, and sustained over continued crises" or the system will be transformed back to its old practices (p. 127). According to Clay there is a strategic balance that systems require in order to maintain themselves.

Strong leadership is essential to successful reform and leaders are considered "change agents." Rogers (1995) defines change agent as "an individual who influences clients' innovation decisions in a direction deemed desirable by a change agency" (p. 335). Key to this role is the function of "linker"—facilitating "the flow of innovations from a change agency to an audience of clients" (p. 336). The change agent's role can include seven steps in relation to the innovation: developing a need for change, establishing an information exchange relationship, diagnosing problems, creating an intent in the client to change, translating intent into action, stabilizing adoption and preventing discontinuance of the innovation, and achieving a terminal relationship in which the innovation is self-renewing (p. 337). Factors in the change agent's success include communication, timing, orientation in relation to client, compatibility of the innovation with the client's needs, empathy with the client, similarity with the client, involvement of opinion leaders, the client's evaluative abilities, and the nature of the diffusion process—whether it is centralized or decentralized (pp. 336–370).

There are many models of reform but "the difficulty comes, it seems, in transporting these practices from the sites where they are invented and demonstrated to other sites. The history of education is replete with examples of successful experiments that are abandoned after they proved their worth. In business this is referred to as the problem of 'going to scale'" (Schlechty, 1997, p. 83). Scaling means that an innovation can be expanded into multiple implementation sites of varying sizes and settings—small, medium, and large districts, urban, suburban, and rural districts. A variety of factors influence the scalability of an innovation. These include clarity of purpose, school buy-in, district commitment, strong leadership, training and support, sense of connectedness, quality control (Olson, 1994; Stringfield in Olson, 1994), and continuous improvement and redesign (Wilson & Daviss, 1994).

## Reading Recovery as an Example of Innovation

An educational innovation that has been considered "one of the most successful educational reforms to appear in U.S. schools—one thoroughly grounded in the process of redesign" (Wilson & Daviss, 1994) is Reading Recovery. Reading Recovery is a short-term, early intervention tutoring program for first-grade students who are at the lowest level of achievement in reading and writing in their classrooms. The intervention includes thirty-minute, daily lessons for up to 20 weeks. The purpose of Reading Recovery is to accelerate children's learning to enable them to catch up with their average-achieving peers and to sustain their own learning as they benefit from regular classroom instruction.

The design of Reading Recovery is intended to achieve the results expected by the host system in order to foster institutionalization. The design provides for a pedagogical plan for implementation that includes key personnel (teacher leader and site coordinator in particular) with responsibility for helping the system learn what is needed to implement Reading Recovery. The plan is sustained over time by the efforts of the teacher leader and his or her colleagues as they work to balance the vital processes existing in the system with the changes required for a successful implementation of Reading Recovery.

The factors influencing the scalability of an innovation mentioned above are also included in the design of this early intervention program. In Reading Recovery, looking at results and making modifications means looking at two fundamental questions: (a) Are enough children being served with results that demonstrate that the children are getting "discontinued;" that is, reading and writing at a level that is within the average band of their respective classes and demonstrating a self-extending system that will enable them to continue to be successful in their classroom program? and (b) Is Reading Recovery meeting its one clear goal: ". . . to dramatically reduce the number of learners who have extreme difficulty with literacy learning and the cost of those learners to educational systems" (Clay, 1994a)?

Clay (1994b) has identified the teacher leader as playing a key role in the scaling up of the program. Reading Recovery's three-tier "trainer of trainers" model creates what Clay (building upon Goodlad, 1984) describes as a "redirecting system." The model provides for professionals with specific roles at the university, school system, and school level to collaborate to support the educational innovation.

Clay (1994b) describes five key points that characterize the teacher leader role in Reading Recovery:

- A full year of training provides teacher leaders with an understanding of the changes that occur over the year of training in Reading Recovery teachers.
- Teacher leaders "test practice against theory" in their work with children and teachers.
- Teacher leaders collaborate with teachers in assisting and guiding them in their efforts to teach the lowest achieving children.
- Teacher leaders develop understanding and thorough knowledge of the program in the educational system in which it occurs.
- Teacher leaders in training observe other teacher leaders and teachers and practice their own skills throughout their year of training and their ongoing professional development. (p. 126)

In essence then, teacher leaders are change agents, as described above by Rogers (1995). The teacher leaders function as a "redirecting system" as they "teach children, train teachers, educate the local educators, negotiate the implementation of the program, act as advocates for whatever cannot be compromised in the interests of effective results, and talk to the public and the media, correcting misconceptions" (Clay, 1994b, p. 127).

## Purpose of the Study

Any effort to implement reform or innovation in education or in other systems requires the key element of leadership. Leadership may come from the change agent or from another individual involved in the change process. Whichever the case may be, and it is likely to be a combination of leadership from many sources, there is much to learn from studying the leadership role in the scaling up of reform designs and innovations. Reading Recovery represents an ideal setting in which to study the role of the key individuals who serve in the role of teacher leader.

The purpose of this study was to examine the role of teacher leader in the implementation of Reading Recovery as an educational innovation. Of interest is what teacher leaders do to move the implementation of Reading Recovery from adoption to "full implementation," meaning there are enough teaching slots available to meet the identified need for Reading Recovery.

Since Reading Recovery is deemed to have an impact on the culture and operation of schools, the role of the teacher leader as a change agent is explored with regard to the relationships that are created and the strategies that are employed by the teacher leader in support of Reading Recovery implementation.

Specifically, the two fundamental research questions were: What do teacher leaders say they do to make scaling up of an educational innovation effective? What is the profile of the teacher leader who successfully leads the scaling up of Reading Recovery at his or her site?

## Theoretical Frameworks for Exploring Innovation

Three basic approaches for consideration of the process of innovation in organizations emerge from the research literature. The first is the *traditional theoretical approach to innovation* (Rogers, 1995), which serves as the framework that anchors this study. Rogers' theory is based on highly personalized interactions within a social system to influence the adoption and confirmation or rejection of innovations. Innovations must be compatible with the belief structures within the social system. Opinion leaders, authorities, and change agents all influence the adoption and confirmation process. The change agent, in this study the teacher leader, must operate in a delicately balanced manner to represent the innovation in such a way as to gain confidence and credibility from the adopters and to support the implementation of the innovation with faithfulness to the innovation and respect for the host system. Figure 1 outlines Rogers' model of the "Innovation-Decision Process." Figure 2 presents Rogers' model of the "Five Stages in the Innovation Process in an Organization."

Other researchers (e.g., Huberman & Miles, 1984; Levine, 1980; Sarason, 1971) acknowledge fundamental elements of the innovation process. One involves the steps of recognizing the need, formulating a plan to meet the need, initiating and implementing the plan, and institutionalizing or terminating the innovation. Another element is the highly interactional nature of the innovation process particularly with regard to contextual antecedents, interpersonal relationships, past practices, and perceived "fit" with individual and organizational interests. The third element is the complexity of the innovation process and the impact variation that occurs from one individual to another and the resulting decisions that are made within the social context. Finally, the fourth element is the critical role of the change agent in understanding the context and the individual perspectives during the change process.

The *"cookbook"* or *"how-to" approaches to organizational change* appear to be growing out of recent federal initiatives toward school reform (e.g., Bodilly, 1996, 1998; Bowman, 1999; Cawelti, 1999; Educational Research Service, 1998; Education Funding Research Council, 1999; Hayes, Grippe, & Hall, 1999; Herman & Stringfield, 1997; Horsley & Kaser, 1999). While not all of the suggestions from these approaches seem relevant here, several contribute to the discussion of innovation and school reform in positive ways:

- Time is needed to decide upon the specific innovation desired.
- External factors play an important role in selection of the innovation.
- Time is needed to develop and implement the selected innovation.
- Involvement of all individuals who are affected by the innovation is essential.
- Constant communication and information flow is essential.
- Risk taking must be encouraged and supported.
- The design selected must be consistent with organizational practices and instructional approaches.
- Clarity of vision about the design and its fit with the school is essential.
- Leaders must provide initial and ongoing support, but consensus building about the vision is important to sustain the innovation in the face of changes in leadership.

# A Model of the Stages in the Innovation-Decision Process

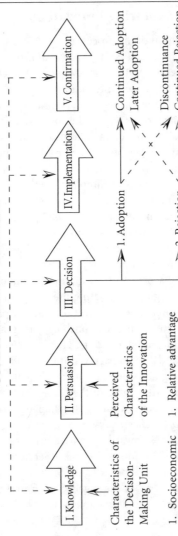

**COMMUNICATION CHANNELS**

**PRIOR CONDITIONS**

1. Previous practice
2. Felt needs/problems
3. Innovativeness
4. Norms of the social systems

| I. Knowledge | II. Persuasion | III. Decision | IV. Implementation | V. Confirmation |

Characteristics of the Decision-Making Unit

1. Socioeconomic characteristics
2. Personality variables
3. Communication behavior

Perceived Characteristics of the Innovation

1. Relative advantage
2. Compatibility
3. Complexity
4. Trialability
5. Observability

1. Adoption → Continued Adoption / Later Adoption

2. Rejection → Discontinuance / Continued Rejection

The innovation-decision process is the process through which an individual (or other decision-making unit) passes from first knowledge of an innovation to forming an attitude toward the innovation, to a decision to adopt or reject, to implementation of the new idea, and to confirmation of this decision. (Rogers, 1995, p. 163)

**Figure 1.** Rogers' Model of the Innovation-Decision Process
*Note:* From *Diffusion of Innovations* by E. M. Rogers, 1995, New York: The Free Press.

# Five Stages in the Innovation Process in an Organization

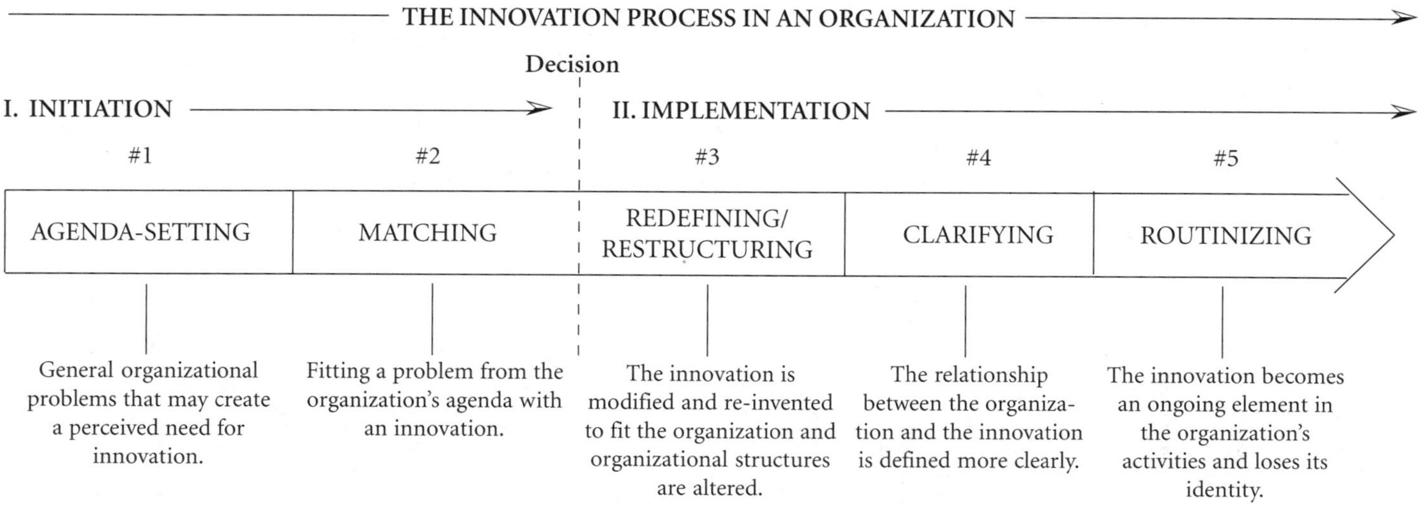

——— THE INNOVATION PROCESS IN AN ORGANIZATION ———→

Decision

| I. INITIATION | | II. IMPLEMENTATION | | |
|---|---|---|---|---|
| #1 | #2 | #3 | #4 | #5 |
| AGENDA-SETTING | MATCHING | REDEFINING/ RESTRUCTURING | CLARIFYING | ROUTINIZING |
| General organizational problems that may create a perceived need for innovation. | Fitting a problem from the organization's agenda with an innovation. | The innovation is modified and re-invented to fit the organization and organizational structures are altered. | The relationship between the organization and the innovation is defined more clearly. | The innovation becomes an ongoing element in the organization's activities and loses its identity. |

The innovation process in an organization consists of two broad activities: (1) *initiation*, defined as all of the information gathering, conceptualizing, and planning for the adoption of an innovation, leading up to the decision to adopt, and (2) *implementation*, all of the events, actions, and decisions involved in putting an innovation into use. The decision to adopt (shown as a vertical dotted line in the figure above) divides initiation, composed of agenda-setting and matching stages from implementation, composed of the three stages of redefining/restructuring, clarifying, and routinizing. (Rogers, 1995, p. 392)

**Figure 2.** Rogers' Five Stages in the Innovation Process in an Organization
*Note:* From *Diffusion of Innovations* by E. M. Rogers, 1995, New York: The Free Press.

- Cultural alignment and revision of the infrastructure may be needed to support the innovation on an ongoing basis.
- A stable environment supports durability of the innovation.
- Technical support, professional development, and ongoing networks of support are essential for successful institutionalization of an innovation.
- Accountability must balance patience and progress, particularly early in the innovation adoption process.

The *human side of change theories* emphasize the impact of change on the individual and view the individual as the only or key element of hope for school reform. Hargreaves (1997) views teaching and school reform as emotional work, driven by moral purpose, and creating the day-to-day foundation for school change. Fullan (1997) identifies the new messages about supporting change as follows: Have good ideas, but listen with empathy. Create time and mechanisms for personal and group reflection. Allow intuition and emotion a respected role. Work on improving relationships. Realize that hope, especially in the face of frustrations, is the last healthy virtue. Evans (1996) describes the change process as one of loss and grief that moves from there to a new commitment, new competencies, new coherence, and consensus about the value of the change. Goodlad (1984) describes the relationship between the teacher and the student as the bridge of relationships that makes the school effective in its mission. These three approaches to the process of innovation in organizations provide impetus to the study of teacher leaders as change agents in the implementation of Reading Recovery in educational systems. Each approach emphasizes the important role of leadership in initiating and sustaining the innovation. Hence, each provides critical context for the study presented here.

## Methodology

Both qualitative and quantitative approaches were used to explore the role of teacher leader in the implementation of Reading Recovery as an educational innovation. A questionnaire was developed based largely upon Rogers' (1995) theory of diffusion of an innovation, including the role of the change agent in the innovation process. In addition, in-depth interviews were conducted with nineteen questionnaire respondents in order to develop a richer perspective regarding the questionnaire responses.

### Survey Questionnaire

Using Rogers' theory and supplementing it with other findings from the literature review and from a review of the syllabi from seven university training centers for teacher leaders, a questionnaire (see Appendix) was designed to collect data from the entire population of teacher leaders ($N = 756$). A pilot survey of teacher leaders ($N = 17$) was conducted prior to the full administration of the survey. As a result, instructions for completing the questionnaire were revised and one question was eliminated. The revised questionnaire was administered at the 1999 Teacher Leader Institute (early June) so that all teacher leaders would be available to participate. Survey responses were obtained from 154 teacher leaders during this process. In addition, following the Teacher Leader Institute, the questionnaire was mailed to all teacher leaders who had not completed the survey at the Institute ($n = 588$). An additional 91 surveys were obtained through this mechanism. A total of 262 surveys were obtained for a response rate of 35%.

The purpose of the survey was to collect data from teacher leaders regarding perceptions of their role and the environmental factors that affect it in the scaling up of Reading Recovery. Particular attention was given to those factors that characterize the change agent's role in the adoption and implementation of an educational innovation. In addition, attention was given to those factors that teacher leaders identified as contributing to the full implementation of Reading Recovery and to the teacher leader role in that implementation. The questionnaire was developed in collaboration with several teacher leaders and university trainers who agreed to assist in the development process.

The questions were divided into two groups. The first group involved questions regarding the teacher leader's involvement in the adoption of Reading Recovery. Since frequently teacher leaders have had limited involvement in the adoption phase, these questions were placed at the back of the questionnaire document and printed on a different color of paper so that teacher leaders could easily distinguish between the two sections of the questionnaire. The second group of questions was presented at the front of the questionnaire since all teacher leaders are by definition involved in the implementation process and all respondents were requested to complete this section.

The questionnaire consisted of twenty-two questions including five on the adoption of Reading Recovery (the first group described above). Four questions were open-ended and provided opportunity for participants to respond in any way they wished. The remaining questions provided a list of responses and asked the respondents to check their preferred response on a scale of zero to ten or a scale of zero to five. These questions also provided an option of "Other," which the respondent was asked to specify and rank.

## Teacher Leader Interviews

The purpose of the in-depth interviews was twofold: (a) to assess the relationship of the theories examined in the literature review to actual experience of teacher leaders, and (b) to provide grounding for further analysis of the questionnaire results. The in-depth interviews were conducted using a semi-structured format with questions providing for open-ended responses. These interviews solicited a broad range of information from the teacher leaders regarding how they see their role in the scaling up of Reading Recovery.

The process used for selecting the teacher leaders for the interviews was to inquire among all the university trainers for their recommendations regarding teacher leaders who have been successful in full implementation of Reading Recovery at their respective sites. Forty-five teacher leaders were identified in this process. A second request to trainers asked for names of teacher leaders who had struggled greatly in the implementation process. Fourteen teacher leaders were named in this round. From the names suggested by the trainers, those teacher leaders who had not responded to the questionnaire were eliminated. Additional teacher leaders were eliminated who were from the same state or geographic region in a state. As a result of this process, 19 teacher leaders were interviewed. Of these, two were identified as having struggled greatly with the implementation process.

## Results

The 262 respondents to the questionnaire reflected a very uniform sample of teacher leaders. The respondents were predominantly white women with English as their native language, educated at the post-masters degree level, with many years of experience in education (21+ years), and extensive experience in Reading Recovery (5+ years). Most teacher leaders (77%) had served at only one Reading Recovery site, and fewer than half of the teacher leaders (40%) had been involved in the adoption of Reading Recovery at their site. Table 1 includes the levels of experience of the teacher leader respondents and Table 2 presents a summary of their characteristics.

**Table 1.** Levels of Experience of Teacher Leader Respondents

|  | N | LOWEST | HIGHEST | MEAN | S D |
|---|---|---|---|---|---|
| Years of Employment in Education | 262 | 2 | 46 | 21.8 | 7.32 |
| Years in Reading Recovery | 262 | 1 | 14 | 5.77 | 2.70 |

According to questionnaire responses, the teacher leaders' reported behaviors present a picture that is very positively skewed toward activities that are deemed in the literature to promote the implementation of an educational innovation. For example, on all the behavioral questions, teacher leaders reported their behaviors include frequent use of strategies designed to develop ongoing support for Reading Recovery implementation, to establish their credibility and trustworthiness in relation to others in the implementation of the program, to work with opinion leaders toward full implementation, to demonstrate the effectiveness of Reading Recovery, to assist the site in evaluating its effectiveness, and to maintain the quality of the implementation in relation to the Standards and Guidelines of the Reading Recovery Council of North America.

On the behavioral questions related to teacher leader involvement in the process of adoption of Reading Recovery at their sites, the teacher leaders also reported they frequently used strategies designed to promote the adoption of Reading Recovery as an educational innovation. During the adoption process, teacher leaders were involved in the process, established rapport with the schools, took actions that promoted adoption, worked with decision-makers, and had frequent contact with those decision-makers.

Teacher leaders evaluated the involvement of school related individuals in the implementation of Reading Recovery. They concluded that assistant superintendents, federal program directors, and principals dominated the process and that classroom teachers, superintendents, and school board members were involved to lesser extents. Teacher leaders reported that their contacts with these decision-makers occurred frequently (48.6% at a response of 3 of 5), quite frequently (23.7% at a response of 4 of 5), to very often (9.3% at a response of 5 of 5).

**Table 2.** Summary of Characteristics of Teacher Leader Respondents

| CHARACTERISTIC | N | % |
|---|---|---|
| Source | 17 Pilot | 6.5 Pilot |
| | 154 Institute | 58.8 Institute |
| | 91 Mail | 34.7 Mail |
| Gender | 9 Male | 3.0 Male |
| | 253 Female | 97.0 Female |
| Ethnicity | 9 Black | 3.4 Black |
| | 12 Hispanic | 4.6 Hispanic |
| | 241 White/Pacific Islander | 92.0 White/Pacific Islander |
| Education | 7 Bachelors | 2.7 Bachelors |
| | 37 Masters + | 90.5 Masters + |
| | 18 Doctorate | 6.8 Doctorate |
| RR/DLL Training | 246 RR only | 93.8 RR only |
| | 16 RR/DLL | 6.2 RR/DLL |
| | 0 DLL only | 0 DLL only |
| Status | 252 Trained/Active | 96.0 Trained/Active |
| | 5 Trained/Returning | 2.0 Trained/Returning |
| | 5 Training/Completed | 2.0 Training/Completed |
| Number of Sites Served | 200 One | 77.0 One |
| | 36 Two | 14.0 Two |
| | 26 Three or more | 9.0 Three or more |
| Involved in Adoption | 105 Yes | 40.0 Yes |
| | 157 No | 60.0 No |

In assessing the barriers to achieving and maintaining full implementation of Reading Recovery, teacher leaders gave a ranking of 10 (a substantial problem) to funding (71% of respondents) as the most substantial problem. This problem is followed by the perceived high cost of the program (44%), large numbers of students who need additional support (25.9%), and political problems in the district (20.6%). In order to address these barriers, teacher leaders report they most often use the following strategies (ranking of 10):

- Explain why a safety net program needs high priority (43.8%)
- Provide information to administrators (40.6%)
- Support classroom program development (40.6%)

- Provide regular reports to decision-makers (40%)
- Explain how Reading Recovery is a part of a comprehensive program (38%)
- Provide in-service training for classroom teachers (38%)
- Document performance of former Reading Recovery students on proficiency tests (32.6%)
- Conduct awareness sessions in the district (30%)

When asked to identify areas in which universities provide support, teacher leaders rated four areas high. University trainers provide relevant and timely professional development sessions, provide updated information about implementation issues, assist with problem solving around issues of compliance with Reading Recovery Standards and Guidelines, and organize Reading Recovery conferences. Teacher leaders reported lower levels of university support in the following areas: (a) supporting and promoting communication and networking among Reading Recovery teachers and teacher leaders associated with the center, (b) assisting with problems related to teaching the most difficult to accelerate children, and (c) meeting with school officials as needed to discuss implementation issues.

Teacher leaders believe they need additional support from the university training centers. They would like greater advocacy with state and local funding sources and administrators as well as advocacy with administrators and decision-makers. Teacher leaders also perceive that they need assistance from trainers around a wide variety of implementation issues.

The open-ended questions provided the teacher leaders with opportunities to tell their stories in their own words. The responses were rich and reflect the commitments, frustrations, and passions of the teacher leaders. When asked what type of assistance they needed to support the implementation of Reading Recovery at their sites, the teacher leaders responded with implementation issues to be addressed (23.3%), support for administrators and the state for funding (20.2%), advocacy by trainers with administrators and decision-makers (16.8%), opportunities to network with other teacher leaders (2.7%), and development of classroom programs by trainers (1.1%).

Teacher leaders identified factors they believe have contributed to success at their sites. These factors included collaborations outside Reading Recovery (30.9%), advocacy through presentations and reports to decision-makers (23%), the achievement of full implementation as a strategy for seeing the results and maintaining the success (21.8%), teamwork inside Reading Recovery (9.6%), the caliber and commitment of the Reading Recovery teachers (9.1%), and the process of networking with teacher leaders from other sites as well as with administrators (5.6%).

Teacher leaders identified six fundamental areas they considered as their greatest accomplishments or about which they felt the greatest pride. These areas included their success in implementing Reading Recovery (38.5%), their work with teachers (30.5%), the impact of Reading Recovery beyond itself in the educational system (25.6%), the impact of Reading Recovery on children (21%), their personal and professional development and accomplishments as a teacher leader (9.5%), and their professional relationships (2.3%). [Many teacher leaders gave more than one response to this question.]

Finally, teacher leaders identified the most compelling reason to continue in their roles as teacher leaders, with many offering more than one. Reasons included the children and parents (77.9%), the teachers with whom they work (41.6%), their professional and personal successes and satisfaction (30.9%), and the impact Reading Recovery has on the system (10.7%).

The teacher leader interviews provided for greater depth of information regarding how teacher leaders perceive their role. The interviews confirmed the questionnaire results that serving children and working with teachers are the greatest attractions of the position. In addition the teacher leaders' passion for their work sustained them in times of frustration. Teacher leaders described the stress of their positions and the multiple roles involved as creating incredibly busy work lives that were constantly in need of balancing efforts. The teacher leaders also described the demands on their responsibilities outside Reading Recovery. Nearly every teacher leader who was interviewed had responsibilities in addition to his or her teacher leader role. These additional responsibilities provided access and information that otherwise would be less readily available to Reading Recovery, and these additional responsibilities frequently resulted in greater respect and ongoing support (including funding) for Reading Recovery; however, the additional work created stress and tensions for those teacher leaders who value their performance as teacher leaders most highly.

In summary, the teacher leader respondents are highly motivated and highly committed to the delivery of Reading Recovery services to children. This work occurs through an interpersonal network of trained Reading Recovery professionals working in collaboration with school and district level teachers and administrators. The teacher leaders' reported behaviors align with those considered in the literature to promote the implementation and institutionalization of educational innovations.

## Discussion

Teacher leaders operate in a complex role within complex social (educational) systems. The role involves operating as a change agent within an environment of multiple schools and frequently multiple school districts. The role involves operating in a limbo status generally without administrative authority but always with educational responsibility. The role is dependent upon many different relationships to insure the quality of the implementation through teaching teachers, teaching children, and getting results. In addition, many school districts expect teacher leaders to assume responsibilities for non–Reading Recovery educational functions, further complicating their roles.

Based on the data gathered from the teacher leaders through the questionnaires and the in-depth interviews, Figure 3 illustrates the adaptation of Rogers' (1995) innovation-decision process to a school system's decision-making process in relation to adopting and implementing Reading Recovery as an educational innovation. Figure 4 presents an adaptation of Rogers' model of the five-stages in the innovation process in an organization to the initiation and implementation of Reading Recovery in a school district.

The questionnaire itself was designed to gather information regarding the teacher leaders' behaviors during the seven stages of adoption and implementation of an innovation as defined by Rogers. Figure 5 presents the data describing the Reading

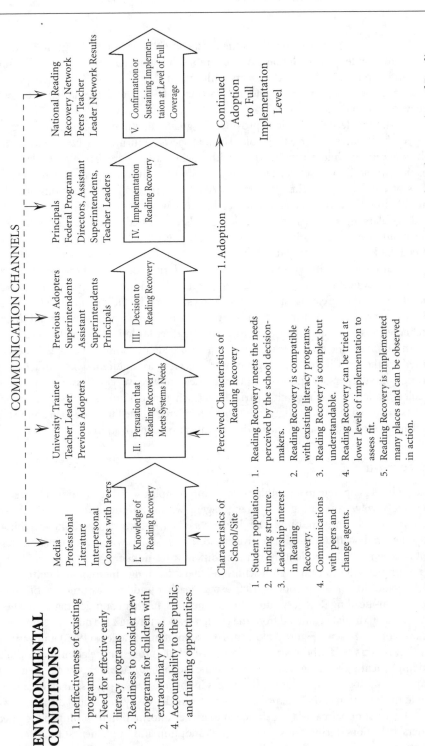

**Figure 3.** Adaptation of Rogers' model of the innovation-decision process as applied to the adoption and implementation of Reading Recovery as an educational innovation

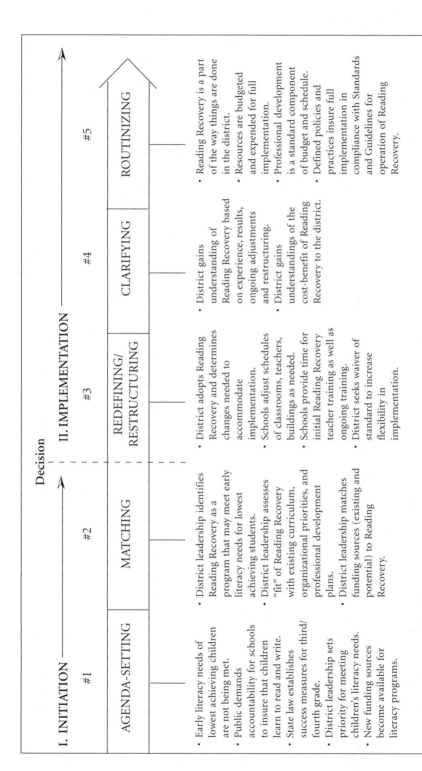

**Figure 4.** Adaptation of Rogers' Model of the Five Stages in the Innovation Process in an Organization to the Initiation and Implementation of Reading Recovery in a School District

| I. Develop a need for change. | II. Establish an Information Exchange Relationship. | III. Diagnose Problems. | IV. Create an Intent in the Client to Change | V. Translate Intent into Action. |
|---|---|---|---|---|
| Identified and presented information on Reading Recovery as a solution to early literacy problem. | Created awareness of needs through presentations to others of the information identified about Reading Recovery.<br><br>Worked first with colleagues who knew me to be credible, competent, and trustworthy.<br><br>Held awareness sessions for interested individuals in the school system and community.<br><br>Provided additional information upon request. | Gathered and shared information about Reading Recovery as a possible solution.<br><br>Presented information about alternatives and why they would not be successful in comparison to Reading Recovery. | Presented information about how everyone who wanted to be involved could be involved.<br><br>Met with colleagues to persuade them to support adoption.<br><br>Met with opinion leaders to persuade them to support adoption. | Convinced other school personnel that Reading Recovery could help.<br><br>Met with additional colleagues and system decision-makers about Reading Recovery.<br><br>Problem-solved with decision-makers about potential problems they saw in implementing Reading Recovery.<br><br>Met with decision-makers to encourage them to adopt.<br><br>Wrote letters of support. |

**Figure 5.** The Reading Recovery Teacher Leader as Change Agent in Rogers' Sequence of Change Agent Roles

| VI. Stabilize Adoption and Prevent Discontinuance | | | | | | VII. Achieve a Terminal Relationship |
|---|---|---|---|---|---|---|
| | | | | | | Not assessed. |
| Developed ongoing support for implementation by: Providing data on student performance. Problem-solving around difficult to teach children. Problem-solving around scheduling lessons. Assisting in building Reading Recovery teams. Communicating promptly. Staying available for consultation to teachers. Making in-service presentations. Serving as a clearinghouse for early literacy information. | Established credibility and trustworthiness by: Listening to needs as expressed by teachers and administrators. Problem-solving around a variety of issues. Providing accurate information. Sharing personal experiences in Reading Recovery. Linking decision-makers with other Reading Recovery implementers. Sharing common interests with decision-makers. | Worked with opinion leaders by: Providing information. Answering questions. Enlisting endorsement for ongoing implementation. Sharing children's success stories. Describing the relationship between Reading Recovery and classroom programs. | Demonstrated effectiveness by: Providing opportunities for observation of lessons and professional development sessions. Providing written materials documenting Reading Recovery success. Providing supporting statements from teachers, parents, and others in other adopting districts. Providing data from the site and comparing it with state and/or national data. | Evaluated effectiveness by: Providing annual site report of progress. Analyzing cost-benefit in relation to retention and referral of comparison groups. Assisting in determination of "full implementation." Providing rationales for Standards and Guidelines. Providing forums for discussion of results at school and district levels. | Maintained the quality of the implementation by: Articulating Standards, Guidelines, and rationales. Providing examples of school or district level decisions that affect quality of implementation. Applying to university training center for one-time waiver of a Standard. Problem-solving a variety of situations to maintain compliance Monitoring quality of implementation and children's programs at school and site level. | |

**Figure 5.** (Continued)

Recovery teacher leader as change agent in Rogers' "Sequence of Change Agent Roles." The data are consistent with behavioral strategies for effective initiation and implementation of an educational innovation as gathered from the research literature.

The responsibility for maintaining the quality of the implementation of Reading Recovery places the teacher leader in the nexus between the innovation and the system. To the extent the teacher leader as change agent is perceived to have greater affinity with the school system, the teacher leader is likely to be more effective in insuring the effectiveness of the implementation (Rogers, 1995). In order to assess the teacher leader's perception of affinity to employer (the client) versus to Reading Recovery (the innovation), the questionnaire included two specific questions. In response to the question of "How important is it to you to continue being a Reading Recovery teacher leader?", an astonishing 72.1% of the teacher leaders responded that it is very important (the highest rating). In contrast, in response to the question of "How important is it to you to continue being in your current district for employment?", only 45% of the teacher leaders responded in like manner.

Given the substantial difference in affinity to Reading Recovery (the innovation) in comparison to affinity to current employer (the client or host), and given the stressful nature of the teacher leader position as described by the interviewees, the question arises: Why is there such a difference? One hypothesis is that the teacher leaders are teachers at their core, and their motivations for service to children largely exceed their loyalty to any particular employer. The passion and commitment described by teacher leaders in response to the open-ended questions on the questionnaire and in the interviews lend credence to this hypothesis. The theories of the human side of the change process (Evans, 1996; Fullan, 1997; Goodlad, 1984; Hargreaves, 1997) speak to the passion and engagement required of individuals (teachers and administrators) and systems in order to sustain change in an institution. Teacher leaders appear to have such passion and engagement, and their success in implementing and sustaining Reading Recovery is evidence.

Another hypothesis for the differences in allegiance is that the teacher leader's professional and personal development offers such satisfaction that losing that sense of reward for the purposes of ongoing employment in the current district is the less desirable option. Goodlad (1984) speaks to the quality of relationships as indicators of satisfaction. The teacher leaders' descriptions of their professional and personal relationships with colleagues, children, and parents appear to drive the level of satisfaction that teacher leaders obtain from their work in Reading Recovery.

A third hypothesis is that the teacher leaders in many instances are in a position to cross organizational boundaries in order to serve children. In nearly all situations, teacher leaders serve multiple schools. In many situations they serve multiple school districts (in the case of consortia of school districts). This level of service provides teacher leaders with the opportunity to focus beyond one situation (even as they continue to teach individual children) to the bigger picture of service to many children and to many teachers. The role places teacher leaders in the position of helping children regardless of their local organizational affiliation. It also requires teacher leaders to support the ongoing implementation of Reading Recovery in different host systems with attention to the quality and integrity of the implementation in each. Since host systems will attempt to change the innovation to suit their needs, the teacher leader must focus on how to accomplish the implementation while maintaining the quality and integrity of Reading Recovery. This process lends itself to the teacher leader's focusing on his or her role in Reading Recovery (the innovation) rather than in the institution.

The teacher leaders' responses create a profile of the teacher leader as an activist change agent, constantly working for the successful adoption and effective implementation of Reading Recovery as a high quality, results-oriented educational innovation. The behaviors the teacher leaders report create a repertoire of strategies that foster the full implementation and institutionalization of Reading Recovery so that all children who need assistance have the opportunity to participate.

Not all the behaviors in the repertoire are practiced to the fullest extent, however. Teacher leaders report frequent engagement with teachers and teaching, with providing information and responding to inquiries about Reading Recovery, and with problem solving around issues related to implementation. Teacher leaders appear to have developed a high level of comfort in performing these functions that surround the practice and teaching of Reading Recovery. In contrast, teacher leaders report less frequent involvement in activities that span the administrative structures or place teacher leaders in an advocacy role. For example, teacher leaders are more likely to respond to requests for information than to initiate the creation of reports and analyses such as cost-benefit analyses or analyses of the performance of Reading Recovery children in comparison to non–Reading Recovery children on such factors as retention, referral, and performance on proficiency tests. Although teacher leaders identify that funding is the most substantial barrier to achieving and maintaining full implementation, fewer than half the respondents reported they have submitted applications for funding from non-school sources. In addition, teacher leaders report they were unprepared for the extent of the role of spokesperson for Reading Recovery that the teacher leader position in practice requires of them. Thus, while most teacher leaders report using the full repertoire of strategies to support the implementation of Reading Recovery, there appear to be levels of comfort that differ from one type of strategy to another.

Finally, the teacher leaders' responsibility to practice Reading Recovery as a teacher while also serving as the change agents or "carriers" of the innovation may be one of the sources of success for Reading Recovery. As practitioners, teacher leaders constantly demonstrate their mastery of the practice of the Reading Recovery lesson. Their practice informs their teaching through their constant assessment of the strategies they use as they teach children. This assessment provides insights into teaching children that the teacher leaders can use in helping Reading Recovery teachers be successful in their teaching. Furthermore, the experience of teaching children and teaching teachers provides a solid base from which teacher leaders can address system barriers to the achievement and maintenance of full implementation of Reading Recovery. This experience-based position may add credibility to the teacher leader's role as change agent in securing high quality implementation of Reading Recovery.

Figure 6 presents a graphical description of the complexity of the teacher leader role as described in the preceding paragraphs.

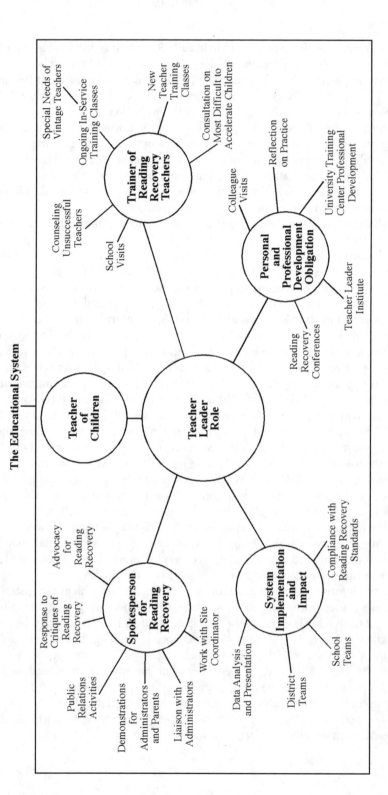

**The Educational System**

Special Needs of Vintage Teachers

Ongoing In-Service Training Classes

New Teacher Training Classes

Consultation on Most Difficult to Accelerate Children

Counseling Unsuccessful Teachers

**Trainer of Reading Recovery Teachers**

School Visits

Colleague Visits

Reflection on Practice

University Training Center Professional Development

**Personal and Professional Development Obligation**

Teacher Leader Institute

Reading Recovery Conferences

**Teacher of Children**

**Teacher Leader Role**

Response to Critiques of Reading Recovery

Advocacy for Reading Recovery

Public Relations Activities

**Spokesperson for Reading Recovery**

Demonstrations for Administrators and Parents

Liaison with Administrators

Work with Site Coordinator

Compliance with Reading Recovery Standards

**System Implementation and Impact**

School Teams

District Teams

Data Analysis and Presentation

Figure 6. Reading Recovery Teacher Leader Role as Described by Interviewees (Excluding non–Reading Recovery responsibilities)

## Implications for Reading Recovery as an Educational Innovation

Prior to addressing the implications of this research for Reading Recovery as an educational innovation, it is important to remind the reader that the research is based on self-reports from teacher leaders who may represent the most vested (as evidenced by the questionnaire return rate of 35%) among the total population of 756 teacher leaders who were eligible to respond to the questionnaire. In addition, the teacher leaders were encouraged to respond because the staff director of the national association for Reading Recovery was the researcher, and the research advisor was one of the founders of Reading Recovery in North America. Accordingly, the results must be interpreted and used with caution. It is possible that teacher leaders who chose not to respond to the questionnaire may have substantially different perspectives and chose not to share them. There is, however, no evidence or other reason to believe that the non-respondents are remarkably different from the respondents.

The results of this research appear to support the continued development of the teacher leader role as change agent in the process of introducing and sustaining Reading Recovery as an educational innovation. The teacher leaders are highly educated and trained as teachers of teachers. Their self-reports of the functions they perform to support the ongoing implementation of Reading Recovery are consistent with the research on change in educational systems. The teacher leaders' detailed reports of their problem solving behaviors provide evidence of their ability to work within systems to meet the needs of children. Teacher leaders build relationships within their sites that are essential to their continuing success. They are passionate about their work and bring a commitment to the innovation of Reading Recovery that exceeds expectations.

In relation to the teacher leader role, respondents identified three areas as critical to the ongoing success of Reading Recovery as an educational innovation. The three areas are role diversity and scope, support, and funding. Each is described below.

In relation to role diversity and scope, the teacher leaders perform a wide range of functions and responsibilities within the defined Reading Recovery role. As the role is implemented in many educational systems, however, teacher leaders also have responsibility for many non–Reading Recovery functions and responsibilities. If Reading Recovery is to continue to grow and succeed in teaching children to learn to read and write, the complexities of the teacher leader role must be addressed by the leadership of Reading Recovery. Some questions to consider are: Must teacher leaders be solely committed to Reading Recovery? If so, how can Reading Recovery address the issues of resource allocation and return on investment from the perspective of the host systems? If teacher leaders are encouraged to perform non–Reading Recovery functions and responsibilities, what changes would be needed in the Standards and Guidelines for Reading Recovery that govern the role of teacher leader? What options are possible for changing the scope of the teacher leader role without diminishing the effectiveness of the teacher leader as change agent? What are the implications of potential teacher leader role changes for the relationship of Reading Recovery to the host systems?

A second series of questions related to the teacher leader's role as change agent includes such questions as: How can teacher leaders be trained to understand their role as change agent and to assume that role in addition to their role as teacher of teachers and teacher of children? How can the initial training and ongoing professional development for teacher leaders address their responsibilities as change agents and as "public relations" agents?

The second area that appears to be critical for the ongoing success of teacher leaders in implementing Reading Recovery is support. The current Reading Recovery organizational structure vests the primary responsibility for supporting teacher leaders in the university training centers. The teacher leaders have indicated in their responses to the questionnaire that they need additional support from the university training centers in working on issues related to implementation and advocacy at the local level and on networking with other teacher leaders. The university training centers, working through the North American Trainers Group, may wish to address the issue of support available to teacher leaders. The next question, of course, is how will the university training centers be supported to provide additional support to the teacher leaders?

The host systems are also a source of support for the teacher leaders. Many teacher leaders reported strong administrative leadership and advocacy as factors in the success of the Reading Recovery implementation at their sites. Strategies should be developed by Reading Recovery to support the work of administrators and to encourage them to work in support of Reading Recovery. Examples of such support could include materials describing Reading Recovery implementation as a part of comprehensive literacy or school reform programs, networks with other administrators who value Reading Recovery, and conferences and events where administrators can learn from others about Reading Recovery.

The third area that appears to be critical for the ongoing success of teacher leaders in implementing Reading Recovery is funding. Teacher leaders identified funding as the greatest barrier or problem in achieving and maintaining full implementation of Reading Recovery. Suggestions for addressing this barrier include the following:

- Reading Recovery must find new ways to demonstrate its effectiveness as a one-to-one tutorial intervention.
- Reading Recovery must strongly promote its philosophy of service to the lowest achieving children as a value that school districts should embrace in order to meet the needs of all of the children who attend schools in those districts.
- Reading Recovery must find new ways of articulating its role in comprehensive literacy programs and in comprehensive school reform efforts.
- Reading Recovery must embrace the anecdotal evidence of its impact on systems change and find ways to articulate its value in relation to effective change.

While these suggestions do not directly address the issue of new or more funds for Reading Recovery, the suggestions are strategies that may make it possible for Reading Recovery to be better understood by school leaders as an innovation and, hence, lead to more funding. From a more traditional perspective, Reading Recovery can gather together all the information available about current sources of funding for the program and share that information and analysis throughout the Reading Recovery constituency. Reading Recovery also can be deliberate in approaching states and federal agencies for ideas and information that may support the ongoing funding of Reading Recovery.

## Recommendations for Further Study

This study generates a number of interesting possibilities for further study. First, the development of a measure of implementation at the site level as an alternative to the school level could strengthen the researcher's ability to draw conclusions about the relationship between the teacher leaders' reported behaviors and extent of the implementation.

Also, observing teacher leaders' behaviors in the field, at the site, on a first-hand basis rather than depending on self-reports could provide further opportunities for analysis of the relationship between the behaviors and the extent of the implementation. Field studies would also help control for pro-innovation bias from self-reports and recall problems associated with self-reports.

Analysis of the difference between implementing Reading Recovery in a single district site in comparison to implementing the program in a consortium of multiple districts could provide further insight into the complexity of the responsibilities of the teacher leader. Such analysis also could provide valuable information regarding collaboration and coalition building to support an educational innovation as well as about the scale of the implementation required to sustain the teacher leader role.

Embedding Reading Recovery into the educational system in many instances has been dependent upon its development of relationships with other programs. A study of how these relationships are formed and what other programs are involved could provide insight into ways to insure the ongoing support for Reading Recovery implementation and institutionalization.

The role of leaders as decision-makers and the role of opinion leaders in influencing decisions call for additional study from the perspective of educating leaders and building ownership for Reading Recovery through a succession of leaders in a particular school, district, or site. Given the strength of the teacher leaders' responses concerning the importance of these roles, and given the literature on the importance of these roles, such a study could provide valuable information about sustaining the implementation in the face of changes in leadership. Particular attention could be paid to the role of the principal and how teacher leaders could assist Reading Recovery teachers in working with principals. Another variation for research with this particular important group could be to research these leaders' perceptions of the teacher leader's role.

Obtaining responses from additional teacher leaders could help address the issue of response by 35% of the population in this study. Research through the use of focus groups or additional surveys from the non-responding teacher leaders to gather their assessment of the data collected in this study could provide additional insight into the change process and the teacher leader role in that process.

Further investigation of the data collected in this study on several different dimensions could be interesting. Examples of these dimensions include the length of time a teacher leader has been in his or her role and the length of time the school or/ and site has been involved in Reading Recovery.

Separate investigations of subgroups of the teacher leader population might also be informative with regard to the change process. Given that the respondents in this research were largely white women (including 18 of 19 interviewees), further research targeted to under-represented groups (particularly African Americans and Hispanics) and to male teacher leaders could provide additional insight into the role of teacher leader and to particular circumstances experienced by these teacher leaders.

Finally, further assessment of the various responsibilities within the complex role of the teacher leader is desirable. Learning how teacher leaders actually spend their time could provide valuable information about the teacher leader's role in the change process. In addition, research regarding the responsibilities that teacher leaders perform outside their Reading Recovery role is warranted given the responses to the open-ended questions in the questionnaire as well as the data collected during the interview process.

## References

Allington, R. L. (1995). Literacy lessons in the elementary schools: Yesterday, today, and tomorrow. In R. L. Allington & S. A.Walmsley (Eds.), *No quick fix: Rethinking literacy programs in America's elementary schools* (pp. 1–18). New York: Teachers College Press.

Allington, R. L., & Walmsley, S. A. (1995). No quick fix: Where do we go from here? In R. L. Allington & S. A. Walmsley (Eds.), *No quick fix: Rethinking literacy programs in America's elementary schools* (pp. 253–264). New York: Teachers College Press.

Askew, B. J., Fountas, I. C., Lyons, C. A., Pinnell, G. S., & Schmitt, M. C. (1998). *Reading Recovery review: Understandings, outcomes and implications.* Columbus, OH: Reading Recovery Council of North America.

Atkinson, R. C., & Jackson, G. B. (Eds.). (1992) *Research and education reform.* Washington, D.C.: National Academy Press.

Bodilly, S. (1996). *Lessons from New American Schools' development corporation phase.* Santa Monica, CA: RAND.

Bodilly, S. (1998). *Lessons from New American Schools' scale-up phase: Prospects for bringing designs to multiple schools.* Santa Monica, CA: RAND.

Bowman, R. F. (1999). Change in education: Connecting the dots. *The Clearing House, 72*(5), 295–297.

Cawelti, G. (1999). *Portraits of six benchmark schools: Diverse approaches to improving student achievement.* Arlington, VA: Educational Research Service.

Clay, M. M. (1994a). Report on meeting on Reading Recovery implementation. Raleigh, NC.

Clay, M. M. (1994b). Reading Recovery: The wider implications of an educational innovation. *Literacy, Teaching and Learning: An International Journal of Early Literacy, 1*(1), 121–141.

Dalin, P. (1978). *Limits to educational change.* New York: St. Martin's Press.

Education Funding Research Council (1999). First CSRD grantees present strategies for success. *Title I Monitor* (1999, August), *1,* 11–12.

Educational Research Service. (1998). *Comprehensive models for school improvement: Finding the right match and making it work.* Arlington, VA: Author.

Evans, R. (1996). *The human side of school change: Reform, resistance, and the real-life problems of innovation.* San Francisco: Jossey-Bass.

Fullan, M. (1997). Emotion and hope: Constructive concepts for complex times. In A. Hargreaves (Ed.), *Rethinking educational change with heart and mind: 1997 ASCD yearbook* (pp. 216–233). Alexandria, VA: Association for Supervision and Curriculum Development.

Fullan, M. (1993). *Change forces: Probing the depths of educational reform.* London: The Falmer Press.

Goodlad, J. I. (1984). *A place called school.* New York: McGraw Hill.

Hargreaves, A. (1997). Rethinking educational change: Going deeper and wider in the quest for success. In A. Hargreaves (Ed.), *Rethinking educational change with heart and mind: 1997 ASCD yearbook* (pp. 1–26). Alexandria, VA: Association for Supervision and Curriculum Development.

Hayes, C., Grippe, P., & Hall, G. H. (1999). Firmly planted. *Journal of Staff Development, 20*(4), 17–21.

Herman, R., & Stringfield, S. (1997). *Ten promising programs for educating all children: Evidence of impact.* Arlington, VA: Educational Research Service.

Hinds, M. C. (1999). Public schools: Is there a way to fix them? *National issues forums.* Dubuque, IA: Kendall/Hunt.

Horsley, D., & Kaser, J. (1999). How to keep a change initiative on track. *Journal of Staff Development, 20*(4), 40–45.

Huberman, A. M., & Miles, M. B. (1984). *Innovation up close: How school improvement works.* New York: Plenum Press.

Levine, A. (1980). *Why innovation fails.* Albany, NY: State University of New York Press.

National Research Council. (1999). *Improving student learning: A strategic plan for educational research and its utilization.* Washington, DC: Author.

Ohio State University (2000). *Draft national data report 1984–1999.* Columbus, OH: The Ohio State University—Unpublished Report.

Olson, L. (1994). Learning their lessons. *Education Week, November 2, 1994,* 43–46.

Rogers, E. M. (1995). *Diffusion of innovations* (4th ed.). New York: The Free Press.

Sarason, S. B. (1971). *The culture of the school and the problem of change.* Boston: Allyn and Bacon.

Schlechty, P. C. (1997). *Inventing better schools: An action plan for educational reform.* San Francisco: Jossey-Bass.

Wilson, K. G., & Daviss, B. (1994). *Redesigning education.* New York: Teachers College Press.

# Appendix

## A Survey on the Role of the Teacher Leader in the Scaling Up of an Educational Innovation

*Read the instructions for response for each individual question carefully prior to indicating your response. When selecting "Other (Specify)," be sure to check the ranking box. (Note: Throughout this survey, "implementation" refers to the period of time that includes the first year and subsequent years of teacher training at the site.)*

1. How do you develop *ongoing support* for Reading Recovery implementation at your site? (Check ranking from 0 to 10 where 0 = *never*, and 10 = *very often*.)

|  | 0 | 1 | 2 | 3 | 4 | 5 | 6 | 7 | 8 | 9 | 10 |
|---|---|---|---|---|---|---|---|---|---|---|---|
| Provide data on student performance | | | | | | | | | | | |
| Assist with problem-solving around difficult to teach children | | | | | | | | | | | |
| Assist with problem solving around scheduling of lessons | | | | | | | | | | | |
| Assist in building school and district Reading Recovery teams | | | | | | | | | | | |
| Communicate promptly | | | | | | | | | | | |
| Stay available for consultation to teachers | | | | | | | | | | | |
| Make in-service presentations | | | | | | | | | | | |
| Serve as a clearinghouse for early literacy information | | | | | | | | | | | |
| Other (Specify) | | | | | | | | | | | |
| Other (Specify) | | | | | | | | | | | |
| Other (Specify) | | | | | | | | | | | |

2. Who are the *decision-makers* with whom you work in the implementation process and to what extent are they involved? (Check ranking for each decision-maker category listed below from 0 to 5 where 0 = *not involved*, and 5 = *very involved*.)

|  | 0 | 1 | 2 | 3 | 4 | 5 |
|---|---|---|---|---|---|---|
| School board members | | | | | | |
| Superintendent | | | | | | |
| Assistant Superintendent | | | | | | |
| Federal Programs Director | | | | | | |

|  | 0 | 1 | 2 | 3 | 4 | 5 |
|---|---|---|---|---|---|---|
| Principals | | | | | | |
| Classroom Teachers | | | | | | |
| School Teams | | | | | | |
| District Teams | | | | | | |
| Other (Specify) | | | | | | |
| Other (Specify) | | | | | | |
| Other (Specify) | | | | | | |

3. Check one response only.

*Never = 0*      *Frequently (Daily) = 5*
   0    1       2    3    4    5

Describe the *number of contacts with decision-makers* at your site that you have during the ongoing implementation process.

4. How do you establish your *credibility/trustworthiness* in relation to others in the implementation of Reading Recovery? (Check ranking from 0 to 10 where 0 = *never*, and 10 = *very often*.)

|  | 0 | 1 | 2 | 3 | 4 | 5 | 6 | 7 | 8 | 9 | 10 |
|---|---|---|---|---|---|---|---|---|---|---|---|
| Listen to needs as expressed by teachers and administrators | | | | | | | | | | | |
| Engage in problem solving around a variety of issues | | | | | | | | | | | |
| Provide accurate information about Reading Recovery | | | | | | | | | | | |
| Share information about my personal experience in Reading Recovery | | | | | | | | | | | |
| Link decision-makers with others who have implemented Reading Recovery | | | | | | | | | | | |
| Emphasize my common interests with those of the decision-makers | | | | | | | | | | | |
| Other (Specify) | | | | | | | | | | | |
| Other (Specify) | | | | | | | | | | | |
| Other (Specify) | | | | | | | | | | | |

5. How do you work with *opinion leaders* (people who influence decisions even though they may not be the decision-makers) toward full implementation of Reading Recovery? (Check ranking from 0 to 10 where 0 = *never*, and 10 = *very often.*)

|  | 0 | 1 | 2 | 3 | 4 | 5 | 6 | 7 | 8 | 9 | 10 |
|---|---|---|---|---|---|---|---|---|---|---|---|
| Contact opinion leaders with information | | | | | | | | | | | |
| Answer questions about Reading Recovery from opinion leaders | | | | | | | | | | | |
| Enlist opinion leaders in endorsing the ongoing implementation of Reading Recovery | | | | | | | | | | | |
| Tell success stories of children's experiences in Reading Recovery | | | | | | | | | | | |
| Describe the relationship between Reading Recovery and the classroom program | | | | | | | | | | | |
| Other (Specify) | | | | | | | | | | | |
| Other (Specify) | | | | | | | | | | | |
| Other (Specify) | | | | | | | | | | | |

6. Prior to a formal evaluation process, how do you *demonstrate the effectiveness* of Reading Recovery? (Check ranking from 0 to 10 where 0 = *never*, and 10 = *very often.*)

|  | 0 | 1 | 2 | 3 | 4 | 5 | 6 | 7 | 8 | 9 | 10 |
|---|---|---|---|---|---|---|---|---|---|---|---|
| Provide opportunities for school personnel, opinion leaders, and decision-makers to observe a Reading Recovery lesson and a behind the glass session | | | | | | | | | | | |
| Provide written materials that document the success of Reading Recovery | | | | | | | | | | | |
| Provide statements from teachers, parents, and others in districts that have adopted Reading Recovery | | | | | | | | | | | |
| Provide data from the site and compare it with state and/or national data | | | | | | | | | | | |
| Other (Specify) | | | | | | | | | | | |
| Other (Specify) | | | | | | | | | | | |
| Other (Specify) | | | | | | | | | | | |

7. How do you assist your site (across the district(s) or at the school level) in *evaluating* the effectiveness of Reading Recovery? (Check ranking from 0 to 10 where 0 = *never*, and 10 = *very often*.)

|  | 0 | 1 | 2 | 3 | 4 | 5 | 6 | 7 | 8 | 9 | 10 |
|---|---|---|---|---|---|---|---|---|---|---|---|
| Provide annual site report with information about the progress of the program | | | | | | | | | | | |
| Provide analysis of cost-benefit in relation to retention and referral of Reading Recovery children in comparison to non-Reading Recovery children | | | | | | | | | | | |
| Provide information about how to determine "full implementation" in each school | | | | | | | | | | | |
| Provide rationales for Standards and Guidelines in Reading Recovery | | | | | | | | | | | |
| Provide forums for discussion of Reading Recovery results in schools and at the district level | | | | | | | | | | | |
| Other (Specify) | | | | | | | | | | | |
| Other (Specify) | | | | | | | | | | | |
| Other (Specify) | | | | | | | | | | | |

8. After demonstrating effectiveness, how do you *maintain the quality* of the implementation in relation to the Standards and Guidelines for Reading Recovery? (Check ranking from 0 to 10 where 0 = *never*, and 10 = *very often*.)

|  | 0 | 1 | 2 | 3 | 4 | 5 | 6 | 7 | 8 | 9 | 10 |
|---|---|---|---|---|---|---|---|---|---|---|---|
| Articulate the Standards and Guidelines and rationales so that they were understood by all | | | | | | | | | | | |
| Provide examples of how decisions at the school or district level created problems with the quality implementation of Reading Recovery | | | | | | | | | | | |
| Apply to University Training Center for one-time waiver of a Standard | | | | | | | | | | | |
| Problem-solve a variety of situations at the school and district levels in order to maintain compliance with the Standards and Guidelines | | | | | | | | | | | |
| Monitor quality of implementation and children's programs at school and site level | | | | | | | | | | | |
| Other (Specify) | | | | | | | | | | | |
| Other (Specify) | | | | | | | | | | | |
| Other (Specify) | | | | | | | | | | | |

9. What are the greatest *barriers or problems* in achieving and maintaining full implementation? (Check ranking from 0 to 10 where 0 = *not a problem*, and 10 = *a substantial problem*.)

| | 0 | 1 | 2 | 3 | 4 | 5 | 6 | 7 | 8 | 9 | 10 |
|---|---|---|---|---|---|---|---|---|---|---|---|
| Funding | | | | | | | | | | | |
| Competing programs | | | | | | | | | | | |
| Low priority | | | | | | | | | | | |
| Emphasis on proficiency tests | | | | | | | | | | | |
| Scheduling regular lessons | | | | | | | | | | | |
| Documenting success | | | | | | | | | | | |
| Responding to negative critiques of Reading Recovery | | | | | | | | | | | |
| Perceived high cost of program | | | | | | | | | | | |
| Limited program understanding in the district | | | | | | | | | | | |
| Not a comprehensive program | | | | | | | | | | | |
| Lack of attention from decision makers | | | | | | | | | | | |
| Low interest among classroom teachers | | | | | | | | | | | |
| Lack of administrative support | | | | | | | | | | | |
| Political problems in the school district | | | | | | | | | | | |
| Student mobility | | | | | | | | | | | |
| Large number of students who need additional support | | | | | | | | | | | |
| Perceived incompatibility of Reading Recovery with the predominant approach to literacy instruction | | | | | | | | | | | |
| Other (Specify) | | | | | | | | | | | |
| Other (Specify) | | | | | | | | | | | |
| Other (Specify) | | | | | | | | | | | |

10. What *strategies* do you use to overcome *barriers or problems* with implementation? (Check ranking from 0 to 10 where 0 = *never*, and 10 = *very often*.)

| | 0 | 1 | 2 | 3 | 4 | 5 | 6 | 7 | 8 | 9 | 10 |
|---|---|---|---|---|---|---|---|---|---|---|---|
| Apply for funds from non-school sources | | | | | | | | | | | |
| Provide information to demonstrate Reading Recovery effectiveness in relation to other early intervention programs | | | | | | | | | | | |
| Explain why a safety net program needs high priority | | | | | | | | | | | |

|  | 0 | 1 | 2 | 3 | 4 | 5 | 6 | 7 | 8 | 9 | 10 |
|---|---|---|---|---|---|---|---|---|---|---|---|
| Document performance of former Reading Recovery students on proficiency tests | | | | | | | | | | | |
| Work with classroom teachers and principals to increase the frequency of daily lessons | | | | | | | | | | | |
| Develop and distribute school reports documenting success of Reading Recovery students in the classroom | | | | | | | | | | | |
| Provide information about Reading Recovery in response to critiques | | | | | | | | | | | |
| Work with teachers and principals to develop cost-benefit scenarios for Reading Recovery | | | | | | | | | | | |
| Conduct awareness sessions in the district | | | | | | | | | | | |
| Explain how Reading Recovery is a part of a comprehensive program | | | | | | | | | | | |
| Provide regular reports to decision-makers | | | | | | | | | | | |
| Provide in-service training for classroom teachers | | | | | | | | | | | |
| Convene meetings of classroom and Reading Recovery teachers | | | | | | | | | | | |
| Provide information to administrators | | | | | | | | | | | |
| Avoid involvement in political processes | | | | | | | | | | | |
| Support classroom program development | | | | | | | | | | | |
| Consult with university training center for assistance | | | | | | | | | | | |
| Other (Specify) | | | | | | | | | | | |
| Other (Specify) | | | | | | | | | | | |
| Other (Specify) | | | | | | | | | | | |

11. Check one response only.        *Not Important = 0*        *Very Important = 5*

                                                  0    1           2   3   4   5

How important is it to you to continue being a Reading Recovery teacher leader?

12. Check one response only.        *Not Important = 0*        *Very Important = 5*

                                                  0    1           2   3   4   5

How important is it to you to continue being in your current district for employment?

13. What does your university training center do to support implementation at your site? (Check ranking from 0 to 10 where 0 = *never*, and 10 = *very often*.)

|  | 0 | 1 | 2 | 3 | 4 | 5 | 6 | 7 | 8 | 9 | 10 |
|---|---|---|---|---|---|---|---|---|---|---|---|
| Provides relevant and timely professional development sessions | | | | | | | | | | | |
| Provides updated information about implementation issues | | | | | | | | | | | |
| Assists with problem solving around issues of compliance with Reading Recovery Standards and Guidelines | | | | | | | | | | | |
| Assists with problems related to teaching the most difficult to accelerate children | | | | | | | | | | | |
| Meets with school officials as needed to discuss implementation issues | | | | | | | | | | | |
| Supports and promotes communication and networking among Reading Recovery teachers and teacher leaders associated with it | | | | | | | | | | | |
| Organizes Reading Recovery conference | | | | | | | | | | | |
| Other (Specify) | | | | | | | | | | | |
| Other (Specify) | | | | | | | | | | | |
| Other (Specify) | | | | | | | | | | | |

14. What additional help would you like to have in implementing Reading Recovery at your site? Who could provide that help?

15. Describe two things you did that you consider very successful in making Reading Recovery work well at your site. These need not be "traditional" things you learned in your training. It could be "lucky accidents," people you know, advantages in a particular situation.

16. What are you most proud of in your work at your Reading Recovery site? What is your proudest accomplishment?

17. What has been most rewarding to you in your work in Reading Recovery? In other words, what is the most compelling reason for continuing your work in Reading Recovery? Write as much as you can.

*Complete questions 18 through 22 only if you have participated in the process of* adopting *Reading Recovery (i.e., when the commitment was made at the site to train the first teacher leader).*

18. How were you involved in the *adoption* of Reading Recovery at your site? (Check ranking from 0 to 10 where 0 = *never*, and 10 = *very often*.)

|  | 0 | 1 | 2 | 3 | 4 | 5 | 6 | 7 | 8 | 9 | 10 |
|---|---|---|---|---|---|---|---|---|---|---|---|
| Identified and presented information on Reading Recovery as a solution to our early literacy problem | | | | | | | | | | | |
| Created awareness of needs through presentations to others of the information I identified | | | | | | | | | | | |
| Presented information about alternatives and why they would not be successful | | | | | | | | | | | |
| Presented information about how everyone who wanted to be involved could be involved | | | | | | | | | | | |
| Convinced other school personnel that Reading Recovery could help | | | | | | | | | | | |
| Other (Specify) | | | | | | | | | | | |
| Other (Specify) | | | | | | | | | | | |
| Other (Specify) | | | | | | | | | | | |

19. How did you *establish rapport* with the schools in order to promote the *adoption* of Reading Recovery? (Check ranking from 0 to 10 where 0 = *never*, and 10 = *very often*.)

|  | 0 | 1 | 2 | 3 | 4 | 5 | 6 | 7 | 8 | 9 | 10 |
|---|---|---|---|---|---|---|---|---|---|---|---|
| Worked first with colleagues who knew me to be credible, competent and trustworthy | | | | | | | | | | | |
| Gathered and shared information about Reading Recovery as a possible solution | | | | | | | | | | | |
| Held awareness sessions for interested individuals in the school system and community | | | | | | | | | | | |
| Met with additional colleagues and system decision-makers (principals, administrators, board members) about Reading Recovery | | | | | | | | | | | |
| Problem-solved with decision-makers about potential problems they saw in implementing Reading Recovery | | | | | | | | | | | |
| Other (Specify) | | | | | | | | | | | |
| Other (Specify) | | | | | | | | | | | |
| Other (Specify) | | | | | | | | | | | |

20. What *action* of yours was the most *important factor* in influencing schools to *adopt* Reading Recovery? (Check ranking from 0 to 10 where 0 = *never*, and 10 = *very often*.)

0 1 2 3 4 5 6 7 8 9 10

Met with colleagues to persuade them to
support adoption

Met with opinion leaders (people who influence
decisions even though they may not be the
decision-makers) to persuade them to support
adoption

Met with decision-makers (school board members,
superintendent, principals, or others who make policy
decisions for the district) to encourage them to adopt

Provided additional information upon request

Wrote letters of support

Other (Specify)

Other (Specify)

Other (Specify)

21. Who are the *decision-makers* in the *adoption* process and to what extent were they involved? (Check ranking for each decision-maker category listed below from 0 to 10 where 0 = *not involved*, and 5 = *very involved*.)

0 1 2 3 4 5

School board members

Superintendent

Assistant Superintendent

Federal Programs Director

Principals

Classroom Teachers

School Teams

District Teams

Other (Specify)

Other (Specify)

Other (Specify)

22. Check one response only.        *Never = 0*     *Frequently (Daily) = 5*

0 1        2 3 4 5

Describe the number of contacts with
decision-makers you had during the *adoption* stage.

# An Examination of Sustaining Effects in Descubriendo la Lectura Programs

Kathy Escamilla, Martha Loera, *University of Colorado at Boulder*
Olivia Ruiz, *the Tucson Unified School District*
Yvonne Rodríguez, *Texas Woman's University*

## ABSTRACT

*The study discussed herein examined the long-term impact of Descubriendo la Lectura (DLL) programs on second and third grade Spanish speaking students. The purpose of the study was to determine whether former DLL students sustain the gains they made in the program as they moved through the grades. Subjects included 264 students (184 second graders and 80 third graders). One-half of the subjects were former DLL students and one-half were students who were randomly selected from the grade cohort. Former DLL students and random sample students were compared on qualitative and quantitative measures. Results on all measures indicated that DLL students were either on par or ahead of random sample students, suggesting that DLL programs have sustaining effects for Spanish speaking students just as Reading Recovery programs have for English speaking students.*

Reading Recovery programs in English have demonstrated much success in helping students who are struggling to learn to read (Clay, 1989; Pinnell, Lyons, DeFord, Bryk, Seltzer, 1994). The program consists of an average of 12 to 15 weeks of individually tailored instruction provided by a highly trained certified teacher. Reading Recovery programs are specifically designed for first grade students. The impact of Reading Recovery programs in English has been well documented and has indicated that the majority of children in Reading Recovery programs make accelerated progress while they are in the program. Their accelerated progress enables them to catch up with their peers, and exit the program in a short amount of time. In addition to accelerated progress, and a high rate of discontinuation, Reading Recovery programs in English have demonstrated that three years after successfully leaving the program, children still retain their gains. That is, they continue to make average progress and are on par with grade level peers even though they are no longer receiving individual attention or other special reading programs (e.g., Clay, 1985; DeFord, Pinnell, Lyons, & Young, 1987; Lyons, Pinnell, McCarrier, Young, & DeFord, 1988; Rowe, 1995).

In 1988, the Reading Recovery program in English underwent a reconstruction into Spanish, and has continued to evolve. The Spanish reconstruction has been named Descubriendo la Lectura (DLL) and is now being implemented in eight states in the

United States. Research on student acceleration in Descubriendo la Lectura programs has demonstrated that DLL, like English Reading Recovery, does enable students to catch up to their grade level peers (Escamilla, 1994a). To date, however, little research exists that examines the sustaining effects of Descubriendo la Lectura on Spanish speaking students after they leave the DLL program and continue through the grades.

The purpose of this study, then, was to assess the sustaining effects of DLL programs on students who had the program in the first grade and were in second and third grades during school year 1996–97. This study was an initial attempt to examine the long-range effectiveness of DLL.

As part of this study, it was also important to examine additional variables that apply to the teaching of Spanish speaking children in the United States that are peculiar to them and do not occur with English speaking students. For example, in the United States, English speaking students who received and were discontinued from English Reading Recovery programs continue to receive English reading instruction throughout their school years (through secondary school and college). Such is not the case for Spanish speaking students, the majority of whom are in Transitional Bilingual Education Programs in U.S. schools (Fradd & Tikunoff, 1987). In these programs, students are expected to transfer, at some point in their elementary careers, from reading in Spanish to reading in English.

The criteria for transfer from Spanish to English reading vary by school and by school district, with some school districts transitioning children as early as second grade and others as late as sixth grade. It is important to note that children can also be in classrooms labeled as bilingual classrooms and yet no longer be reading in Spanish.

Therefore, in examining sustaining effects of DLL programs in Spanish, it is important to study children's success vis-a-vis their continuing opportunities to learn to read in their native language (Spanish), as well as to examine whether any of their Spanish reading gains transfer as they begin to learn to read in English.

Given the above, a second purpose of this study was to examine the reading environments of children who have been discontinued from DLL to study how such environments may affect student progress in learning to read in Spanish and English.

During the 1996–97 school year, 2,924 Spanish speaking students parti-cipated in DLL programs across the United States (National Data Evaluation Center, 1997). Of these students, 1,575 or 81% were discontinued successfully from the DLL program. The number of DLL programs continues to grow, as does the number of Spanish speaking children entering public schools in the United States. The growth of such programs, along with an increase in the number of children in need of them, makes it imperative to study long-term effects.

## The Study

### Participants

This study involved schools and teachers from certified Descubriendo la Lectura Programs in California, Arizona, and Texas. The study included 264 students (184 second graders and 80 third graders). Students were divided into groups as follows: (a) Descubriendo la Lectura (DLL) children who were served and discontinued from the program (n = 89 second graders; n = 42 third graders); and (b) random sample children drawn from second and third grade classrooms in the schools participating in the study (n = 95 second graders; n = 38 third graders). The study also included 39 schools and 63 teachers from the three participating states.

All sites are members of the Descrubriendo la Lectura Collaborative, which is a membership organization of school districts with DLL teacher leaders and teachers who are implementing certified DLL and bilingual education programs. Members of the collaborative, the purpose of which is to assure quality implementation of DLL and bilingual education programs, meet twice a year at different locations to discuss issues related to the implementation. As a part of membership, school districts sign a set of assurances to guarantee quality program implementation. Among these assurances are the following:

1. Members of the collaborative agree to participate in research on program effectiveness, particularly longitudinal research.

2. Members of the collaborative agree that Spanish speaking students in bilingual programs will continue to receive Spanish reading instruction through the third grade, although it is strongly recommended that the students continue their literacy development in Spanish beyond the third grade.

3. DLL teachers will have strong academic and instructional backgrounds in both Bilingual Education and Reading Recovery theory. They will be certified in DLL and hold bilingual and bicultural endorsements (Guidelines for Participating in Reading Recovery in Spanish, 1995).

The guidelines above reflect standards and expectations for teachers implementing DLL programs, but do not cover basic bilingual classroom teachers. In English only classrooms in the United States, the majority of teachers are native speakers of English and have completed state approved programs to obtain teaching licenses. Such is not the case in Spanish language bilingual education classrooms. In many cases, bilingual education classrooms have personnel consisting of an English speaking teacher and a bilingual paraprofessional. In these classes, the paraprofessional is responsible for all Spanish language instruction including reading and writing. In other cases, bilingual classroom teachers hold licenses to teach, but have not obtained state bilingual endorsements. Thus, they may not be well versed in bilingual teaching methodology, including the teaching of reading and writing in Spanish.

Given the above, it is important, in studies such as this one, to consider the qualifications and experiences of the persons who are directly teaching Spanish speaking children (i.e., the basic bilingual education teachers). For this study, all bilingual teachers were asked to complete a survey to determine whether they were native speakers of Spanish, and if they held full bilingual endorsements. A sample survey is included in Appendix A. Table 1 presents results of attributes of second and third grade teachers who participated in the study. Data are separated by state, and do not include DLL teachers.

**Table 1.** Attributes of Second and Third Grade Basic Bilingual Classroom Teachers

| STATE | GRADE | NATIVE SPANISH | BILLINGUAL ENDORSEMENT | N |
|---|---|---|---|---|
| Arizona | Second | 8 | 10 | 10 |
| | Third | 6 | 5 | 6 |
| California | Second | 4 | 8 | 13 |
| | Third | 7 | 5 | 10 |
| Texas | Second | 17 | 18 | 21 |
| | Third | 3 | 3 | 3 |
| Total | | 45 | 49 | 63 |

Table 1 illustrates that 72% of the teachers in the basic bilingual classrooms in the study were native Spanish speakers and 80% held bilingual endorsements. The caliber of classroom teachers in this study helped to insure that former DLL students and other bilingual students had opportunities to continue to learn to read in Spanish in classrooms where instruction was provided by fully qualified, bilingual teachers. It should be noted, however, that these classrooms do not necessarily represent typical bilingual classrooms.

## Research Questions

Research questions addressed in the study were as follows:

1. Are former DLL students continuing to read in Spanish in second and third grades?
2. How does the performance of discontinued DLL students compare with the performance of random sample students in Spanish reading in second and third grades based on informal measures?
3. How does the performance of DLL students compare with the performance of random sample children on the end-of-year assessment of Text Reading in Spanish?
4. How does the performance of DLL students compare with the performance of random sample children on an end-of-year standardized reading achievement test in Spanish?
5. What proportion of DLL students achieve end-of-the-year scores that are at least within the average band for their grade level in participating schools in the study?
6. What proportion of DLL students and random sample students have been transitioned from reading in Spanish to reading in English? At what grade level did the transition take place?

The following definitions serve to clarify the various categories of children, teachers, and classrooms:

**Discontinued Descubriendo la Lectura Children:** Children who successfully completed the program and who were officially released from the program during the year or who were identified by the DLL teacher at the end of the year as having reached a performance level satisfactory for discontinuing.

**Random Sample Children:** Children who are Spanish readers and who were in the same bilingual classrooms as DLL children, but who did not receive the program.

**Bilingual Classroom:** A classroom where Spanish and English are used for instruction in all content areas and literacy for all or part of the school day. Children in bilingual classrooms receive their literacy instruction in their dominant or strongest language (in this case Spanish).

**Descubriendo la Lectura Teacher:** A teacher who has been fully trained and certified as a DLL teacher and whose training program focused on DLL.

## Data Collection and Procedures

All students (DLL Program and Random Sample) who participated in the study were given two separate measures to assess Spanish reading achievement. These included: (a) Spanish Text Level Reading (developed for use with DLL program students and students who have discontinued from DLL programs); and (b) the SABE-2 Spanish Reading Achievement Test (CTB Macmillan/McGraw-Hill, 1994). In addition, schools that had transitioned children from reading in Spanish to reading in English were asked to administer two additional measures. These were: (a) the English Text Level Reading (developed for use with Reading Recovery students and former Reading Recovery students); and (b) the Gates MacGinitie Standardized English Reading Test. All subjects were given some or all of these measures at the end of the 1997 school year (the end of the school year varied by state and ranged from mid-May until mid-June). Both English and Spanish Text Level Reading measures were administered by certified DLL teachers. The SABE-2 Spanish reading achievement test and the Gates-MacGinitie English reading achievement tests were administered by classroom bilingual teachers.

In addition to the above, the research team created a survey for use in collecting information relating to student reading performance in bilingual classrooms. The Student Information Survey is included in Appendix B. The survey was designed to gather additional information related to classroom reading behaviors of Spanish speaking students. This survey provided information such as, which children were reading in Spanish, which were reading in both Spanish and English, and which had been transitioned to English reading. Information about other program interventions such as ESL, special education, Title I, and other programs was also gathered. The survey was also used to gather teacher judgment data related to classroom reading and writing performance of former DLL and random sample students.

## Results and Analysis

*Research Question 1: Are former DLL students continuing to read in Spanish in second and third grades?*

Data to address research question 1 were gathered from two sources. The first source was the data base established for all project sites using all four reading measures. Subjects who took the two Spanish reading measures were counted as being students who were continuing to read in Spanish. Students who took all four measures (two in Spanish and two in English) were counted as students who had either transitioned from Spanish reading to English reading or had added English reading to Spanish reading. From this data base, it was noted that all 264 children in the study were continuing to read in Spanish in the second and third grades. It was also noted that 62 students (23%) had been given the English language assessment measures as well as the Spanish language assessment measures. Further, all of the students who were assessed both in Spanish and English came from the same school district in Texas. Therefore, from these data, it would appear that the majority of students are continuing to read in Spanish and thus complying with the DLL collaborative agreements (please refer to the collaborative agreements explained earlier). Table 2 presents a breakdown of students for whom data on reading achievement in both Spanish and English were collected.

The second source of data to examine continuing opportunities to read in Spanish was taken from questions 1 and 3 from the follow-up Student Survey (see Appendix B). These questions asked classroom teachers to report in which languages students were reading and in which reading groups they were participating. Student Survey data were collected for 259 of 264 subjects. Classroom teachers did not know who the random sample and DLL students were when they completed the teacher survey forms. These data serve to verify further that the vast majority of students (both DLL and random sample) are continuing to read in Spanish in the second and third grades. Further, most of the students who were reported to be reading in English were also reading in Spanish. However, it is noteworthy that a very small number of students in both second (n = 6) and third (n = 8) grades have been transitioned to reading only in English. Table 3 presents summary results of these sections of the Student Survey.

**Table 2.** Students Taking Both Spanish and English Reading Achievement Measures

| GRADE | STATUS | SPANISH ONLY DATA | STATUS | SPANISH/ENGLISH DATA |
|---|---|---|---|---|
| Second | DLL | 71 | DLL | 20 |
| | Random | 74 | Random | 21 |
| Third | DLL | 31 | DLL | 11 |
| | Random | 28 | Random | 10 |
| Total | | 204 | | 62 |

**Table 3.** Language(s) for Reading Instruction During Spring 1997

| GRADE | STATUS | SPANISH ONLY | ENGLISH ONLY | BOTH | |
|-------|--------|--------------|--------------|------|--|
| Second | DLL | 71 | 2 | 21 | |
| | Random | 74 | 4 | 24 | |
| Third | DLL | 18 | 4 | 7 | |
| | Random | 24 | 4 | 6 | |
| | Total | 187 | 14 | 58 | 259 |

*Research Question 2: How does the performance of discontinued DLL students compare with the performance of random sample students in Spanish reading in second and third grades based on informal measures?*

To address this question, results of the Student Survey were compared across groups (DLL and Random). Informal measures consisted of obtaining teacher judgments regarding student classroom reading performance with respect to a variety of issues including: (a) special services students were receiving; (b) reading group participation; and (c) teacher judgment to predict future student performance, and to assess current attitudes toward reading and writing. To collect these informal data, classroom teachers completed a survey for each student in their classroom who was a part of the study. Student surveys were completed on 259 of the 264 total study subjects. Results of the informal assessment of student progress are presented below.

## Special Services Received by Students

Data were collected to determine whether former DLL students needed or were referred to more special services than random sample students. Data presented below indicate there are no major differences in the participation of DLL students and random sample students in special programs. More than half of DLL and random sample students receive ESL as a service. This is to be expected since both groups of students are still learning English, and ESL is a basic part of a bilingual education program. All other special services such as Title I and Special Education have minimal participation by either group of subjects. From these criteria, presented in Table 4, former DLL students are doing as well as random sample students.

## Reading Group Participation

An interesting finding from the survey was that the vast majority of bilingual classroom teachers in the study continue to use ability grouping as the predominate means of grouping students for instruction. However, they use a variety of assessment techniques to make group placement decisions. Survey information indicated that bilingual classroom teachers used the following information to place students in reading

**Table 4.** Special Services Received by Students

| SERVICE | DLL | | RANDOM SAMPLE | |
|---|---|---|---|---|
| | NUMBER | PERCENT | NUMBER | PERCENT |
| ESL | 80 | 61% | 78 | 59% |
| Title 1 | 35 | 26% | 28 | 21% |
| Speech | 5 | 3% | 8 | 6% |
| Special Education | 1 | 1% | 3 | 2% |
| Other | 18 | 13% | 18 | 13% |
| None | 16 | 12% | 19 | 14% |

**Table 5.** Reading Group Participation

| GROUP | DLL | | RANDOM SAMPLE | |
|---|---|---|---|---|
| | NUMBER | PERCENT | NUMBER | PERCENT |
| High | 74 | 59% | 69 | 54% |
| Average | 50 | 39% | 46 | 36% |
| Low | 1 | 1% | 10 | 8% |
| Other[a] | 1 | 1% | 3 | 2% |

[a]Class does not group for instruction

groups, and that these methods were the same for both former DLL students and random sample students. Techniques used in order of their frequency were: (a) teacher observation, 66%; (b) informal reading inventory, including Running Records, 54%; (c) other information (e.g. previous teacher recommendation), 27%; (d) placement test from a basal reader series, 23%; (e) information from a student's previous report card, 15%; and (f) standardized reading test, 3%.

Using the above information, teachers reported the data presented in Table 5 with regard to student grouping for Spanish reading instruction.

These data provide further evidence that DLL students are faring well in bilingual education classrooms in Spanish reading. These data indicate that over half of the former DLL students are in the high reading groups in their second and third grade classrooms, and that DLL and random sample students are found in the high reading group in roughly equal percentages. The same can be said for the average and low groups. Again, using the criteria of reading group assignment, former DLL students are faring as well as random sample students.

## Prediction Regarding Future Reading Performance

Bilingual classroom teachers were also asked to predict how well they thought their students would do in reading in subsequent school years. These data are presented in Table 6.

Once again, these data suggest that classroom teachers predict DLL students will fare very well or satisfactorily at even higher rates than random sample students. They also predict that fewer DLL students will require supplementary assistance.

## Reading and Writing Attributes

Finally, bilingual classroom teachers were asked to rank, on a scale of 1–5, each one of the students in the study using the following attributes relative to reading and writing. The data presented in Table 7 indicate the mean ranking for DLL and random sample students on each attribute.

Drawn from teachers' perspectives, these data suggest there are no major differences in student reading and writing attitudes and abilities between former DLL and random sample students. In sum, all data indicate, in the view of teachers, that former DLL students are performing as well as other students in classroom literacy activities.

*Research Questions 3 and 4: How does the performance of DLL students compare with the performance of random sample children on the end-of-year assessment of Text Reading in Spanish? How does the performance of DLL students compare with the performance of random sample children on an end-of-year standardized reading achievement test in Spanish?*

For research questions 3 and 4, data were collected by administering the Spanish Text Level Reading assessments to all second and third grade subjects. These reading assessments have been especially developed for use with students in Descubriendo la Lectura programs. The text level reading measure was administered individually to children by a certified DLL teacher. Children were asked to read stories aloud while the DLL teacher took a Running Record of reading behavior and calculated an accuracy level. Children continued reading at higher levels until they reached a level where they read below 90% accuracy. The score on text level reading is the highest level read with at least 90% accuracy. Levels range from A–30.

**Table 6.** Teacher Prediction Regarding Future Reading Performance

| TEACHER PREDICTION | DLL NUMBER | DLL PERCENT | RANDOM SAMPLE NUMBER | RANDOM SAMPLE PERCENT |
|---|---|---|---|---|
| Very Well | 66 | 50% | 54 | 40% |
| Satisfactory | 50 | 38% | 45 | 33% |
| Will Need Extra Help | 12 | 9% | 26 | 20% |

**Table 7.** Reading and Writing Attributes

| ATTRIBUTE | DLL MEAN | RANDOM SAMPLE MEAN |
|---|---|---|
| Reading Ability | 3.8 | 3.8 |
| Writing Ability | 3.2 | 3.4 |
| Attitude Toward Reading | 4.2 | 4.2 |
| Attitude Toward Writing | 3.6 | 3.5 |
| Chooses to Read | 3.7 | 3.6 |
| Selects Books at his/her Level | 4.2 | 4.2 |
| Independent in Class Work | 3.5 | 3.9 |
| Tries Hard | 3.5 | 3.8 |
| Completes Work | 3.8 | 3.7 |
| Attends Well In Class | 3.7 | 3.7 |
| Responds in Group Discussion | 3.4 | 3.6 |

All subjects also took the SABE-2 Spanish achievement test in reading. These tests were group administered by classroom bilingual teachers. Scores obtained were from the Total Reading score of the test. For the Spanish Text Level Reading, mean reading levels were calculated for each group and each grade. For the SABE-2 test, mean reading levels were calculated for each group and each grade two times—one time using raw scores and a second using percentiles. A two-tailed $t$ test was used to test for significant differences between group means. Tables 8 and 9 present results for the Spanish Text Level Reading measure and the SABE-2 test measures.

From the calculated means of Spanish Text Level Reading, it is noted that the DLL students were above their random sample counterparts in both second and third grades. For both second and third graders, $t$ test results indicated that the differences were statistically significant for second graders ($t = 1.87$, $p < .001$) and for third graders ($t = 2.44$, $p < .001$). These findings provide support for the notion of sustaining effects. Former DLL students are continuing to progress in their acquisition of literacy without additional special program support. In fact, their achievement in Spanish reading is higher than the random sample students.

**Table 8.** Results of Spanish Text Level Reading

| GRADE | STATUS | MEAN | SD | N |
|-------|--------|------|-----|-----|
| Second | DLL | 25.6 | 5.2 | 89 |
| | Random | 23.9 | 7.0 | 95 |
| Third | DLL | 28.4 | 4.0 | 42 |
| | Random | 24.9 | 8.0 | 36 |
| Total | | | | 262 |

**Table 9.** Results of SABE-2

| MEAN GRADE | MEAN STATUS | RAW SCORE | SD | STANINE | N |
|------------|-------------|-----------|-----|---------|-----|
| Second | DLL | 31.6 | 7.8 | 5 | 81 |
| | Random | 31.9 | 8.5 | 5 | 86 |
| Third | DLL | 39.1 | 8.0 | 5 | 34 |
| | Random | 38.0 | 9.8 | 4 | 40 |
| Total | | | | | 241 |

From the calculated means of the raw scores on the SABE/2 Spanish Reading Achievement Test, it is noted that the DLL students also performed above their random sample counterparts in third grade, and at a roughly equivalent level in the second grade. In the second grade both groups were in the fifth stanine, and in the third grade both groups were in the fourth stanine. A *t* test was conducted using the raw score data to ascertain whether these differences were statistically significant. For both second and third graders, *t* tests did not indicate that the differences between former DLL program students and randomly selected students were statistically significant. These data provide solid evidence to support the notion of sustaining effects. Specifically, former DLL students were selected for the program because they were performing far behind their peers in first grade. These data suggest they are no longer far behind, but rather reading at a level that is equivalent to their peers. These data provide further evidence that former DLL students are continuing to progress in their acquisition of literacy without additional special program support.

It is further significant to note that, at the second grade level, mean percentile scores for both DLL and random sample students are above the 50th percentile (54.2 for DLL; 55.5 for the random sample). This is an indication that DLL students are not only keeping pace with random sample students in the study, but also are achieving on par with national norms. At the third grade level, mean percentiles for DLL and random students are also similar (23.8

for DLL; 26.7 for the random sample). However, scores for both groups are below the 27th percentile. Achievement levels for both groups are well below national norms and represent a significant decrease in achievement from the second grade.

The exact causes of this decline in scores cannot be determined from the data presented in this study. However, it might be important to consider the role played by language status differences between English and Spanish. It has been well documented that, in most bilingual programs in the U.S., there is an unequal status between English and Spanish (Escamilla, 1994b; Shannon, 1995). English is the high status language, while Spanish has a lower status. As a result, after several years in U.S. schools, students begin to think there is no value in knowing Spanish. As a result, they begin to reject Spanish and resist learning in Spanish. This resistance develops at the same time that schools are putting pressure on teachers to transfer students from Spanish to English reading, and to exit them from bilingual programs.

Given this situation, it may be that the decline in Spanish reading achievement is a reaction to the message that learning in Spanish is not as important as learning in English. As Shannon (1995) reports, children and teachers respond in real ways to the "hegemony of English." It is important that any report on student achievement in Spanish in bilingual programs in the U.S. consider language status differences and the context in which bilingual education programs are implemented as they undertake studies such as this one.

*Research Question 5: What proportion of DLL students achieve end-of-the-year scores that are at least within the average band for their grade level in participating schools in the study?*

Research question 5 examined the proportion of DLL students who achieved end-of-the-year scores that were at least within the average band for their grade level in the schools in the study. To address this question, an average band of performance was calculated using the random sample of second grade children in this study. An average band was also calculated for third grade using the random sample third graders in the study. Average bands were calculated using both Spanish Text Reading and SABE-2 raw scores. The average band was calculated as ± .5 standard deviations from the mean. This calculation determined the upper and lower band of average performance. The numbers of students who achieved or exceeded average band performance and the percentages of total DLL students are presented in Table 10. The vast majority of DLL students both in second and third grades achieved or exceeded average band performance on both measures (Spanish Text Reading and SABE-2 Raw Scores). These data provide further support for the notion that the initial positive impact of Descubriendo la Lectura Programs is sustained across grade levels.

*Research Question 6: What proportion of DLL students and random sample students have been transitioned from reading in Spanish to reading in English? At what grade level did the transition take place?*

Research question 6 was meant to investigate whether or not sustaining effects of DLL in Spanish may have transfer effects as Spanish speaking students begin to learn to read in English. To address the question, data were collected on DLL program students

**Table 10.** Numbers and Percentages of DLL Children in End-of-Year Average Band on Spanish Text Reading and SABE-2 Spanish Reading Test

| GRADE | MEASURE | AVERAGE BAND | MET AVERAGE BAND NUMBER PERCENT | EXCEEDED AVERAGE BAND NUMBER PERCENT | N |
|---|---|---|---|---|---|
| Second | Spanish Text Reading | 20.45–27.48 | 39  43.8% | 43  48.3% | 89 |
| Second | SABE-2 Raw Scores | 27.62–36.21 | 37  45.6% | 24  29.4% | 81 |
| Third | Spanish Text Reading | 20.93–29.01 | 6  14.4% | 33  78.6% | 42 |
| Third | SABE-2 Raw Scores | 33.13–42.93 | 17  50.0% | 10  29.2% | 34 |

and random sample students who had been transitioned from reading in Spanish to reading in English. Transitioned students were given the Gates MacGinitie English Achievement Test to assess their progress in English reading.

Of the 39 schools participating in the study, only one school in one school district reported transitioning students from Spanish to English reading in either the second or the third grade. In this district, transition data were reported in second grade for 20 DLL students and 21 random sample students. The same district reported transition data in third grade for 11 DLL students and 11 random sample students.

With only one district and one school reporting transition data, it was not appropriate to do extensive data analysis, as data reported were not representative of the larger group of DLL and random sample students. Further, in this particular school district, all Spanish speaking children transition to English reading in the second grade and thus the proportion of DLL students making the transition is exactly the same as English language students. The policy is applied to all Spanish speaking students regardless of special program category.

The fact that only one district and school reported data on transition from Spanish to English and on English language achievement it is not viewed as a problem in this study. In fact, according to the guidelines for participating in Descubriendo la Lectura, school districts commit to keeping students in Spanish reading through the third grade. The majority of districts in this study are simply choosing not to transition students to English reading until the fourth grade or beyond.

The question about sustaining effects of DLL program and their potential for transfer to English reading programs is an important one. However, it will need to be addressed in future longitudinal studies that look at reading achievement of former DLL students in fourth grade and beyond. The majority of districts in this study are simply choosing not to transition students to English reading until the fourth grade or beyond.

**Table 11.** English Reading Achievement of DLL and Random Sample Students Transitioned from Spanish to English Reading

| GRADE | PROGRAM | N | MEAN/ SD VOCABULARY | MEAN/ SD COMPREHENSION |
|---|---|---|---|---|
| Second | DLL | 20 | 28.05/28.06 | 27.55/28.47 |
| | Random | 21 | 30.29/22.11 | 28.70/22.00 |
| | Total | 41 | | |
| Third | DLL | 11 | 21.46/28.13 | 21.36/24.81 |
| | Random | 10 | 10.3/13.73 | 9.90/13.99 |
| | Total | 21 | | |

Data on the English Reading Achievement of transitioned students are presented in Table 11. Data are presented only as descriptive statistics. Because of the low numbers of students and the fact that they all came from the same school district, no statistical analyses were conducted with these data and they should be discussed only in a very preliminary way. While they provide a snap-shot that suggests former DLL students are doing as well in English reading as a random sample of second graders, it must be noted that the achievement of both groups in English reading is low. Similarly, in third grade, former DLL students are doing much better in English reading than random sample students, however, achievement in both groups is low. Again, because of the low number of students in each group, these findings should be considered with caution.

## Discussion

The data reported here establish that the DLL program achieved sustaining effects with Spanish speaking students who had been in DLL programs in first grade, who had been discontinued from these programs, and who were continuing to read in Spanish in second and third grades. Results of this study, considered collectively with research on acceleration of Spanish speaking students in DLL programs (Escamilla, 1994a), establish that Descubriendo la Lectura is having a positive impact on Spanish speaking students in much the same way that Reading Recovery is impacting English speaking students.

DLL children could be considered as ones in need of long-term interventions beyond DLL. As second language learners of English, they will need continued support in both their first and second languages to insure their long-term success in U.S. schools. Aside from language, children who participate in DLL have other social needs. They often are among the poorest of all school-aged children in the United States. They most likely attend large urban schools that are overcrowded and lacking in resources, and they are likely to be in classrooms with teachers who have no preparation in how to teach them. DLL is having a positive impact on these students, however, issues affecting their academic success may extend far beyond literacy instruction. DLL is helping these children become literate, but this program cannot solve the social and societal issues that are part and parcel of growing up in the United States as members of a cultural and linguistic group that is marginalized and undervalued by the larger society.

Evidence of sustaining effects presented in this study include both qualitative and quantitative data. Qualitative data indicate that former DLL students in both second and third grades do not require special services such as Title I at higher rates than random sample students, they are as likely to be in the average or high reading group in their classrooms as random sample students, and their teachers report that their achievement in and attitude toward reading and writing are very similar to random sample students. Their teachers perceive them just as likely to be successful in reading and writing as they perceive other Spanish speaking students.

Quantitative data gathered on Spanish reading achievement on the DLL Spanish Text Level Reading indicated that former DLL students were achieving at higher rates than randomly selected students both in the second and third grades and that these differences were statistically significant in favor of former DLL students. Mean scores for the former DLL students in second grade were at level 25 on Spanish Text Reading. Mean scores for the former DLL students in third grade were at level 28 on Spanish Text Reading. Third grade results are promising in that they also provide evidence for sustaining effects of the DLL program two years after discontinuation from the program, and indicate that former DLL students are continuing to progress in Spanish reading without further program assistance.

All subjects were also given the SABE-2 Spanish Reading Achievement Test. Again, DLL students were achieving at levels that were at or above their random sample counterparts in both second and third grades. For these measures, achievement differences between DLL and random sample students were not statistically significant, providing support for the notion of sustaining effects since the achievement of DLL students is similar to that of randomly sampled students. This is true because when first selected to participate in DLL, this group's achievement was far below that of all other students. The goals of DLL are to have children reach the average of their class in reading and writing, while at the same time to develop independent learning strategies. Results of this study indicate the children are achieving these goals.

Further evidence of sustaining effects is apparent in second graders' achievement on the SABE-2 where their mean was at the 54th percentile. The third graders' mean percentile on the SABE-2 was only at the 23rd percentile, representing a significant decrease from the second grade. However, this decline occurred in the third grade for both DLL and random sample students. When interpreting these data for Spanish speaking students, it is important to consider the role that language status may play in both student and teacher beliefs about the importance of literacy in Spanish.

Achievement of discontinued DLL students in second and third grades was further examined by calculating the number and percentage of former DLL students who were achieving within or above the average band of reading on the Spanish Text Level Reading measure and on the SABE-2 Test. In second grade, 92% of the former DLL students were achieving within or above the average band on Spanish Text Level Reading and 75% were achieving within or above the average band on the SABE-2 Spanish Reading Achievement Test. In third grade, 93% of the former DLL students were achieving within or above the average band on Spanish Text Level Reading and 79% were achieving within or above the average band on the SABE-2 Spanish Reading Achievement Test.

A very small number of former DLL students in the study, who were from the same school district, were transitioned from Spanish reading to English reading during the course of the study (n = 20 second graders and n = 10 third graders). These low numbers indicate that school districts participating in the implementation of Descubriendo la Lectura are following implementation guidelines and not transitioning students before the end of the third grade. Data on English reading achievement were presented herein, however, no statistical analyses were conducted. Collecting and analyzing data on former DLL students as they transition from Spanish to English reading is of critical importance to future longitudinal studies dealing with the impact of DLL on students. However, such data should not start being collected until fourth grade, and must include only students who have had consistent and continuous instruction in Spanish reading until the fourth grade or until they have met academic criteria for transition.

## Summary

In summary, results presented herein, indicate that DLL programs are affecting former students in a positive way after they are successfully discontinued from program services. Data presented here establish that the DLL program has sustaining effects in much the same manner as Reading Recovery programs in English. It must be noted that this study is the first of its kind, and there is a crucial need for further studies addressing these issues for Spanish speaking students.

Finally, it is important to state, once again, that research on Descubriendo la Lectura programs and children cannot and should not consist of simple replications of studies conducted on English Reading Recovery programs. The implementation of Spanish DLL programs has a political and social reality that is quite different from English Reading Recovery. This unique political and social reality must be considered in future research studies, in order to insure valid and reliable interpretation of study results.

As an example, in all likelihood, students who participate in and are discontinued from English Reading Recovery will continue to receive English reading instruction throughout their school careers. Such is not the case for Spanish speaking students. In many cases, basic literacy instruction for Spanish speaking students is inconsistent and often interrupted. For example, it is not unusual to find school and bilingual programs where students receive literacy instruction in Spanish one year, in English the next year, and then Spanish the following year. It is also not unusual to find programs where students are prematurely transitioned into English (Cziko, 1992; Escamilla, 1994c).

In addition, the overwhelming majority (95%) of Spanish/English bilingual programs in the United States are transitional in nature (Fradd & Tikunoff, 1987). This means that Spanish speaking students will receive Spanish reading for only three or four years or until they are transitioned into English reading. There is strong research evidence that literacy skills and strategies transfer from one language to another (Escamilla, 1987; Krashen & Biber, 1988; Lesher-Madrid & García, 1985; Rodríguez, 1988). However, this research base must be extended to include students who were former DLL students. Future studies in this area that look at former DLL students as they begin to read in English must consider both the quantity and quality of Spanish reading instruction after students were discontinued from DLL programs. While English Reading Recovery programs will not likely be scrutinized to see if former students are applying reading skills and strategies in a second language, Descubriendo la Lectura programs most assuredly will be studied vis-a-vis transfer to the students' second language. Moreover, it is important that future studies investigate former DLL students in the upper elementary grades and examine their English reading achievement as well as their Spanish achievement.

Research in the area of Descubriendo la Lectura is promising, but must be considered to be in its infancy. Much remains to be studied. However, if basic bilingual programs are inconsistently implemented or are not operating using sound pedagogy, then the efficacy of Descubriendo la Lectura programs will also most likely be affected. It is critical, therefore, for future research to study DLL in the context of the larger school's implementation of bilingual education, as well as in the context of the sociolinguistic realities of the status of Spanish and Spanish speaking populations in the United States.

## References

Clay, M. M. (1985). *The early detection of reading difficulties.* Portsmouth, NH: Heinemann.

Clay, M. M. (1989). Concepts about print in English and other languages. *The Reading Teacher, 42,* 268–276.

Cziko, G. (1992). The evaluation of bilingual education. *Educational Researcher, 21,* 10–15.

DeFord, D. E, Pinnell, G. S., Lyons, C. A., & Young, P. (1987). *Report of the Follow-up Studies.* Columbus, OH: Ohio Reading Recovery Project.

Escamilla, K. (1994a). Descubriendo la Lectura: An early intervention literacy program in Spanish. *Literacy Teaching and Learning:* An International Journal of Early Literacy, *1,* 57–85.

Escamilla, K. (1994b). The sociolinguistic environment of a bilingual school: A case study introduction. *Bilingual Research Journal, 18,* 21–47.

Escamilla, K. (1994c). Issues in bilingual program evaluation. In R. Rodríguez, N. Ramos & J. Ruiz-Escalante (Eds.), *Compendium of readings in bilingual education: Issues and practices* (pp. 74–83). San Antonio, TX: Association for Bilingual Education.

Escamilla, K. (1987). *The relationship of native language reading achievement and oral English proficiency to future achievement in reading English as a second language.* Unpublished doctoral dissertation, University of California, Los Angeles.

Fradd, S., & Tikunoff, W. (1987). *Bilingual education and bilingual special education: A guide for administrators.* Boston: College Hill.

*Guidelines for participating in Reading Recovery in Spanish.* (1995). Tucson, AZ: Tucson Unified School District, Title I, Descubriendo la Lectura Project.

Krashen, S., & Biber, D. (1988). *On course: Bilingual education's success in California.* Sacramento, CA: California Association for Bilingual Education.

Lesher-Madrid, D., & García, E. (1985). The effect of language transfer on bilingual proficiency. In E. García & R. Padilla (Eds.), *Advances in bilingual education research* (pp. 53–70). Tucson: The University of Arizona Press.

Lyons, C. A., Pinnell, G. S., McCarrier, A., Young, P., & DeFord, D. E. (1988). *The Ohio Reading Recovery project — Year 2*. Columbus, OH: Ohio Reading Recovery Project.

National Data Evaluation Center for the Study of Reading Recovery. (1997). *Reading Recovery Executive Summary*. Columbus, OH: The Ohio State University.

Pinnell, G. S., Lyons, C. A., DeFord, D. E., Bryk, A., & Seltzer, M. (1994). Comparing instructional models for the literacy education of high-risk first graders. *Reading Research* Quarterly, *29*, 8-39.

Rodríguez, A. (1988). Research in reading and writing in bilingual education and English as a second language. In A. Ambert (Ed.), *Bilingual education and English as a second language*. New York: Garland Publishing.

Rowe, K. J. (1995). Factors affecting students' progress in reading: Key findings from a longitudinal study. *Literacy, Teaching and Learning: An International Journal of Early Literacy, 1*, 57–110.

Shannon, S. (1995). The hegemony of English: A case study of one bilingual classroom as a site of resistance. *Linguistics and Education: An International Research Journal, 7*, 177–202.

## Acknowledgments

The authors wish to acknowledge with gratitude the financial support for this project that was granted by the Reading Recovery Council of North America. Also, special appreciation goes to Carlos Manrique of the El Monte Unified School District in El Monte, California, for the countless hours of help in mailing and distributing materials for this project.

We extend our gratitude to all of the tireless Descubriendo la Lectura teacher leaders and teachers who made this project a priority when they were already overworked and over-committed. Without their willingness to help collect data for this study, it would never have been completed. Their commitment to the cause of quality educational experiences for Spanish speaking children is commendable. Otra vez, muchisimas gracias.

In addition, we wish to acknowledge the following school districts that participated in this research project:

**Arizona**
Tucson Unified School District

**California**
ABC Unified School District
Bakersfield City Schools
Baldwin Park School District
Cajon Valley School District

Chula Vista School District
Corcoran Unified School District
Delano School District
Fresno Unified School District
Hilmar Unified School District
Lindsay Unified School District
Los Angeles County Office of Education
Long Beach Unified School District
Los Nietos School District
Madera Unified School District
Napa Valley Unified School District
Patterson School District
Planada School District
Pomona Unified School District
Porterville Unified School District
San Diego City Schools
San Diego Unified School District
Santa Rosa Unified School District
Sonoma Unified School District
Vacaville Unified School District
Visalia Unified School District Texas
Carollton-Farmer's Branch Independent School District
Fort Worth Independent School District
McAllen Independent School District
Spring Branch Independent School District
United Independent School District (Laredo)

## Appendix A

### Descubriendo la Lectura Follow-Up Study 1996–97
### Teacher Information Form

DLL Teacher Leader: Please complete the following information for each classroom teacher from whom you have taken children for this study. This includes teachers who teach former DLL students and randomly selected students.


Teacher Name: _____

Grade: _____ District: _____

Address: _____

State Bilingual Endorsements: _____ Yes _____ No

Native Spanish Speaker: _____Yes _____ No

Number of Years Experience as a Bilingual Teacher _____

Comments:

# Appendix B

## Descubriendo la Lectura Follow-Up Study 1996–97
## Student Survey

Complete for each student in the DLL study (former DLL and random sample students).

Child's Name: _____

Grade: _____  School: _____

District: _____

1. Student is currently reading in:
   ____ Spanish   ____ English   ____ Both

2. What special services are currently being received by the student:
   ____ ESL
   ____ Title 1
   ____ Speech
   ____ Special Education
   ____ Other (Please specify)
   ____ None

3. In what reading group is the student currently participating?

   | Spanish | English (if applicable) |
   |---------|--------------------------|
   | ____ High | ____ High |
   | ____ High Average | ____ High Average |
   | ____ Average | ____ Average |
   | ____ Low Average | ____ Low Average |
   | ____ Low | ____ Low |
   | ____ Other (e.g., no ability groups) | ____ Other (e.g., no ability groups) |

4. What information did you use to place students in these reading groups?

   | Spanish | English (if applicable) |
   |---------|--------------------------|
   | ____ Basal Reader Test | ____ Basal Reader Test |
   | ____ Standardized Reading Test | ____ Standardized Reading Test |
   | ____ Informal Reading Inventory | ____ Informal Reading Inventory |
   | ____ Teacher Observation | ____ Teacher Observation |
   | ____ Previous Student Report | ____ Previous Student Report |
   | ____ Other (Please describe) | ____ Other (Please describe) |

5. What grade did the child receive in reading on the last report card? (Explain your assessment system if it is other than grades)?

6. In what basal reader is the child currently reading? (Indicate grade level) If no basal reader is used, approximately what grade level is the child reading? How did you determine this?

7. How do you predict the child will perform in reading next school year?
___ very well
___ satisfactory
___ will need extra help

8. Rate the attributes that best describe this child by rating him/her on a scale of 1–5 (1 = weak; 5 = strong).

Spanish
___ Reading Ability
___ Writing Ability
___ Attitude Toward Reading
___ Attitude Toward Writing
___ Chooses to Read When Time
    Allows
___ Selects Books on His/Her Own
___ Independent in Class Work
___ Tries Hard
___ Completes Work
___ Attends Well in Class Work
___ Responds in Group Discussions

English (if applicable)
___ Reading Ability
___ Writing Ability
___ Attitude Toward Readingg
___ Attitude Toward Writing
___ Chooses to Read When Time
    Allows
___ Selects Books on His/Her Own
___ Independent in Class Work
___ Tries Hard
___ Completes Work
___ Attends Well in Class Work
___ Responds in Group Discussions

9. Other comments about the student as a learner of two languages:

# Reading Recovery in the United States: More than a Decade of Data

Carol A. Lyons, *The Ohio State University*

## ABSTRACT

*There is considerable information available to evaluate Reading Recovery's impact on children's literacy development and the professional development of teachers. The purpose of this article is to review the thirteen years of replication data that support Reading Recovery's effectiveness, as well as to address the questions most often raised by critics regarding (a) the length of the teacher training program, (b) the cost of implementation, and (c) the long-term effects of the program for children. Rationales are explicated for leaders of the program requiring that certified teachers enroll in a year of academic coursework and participate in continued professional development, teach the lowest achieving children one-on-one, and collect and report data on a daily basis to document the effectiveness of the program.*

Reading Recovery (RR), an early intervention literacy program, has been operating in the United States for more than a decade. During that time, nearly a half million children have received instruction and 15,000 teachers have participated in training. Because of the extent of the development of this program, there is considerable information available to evaluate its impact on children's literacy development and the professional development of teachers.

The purpose of this article is to review the extensive replication data that support RR's effectiveness, as well as to address the questions most often raised by critics regarding (a) the length of the teacher training program, (b) the cost of implementation, and (c) the long-term effects of the program for children. After a brief history of the development of RR, each of these areas will be discussed separately, and there will be a general call for programs to substantiate their effectiveness in the quest toward literacy for all children.

## A Brief History of Reading Recovery

In September 1984, Professor Marie M. Clay, a New Zealand researcher and educator who originally designed the program, and Barbara Watson, current National Director in New Zealand, introduced RR to faculty at The Ohio State University and sixteen teachers in the Columbus Public Schools. This early intervention program provided intensive, individual help to the lowest achieving first grade students in six Columbus,

215

Ohio, schools. End-of-year data revealed that during the initial year of implementation, when all of the educators were learning the program, 67% of the lowest achieving children developed effective strategies for reading and writing and reached average classroom levels after 12–20 weeks of one-to-one instruction.

In July 1985, the successful results of the pilot study led the Ohio General Assembly to provide funding to establish teacher training sites in Ohio and to begin implementing the program throughout the state. By the start of the 1987 school year, RR was operating in 182 school districts throughout Ohio. When the number of low-progress first grade children who were reaching average reading levels increased from 73% in 1986 to 79% in 1987, long-term benefits of the RR program became a possibility. The Ohio General Assembly and the Ohio Department of Education have continued to fund the training and ongoing professional development of RR teachers and teacher leaders for 12 years.

In 1987, the U.S. Department of Education's National Diffusion Network (NDN) recognized RR as an exemplary research-based program and provided funding to make the program available to school districts in other states. Four educators from outside of Ohio enrolled in the year-long RR teacher leader course at The Ohio State University during the 1987–1988 academic year. These educators returned to their home sites the following year to begin training teachers to deliver the program to children. In 1996–97, the United States RR program was operating in 48 states, the District of Columbia, and some U.S. Defense Department Schools overseas. As reported in Table 1, the RR network by 1996–1997 includes 42 university trainers, 667 teacher leaders, 15,483 teachers, 3,241 school districts, and 9,815 schools.

**Table 1.** U.S. University Trainers, Teacher Leaders, Teachers, School Districts, and Schools Participating in Reading Recovery from 1984–1997

| UNIVERSITY YEAR | TEACHER TRAINERS | LEADERS | SCHOOL TEACHERS | DISTRICTS | SCHOOLS |
|---|---|---|---|---|---|
| 1984-85 | 0 | 0 | 16 | 1 | 6 |
| 1985-86 | 1 | 3 | 58 | 23 | 35 |
| 1986-87 | 3 | 2 | 280 | 108 | 255 |
| 1987-88 | 3 | 45 | 531 | 143 | 227 |
| 1988-89 | 6 | 43 | 732 | 265 | 623 |
| 1989-90 | 11 | 54 | 1,163 | 332 | 892 |
| 1990-91 | 13 | 80 | 1,850 | 508 | 1,406 |
| 1991-92 | 19 | 155 | 3,164 | 798 | 2,336 |
| 1992-93 | 24 | 259 | 5,343 | 1,246 | 3,731 |
| 1993-94 | 33 | 388 | 8,182 | 1,905 | 5,523 |
| 1994-95 | 39 | 510 | 12,084 | 2,543 | 7,784 |
| 1995-96 | 39 | 625 | 14,153 | 2,939 | 9,062 |
| 1996-97 | 42 | 667 | 15,843 | 3,241 | 9,815 |

*Note:* Data from the National Evaluation Data Center, The Ohio State University

## Reading Recovery Evaluation Data: Replication Methodology

Replication of results represents a vital component of research and an important concept in the history and theory of research design (Campbell & Stanley, 1963; Kratochwill, 1978). Intervention research in such fields as medicine, social work, psychology, and education seemingly requires replication of results to an even greater degree (Hersen & Barlow, 1976; Neuman & McCormick, 1995). There are two main approaches to replication: (a) Systematic replication, which involves different investigators conducting the same study on different subjects with the same problem at a different location and at a later time, and (b) simultaneous replication, which is similar to the former, but being conducted at the same time (Gay, 1987).

While replication at a later time (i.e., systematic) is the standard approach, simultaneous replication, a research methodology designed by Frymier, Barber, Gansneder, and Robertson (1989), has been used effectively to assess students' academic achievements in widely separated geographical settings. For example, simultaneous replication was successfully tested as a methodology in the Phi Delta Kappa Study of Students at Risk (Frymier et al., 1989) by subjecting to common analytic procedures data that were collected in common ways with common instruments in 87 separate sites. The study enabled researchers from urban, rural, and suburban school districts to verify results by focusing on local analyses of data collected at the school level while still contributing to a large-scale study. To determine program effectiveness, RR has employed both types of replication methodology.

Data evaluating the original design of the program are monitored annually in New Zealand by the Ministry of Education (Kerslake, 1996). Since 1985 in the United States, the effect of the RR program has been replicated hundreds of thousands of times in thousands of schools with hundreds of thousands of individual subjects. In that time, approximately 15,000 RR teachers working individually with more than 435,000 low achieving first grade children from different cultures in urban, suburban, and rural school districts have documented similar results. That is, RR teachers, using the RR teaching procedures they learned through standardized professional training, have helped the lowest achieving first grade students reach average band reading levels after 12 to 20 weeks of individually designed and individually delivered instruction (Lyons, 1997). Essentially, children who were initially labeled "slow" learners were shown to be performing at average levels in reading, and some reports have indicated profits in other subject areas, as well (Lyons & Beaver, 1995). Furthermore, RR teachers in other countries such as Australia, Canada, The United Kingdom, New Zealand, and the U.S. Defense Department Schools overseas have produced notably similar results. According to Kratochwill (1978), repeatedly producing the same effect with different students in different settings increases confidence in a treatment or intervention, thereby providing substantial evidence of the effectiveness of RR tutoring.

As reported in Table 2, from 1985–1997, the RR program served a total of 436,249 children. Of that group, 313,848 had sufficient time to experience a complete program (defined as 60 lessons) and 81% reached criteria for successful release from the program; that is, they were performing within the average band reading group of their classroom. Such numbers represent extensive replication documentation, a hallmark of research reliability. Data documenting the impact of RR on student achievement

**Table 2.** U.S. Reading Recovery Children Served, Program Children and Percentage of Children Discontinued from 1984–1997

| YEAR | SERVED** | PROGRAM*** | DISCONTINUED**** | % |
|------|------|------|------|------|
| 1984-1985* | 110 | 55 | 37 | 67% |
| 1985-1986 | 230 | 136 | 99 | 73% |
| 1986-1987 | 2,048 | 1,336 | 1,059 | 79% |
| 1987-1988 | 3,649 | 2,648 | 2,269 | 86% |
| 1988-1989 | 4,772 | 3,609 | 2,994 | 83% |
| 1989-1990 | 7,778 | 5,840 | 4,888 | 84% |
| 1990-1991 | 12,605 | 9,283 | 8,126 | 88% |
| 1991-1992 | 21,821 | 16,026 | 3,499 | 84% |
| 1992-1993 | 36,443 | 26,582 | 22,109 | 83% |
| 1993-1994 | 56,077 | 40,493 | 33,243 | 82% |
| 1994-1995 | 81,220 | 57,712 | 46,637 | 81% |
| 1995-1996 | 99,617 | 71,193 | 59,266 | 83% |
| 1996-1997 | 108,876 | 78,935 | 65,551 | 83% |
| Totals | 436,249 | 313,848 | 259,777 | 81% |

*Note:* Data from the National Evaluation Data Center, The Ohio State University

*Pilot year: RR teachers were in training.

**Served: Program children and children who entered Reading Recovery but did not receive a minimum of 60 lessons because they moved, were absent for extended periods of time, or the school year ended prior to completion of lessons. Column 1 is inclusive of the subcategory Program Children, column 2.

*** Program: RR children who received a minimum of 60 lessons or were discontinued prior to receiving 60 lessons.

****Discontinued: RR children who were released from the RR program reading within average band reading levels of the class.

are reported each year in local, state, and national evaluation reports. In addition, several other reports produced by RR professionals and others provide data to document three claims related to the effectiveness of the RR program.

*Claim 1: Within 12–20 weeks of daily, one-to-one instruction, the majority of the lowest achieving first grade students can be placed in an average reading group in their respective first grade classrooms.* Since 1984, data for every child served in the U.S. have been reported to the Reading Recovery National Data Evaluation Center at The Ohio State University and forwarded to the United States Department of Education. If we consider all students served, even for one day, 60% met the stringent exit criteria for success.

There is no checklist of specific criteria to determine that a child is ready for discontinuing because the goal of the program is to place the child in a classroom reading group in which he or she is predicted to make progress without further individual instruction. The level of performance will differ from child to child and from school to school (Clay, 1993). If the child is to continue to make progress, however, RR teachers must consider whether that child has acquired a system of strategies that helps him or her learn from further attempts to read and write. This system of strategies includes the ability to (a) control left to right directional movement, (b) match spoken to written words, (c) notice and correct errors when reading and writing, (d) notice discrepancies in responses by cross-checking one source of information (e.g., visual) with a different source of information (e.g., meaning or structural cues), (e) use many sources of information, and (f) detect and self-correct errors (Clay, 1993). If RR students acquire these strategies, assuming these strategies are the ones beginning readers must acquire, they should continue to make average progress in reading in the years after they complete RR.

*Claim 2: Reading Recovery is more effective when compared to traditional one-to-one and small group remedial programs targeting low-achieving first grade students.* Researchers Wasik and Slavin (1993) compared RR to four other one-to-one tutoring models that have been used to improve the reading skills of first graders who were at risk of failure: Success for All, Prevention of Learning Disabilities, The Wallach Tutoring Program and Programmed Tutorial Reading. Sixteen studies evaluating the effect of these models on student achievement revealed substantial positive effects of one-to-one tutoring in comparison to small group instruction. Wasik et al., (1993) reported "follow-up studies found that effects of tutoring were generally lasting and the results were more positive when reading instruction was based on a more comprehensive model of reading and when certified teachers (rather than paraprofessionals) were the tutors" (p. 178). The researchers also reported that RR is the only program that has documented long-term success without additional intervention and the only program that has assessed the quality of implementation across tutoring sessions and the effect this has on outcome data. Wasik and Slavin (1993) concluded that when compared to other one-to-one interventions, RR is at least as effective as the others, but one well-wrought study found it is more effective.

In 1988, the John D. and Catherine T. MacArthur Foundation funded an experimental study (Pinnell, Lyons, DeFord, Bryk, & Seltzer, 1994) designed to compare the effect of RR to two alternative one-to-one treatments and one small group treatment, with Title 1 programs as control groups. The results of the study indicated that RR was the only group for which the mean treatment effect was significant on four measures: Dictation 2 (Clay, 1993); text reading (Scott Foresman, 1979); and two standardized tests, the Gates-MacGinitie Reading Test (1989) and the Woodcock Reading Mastery Test (1990). While the effectiveness of RR is not challenged, we need to know more about qualitative differences that exist between the teacher-student interaction during RR lessons and how to maximize Reading Recovery's effectiveness while minimizing the cost.

*Claim 3: Reading Recovery greatly reduces the number of children targeted for placement in learning disability (LD) classrooms.* Several studies have demonstrated that once RR is introduced into a school system, there is a sharp decline in the number of first grade students referred for learning disability screening and placement. For example, Lyons and Beaver (1995) reported that in the State of Ohio the number of RR program students referred for learning disability screening decreased from 1.26% to just 0.51% over a five year period. Furthermore, a national study demonstrated that the number of first grade students targeted to receive LD services was cut in half two years after RR was implemented. Specifically, prior to RR implementation, 59 (2.3%) of the 2,569 first grade students in the ten districts were referred for LD services. One year after RR intervention, 53 (2%) of 2,602 first grade students were referred for LD services and only 34 (1.3%) of 2,572 students were referred for LD services two years after the program was implemented (Lyons, 1994). Data reported to the United States Office of Education (Lyons, 1997) for the 1995–1996 academic year, indicated that only .02% of the 71,193 RR children who received full programs were referred for LD assessment.

Research suggesting that RR has the potential to reduce the escalating number of students retained and referred for learning disability testing and placement was cited in a report to the International Reading Association (IRA). The IRA report, *Learning Disabilities—A Barrier to Literacy Instruction* (1995), stated that "RR effectively teaches children to read. . . . Not only does it reduce the number of children who are labeled with learning disabilities, but it also significantly reduces the number of children who are retained in remedial reading programs" (p. 45). Furthermore, the program enables educators to separate first grade children who may be low achieving from those with more severe learning problems (Lyons, 1994).

Essentially, there is no question that RR works. Consider, for example, that Hiebert (1994) noted ". . . a high percentage of Reading Recovery tutees can orally read a first-grade text at the end of Grade 1. . . " (p. 21). Shanahan and Barr (1995) concluded, "Evidence firmly supports the conclusion that Reading Recovery does bring the learning of many children up to that of their average-achieving peers. Thus, in answer to the question 'Does Reading Recovery work'? we must respond in the affirmative" (p. 989). Most strongly, in *Classrooms That Work*, Cunningham and Allington said, "No other remedial program has ever come close to achieving the results demonstrated by Reading Recovery" (1996, p. 254). What is most often questioned, however, is the need for year-long training and continued professional development of teachers, the costs associated with the program, and evidence of the long-term effects of the early intervention using standardized measures. In the following sections I will address these three issues.

## Year-Long Training and Continued Professional Development

Unlike many other programs for low progress students, RR is not based on one procedure or a set of materials to use for instruction. Rather, it is dependent on the customized instruction designed by a specially trained teacher who has developed a systematic knowledge and understanding of possible progressions in acquiring a reading and writing process. The teacher assists the reader in acquiring the strategies employed by successful readers.

In order to implement the RR program, qualified teachers enroll in a year-long course taught by a certified teacher leader at a training site in or near their school district. Through close observation of teacher and student interactions, guided by a skilled teacher leader, RR teachers learn to use observation techniques to determine where the student's literacy processing is breaking down and why. Extensive use is made of a one-way glass for demonstration and observation. By observing each other working with children behind the one-way glass, teachers become sensitive observers of children's reading and writing behaviors and develop skill in making moment-to-moment teaching decisions that help children use what they know to generate further understandings.

The RR teacher is responsible for teaching children who, despite one year of kindergarten, remain at the lowest achieving level of the first grade class. In order to accomplish this feat, teachers must customize every lesson to meet the idiosyncratic needs of the child by selecting from a wide range of books and helping individuals use their writing to assist in reading. Teachers also perform and record their own assessments of a student's progress in reading. During reading and writing tasks, teachers must select from an array of special techniques those that will help children develop effective problem-solving strategies that independent readers use. Students are taught how to predict, confirm, and understand what they read using all sources of information (e.g., visual, semantic, etc.). As they write, they develop strategies for hearing and recording sounds in words, composing messages, and for monitoring and checking their own reading and writing. During each lesson, the teacher carefully observes the child acting on a variety of texts and systematically records these observations to form the basis for the next lesson. Learning such a complex role takes time, commitment, much energy, and a rigorous training program.

Teachers in training continue working full-time in their school as they receive instruction in RR techniques. The most common arrangement during the training year and subsequent years is for teachers to spend one half day teaching RR students and the other half day performing other assigned duties (e.g., kindergarten, first grade, Title 1 teacher). Reading Recovery teachers working with four or five students for one half day will teach a total of 7 to 10 children, on average, every year. This represents 14–20 children per 1.0 FTE annually.

Following the training year, teachers meet several times annually with their teacher leader for continued professional development. In these sessions, teachers sharpen their observation skills and learn how to use these observations to design efficient lessons that will most effectively accelerate students' progress. Teachers are also given the opportunity to attend the annual national RR conference and a number of regional professional development institutes to further their theoretical and practical understandings of the reading and writing processes.

Leading authorities in school reform have recognized the quality of the RR training. In a discussion of the use of standards and assessments to support student learning, Darling-Hammond and Falk (1997) singled out RR as effective in helping students gain skills that make them successful and confident readers, including students whose first language is not English and many who have been identified for special education. Allington and Cunningham (1996) noted that "Planned professional development of this intensity is rarely encountered in school improvement efforts" (p.32). The knowledge and skill of the trained teacher is the critical element to RR; the element that distinguishes RR from other programs designed for low progress children; the element that may very well be the deciding factor that allows for the program's success.

After conducting a three-year study of RR, Kenneth Wilson (Wilson & Daviss, 1994), a Nobel Prize winning physicist and educational reformer, concluded that in three ways the program can encourage the process of educational redesign:

> First, it proves that a well-designed educational program can be replicated among teachers and schools across as wide array of locations and cultures and still yield uniformly superior results. Second, it indicates that an investment of money and effort in educational design can earn dramatic rewards— if it's made in a properly researched and designed program that offers thorough teacher training and support. Third, it shows that when educators find a program that meets these two criteria and proves that it can earn a good return, schools are willing to make its adoption a budget priority. Reading Recovery is the best evidence yet of the direct link between good design and educational excellence (p. 76).

American society prides itself on the advancement of technical skills in medicine. Physicians are expected to engage in life-long learning through continuous professional development; some physicians (e.g., surgeons) require more advanced, long-term training than others. You would not want a surgeon performing a heart transplant on a loved one using the same techniques he or she learned 20 years ago in medical school. You would expect the surgeon to use more effective, proven procedures that he or she learned in advanced surgical training institutes. Advanced life-long professional development for teachers is rare. Some teachers continue to use the same teaching methods they learned in undergraduate teacher education programs.

Reading Recovery teachers should have more specialized continuous professional development because they are required to work with the most difficult to teach students. In order to do so successfully, teachers must learn specialized skills which require specialized training. The RR initial and ongoing professional development program for teachers breaks away from the expected norm. In doing so, there are long term gains for school districts, administrators, teachers, students, and parents.

The best investment this nation can make is in massive ongoing professional development for teachers. Renewing, re-educating, extending, and enhancing the professional expertise of the teachers who carry out the daily work of educating children is critical to school reform. In her presidential address at the American Education Research Association annual meeting, Linda Darling-Hammond (1996) stated that "recent research illustrates that money makes a difference in the quality of education, especially as it is used to pay for more expert teachers, whose levels of participation and skill prove to be the single most important determinant of student achievement (Armour-Thomas et al., 1989; Ferguson, 1991). Furthermore, students' right to learn is directly tied to their teachers' opportunities to learn what they need to know to teach well" (p. 6).

## The Cost of Reading Recovery

In *No Quick Fix: Rethinking Literacy Programs in America's Elementary Schools*, Allington & Walmsley (1995) concluded that ". . . the more expensive RR program provides the best evidence of long-term success for the largest population of at-risk students served" (p. 262). However, some researchers (Hiebert, 1994; Shanahan & Barr, 1995) report RR costs too much. Others (Dyer & Binkney 1995; Lyons & Beaver, 1995, Moriarty, 1997; Pinnell, Lyons & Jones, 1996) argue that it costs much less than retention and long-term placement in learning disability, special education, or remedial reading resource rooms. Furthermore, the initial start-up cost of the program (i.e., teacher leader training, installation of a one-way mirror, tuition, books and materials, and the initial training of RR professionals) is a one-time expense.

Can the cost for RR be justified? Those who agree it can be justified weigh the cost of a 30-minute RR lesson for 12 to 20 weeks against the cost of 45 minutes of daily remedial reading groups for more than 1 year. They weigh the cost of a 30-minute RR lesson for 12 to 20 weeks against 5 hours of daily learning disability (LD) classes for 4 to 5 years. They weigh the cost of a 30-minute RR lesson for 12 to 20 weeks against a year of repeating first grade. Educators can expect to spend about 50 percent more to educate a low achieving child (Levin, 1989). The Massachusetts State Legislature reached a similar conclusion after conducting a study of five years of special education placements in the state. The study revealed that between FY 1990 and FY 1995, total enrollment in special education increased by 8.3% statewide (MA Superintendents Association Task Force, 1997).

Furthermore, an examination of the relative cost of the increased enrollment in regular and special education during this period revealed that expenditures per full time equivalent (FTE) enrollments in special education increased by almost $4,000 from FY 1990 to FY 1995, while they increased by only $305 in regular education. The impact of these increases statewide has been dramatic, resulting in an additional expenditure of $61 million on special education in FY 1995 alone. The report also revealed that expenditures for special education increased at a greater rate than expenditures for regular education in 71% of the Massachusetts school districts with only 3% of the districts reporting a decline in special education expenditures between FY 1990 and FY 1995.

A cost-effectiveness study of special education referrals, Title 1 placement, and retention was conducted in Fall River, Massachusetts (Assad & Condon, 1996). The report revealed that over a two-year period (1993–94, 1994–95) the Fall River RR project served 186 students at an actual cost of $2,362 per pupil. Based on school history, it was estimated that without the RR program, 45%–50% of the students would have been referred for Special Education; 45%–50% would have been referred for Title 1 services and approximately 5.7% of the students would have been retained. Total cost for special education services in this school district is $17,830 per pupil; total cost of Title 1 services per pupil is $4,860; total per pupil cost for retention is $3,843. Using this information, Fall River administrators determined a projected five year cost of $1,746,145 if RR had not been operating in the district. The RR intervention for this same five year period would cost $483,271, creating a net savings of $1,262,874 that could be reallocated for a variety of other services needed for students within the district.

Similar cost savings were calculated in Medford, Massachusetts. Data collected in this urban school district over a five-year period revealed that five of the 175 first graders who were successfully released from RR, representing fewer than 3%, have been referred to Special Education. Prior to RR implementation, it was estimated that the vast majority of these students would have been targeted for special education (Moriarty, 1996).

After conducting a seven month investigation, the Massachusetts legislative team concluded that RR research shows a high degree of success in teaching low progress children how to read and write; defers children from special education, reduces the number of children retained, and is cost effective because for every $3 invested in RR, a school system saves $5. In 1997, the Massachusetts legislature allocated $500,000 for early intervention and identified RR as a research-based program that would qualify for funding (Moriarty, 1997).

When examined as a whole, the net costs of RR are justified by the value of all that is saved. First of all, the program is producing effective results time and time again, as evidenced by replication data. Second, the program cuts the cost of retaining a child or placing a child in a learning disability resource room for up to 4 and 5 years. Third, the program cuts the cost of long-term help in remedial reading resource rooms. Fourth, in preventing more serious problems from occurring, the program cuts the cost of on-going expensive psychological assessment and treatment. The school district saves money in the long run. To all of these monetary savings, however, must be added the incalculable value of what the program does for the thousands of boys and girls who are spared from a lifetime of feeling inadequate because they cannot read and write well enough to keep up with peers and benefit fully from classroom experiences.

## Evidence of the Long-Term Effects of Reading Recovery Using Standardized Measures

Even since the early years of RR in the U.S., there has been interest in determining whether children who are successfully released from the RR program continue to make average band progress in reading and writing. In 1988, the Ohio Department of Education commissioned an outside evaluation team to evaluate long-term effects of the RR program (Anderson, 1988). Over a three-year period (1984–1987), the evaluation team examined the effect of RR on the lowest achieving first grade Ohio children's reading progress. The evaluation team was comprised of nationally known experts in literacy and chaired by Dr. Richard Anderson, at that time the Director of the Center for the Study of Reading at the University of Illinois. The report revealed that 81.8% of RR children who received a full program made accelerated progress and performed within the average band range for their classes. Furthermore, Anderson (1988) found that children "retain their gains and continue to make progress at least 2 years after the intervention" (p. 42).

The long-term effects of any intervention are difficult to measure because there are many intervening variables which can influence children's progress (e.g., quality of subsequent classroom instruction, promotion and disciplinary policies, student's health, mobility, and individual life circumstances). As a matter of fact, few implementers or proponents of any intervention programs collect follow-up data. Critics of RR argue that most follow-up studies use Clay's assessments to document long-term effects of the program. However, a number of state-wide follow-up studies conducted in the United States have utilized standardized measures to document that former RR children maintain their literacy gains and make average or better progress up to three, four and five years after the intervention ended.

Researchers at New York University tested a total of 1,596 second grade children and 604 third grade children who were successfully discontinued from RR between 1990–1993. The nationally standardized Slosson Oral Reading Test (1990) was administered to the total number of RR children and random sample children who participated in a follow-up study in the state of New York. The findings revealed that RR children's mean achievement levels on the Slosson word recognition test reflected average performance for students who were at the end of second grade, and slightly higher than average performance for those at the end of third grade, based on national norms. These results are impressive given that, only one and two years before, they were the lowest achieving students in their first grade classrooms.

Furthermore, 93% of the second graders and 98% of the third graders scored at or above grade level on a measure of text reading. The results of the four-year study demonstrate that the majority of the children in New York who had a full series of lessons and were successfully discontinued from RR in first grade sustained their gains and performed as well as their grade-level peers one and two years after completing the program. These results indicate that RR students in New York, after becoming average or better readers in first grade, continued to make significant progress in reading after the specialized teaching is discontinued (Jaggar, Smith-Burke, Ashdown, Simic, 1996).

A follow-up study conducted in the state of Massachusetts (RR Annual Report, 1996) produced similar results. In the Spring of 1995, 122 children who had successfully discontinued from RR during 1993–1994 and 143 non-RR children were randomly selected for a grade two study. The two groups of second grade children were compared on four measures: text reading, a story retelling, a dictation task, and the Slosson Oral Reading Test (1990). When compared with randomly selected non-RR students, the discontinued second grade RR students performed within the average band of achievement on text reading, story retelling, and the word recognition subtest on the Slosson. In May 1996, in addition to the same four measures, the Gates MacGinitie Reading Test (1989) was administered to the same groups of children who, at this time, were completing third grade. The achievement of discontinued RR students was compared to that of a random sample of third graders. The mean text reading level of 30.7 (roughly equivalent to a grade 4 basal reader level) was achieved for former RR students and 31.0 for the random sample students providing evidence that both groups of students were reading well above grade level.

Furthermore, the former RR students, who were identified as the lowest achievers in grade one, were more successful at retelling stories than their random sample peers. Ninety-five percent of RR students and 92% of random sample students retold an end-of-grade-three story at an adequate to exceptional level. Scores from the Slosson Oral Reading Test (1990) and the Gates MacGinitie Comprehension Test (1989) demonstrated that the former RR students performed within the random sample's average band of achievement.

In a cross-sectional evaluation, researchers at Texas Woman's University (RR Texas State Report 1988–1996) studied second, third, and fourth graders who had successfully discontinued from Reading Recovery during their first grade year. Four assessments were used to measure the literacy performance of former RR students: a test of text reading, a written retelling, the comprehension test of the Gates MacGinitie

Reading Tests (1987), and the reading subtest of the Texas Assessment of Academic Skills (TAAS). The results indicated that when compared to a random sample of their peers, former RR students placed well above grade level in text reading and written retelling and maintained their gains through fourth grade. Additionally, by fourth grade, former RR students compared well with their peers on the TAAS: 69% of the RR students and 76% of the random sample group of students had passing scores on TAAS. On the Gates MacGinitie Comprehen-sion Test (1989), 67% of the RR students and 71% of the random sample of fourth grade students had comprehension scores within the average range. These results indicate that former RR students are more similar to a random sample of peers on standardized measures when in grade four.

The follow-up studies from New York, Massachusetts, and Texas report on former RR students who were discontinued from RR; that is, these children reached the average reading levels of their peers and thus successfully completed the program in first grade. Due to limited resources, researchers in these three states could not follow every RR student who was served in the program in first grade. An Ohio fourth grade follow-up study, however, reports data on three groups of RR students: (a) those who were successfully discontinued from the RR program in grade one, (b) those who were referred for additional support, and (c) those who were served in RR but received fewer than 60 lessons (State of Ohio 1996–1997 Report).

The researchers in the Ohio study examined two cohorts of these three types of students: the first cohort received RR services in 1991–1992; the second cohort received RR services in 1992–1993. The children's overall proficiency scores on the Ohio Test of Fourth Grade Proficiency were examined for each cohort. The results revealed that when compared to all fourth grade children in the State of Ohio, 71% of the total group of RR students (including those who had fewer than 60 lessons, whether they were discontinued or not) in the first cohort scored above proficiency in reading and 72% scored above proficiency in writing. Similar results were reported for the second cohort of children. Seventy-five percent of all RR students who were in first grade in 1992–1994 scored above proficiency on reading and 67% performed above proficiency on the writing measures. These findings suggest that the total number of RR students served made substantial gains in reading and writing by fourth grade.

When one considers that in every follow-up study, the random sample comparisons are drawn from a general population of regular education students who were not selected for RR and compares these students with former RR students who were once the lowest achievers in a first grade classroom, it is clear that the program does what was it was designed to do—brings the hardest-to-teach children to a level of literacy achievement where they are full participants in classroom literacy programs. Furthermore, scores on two nationally standardized tests, the Slosson Oral Reading Test (1990) and the Gates MacGinitie Reading Test (1989), and on two statewide assessments, the Texas Assessment of Academic Skills and the Ohio Test of Fourth Grade Proficiency, collected at the end of grades two, three, and four, suggest that former RR students, in particular those that have been successfully discontinued (released) from the program, maintain their gains and continue to make reading and writing progress.

## Conclusion

We are continually inundated with media reports that the number of school-aged children who cannot read and write continues to rise. Local, state, regional, and federal legislators, parents, business owners, and other stakeholders are demanding changes in school curricula and practices to remedy the situation. In a comprehensive review of literacy programs in America's elementary schools, Allington and Walmsley (1995) argue that early reading achievement predicts future success or failure in life and strongly recommend early intervention programs for students who are failing to learn how to read.

Within this growing consensus for early intervention, there is continuing disagreement about several issues, including: (a) using professionals or paraprofessionals, (b) the amount of training necessary, (c) whether and how to monitor the fidelity of the local implementation of the program, (d) student-teacher ratio (e.g., one-to-one or small group), and (e) whether and how to collect data to document individuals' progress. Reading Recovery is decidedly consistent on all of these. Reading Recovery uses professionals who are required to be trained for a year, the pupil-teacher ratio is one-to-one, the local implementation is carefully monitored on a constant basis, and data are collected on individuals' reading and writing progress on a daily basis and reported annually to document the effectiveness of the program.

Any primary teacher can attest to the enormous range of differences in what children know and can do when they begin schooling. These individual differences suggest that the quantity, quality, and intensity of instruction needed to meet a child's idiosyncratic needs must differ. Allington and Walmsley (1995) encourage educators "to think of individual differences less as indicators of how much or how little children might learn, and instead think of them as indicating how much intensive instruction will be needed to accelerate their literacy development and move them alongside their peers. As long as we believe that not all children can learn to read on schedule, we will fail to embrace instructional programs that demonstrate how wrong that tradition is" (p. 6). Perhaps that is what is happening in American elementary schools today— Reading Recovery supporters are challenging 100 years of conventional school organization and instructional practice.

In summary, RR operates within educational systems through three key program elements: (a) an intensive, daily, one-to-one, thirty minute program for the lowest achieving children in grade one; (b) an initial graduate level year-long training and continuous professional development program through which teachers refine their knowledge and skills in using proven techniques; and (c) a standard research program whereby individual data are collected on all students, even those who are served for one day, to monitor results continuously, to provide support for participating teachers, and to develop guidelines for implementing the program with integrity.

Reading Recovery has an approach to program evaluation that is coherent and which has employed both systematic and simultaneous replication extensively. I would encourage those who question RR to publish their program descriptions and their data along with replication information so that stakeholders will have substantive information for decision-making.

Essentially, after all of the objections to RR have been identified, after all of the arguments against the program have been weighed, we must face the hard and simple fact that no other program currently operating in the United States can produce thirteen years of data on every single child who was served in the program to document its success. At no time in recent history has there been more pressure to produce results. At no time in our history has there been a program that can produce more than a dozen years of replication data to document successful results.

# References

Anderson, R. C. (1988). *The Ohio Reading Recovery project: Preliminary report of the national evaluation panel.* Columbus, OH: Department of Education.

Allington, R. L. (1994). What's special about special programs for children who find learning to read difficult? *Journal of Reading Behavior, 26,* 95–115.

Allington, R. L., & Walmsley, S. A. (1995). *No quick fix: Rethinking literacy programs in America's elementary schools.* New York: Teachers College Press and International Reading Association.

Armour-Thomas, E., Clay, C., Domanico, R., Bruno, K., & Allen, B. (1989). *An outliner study of elementary and middle schools in New York City: Final report.* New York: City Board of Education.

Assad, S., & Condon, M. A. (1996). Demonstrating the cost effectiveness of Reading Recovery: Because it makes a difference. *Network News, 2,* 10–14.

Campbell, D. T., & Stanley, J. C. (1963). Experimental and quasi-experimental designs for research. Chicago: Rand-McNally.

Clay, M. M. (1993). *Reading Recovery: A guidebook for teachers in training.* Portsmouth, NH: Heinemann.

Cunningham, P. M., & Allington, R. L. (1996). *Schools that work: Where all children read and write.* New York: Harper Collins.

Darling-Hammond, L. (1996). The right to learn and the advancement of teaching: Research, policy, and practice for democratic education. *Educational Researcher, 25,* 5–18.

Darling-Hammond, L., & Falk, B. (1997). Using standards and assessments to support student learning. *Phi Delta Kappan, 79,* 190–201.

Dyer, P., & Binkney, R. (1995). Estimating cost effectiveness and educational outcomes: Retention, remediation, special education, and early intervention. In R. L. Allington, & S. A. Walmsley (Eds.), *No quick fix: Rethinking literacy programs in America's elementary schools.* NY: Teachers College Press and the International Reading Association.

Ferguson, R. E. (1991). Paying for public education: New evidence how and why money matters. *Harvard Journal of Legislation, 28,* 465–498.

Frymier, J., Barber, L., Gansneder, B., & Robertson, N. (1989). Simultaneous replication: A technique for larger-scale research. *Phi Delta Kappan, 71,* 228–231.

Gates & MacGinitie, (1989). [Gates MacGinitie Reading Tests] (3rd ed.). New York: Columbia University and Teachers College Press.

Gay, L. R. (1987). *Educational research: Competencies for analysis and application.* Columbus, OH: Merrill Publishing.

Hersen, M., & Barlow, D. H. (1976). *Single case experimental designs: Strategies for studying behavior change.* New York: Pergamon.

Hiebert, E. H. (1994). Reading Recovery in the United States: What difference does it make to an age cohort? *Educational Researcher, 23,* 15–25.

Jaggar, A. M., Smith-Burke, M. T., Ashdown, J., & Simic, O. (1996). *A four-year follow-up study of Reading Recovery children in New York state: Preliminary report.* New York: New York University. *

Kerslake, J. (1997). *A summary of the 1996 Data on Reading Recovery.* Research and Statistics Division Bulletin, No. 9. Wellington, NZ: Ministry of Education.

Kratochwill, T. R. (1978). *Single subject research: Strategies for evaluating change.* New York: Academic Press.

*Learning disabilities—A barrier to literacy instruction.* (1995). Washington, DC: International Reading Association.

Levin, H. (1989). Financing the education of at-risk students. *Educational Evaluation and Policy Analysis, 11,* 47–60.

Lyons, C. A. (1994). Reading Recovery and learning disability: Issues, challenges and implications. *Literacy, Teaching and Learning: An International Journal of Early Literacy, 1,* 109–120.

Lyons, C. A. (1997). Final report of the Reading Recovery program 1995–1996. Columbus, OH: The Ohio State University.

Lyons, C. A., & Beaver, J. (1995). Reducing retention and learning disability placement through Reading Recovery: An educationally sound, cost-effective choice. In R. L. Allington & S. A. Walmsley (Eds.), *No quick fix: Rethinking literacy programs in America's elementary schools* (pp. 116–136). NY: Teachers College Press and the International Reading Association.

Massachusetts Superintendents Association Task Force. (1997). *The impact of special education on educational reform: Final report of the Task Force on Special Education.* Boston: The Massachusetts Association of School Superintendents.

Moriarty, D. (1996). *Report to the Massachusetts superintendents task force on special education.* Medford, MA: Medford, MA Public Schools.

Moriarty, D. (1997). A message to Congress: Redefining special education. *Network News, 1,* 16–17.

Neuman, S. B., & McCormick, S., eds. (1995). *Single-subject experimental research: Applications for literacy.* Newark, DE: International Reading Association.

Pinnell, G. S., Lyons, C. A., DeFord, D. E., Bryk, A., & Seltzer, M. (1994). Comparing instructional models for the literacy education of high-risk first graders. *Reading Research Quarterly, 29,* 8–39.

Pinnell, G. S., Lyons, C. A., & Jones, N. (1996). Response to Hiebert: What difference does Reading Recovery make? *Educational Researcher, 25,* 23.

Reading Recovery in Massachusetts (1996). *Technical State Report 1995–1996* Cambridge, MA: Lesley College. *

Reading Recovery in Ohio (1996). *Technical State Report 1995–1996.* Columbus, OH: The Ohio State University. *

Reading Recovery in Texas (1996). *Technical State Report 1995–1996*. Denton, TX: Texas Woman's University.*

Scott-Foresman and Company (1979). *Special Practice Books.*

Shanahan, T., & Barr, R. (1995). Reading Recovery: An independent evaluation of the effects of an early intervention for at-risk learners. *Reading Research Quarterly, 30,* 958–997.

Slosson, R.T. (1990). *Slosson Oral Reading Test* (3rd. ed.). East Aurora, NY: Slosson.

Wasik, B. A., & Slavin, R. E. (1993). Preventing early reading failure with one-to-one tutoring: A review of five programs. *Reading Research Quarterly, 28,* 178–200.

Wilson, K., & Daviss, B. (1994). *Redesigning education*, New York: Henry Holt.

Woodcock Reading Mastery Test-Revised. (1989). New York: American Guidance Service.

---

* follow-up studies

# The Effects of Reading Recovery on Children's Home Literacy Experiences

Christine A. Marvin, *University of Nebraska*
Janet S. Gaffney, *University of Illinois*

## ABSTRACT

*One hundred thirty parents completed a literacy survey in the fall of the school year and again in the spring as their children completed first grade. At both times, parents were asked about the type and frequency of literacy activities in which the children engaged at home. Responses in the spring were compared across three groups of parents representing children who had been (a) enrolled in Reading Recovery, (b) identified in the fall as experiencing reading difficulties but received no special reading instruction, and (c) identified as having grade-level reading skills at the start of first grade. Responses provided by parents in the spring were compared to responses they gave to the same questions as their children began first grade the previous fall.*

*All children showed growth in literacy skills at home over the course of the year. Children who participated in Reading Recovery made significant changes in the frequency with which they read aloud to adults and with which they read independently at home. Furthermore, parents reported more frequent writing of words and simple sentences at home by the Reading Recovery children as the year progressed. Results are discussed relative to the role home literacy experiences play in early reading and writing and the reciprocal influences that home and school literacy experiences may have on each other.*

All parents expect that their children will learn to read and write once they begin school. For some parents, however, this expectation is not fulfilled. Some children finish their primary school years without satisfactory achievement in reading and writing (Juel, 1988). Recent research on the home environments of young children has suggested that significant limitations in some children's exposure to functional reading and writing materials and activities at home during the preschool years may contribute to these difficulties. The cause of such limited experiences, however, is not always clear.

For example, some children from economically disadvantaged homes have often been described as lacking access to reading and writing materials, to shared book-reading with competent adult readers, and to family members whose own reading and writing skills model or promote reading and writing as functional skills in everyday life (Heath, 1983; Marvin & Mirenda, 1993; Purcell-Gates, 1996; Sonnenschein, Brody, & Munsterman, 1996; Teale, 1986). In addition, preschool children who demonstrate cognitive abilities appropriate for their age, but show delays or impairments in speech-language skills, reportedly have fewer experiences with nursery rhymes, poems, interactive book reading, and writing and drawing activities at home than do children without disabilities or even children from economically disadvantaged homes (Katims, 1991; Light & Kelford-Smith, 1993; Marvin, 1994; Marvin & Mirenda, 1993; Marvin & Wright, 1997). These data suggest that family socio-economic status and children's biological make-up could independently or collectively interact to affect not only the literacy opportunities provided to young children at home but also the children's preparedness for formal instruction in reading and writing once they begin school.

Clearly, some children may require greater support at home in the form of more frequent exposure to print with supportive family members, while others, already rich in their home experiences may need direct intervention at school to increase skills in generating meaning from print. For some children, both are needed if reading and writing skills are to improve quickly enough to be useful in academic endeavors in the primary grades. The Reading Recovery program proposes to improve children's reading abilities, despite limited ability and/or experience with print as the children begin first grade. This study was designed to examine what changes occur in children's home literacy activities and behaviors as a result of participation in Reading Recovery during first grade.

## Reading Recovery

Reading Recovery is a school-based, early intervention program that is designed to teach first-grade children who are experiencing literacy difficulties how to read and write early in their school careers (Clay, 1993). Children are individually taught for 30 minutes per day by a specially trained teacher. The teaching goal is to assist the lowest-achieving children in quickly developing competency in reading and writing so that they can "catch up" to their peers.

Teachers are encouraged to elicit the parents' support for their children's consistent school attendance, to invite parents to observe lessons, if possible, and to share their insights about their children's interests and strengths. During the Reading Recovery program, teachers will send home "little books" the children enjoy and can read with ease. Children benefit from the additional opportunities to read books on which they have demonstrated success, and parents have a "window" for viewing their children's reading progress across the weeks the children participate in the program. Also, children will often bring home a message (one or two sentences) that they wrote with the teacher's support during a lesson at school. The teachers cut the printed message into phrases, words, or word parts for the children to remake in class and again at home. The teachers write the complete message on the outside of an envelope so that the children have a model and a way to check the story arrangement at home. The transfer of these literacy materials between school and home on a daily basis serves both as a vehicle for communication between the parents and teachers and for the children's skill transfer and generalization; the children have the opportunity to read familiar text in different contexts and with different audiences.

## Literacy Socialization

It is generally accepted that the development of literacy begins long before young children participate in formal school instruction. Adult-child interactions at home and exposure to printed materials can provide young children with the opportunity to see the various forms in which messages can be conveyed. Home environments in which children (a) are read to regularly, (b) frequently see others reading for pleasure or to complete daily tasks, (c) have easy access to reading and writing materials, and (d) are encouraged to interact during reading and writing activities are considered fundamental to the development of reading and writing skills (Anderson & Stokes, 1984; Bissex, 1980; Cochran-Smith, 1984; Heath, 1983; Purcell-Gates, 1996; Scarborough & Dobrich, 1994; Snow, 1983; Teale & Sulzby, 1987, 1989; Thomas, 1985; van Kleeck, 1990; Wells, 1985; Westby, 1985). This philosophy of literacy socialization (Sulzby & Teale, 1991; van Kleeck & Schuele, 1987) has been promoted as important to all young children, including those with high risk factors such as poverty, developmental disabilities, or unspecified delays.

Specific home-related factors that appear to be critical for literacy socialization and are positively correlated with children's ability to be successful in using print for communicating ideas and learning new information include: (a) availability of printed materials and writing utensils in the home and/or child care facility (Cochran-Smith, 1984; Dunn, Beach, & Kontos, 1994; Goelman & Pence, 1987; Thorndike, 1976), (b) guided television watching (Mason, 1980), (c) frequency of book reading at home (Goldfield & Snow, 1985; Wells, 1985), (d) interactive book reading (Bus, van IJzendoorn, & Pellegrini, 1995; Heath, 1983; Snow, 1983; Teale, 1984; Thomas, 1985; Wells, 1985), (e) functional drawing and writing tasks (McLane & McNamee, 1990; Purcell-Gates, 1996), and (f) adult-child interactions with literacy materials prior to school age (Anderson & Stokes, 1984; Bissex, 1980; Cochrane-Smith, 1984; Purcell-Gates, 1996; Teale, 1986; van Kleeck, 1990). Furthermore, non-print activities that foster metalinguistic awareness of words and sounds such as nursery rhymes, finger plays, songs, poems, or stories that contain rhymes, alliterations, or nonsense sound-sequences have been correlated with children's reading competency and success with early reading instruction (Adams, 1990; Catts, 1991; Chaney, 1992; Jusczyk, 1977; van Kleeck, 1994). Finally, parental attitudes toward and aspirations for education have been considered instrumental in fostering a home environment that can support early literacy activities and experiences (Hiebert & Adams, 1987; Marvin & Mirenda, 1993; Sonneschein, Brody, & Munsterman, 1996; White, 1982).

The relationship between these environmental factors and biological factors associated with literacy socialization at home was explored by Marvin and colleagues for various groups of preschool children (Marvin & Mirenda, 1993; Marvin, 1994; Marvin & Wright, 1997). Distinct differences were found in the home experiences of children who presented known disabilities and those from high- and low-risk families. Children enrolled in Head Start programs (without disabilities) and typically developing children from middle class families had far more frequent and more positive literacy experiences at home than did the preschool children with identified special education needs. Parents of children with disabilities placed far less importance on literacy at home for these children, interacted less and qualitatively less effectively during reading or writing/drawing activities with their children, and held lower expectations for their children's development of literacy skills in the future. The authors ruled out SES factors and frequency of reading aloud to children as contributing to these differences. The authors highlighted concern for their findings in light of research that reports positive correlations between parental attitudes and aspirations for educational outcomes and young children's eventual acquisition of reading skills (Auerbach, 1989; Hiebert & Adams, 1987; Koppenhaver, Evans, & Yoder, 1991; White, 1982).

Marvin and Mirenda (1993) noted, however, a high incidence of speech and language impairments (not severe physical, sensory, or cognitive impairments) among the population of disabled children studied. Further analyses of home literacy experiences for the children with speech-language impairments and children with other disabilities suggested differences in key qualities of parent-child interaction during reading and writing activities. There were fewer reports of questions and answers being exchanged between partners during reading and drawing, less mention of fingerplays, songs, and rhymes with the children, and fewer reports of children's "pretend" reading or independent reading to adults at home for the group of children with speech-language impairments. These data suggest possible child-based biological factors that may influence parents' efforts to pursue literacy activities at home. The better able children are at relating to words meaningfully (oral or in print), the greater the variety of literacy experiences at home. Marvin and colleagues, however, did not follow these children into the primary grades to explore how the preschool home literacy experiences, risk factors, and disabilities influenced the children's ability to read and write at grade level.

## Home Literacy Practices in Reading Intervention Programs

A number of programs have demonstrated positive influences on young children's literacy socialization by focusing on home environments as part of their early intervention efforts (Arnold & Whitehurst, 1994; McCormick & Mason, 1986; Toomey & Sloane, 1994). For example, Little Books (McCormick & Mason, 1990) were sent home with preschool age children and kindergarten children in a series of intervention studies aimed at encouraging parent-child reading activities at home and providing an introduction to meaningful, context-supported print for children considered at-risk for reading failure. Consistently, the children who had access to Little Books at home subsequently scored better than control subjects on tests of reading readiness, story comprehension, letter and word recognition, and spelling and emerging literacy concepts (Mason, Kerr, Sinha, & McCormick, 1990; McCormick & Mason, 1986; McCormick & Mason, 1989; Phillips, Norris, Mason, & Kerr, 1990).

Whitehurst and his colleagues also demonstrated positive outcomes in a series of studies in which they used "dialogic reading" programs with parents or adult care-providers and their young children. Children from high-risk environments as well as low-risk (high SES) populations showed notable advances in language development, particularly in the areas of vocabulary, compared to controls following the implementation of this shared book-reading program that emphasized active involvement of the children, parental feedback to expand and praise the children's contributions to the story, and progressive adjustments in parental expectations and prompts for what the children could contribute over time (Arnold & Whitehurst, 1994; Whitehurst, Arnold, Epstein, Angell, Smith, & Fischel, 1994; Whitehurst, Epstein, Angell, Payne, Crone, & Fischel, 1994; Whitehurst, Falco, Lonigan, Fischel, Valdez-Menchaca, & Caulfield, 1988; Valdez-Menchaca & Whitehurst, 1992). Whitehurst and colleagues suggest that the positive influence dialogic reading can have on children's language development is important not only for the children's overall communication skills through the preschool period but well into the primary grades as well. Receptive language abilities at kindergarten age have repeatedly been associated with reading ability at the end of first grade (Pikulski & Tobin, 1989) and expressive language abilities are highly correlated with children's reading ability in second grade (Scarborough, 1989).

The effects of home-based extensions to school-based reading instruction programs for first-grade children have been described in only a few studies. Blum and her colleagues (Blum, Koskinen, Tennant, Parker, Straub, & Curry, 1995) provided nine second-language learners (ages 6 to 7.5 years) with books to take home each day after the students had heard the book read aloud at school and had the opportunity to read the book along with a teacher. Five of the students were provided an accompanying audio-tape of the story and were encouraged to "read along" with the tape at home at least three times before returning the book and tape. Improvements in oral reading fluency as well as letter and word identification skills were documented for all children using the audio-tapes. In addition, the authors reported positive changes in students' attitudes toward reading, more independent reading at home, and an increase in the number of books in English available to the students at home following the nine-week intervention and a nineteen-week follow-up.

Taking a slightly different perspective on the benefits of home-based reading programs, Rubert (1994) described the effects of a three-month, parent-facilitated, home-based reading program for first-grade children on the home literacy environment and reading strategies parents provided for three children. As a complement to a school-based, reading intervention program, Project Prevent staff trained parents to facilitate (a) children's echo-reading after each sentence a parent reads, (b) partner reading, alternating parent-read and child-read sentences, and (c) independent child reading of both parent-selected and teacher-selected story books. Quantitative as well as qualitative data were used to describe two of the three parents' shifts away from an emphasis on phonics and word identification with their children, to the use of contextually based facilitation strategies for oral reading and comprehension of text during the children's reading over the course of the program. Furthermore, the children in these two families demonstrated an increase in independent and shared reading time at home with siblings and parents, reportedly joined siblings in doing homework, and benefited from the family's purchase of more easy-to-read books for the children to read at home.

## Home Literacy and Reading Recovery

Holland (1991) pursued an analyses of the effects of Reading Recovery on the home literacy experiences of first-grade children. She interviewed 13 parents of first-grade children prior to and during the year of the children's enrollment in Reading Recovery.

As the children progressed in their Reading Recovery programs, the home environments took on changes that complemented the skills and interests of the first graders. As children became readers, older and younger siblings, as well as parents, surrendered their roles as readers and became listeners. Children began to read independently the cut-up sentences and selected books sent home each day. Children initiated independent and shared reading sessions with family members and often demanded an audience. Children also began copying the cut-up sentences in an effort to improve their writing skills and began writing (without copying) short sentences as messages to family and friends. Once the children began Reading Recovery, parents appeared to increase their time (a) reading with children, (b) having children read aloud and practice writing, and (c) completing schoolwork with children.

Holland's report of school-related literacy activities in the homes of beginning first graders was similar to those reported by Purcell-Gates (1996) in that introduction to reading and writing assignments at school boosted family literacy activities at home. As the children enrolled in kindergarten and first grade, the home environments included four times as many literacy-related events focused on teaching reading and writing as compared to homes with children still of preschool age. This parental focus on print for the sake of learning to read and write appeared to be prompted by children's homework assignments, but generalized to other print-related interactions with parents as the year progressed.

The tendency for families of all children to shift their emphasis to more advanced literacy activities at home once their children begin reading instruction has not been explored. Holland did not have control subjects (i.e., high-risk readers not enrolled in Reading Recovery) with whom to compare her findings. Nor did Holland have a standard of typical home literacy activities for first-grade students with whom to compare the end of the year accomplishments of her Reading Recovery students. Such studies could offer insight into the secondary benefits of Reading Recovery and help explain the transactional nature of home-school literacy development.

The purpose of the present study was to examine the change in home literacy activities and behaviors of children who had participated in Reading Recovery during their first-grade year at school. This study builds on the findings of Holland (1991) for children enrolled in Reading Recovery, but offers a comparative view of children's experiences at home before and after instruction for three groups of different ability-level readers and for a larger number of families than was reported by Holland. The study also builds on the work of Marvin and colleagues (1993, 1994, 1997) regarding home literacy experiences of preschool children with varying degrees of risk for reading failure; the study compares the home experiences of first-grade children, some of whom had reportedly begun to read and some who had not or were at high risk for not learning to read. The present study used a parent report methodology to survey families at the near-beginning (October) and near-end of the school year (late April). Comparisons of parent-reported home literacy experiences were made for children reading at grade level, for poor readers at risk for reading failure but never enrolled in special reading programs, and for the poorest readers at the beginning of first grade who enrolled in and completed at least sixty sessions of Reading Recovery.

# Method

## Instrument

A six-page survey was used to collect information concerning family demographics, child characteristics, and the home-based opportunities provided to young children relative to early reading and writing/drawing activities (see Appendix). The 32-question survey was an adaptation of one used to survey parents of preschool children by the first author (Marvin & Mirenda, 1993; Marvin, 1994; Marvin & Wright, 1997). A simple multiple choice ("Check one" [n = 24 questions]) or checklist format ("Check all that apply" [n = 8 questions]) was used so that respondents with limited reading and writing skills could easily complete and return the surveys. In addition, respondents were invited to call the primary investigator and complete the survey by phone rather than responding in a written form if they so chose.

Twelve of the survey questions were related to characteristics of the children and families. Two questions addressed the respondents' current goals for their children and future expectations regarding their children's reading and writing abilities. Six questions focused on the children's access to printed materials, writing tools, and non-print literacy activities in the home. Four questions addressed the adults' behaviors during reading and writing activities with their children. The remaining eight questions pursued a description of the children's behaviors during independent and cooperative reading and writing activities at home.

## Procedure

Forty-nine first-grade teachers, employed in 18 different elementary schools in a large midwestern school district were approached in the early fall of the school year and asked to submit the names of the children in their classrooms who (a) were enrolled in Reading Recovery (n = 117), (b) were poor readers who had been referred for assistance with reading but were not currently enrolled in a special reading program (n = 128), and (c) were randomly selected (n = 4 per class) from the remaining class list and who demonstrated grade-level reading abilities (n = 166). Children enrolled in Reading Recovery in the district were selected for participation in that program during the first month of school, based on their poor performance on screening tasks and their bottom ranking from the pool of all children referred and screened for possible reading difficulties from each first-grade classroom.

Survey packets were sent home to the families of these 411 identified first-grade children in October of the fall term. A letter explaining the purpose of the survey, and a stamped, self-addressed envelope were included with the survey. These packets were carried home from school by the children. Three weeks after the initial distribution, follow-up letters and new survey packets were sent home to all the families who failed to respond to the first survey. A final effort was made to increase the return rate by making phone contacts with the families who had failed to return the survey at the end of five weeks, and the survey was read to the parent over the phone (n = 6). Overall, 216 surveys were completed in the fall term, for a return rate of 52%. This represented 58 surveys for children enrolled in Reading Recovery (50% return rate), 63 surveys for poor readers who were not currently enrolled in special reading programs (49% return rate), and 95 surveys for children who were reading at grade level (57% return rate).

The same survey was sent again in late April to all 216 families of first grade children who had completed the survey the previous October. A total of 21 families (10%) had moved out of the district sometime during the school year and were not available for the follow-up study. The available 195 families represented 56 children who had been enrolled in Reading Recovery. In addition, the surveys were sent home to 47 children who were considered poor readers in the fall term but who were never enrolled in a special reading instruction program. Finally, the follow-up survey was sent to the families of 92 children who demonstrated grade-level reading abilities at the start of first grade. If a child's status changed during the school year, the student's fall and spring data were categorized and analyzed according to their status in the spring of the first grade. For example, if a child was identified in the fall as being a poor reader and later in the year participated in Reading Recovery (n = 11), the child's spring and fall data were analyzed with the Reading Recovery group.

Overall, 130 surveys were completed in the spring of the school year for a return rate of 66%. This represented 40 surveys from families associated with Reading Recovery (71%); thirty-five of these surveys represented children who had completed at least 60 Reading Recovery sessions; five students had completed less than 60 sessions at the time the spring survey was completed. Thirty surveys were from families of children who were considered poor readers throughout the school year (62%), and 60 surveys were from families of children who had demonstrated grade-level reading skills at the start of first grade (65%).

## Data Analysis

A pre-post comparison was made of all data collected at the beginning of first grade with the data collected in the spring of the same school year. The samples were matched by the identification number for each respondent and the responses to each survey item were compared using the McNemar test for nonparametric, paired samples of nominal or ordinal data and a binomial distribution, p = .05 (Siegel & Castellan, 1988).

In addition, all completed surveys were coded and analyzed to compare responses across the three groups of children on a number of dimensions related to literacy activities that occurred at home in the spring of the school year. Three-way and two-way comparisons were made across the groups using Chi square for k independent groups a = .05 (Siegel & Castellan, 1988). In order to control for possible Type I errors and keep the overall error rate at .05, an adjusted alpha (.05 / k tests) was calculated for sets of tests that were not orthogonal.

The SPSSx statistical package was used to analyze the data after each survey was coded and entered into a database by a graduate student in special education who was trained in the necessary protocols. To assure reliability of data entry, 40% of the surveys were selected for reentry by a second graduate student within one week of the initial data entry. Point-by-point reliability was 99.9% for data collected in the fall and spring; all of the data-entry errors were typographic in nature and were corrected before the data were analyzed.

## Results

The results are organized in three sections to describe (a) the characteristics of the children and families in each of the three groups, (b) the significant changes in home literacy activities and behaviors reported for the children in Reading Recovery and their parents, and (c) home literacy experiences across the three groups of children as they completed their year in first grade.

### Sample Characteristics

**Families.** The families of the children in the three groups were quite similar. The primary respondents for the children in each group both in the fall and spring of the school year were mothers. The majority of respondents and their spouses were employed in technical or professional settings; one-fourth of the respondents in each group were homemakers who did not work outside the home. English was the primary language spoken in all homes. Approximately one-fourth of each group were reportedly single-parent households. No significant differences were found in the respondents' education levels, with over 50% of the parents in each group reporting completion of college courses and degrees.

In the spring, the majority of respondents in the poor-reader and grade-level reading groups (67 and 78%, respectively) indicated that they expected their children to compete successfully in a college classroom when the children are 21 years of age. Only 50% of the families with a child in Reading Recovery reported such high expectations; forty-eight percent of these parents expected their children to be able to read at a high school level, $X^2$ (6, N = 130) = 13.57, p = .04. These springtime expectations for the parents of children in Reading Recovery were somewhat lower than had been reported by these parents at the beginning of the children's enrollment in first grade when 77% of the parents expected their children to compete in college. These parents had established learning to read, write, and communicate effectively by the end of first grade as priority goals for their children, as did parents of the children in the other two groups. These goals remained priorities from fall through spring for most parents of children in Reading Recovery and the poor readers as well. In the fall of the year, over 84% of the parents in each group had prioritized reading goals for their children; however, significantly fewer parents of grade-level readers (65%) now held reading as the priority for their children, $X^2$ (2, N = 130) = 8.11, p = .02. The parents in this group appeared to shift their priorities from reading, writing, and counting in the fall to having their children communicate effectively in the spring.

**Children.** There were no significant differences relative to age or gender across the three groups. The majority of the children turned seven years old during the school year; nearly half of the children in each group were girls and half were boys; a greater percentage of boys than girls, however made up the sample of children in Reading Recovery.

In the fall of the school year, significant differences were noted across the three groups relative to parent-reported reading and writing skills. Over one fifth of the children in Reading Recovery reportedly could not read at all at the start of first grade compared to only 10% of the poor readers and 1% of the children reading at grade level. More than two thirds of the poor readers and 72% of the children reading at grade level could reportedly read 5–25 words; approximately 20% in each of these groups could read simple text in picture books. In contrast, only one third of the children in Reading Recovery could read any words or text. The largest percentage of children in Reading Recovery were described as having the ability to recognize alphabet letters as their highest reading skill, $X^2$ (14, N = 216) = 38.04, p = .000. Similar differences were noted in the respondents' description of the children's writing abilities at the start of first grade. Significantly fewer children in Reading Recovery (5%) could do more than copy words, which was the most common writing ability across the three groups. However, more children in the other two groups (20–28%) reportedly could write simple notes or sentences, $X^2$ (12, N = 216) = 28.58 p = .004.

Summaries of the children's characteristics as reported by parents at the end of first grade are presented in Table 1. As was noted in the fall of the school year, children with special-education needs were represented in each group, but significantly more children with disabilities (27%) were participating in Reading Recovery. Speech and language disorders were the predominant disability (73%) for the children in Reading Recovery, whereas behavior disorders, hearing impairments, and other unspecified disabilities were more notably represented (20% each) in the poor-reading group, $X^2$ (8, N = 130) = 16.05, p = .04. No children in any group were reported to have autism, mental retardation, or orthopedic, vision, or health-related impairments.

As their children were completing first grade, parents in all groups described their children's reading and writing skills as improved from the beginning of the year. Significant differences remained, however, between the children reading at grade level and the children in the other two groups. Two-way comparisons between the Reading Recovery and poor-reader populations however, revealed no significant differences in the parents' reports of reading or writing skills for their children at the end of the school year, despite significant differences in favor of the poor readers in the fall of the year. These data suggest notable improvements over the year for the children who had participated in Reading Recovery. Although more parents of grade-level readers reported that their children were reading at grade level at the end of first grade, over 75% of the parents of children in the Reading Recovery and poor-reader groups reported that their children were now reading text (picture books, story books, and first-grade stories). Only one third of the children in Reading Recovery and two thirds of the poor readers could read single words when the school year began. Over one half of the parents in these two groups reported that their children were now reading as well as or better than their peers in first grade; over one half of the parents of grade-level readers, however, reported that their children's reading skills exceeded that of their peers.

The children's writing skills were described by their parents as also improved from the beginning of the year. Again, significant differences existed between the grade-level readers and the Reading Recovery and poor-reader groups, but not between these lat-

**Table 1.** Characteristics of Children

| | RESPONDENT GROUPS | | | |
|---|---|---|---|---|
| CHARACTERISTICS | READING RECOVERY PARTICIPANTS *(N = 40)* | POOR READERS *(N = 30)* | GRADE-LEVEL READERS *(N = 60)* | $X^2$ (DF) P |
| Gender | | | | |
| Girls | .45 | .43 | .50 | |
| Boys | .55 | .57 | .50 | |
| *Special Education Need** | .27 | .13 | .07 | 13.2(6) .04 |
| *Spring Reading Skills*[a] | | | | 24.56(12) .02 |
| Recognizes letters | .03 | .03 | .00 | |
| Reads 5–25 words | .05 | .10 | .03 | |
| Reads 25–50 words | .15 | .10 | .03 | |
| Reads text in picture books | .28 | .20 | .10 | |
| Reads simple story books | .20 | .03 | .28 | |
| Reads at 1st grade level | .28 | .53 | .55 | |
| *Comparison with Peers** | | | | 26.8(8) .00 |
| Reading behind peers | .43 | .37 | .12 | |
| Reading like his/her peers | .43 | .43 | .33 | |
| Reading better than peers | .15 | .20 | .55 | |
| *Spring Writing Skills*[a] | | | | 27.18(10) .00 |
| Writes ABC letters | .00 | .03 | .02 | |
| Copies name/familiar words | .30 | .17 | .08 | |
| Writes simple notes | .03 | .20 | .02 | |
| Writes simple sentences | .40 | .33 | .40 | |
| Writes simple stories/answers* | .25 | .27 | .48 | |
| *Comparison with Peers** | | | | 24.55(8) .00 |
| Writing behind peers | .30 | .26 | .09 | |
| Writing like his/her peers | .63 | .63 | .50 | |
| Writing better than peers* | .08 | .10 | .42 | |

* Comparisons were made across groups using chi-square, $p < .05$

[a] These values suggest an improvement from skills reported at the beginning of first grade for all three groups ($p < .05$)

ter two groups. Over 60% of the parents of children in the Reading Recovery and the poor-reader groups reported that their children could now write at least simple sentences, compared to 3% and 5% in each group who reported this level skill in the fall of the year. Nearly one half of the parents in the grade-level readers, however, reported that their children were able to write simple stories or answers to questions; nearly half (42%) of these parents felt their children's writing skills exceeded those of their peers.

## Significant Changes in Reading Recovery Group

Despite the similarities across groups for age, gender, single parent dwellings, parental occupation and education, and parental expectations and goals, the children enrolled in Reading Recovery presented specific deficiencies in home literacy experiences that may have contributed to their having the poorest literacy skills as they began first grade. Table 2 summarizes the significant differences in the three groups in the fall of the school year (n = 216). Compared to other children identified as poor readers and to children reportedly reading at grade level, the children beginning Reading Recovery had less frequent singing activities with adults, listened to books on tape less often, and were less likely to receive books as gifts. They were also less likely to look at photographs or notes, or recognize logos on game boxes, T-shirts or community signs. They were less apt to look at books independently or look for familiar words in print. Fewer of these children had adults spell out words for them to print or encourage them to sound out a word the children did not recognize in print. Furthermore, the children beginning Reading Recovery were less likely to begin first grade having practiced writing words or the alphabet letters.

Pre-Post comparisons were made for each group on the children's home literacy experiences as reported by their parents in the fall and spring of first grade. Statistically significant changes in the responses given by parents of the children in Reading Recovery are noted in the following sections. References to significant changes made by children in the poor- and grade-level reading groups are made where appropriate.

**Children's behaviors.** Parents of children in Reading Recovery reported significant changes in their children's reading and writing behaviors between the fall and spring of the school year. Specifically, the parents reported significant increases in the frequency with which the children read independently and read aloud to adults at home (p = .000). Whereas 24% of the parents in this group reported in the fall that their children never read or looked at books independently, only 13% reported a lack of this activity in the spring; instead, nearly one half of the parents reported that their children read independently on a daily basis and over half reported this activity to be done at least weekly at home. Furthermore, reading aloud to adults at home had been a regular activity for less than one half of the children who participated in Reading Recovery at the beginning of first grade, but all of the children reportedly engaged in this activity at home at least weekly in the spring of the school year. These activities may have influenced the significant change in the parents' reports of their children's reading skills in the spring survey. As was noted previously, only 37% of the parents of children in Reading Recovery had reported that their children could read any words or

**Table 2.** Significantly Different Home Literacy Abilities and Activities for Three Groups of Children at the Beginning of First Grade ($n = 216$).

| CHARACTERISTICS | RESPONDENT GROUPS | | | |
| --- | --- | --- | --- | --- |
| | READING RECOVERY PARTICIPANTS ($N = 58$) | POOR READERS ($N = 63$) | GRADE-LEVEL READERS ($N = 95$) | $X^2$ (DF) P |
| Sings songs | .81 | .94 | .92 | 5.93(2) .05 |
| Listens to books on tape | .71 | .73 | .86 | 6.59(2) .03 |
| Looks at photos | .66 | .87 | .87 | 13.39(2) .00 |
| Looks at notes | .64 | .70 | .82 | 6.82(2) .03 |
| Recognizes logos on games | .59 | .79 | .77 | 8.02(2) .02 |
| Recognizes logos on t-shirts | .57 | .68 | .77 | 6.71(2) .03 |
| Recognizes community signs | .69 | .87 | .90 | 11.91(2) .00 |
| Recognizes own name | .79 | .91 | .95 | 9.12(2) .01 |
| Recognizes family names | .66 | .81 | .93 | 17.9(2) .00 |
| Reads words or simple text* | .37 | .56 | .71 | 38.0(14) .00 |
| Looks at books while alone | .88 | .91 | .98 | 6.44(2) .04 |
| Received books as gift | .69 | .86 | .92 | 13.8(2) .00 |
| Writes alphabet letters* | .88 | .97 | .97 | 6.41(2) .04 |
| Writes words | .69 | .78 | .92 | 13.01(2) .00 |
| Writes phrases or sentences* | .05 | .20 | .28 | 28.6(12) .00 |
| Adult spells words out | .78 | .94 | .93 | 10.29(2) .00 |
| Adult encourages "read the word" | .53 | .57 | .64 | 7.2(2) .03 |
| Adult prompts "sound-it-out" | .76 | .76 | .90 | 6.49(2) .04 |

* Significant differences remain across the three groups for these items in the spring of first grade.

text at the start of first grade; but over 75% reported this level of reading skill or better in the spring, with 48% reporting their children could now read storybooks and first-grade material. Increased read-aloud opportunities for children may have increased the parents' opportunities for observing their children's reading abilities.

The children who had participated in Reading Recovery also demonstrated significant changes in their at-home writing skills over the school year. Children in this group were noted to do significantly less drawing, scribbling, and copying of words at home in the spring (p = .03) and even less compared to their poor-reading peers (p = .03). This decrease in the more basic writing skills was accompanied by a significant increase in more advanced writing skills. Eighty-eight percent of the participants in Reading Recovery were, at a minimum, able to write words independently and 65% could write simple sentences and stories as the school year ended, comparable to that reported for their peers.

**Parental behaviors.** As the children in Reading Recovery developed more advanced reading and writing skills, the parents systematically made changes in how they read to their children. In the spring of the year, significantly fewer parents in this group reported pointing to pictures (p = .001), pointing to letters (p = .02), or asking children to point to pictures while reading books aloud at home (p = .002). The parents of children in Reading Recovery reported significant increases in their use of incorrect reading and waiting for the children to supply the correct word (p = .02), and encouraging the children to sound out words they had difficulty reading (p = .004). No other group demonstrated significant changes in these adult reading behaviors. Furthermore, in the spring of the year, significantly fewer parents of children in Reading Recovery (compared to poor readers) reported having to write the children's names for them (p = .02).

## Home Literacy Experiences Across Three Groups

Despite their progress in reading and writing, the children in Reading Recovery continued to experience literacy events at home that were notably different from those reported for children who were reading at grade level. Very few significant differences remained, however, between the poor-reader and Reading Recovery groups, suggesting notable advancements in home literacy experiences over the year for the latter group.

**Materials used at home.** In the fall of the school year, minor differences were noted across the three groups for the types of literacy-related materials that were available to the children at home. The children in Reading Recovery, however, reportedly used significantly fewer of these materials at home than even the poor readers (see Table 2). In Table 3, a rank ordering of the materials used at home in the spring of the school year is presented for the three groups. As the school year came to a close, children in Reading Recovery looked at picture books, photographs, their names on packages, and comic books as much as children in the poor-reader group. Furthermore, as many children in Reading Recovery reportedly received books as gifts in the spring of the year and took notice of community signs, logos on food boxes and T-shirts, and instructions on games as did children in the other two groups. Finally, the children in Reading Recovery had developed an interest in writing at home over the year and reportedly used pencils (100%), crayons (96%), and markers (88%) comparable to children in the poor- and grade-level reading groups.

**Non-Print literacy activities.** In the fall of first grade, over 80% in each group reported children singing songs, and reciting ABC's and nursery rhymes at home. By spring, fewer families in each group reported that their children engaged in these simple non-print literacy activities. And although more than one half of the families in each group reported that their children participated in reciting poems, rhyming words, telling jokes with puns, singing, and listening to audio-taped stories and oral stories near the end of first grade, significantly more of the poor readers were reportedly engaging in many of these non-print activities. Children in Reading Recovery were more like their grade-level reading peers in their use of nursery rhymes and retelling stories by the spring of first grade. And although all the children increased their attention to compound words, children reading at grade level showed the most signifi-

**Table 3.** Rank Order[a] of Materials Looked at by Children at Home in the Spring of First Grade

| MATERIALS | READING RECOVERY PARTICIPANTS ($N = 40$) | POOR READERS ($N = 30$) | GRADE-LEVEL READERS ($N = 60$) | $X^2$ (DF) $P$ |
|---|---|---|---|---|
| | | RESPONDENT GROUPS | | |
| Reading Materials Used | | | | |
| Story books | 1.00 | .97 | .97 | |
| Picture books* | .96 | .93 | .80[b] | 6.15(2) .04 |
| Community signs | .83 | .87 | .90 | |
| Magazines* | .70 | .87 | .90 | 7.18(2) .03 |
| Letters to child | .70 | .87 | .82[b] | |
| Child's name on packages* | .70 | .90 | .68[b] | 4.07(1) .04 |
| Food boxes | .63 | .67[b] | .82 | |
| Advertisements | .63 | .73 | .77[b] | |
| Birthday cards | .65[b] | .77 | .70[b] | |
| Digital clocks | .60 | .73 | .77 | |
| Photographs | .60 | .63[b] | .75[b] | |
| Notes | .60 | .70[b] | .72[b] | |
| Books as gifts | .55 | .73[b] | .75[b] | |
| Catalogs | .55 | .70 | .67[b] | |
| Newspapers | .58[b] | .60[b] | .57[b] | |
| Game boxes | .50[b] | .63[b] | .65[b] | |
| Words/logos on T-shirts | .53 | .60 | .62[b] | |
| Brand name logos | .40 | .33 | .53 | |
| Comic Books* | .40 | .47 | .25 | 4.29(1) .04 |

*Comparisons were made across groups using chi-square, $p < .05$.

[a] Survey items reportedly used by less than 40% of the children in any group are not listed.

[b] This value is significantly less than the value reported for this group at the beginning of first grade ($p < .04$).

cant increase and use of this type of non-print activity at home. Table 4 summarizes the children's non-print activities at home in the spring of first grade.

**Children's reading activities/behaviors.** More children in all three groups were reading aloud to others or independently at home on a daily or weekly basis by the end of first grade. Over 60% of the children in each group were reported to be finding familiar words in text, asking their parents, "What's this say?", and commenting on what they read. In Table 5, a listing is presented of children's reading behaviors and activities

**Table 4.** Non-Print Literacy Activities at Home in the Spring of First Grade

| | RESPONDENT GROUPS | | | |
| | READING RECOVERY | POOR | GRADE-LEVEL | |
| ACTIVITIES | PARTICIPANTS | READERS | READERS | $X^2$(DF) P |
| | (N = 40) | (N = 30) | (N = 60) | |
|---|---|---|---|---|
| Singing | .68[b] | .73[b] | .75[b] | |
| Telling oral stories | .70 | .70 | .62 | |
| Listening to taped stories | .65 | .77 | .63[b] | |
| Telling jokes with puns | .60 | .70 | .68 | |
| Reciting poems | .53 | .70 | .65 | |
| Rhyming words | .58[b] | .50 | .65 | |
| Saying nursery rhymes* | .35 | .60[a] | .48[b] | 4.31(1) .04 |
| Retelling stories* | .53 | .70 | .47[b] | 4.39(1) .04 |
| Discussing compound words* | .40 | .53 | .70[a] | 9.01(2) .01 |
| Saying ABC's | .50[b] | .50[b] | .37[b] | |
| Finding first letter in name | .43 | .57 | .42 | |
| Doing finger plays | .28[b] | .40 | .33[b] | |

* Comparisons were made across groups using chi-square, $p < .05$
[a] This value is significantly larger than the value reported for this group at the beginning of first grade ($p = .03$).
[b] This value is significantly less than the value reported for this group at the beginning first grade ($p < .05$).
Note: Survey items reportedly used by less than 40% of the children in any group are not listed.

**Table 5.** Children's and Parents' Reading Behaviors at Home in the Spring of First Grade

| | RESPONDENT GROUPS | | | |
| | READING RECOVERY | POOR | GRADE-LEVEL | |
| CHARACTERISTICS | PARTICIPANTS | READERS | READERS | $X^2$ (DF) P |
| | (N = 40) | (N = 30) | (N = 60) | |
|---|---|---|---|---|
| **Children's Behaviors** | | | | |
| Reads aloud to others weekly | 1.00[a] | .97[a] | 1.00[a] | |
| Reads independently weekly | .87[a] | 1.00[a] | 1.00[a] | |
| Recognizes his/her name | .93 | 1.00 | .95 | |
| Chooses books | .95 | .97 | .98 | |
| Recognizes family names | .90 | .97 | .92 | |
| Selects favorite foods at store* | .75 | .97 | .93 | 10.47(2) .005 |
| Selects videos for rent | .85 | .90 | .83 | |
| Listens quietly as adult reads* | .80 | .67[b] | .87 | 5.00(1) .03 |
| Reads familiar lines* | .63 | .73 | .83 | 5.55(1) .02 |
| Finds familiar words | .63 | .73 | .70 | |
| Asks "What's this say?" | .63 | .73 | .60 | |
| Asks questions/comments | .58 | .63 | .70 | |
| Turns pages | .73 | .60 | .55[b] | |
| Announces the title | .58 | .57 | .73 | |
| Reads title page | .53 | .60 | .65[a] | |

**Table 5.** *(Continued)*

| | RESPONDENT GROUPS | | | |
| | READING RECOVERY | POOR | GRADE-LEVEL | |
| CHARACTERISTICS | PARTICIPANTS | READERS | READERS | $X^2$ (DF) P |
| | *(N = 40)* | *(N = 30)* | *(N = 60)* | |
|---|---|---|---|---|
| Visits library* | .48 | .60 | .73 | 6.90(2) .03 |
| Guesses what will happen | .60 | .63 | .43 | |
| Answers adult questions | .48 | .67 | .57 | |
| Points to words you read | .48 | .63 | .52 | |
| Points to pictures* | .73 | .57 [b] | .38 [b] | 11.45(2) .003 |
| Tells story in own words* | .40 | .57 | .35 | 3.84(1) .04 |
| Labels pictures | .30 | .47 [b] | .37 [b] | |
| **Adults' Behaviors** | | | | |
| Reads words in book | .98 | .97 | .97 | |
| Reads title page* | .65 | .73 | .85 | 5.42(1) .02 |
| Encourages "sound it out" | .93 [a] | .90 [a] | .90 | |
| Encourages guessing words* | .55 | .77 | .85 [a] | 11.34(2) .003 |
| Points and reads words aloud | .68 [b] | .73 | .73 | |
| Asks child to read word | .68 | .87 | .70 | |
| Supplies word as child hesitates* | .60 | .80 [a] | .58 | 4.15(1) .04 |
| Relates characters to child's life | .55 | .57 | .62 | |
| Asks "What happened?" | .50 | .67 | .57 | |
| Asks child to "turn page" | .53 | .70 | .55 [b] | |
| Asks child to label pictures* | .55 | .73 | .33 [b] | 13.57(2) .001 |
| Asks child to point to pictures | .50 [b] | .63 [b] | .43 [b] | |
| Asks child to point to word | .55 | .60 | .43 | |
| Asks "What will happen next?" | .50 | .40 | .53 | |
| Points/Labels pictures | .35 | .53 | .43 [b] | |
| Reads incorrectly-waits | .30 [a] | .27 | .30 | |
| Points to ABC letters | .18 [b] | .33 | .18 [b] | |

* Comparisons were made across groups using chi-square, $p < .05$
[a] This value is significantly *higher* than values reported at the beginning of first grade ($p < .05$).
[b] This value is significantly *lower* than values reported at the beginning of first grade ($p < .05$).
*Note:* Survey items reportedly used by less than 50% of the children in any group are not listed.

at home. The vast majority of children in each group could now recognize their own names and those of family members in text and select favorite videos or foods by their labels. Significantly fewer participants in Reading Recovery, however, could demonstrate the latter skill when compared to the poor and grade-level reading groups. And, whereas over 87% in each group attempted to read independently at home and over 70% of the children in the poor-reader group could now read familiar lines independently, significantly fewer children in the Reading Recovery group (63%) could do this at home. Furthermore, significantly fewer children in Reading Recovery were visiting a public library with their families. However, when children from the three groups were compared in the spring of first grade, children in the Reading Recovery group were as likely as grade-level readers to have sat and listened quietly as adults read aloud to them.

**Parents' reading behaviors.** Almost all parents continued to read the precise words in a book rather than using their own words to tell a story in the spring of first grade, but fewer parents asked their children to point to or label pictures, turn the pages, or close the book when reading together. Table 5 provides a summary of the adult reading behaviors used with children at home as the children completed first grade. All parent groups reported an increase in asking children to read the words in a text; parents of children in Reading Recovery did this in the spring as often as the parents in the other groups. In addition, parents of children in Reading Recovery and poor-reader groups significantly increased their use of asking the children to sound out words while reading, matching levels comparable to the grade-level reading group. Finally, approximately 30% of all parents now read words incorrectly and waited for their children to correct them. Parents of children in Reading Recovery, however, were less likely than other parents to read the title page of a book or encourage their children to guess at words. Significantly more parents of children in the poor-reader group reportedly still asked their children to label pictures and supplied words when their children hesitated in reading aloud.

**Children's writing activities/behaviors.** All the children were writing more at home as they approached the end of first grade than they were at the beginning of the school year. According to their parents, only 5% of the children in Reading Recovery "seldom or never" wrote at home; over 95% of the children in all three groups wrote daily at home, and over 80% were able to write their names and other words independently. Significantly more children in Reading Recovery, however, still engaged in pretend writing and wrote their ABCs at home; more children in the poor-reader group copied words that the adults at home wrote first. Grade-level readers, in contrast, were advancing to typing words independently. Table 6 is a ranked listing of the children's writing behaviors and activities at home in the spring of the school year. Although none of the groups reported statistically significant increases in particular writing skills for their children at home, children in Reading Recovery were now reportedly engaging in writing activities and behaviors like their peers in the poor and grade-level reading groups.

**Parents' writing supports.** As the children developed more competence in independent writing tasks at home, parents in all three groups were able to play a less active role in their children's writing efforts. In Table 6, a ranked list is displayed of the adult behaviors that were used to support their children's writing in the spring of first grade. Less than half of the parents of children in Reading Recovery and less than one third of the parents of children in the poor- and grade-level reading groups reported having to write their children's name for them. Over 80% of the parents in each group reported commenting on what the children wrote and asking or answering the children's questions. Parents of children in Reading Recovery were spelling words aloud for their children like the parents in the other two groups and showed a significant increase in the practice of sounding out words for their children to write. However, significantly more parents of children in Reading Recovery (35%) reported still having to position the writing utensils in their children's hands.

**Table 6.** Children's and Parents' Writing Behaviors/Activities at Home in the Spring of First Grade

| CHARACTERISTICS | RESPONDENT GROUPS | | | |
| --- | --- | --- | --- | --- |
| | READING RECOVERY PARTICIPANTS (N = 40) | POOR READERS (N = 30) | GRADE-LEVEL READERS (N = 60) | $\chi^2$ (DF) P |
| **Children's Writing Behaviors** | | | | |
| Writes daily/weekly* | .95 | 1.00 | 1.00 | 11.65(2) .02 |
| Prints his/her name | 1.00 | .97 | .98 | |
| Writes words independently | .88 | .83 | .95 | |
| Draws with markers | .83 [b] | .97 | .82 [b] | |
| Writes ABC letters* | .80 | .67 [b] | .60 [b] | 4.41(1) .04 |
| Copies words adult writes* | .63 [b] | .80 | .57 [b] | 4.75(1) .03 |
| Makes signs to post on doors | .73 | .63 | .75 | |
| Plays with drawing toy | .65 | .53 | .48 | |
| Plays with calculator | .38 | .47 | .53 | |
| Pretends to write under picture* | .68 | .47 [b] | .43 | 5.62(1) .02 |
| Dictates for others to write | .40 | .40 | .30 [b] | |
| Draws on computer | .35 | .23 | .38 | |
| Scribbles left to right | .55 [b] | .37 [b] | .37 [b] | |
| Types words independently* | .25 | .33 | .50 | 6.71(2) .03 |
| **Adult Writing Behaviors** | | | | |
| Comments | .88 | .90 | .92 | |
| Answers child's questions | .80 | .83 | .92 | |
| Asks child to tell what they did | .83 | .83 | .85 [b] | |
| Spells words aloud | .75 | .83 | .88 | |
| Encourages child to do more | .70 | .73 [b] | .67 [b] | |
| Sits silently and watches | .75 | .67 | .68 | |
| Writes words dictated | .53 | .60 [b] | .50 [b] | |
| Sounds-out words for child | .43 [a] | .47 | .32 [b] | |
| Writes child's name | .45 [b] | .27 [b] | .32 [b] | |
| Provides hand-over-hand | .35 | .37 | .08 [b] | |
| Positions writing utensil* | .35 | .20 [b] | .07 [b] | 12.86(2) .001 |

* Comparisons were made across groups using chi-square, $p < .05$

[a] This value is significantly *higher* than the values reported at the beginning of first grade ($p = .05$).

[b] This value is significantly *lower* than the values reported at the beginning of first grade ($p = .05$).

*Note:* Survey items reportedly used by less than 50% of the children in any group are not listed.

## Discussion

The present study complements and extends the findings by Holland (1991). The 40 first-grade students in the present study demonstrated similar changes in their home literacy activities as did Holland's 13 students during enrollment in Reading Recovery. The children reportedly read more at home once they began the program and advanced their literacy activities to include reading aloud to others, reading independently, and writing names and words independently. The results of the study also demonstrate that the changes were in the direction of more mature reading and writing skills and approached the level of home activity reported at the end of first grade for grade-level readers. Although Reading Recovery may not be fully credited with the changes reported here, the association between Reading Recovery efforts and the children's improved home literacy activities and skills should be given some consideration.

As Purcell-Gates (1996) had reported for her kindergarten-1st grade families, the parents of children in the present study made appropriate adjustments in their reading and writing supports and expectations with children at home as the children initiated reading instruction at school and brought home "homework" to complete. The parents of children in Reading Recovery continued to read aloud to children through the year but significantly reduced pointing at words while reading aloud, pointing out letters, or asking children to point at named pictures. Instead, these parents in the spring of the school year were asking children to read the words, encouraging their children to "sound it out," and reading words aloud incorrectly to see if children would catch the mistakes. Without explicit instruction to do so, parents and children made changes in home literacy activities and behaviors that appeared responsive to the children's increased reading and writing abilities. Noteworthy is the fact that Reading Recovery does not purport to influence home literacy activities and, therefore, any positive effects are welcomed indirect outcomes of the program.

Furthermore, the reported shift in the type of parental behaviors used during shared reading and writing activities at home may explain the slight shift some parents in the Reading Recovery group reported in their expectations for their children's future literacy abilities at age 21. These parents may have had somewhat uninformed opinions about their children's abilities and potential for reading in the fall of the school year. Once they began to attend more closely and interact with their children during reading and writing activities, they may have come to recognize the challenges their children faced in learning to read. This new knowledge could explain their lowered, perhaps more realistic, expectation for their children.

Overall, the results of this yearlong investigation lend support to the transactional nature of the relationship between home and school reading environments. Children with greater home-based literacy experiences came to first grade as better readers. As all children increased their reading and writing competencies during first grade, we saw a corresponding change in parents' reading and writing support behaviors and the children's literacy activities at home. This was most evident in the Reading Recovery group where the children had the greatest gains to make during first grade. The children selected for Reading Recovery exhibited the lowest level of literacy skills and had fewer opportunities than other students to use materials and engage in productive literacy-related interactions with adults at home. Evidence from this study indicates that implementation of Reading Recovery services may have had an impact on the activities and interactions these children experienced at home. Subsequently, whether a result of the direct instruction received through Reading Recovery at school, the first grade reading activities in the classroom, or the changed literacy experiences at home, the children enrolled in Reading Recovery reportedly demonstrated improvements over the year in reading and writing at home that were developmentally and often grade-level appropriate. Given the children's lack of skills as they began the school year, participation in Reading Recovery may have influenced both the children's role as reader at home (as active and capable) and the parent's perceptions and support of the children's reading and writing abilities.

The educators who welcome kindergartners and first graders to school know that they must be prepared to greet children with wide-ranging literacy experiences and skills. It is the responsibility of educators in each school to find ways to respond differentially to children with varying levels of competence such that all will have the opportunity to learn to read and write. The implementation of Reading Recovery is one way for schools to address the needs of children who do not arrive in first grade with literacy skills and experiences comparable to their peers. Reading Recovery offers a way for schools to respond to children experiencing difficulties in emerging literacy, extending support directly to the children and indirectly to the families, beyond that which may be provided by an individual first-grade teacher. This attention to children's skills, and indirectly to home literacy environments, makes Reading Recovery unique in its efforts to address the multifaceted factors associated with many children's failure to learn to read.

Future studies are needed to compare quantitative measures and qualitative reports of the children's home-based and school-based reading and writing behaviors at the beginning and end of the first grade. Such studies could confirm or refute the differences noted across groups in this present study and changes reported by parents in home literacy interactions and reading and writing skills for children who enrolled in Reading Recovery. Information about the home literacy environments of children who successfully discontinue Reading Recovery and those who continue unsuccessfully through 60+ lessons would provide insight into the role children's abilities vs. the homework assignments play in changing home literacy environments. Finally, studies that differentially compare the reading and writing progress for Reading Recovery students who had rich home experiences prior to beginning school with those who had limited experiences would be insightful. The results of such studies might provide parents and teachers with additional information that would most likely benefit Reading Recovery efforts.

## References

Adams, M. (1990). *Beginning to read: Thinking and learning about print.* Cambridge, MA: MIT Press.

Anderson, A., & Stokes, S. (1984). Social and institutional influences on the development and practice of literacy. In H. Goelman, A. Oberg, & F. Smith (Eds.), *Awakening to literacy* (pp. 24–37 ). Exeter, NH: Heinemann.

Arnold, D., & Whitehurst, G. (1994). Accelerating language development through picture book reading: A summary of dialogic reading and its effects. In D. Dickinson (Ed.), *Bridges to literacy: Children, families, and schools* (pp. 103–128). Cambridge, MA: Blackwell.

Auerbach, E. (1989). Towards a socio-contextual approach to family literacy. *Harvard Educational Review, 59,* 165–181.

Bissex, G. (1980). *GNYS AT WRK: A child learns to write and read.* Cambridge, MA: Harvard University Press.

Blum, I., Koskinen, P., Tennant, N., Parker, E., Straub, M., & Curry, C. (1995). Using audio-taped books to extend classroom literacy instruction into the homes of second-language learners. *Journal of Reading Behavior, 27*(4), 535–562.

Bus, A., van IJzendoorn, M., & Pellegrini, A. (1995). Joint book reading makes for success in learning to read: A meta-analysis of inter-generational transmission of literacy. *Review of Educational Research, 65,* 1–21.

Catts, H. (1991). The early identification of reading disabilities. *Topics in Language Disorders, 12*(1), 1–16.

Chaney, C. (1992). Language development, metalinguistic skills, and print awareness in 3 year-old children. *Applied Psycholinguistics, 13,* 485–514.

Clay, M. M. (1993). *Reading Recovery: A guidebook for teachers in training.* Portsmouth, NH: Heinemann.

Cochran-Smith, M. (1984). *The making of a reader.* Norwood, NJ: Ablex.

Dunn, L., Beach, S., & Kontos, S. (1994). Quality of the literacy environment in day care and children's development. *Journal of Research in Childhood Education, 9*(1), 24–34.

Goelman, H., & Pence, A. (1987). Some aspects of the relationship between family structure and child language development in three types of day care. *Annual Advances in Applied Developmental Psychology, 2,* 129–146.

Goldfield, B., & Snow, C. (1985). Reading books with children: The mechanics of parental influence on children's reading achievement. In J. Flood (Ed.), *Understanding reading comprehension* (pp. 204–218). Newark, DE: International Reading Association.

Heath, S. (1983). *Ways with words: Language, life and work in communities and classrooms.* New York: Cambridge University Press.

Hiebert, E., & Adams, C. (1987). Fathers' and mothers' perceptions of their preschool children's emergent literacy. *Journal of Experimental Child Psychology, 44,* 25–37.

Holland, K. (1991). Bringing home and school literacy together through the Reading Recovery Program. In D. DeFord, C. Lyons, & G. Pinnell (Eds.), *Bridges to literacy: Learning from Reading Recovery* (pp. 149–170). Portsmouth, NH: Heinemann.

Juel, C. (1988). Learning to read and write: A longitudinal study of fifty-four children from first through fourth grade. *Journal of Educational Psychology, 80,* 437–447.

Jusczyk, P. (1977). Rhymes and reasons: Some aspects of the child's appreciation of poetic form. *Developmental Psychology, 13,* 599-607.

Katims, D. (1991). Emergent literacy in early childhood special education: Curriculum and instruction. *Topics in Early Childhood Special Education, 11*(1), 69–84.

Koppenhaver, D., Evans, D., & Yoder, D. (1991). Childhood reading and writing experiences of literate adults with severe speech and motor impairments. *Augmentative and Alternative Communication, 7,* 20–33.

Light, J., & Kelford-Smith, A. (1993) The home literacy experiences of preschoolers who use augmentative communication systems and of their nondisabled peers. *Augmentative and Alternative Communication, 9*(1), 10–25.

Lucariello, J. (1990). Freeing talk from the here-and-now: The role of event knowledge and maternal scaffolds. *Topics in Language Disorders, 10*(3), 14–29.

Marvin, C. (1994). Home literacy experiences of preschool children with single and multiple disabilities. *Topics in Early Childhood Special Education, 14*(4), 436–454.

Marvin, C., & Mirenda, P. (1993). Home literacy experiences of preschoolers enrolled in Head Start and special education programs. *Journal of Early Intervention, 17*(4), 351–367.

Marvin, C., & Wright, D. (1997). Literacy socialization in the homes of preschool children. *Language, Speech and Hearing Services in the Schools, 28,* 154–163.

Mason, J. (1980). When do children begin to read?: An exploration of four year-old children's letter and word reading competencies. *Reading Research Quarterly, 15,* 203–227.

Mason, J., Kerr, B., Sinha, S., & McCormick, C. (1990). Shared book reading in an early start program for at-risk children. In J. Zutell & S. McCormick (Eds.), *Literacy theory and research analyses from multiple paradigms.* Thirty-ninth yearbook of the National Reading Conference (pp. 189–198). Chicago: National Reading Conference.

McLane, J., & McNamee, G. (1990). *Early literacy.* Cambridge, MA: Harvard University Press.

McCormick, C., & Mason, J. (1986). Intervention procedures for increasing preschool children's interest in and knowledge about reading. In W. Teale & E. Sulzby (Eds.), *Emergent literacy: Writing and reading* (pp. 90–115). Norwood, NJ: Ablex.

McCormick, C., & Mason, J. (1989). Fostering reading for Head Start children with Little Books. In J. Allen & J. Mason (Eds.), *Risk makers, risk takers, risk breakers: Reducing the risks for young literacy learners* (pp. 154–177). Portsmouth, NH: Heinemann.

McCormick, C., & Mason, J. (1990). *Little Books.* Glenview, IL: Scott Foresman.

Phillips, L., Norris, S., Mason, J., & Kerr, B. (1990). Effect of early literacy intervention on kindergarten achievement. In J. Zutell & S. McCormick (Eds.), *Literacy theory and research analyses from multiple paradigms.* Thirty-ninth yearbook of the National Reading Conference (pp. 199–207). Chicago: National Reading Conference.

Pikulski, J., & Tobin, A. (1989). Factors associated with long term reading achievement of early readers. In S. McCormick, J. Zutell, P. Scharer, & P. O'Keefe (Eds.), *Cognitive and social perspectives for literacy research and instruction.* Thirty-eighth yearbook of the National Reading Conference (pp. 123–134). Chicago, IL: National Reading Conference.

Purcell-Gates, V. (1996). Stories, coupons, and the TV Guide: Relationships between home-literacy experiences and emergent literacy knowledge. *Reading Research Quarterly, 31*(4), 406–428.

Rubert, H. (1994). The impact of a parent involvement program designed to support a first-grade reading intervention program. In C. Kinzer, D. Leu, J. Peter, L. Ayre, and D. Frooman (Eds.), *Multidimensional aspects of literacy research, theory and practice.* Forty-third yearbook of the National Reading Conference (pp. 230–239). Chicago: National Reading Conference.

Scarborough, H. (1989). Prediction of reading dysfunction from familial and individual differences. *Journal of Educational Psychology, 81,* 101–108.

Scarborough, H., & Dobrich, W. (1994). On the efficacy of reading to preschoolers. *Developmental Review, 14,* 245–302.

Siegel, S. & Castellan, N. J. (1988). *Non-parametric statistics for the behavioral sciences* (2nd ed.). New York, NY: McGraw-Hill.

Snow, C. (1983). Literacy and language: Relationships during the preschool years. *Harvard Educational Review, 53*(2), 165–189.

Sonneschein, S., Brody, G., & Munsterman, K. (1996). The influence of family beliefs and practices on children's early reading development. In L. Baker, P. Afflerbach, and D. Reinking (Eds.), *Developing engaged readers in school and home communities* (pp. 3–20). Hillsdale, NJ: Lawrence Erlbaum.

Sulzby, E., & Teale, W. (1991). Emergent literacy. In R. Barr, M. Kamil, P. Mosenthal, & D. Pearson (Eds.), *Handbook of reading research: Vol. II* (pp. 727–758). New York: Longman.

Teale, W. (1984). Reading to young children: Its significance for literacy development. In H. Goelman, A. Oberg, & F. Smith (Eds.), *Awakening to literacy* (pp. 110–127). Exeter, NH: Heinemann.

Teale, W. (1986). Home background and young children's literacy development. In W. Teale & E. Sulzby (Eds.), *Emergent literacy: Writing and reading* (pp. 173–206). Norwood, NJ: Ablex.

Teale, W., & Sulzby, E. (1987). Access, mediation and literacy acquisition in early childhood. In D. Wagner (Ed.), *The future of literacy in a changing world* (pp. 173–206). New York: Pergamon.

Teale, W., & Sulzby, E. (1989). *Emergent literacy: Young children learn to read and write.* Newark, DE: International Reading Association.

Thomas, K. (1985). Early reading as a social interaction process. *Language Arts, 62*(5), 469–475.

Thorndike, R. (1976). Reading comprehension in fifteen countries. In J. Merritt (Ed.), *New horizons in reading* (pp. 500–507). Newark, DE: International Reading Association.

Toomey, D., & Sloane, J. (1994). Fostering children's early literacy development through parent involvement: A five-year program. In D. Dickinson (Ed.), *Bridges to literacy: Children, families, and schools* (pp. 129–149). Cambridge, MA: Blackwell.

Valdez-Menchaca, M., & Whitehurst, G. (1992). Accelerating language development through picture-book reading: A systematic extension to Mexican day-care. *Developmental Psychology, 28*(6), 1106–1114.

van Kleeck, A. (1994). Metalinguistic development. In G. Wallach & K. Butler (Eds.), *Language learning disabilities in school age children and adolescents* (pp. 53–101). New York: Macmillan.

van Kleeck, A. (1990). Emergent literacy: Learning about print before learning to read. *Topics in Language Disorders, 10*(2), 25–45.

van Kleeck, A., & Schuele, C. (1987). *Precursors to literacy: Normal development. Topics in Language Disorders, 7*(2), 13–31.

Wells, G. (1985). Preschool literacy-related activities and success in school. In D. Olson, N. Torrance, & A. Hildyard (Eds.), *Literacy, language, and learning: The nature and consequences of reading and writing* (pp. 229–255). Cambridge, MA: Cambridge University Press.

Westby, C. (1985). Learning to talk and talking to learn. In C. Simon (Ed.), *Communication skills and classroom success* (pp. 181–218). San Diego, CA: College-Hill.

White, K. (1982). The relation between socioeconomic status and academic achievement. *Psychological Bulletin, 91*, 461–481.

Whitehurst, G., Arnold, D., Epstein, J., Angell, A., Smith, M., & Fischel, J. (1994). A picture-book reading intervention in day care and home for children from low-income families. *Developmental Psychology, 30*(5), 679–689.

Whitehurst, G., Epstein, J., Angell, A., Payne, A., Crone, D., & Fischel, J. (1994). Outcomes of an emergent literacy intervention in Head Start. *Journal of Educational Psychology, 86*(4), 542–555.

Whitehurst, G., Falco, F., Lonigan, C., Fischel, J., Valdez-Menchaca, M., & Caulfield, M. (1988). Accelerating language development through picture-book reading. *Developmental Psychology, 24*(5), 552–558.

# The Success of Reading Recovery for English Language Learners and Descubriendo la Lectura for Bilingual Students in California

Judith C. Neal, *California State University, Fresno*
Patricia R. Kelly, *San Diego State University*

## ABSTRACT

*The purpose of this study was to determine if Reading Recovery and Descubriendo la Lectura interventions resulted in reading and writing success for two groups of bilingual children: (a) English language learners receiving Reading Recovery instruction (first-grade children acquiring English as a second language concomitantly with developing literacy in English through instruction provided in English-speaking classrooms); and (b) Spanish-speaking children receiving the Descubriendo la Lectura intervention who were in first-grade bilingual classrooms that provided primary language instruction.*

*Pre- and post-test data for the two target populations of first-grade children in California were compared with data for the total English-speaking population of children in Reading Recovery in California for three academic years, 1993–1996, and with end-of-year data from random samples of first-grade children.*

*Results of this study indicate that statistically significant progress was made by both target populations of children, indicating that the interventions enabled low-performing English language learners and Spanish-speaking children to improve their performance on selected indicators of literacy acquisition. The proportion of these children's success rates compared favorably with that of the total population involved in the interventions, and they achieved scores within the average range of a cohort of their peers drawn from a random sample of first graders.*

Early intervention for arresting predicted reading failure of at-risk children is be coming an essential aspect of comprehensive literacy plans for elementary schools (California Department of Education, 1995; Hiebert & Taylor, 1994; Pikulski, 1994). The concept of early intervention is unique in American education in that it is neither a remedial program, a special education program, nor a classroom program, a combination of which has characterized the range of educational options for children in our schools over the past several decades. Intervention, unlike remediation, is not a "wait and see" approach that allows children to fail in order to obtain a two-year discrepancy between grade level and reading achievement. Rather, intervention is pro-active; it identifies children early who need supplemental assistance in order to learn to read and write successfully in the primary grades. By providing a "safety net" for fragile learners before years of failure have fossilized unproductive patterns of responding, intervention seeks to correct quickly young children's misunderstandings of how to operate on print so that future forms of long-term assistance will be greatly reduced or will be unnecessary.

Early intervention is "something more" than classroom instruction alone. Intervention accepts the premise that some children, due to differences in pre-school experiences and/or opportunities to learn, require extra resources to assure their early success in learning to read and write. Hence, an intervention program is supplemental to classroom instruction but does not replace it. Rather, the success of a plan of intervention as extra help is interdependent with a regular classroom program of literacy instruction that operates alongside it. Children are receiving a "double dose," as it were, of literacy instruction.

A program of intervening for literacy success is intended to help screen children who, at a young age, appear to be having difficulties learning to read, yet who cannot be identified with certainty as requiring placement in a long-term assistance program such as special education. In this case, early intervention serves as a pre-referral program to special education to differentiate between children experiencing early confusions related to reading and writing acquisition, and children who have processing difficulties requiring long-term special help.

The crucial issue of extra instructional time for children who are behind in reading was addressed by Kameenui (1998): "The pedagogical clock for students who are behind in reading and literacy development continues to tick mercilessly, and the opportunities for these students to advance or catch up diminish over time" (p. 12). The longer we wait to help children who are behind, the greater the gap between them and their peers. Stanovich (1986) described the increasing gap as the "Matthew effect;" that is, children who have difficulties in the beginning stages of learning to read fall further and further behind their classmates. The "rich get richer and the poor get poorer," so to speak.

In addition to catching children early in their schooling and providing supplemental assistance alongside classroom instruction, intervention programs, to be effective, must focus on powerful instruction that enables slower-performing children to "catch up" with their peers. In traditional thought about children and learning, the idea of taking the lowest-achieving children and moving them more quickly than their peers in order to "recover" the trajectory of progress their classmates have obtained, appears an unlikely, if not impossible, task. However, successful early intervention programs regularly enable children to "accelerate" in their literacy development. The acceleration that children achieve from early identification and intensive supplemental instruction is what makes intervention a short-term program; children "fill in the gaps" of their learning rather quickly and then are released from the supplemental program to continue learning from regular classroom instruction (Allington, 1995; Clay, 1991; DeFord, Lyons, & Pinnell, 1991). In the following section we review the research literature regarding school-based early intervention programs that have been found to be effective.

Although the purpose of this study is to investigate the outcomes of particular early interventions for two specific groups of children (i.e., English language learners and Spanish-speaking students who are participating in Spanish reading instruction), a general review of effective early intervention programs is being provided as background.

## Effective Intervention Programs

### English Intervention Programs

Several programs have been devised that meet the intervention criteria of providing intensive, individual and/or small group, short-term, supplemental instruction to high-risk children. Among these programs are Success for All (Madden, Slavin, Karweit, Dolan, & Wasik, 1991), the Early Intervention in Reading (ERI) Project (Taylor, Short, Shearer, & Frye, 1995), The Winston-Salem Project (Cunningham, Hall, & Defee, 1991), Small Group Literacy Intervention/Boulder Project (Hiebert, 1994), and Reading Recovery (Clay, 1993b; Lyons & Beaver, 1995; Pinnell, 1989, 1995).

Success for All is a total school program that provides both regular classroom instruction and supplemental instruction. The classroom component includes a comprehensive reading program in which students are regrouped for instruction, affording them the opportunity to work with materials that are appropriate for them. For students who are falling behind their peers, a supplemental program is provided. It consists of 20-minute daily individual tutoring sessions conducted by certified teachers or well-qualified paraprofessionals. Consistency is achieved between the classroom program and the tutoring through a focus on the same strategies and skills. Results of a large replication study that evaluated Success for All in 23 sites across the United States showed statistically significant positive effects in reading performance in grades 1 through 5 on every measure used, including standardized tests. Additionally, special education students who were participating in Success for All improved their performance and there was a reduction in special education referrals (Slavin, Madden, & Wasik, 1996).

In the Winston-Salem Project, the traditional ability-grouped basal instruction was replaced by multi-method, multi-level instruction. Classroom instruction was reorganized to include a "four-blocks program" involving guided reading, self-selected reading, working with words, and writing. High-risk students received an additional 45 minutes per day of small group instruction. Results of Informal Reading Inventories and observational data indicated that "after two years of multi-method, multi-level instruction, no child remained a non-reader. Most children, including those at high risk for failure, read at or above grade level" (Hall, Prevatte, & Cunningham, 1995, p. 154).

The Early Intervention in Reading (EIR) Program (Taylor et al., 1995) was developed to accelerate the learning of low-achieving first-grade children. It involves 20 minutes of supplemental, small-group reading instruction taught by the classroom teacher as an addition to the regular daily classroom reading program. While the results of EIR were not as dramatic as those reported by other interventions (Reading Recovery and Success for All), the program helped many low-achieving, emergent readers become readers. By the end of the first year of implementation, 67% of the children served were reading at least on a preprimer level, while 40% were reading on grade level or better. These achievements surpassed a comparison group who did not receive the supplemental instruction. In a follow-up study of these children in March of second grade, 72% of the children who had participated in EIR were reading second-grade-level texts while 65% of the children in the comparison group were reading on grade level. This intervention demonstrated that classroom adaptations by teachers can positively affect the reading development of children experiencing difficulty in first grade, even though it does not meet the needs of every child who requires special assistance (Taylor et al., 1995).

Another intervention program that reported promising results modified Title 1 instruction to focus on rereading of predictable books, word identification strategies, word pattern instruction, and writing. The intervention was provided to groups of three children for 30 minutes daily by paraprofessionals and teachers (Hiebert, 1994). According to the author, the majority of children who were initially in the bottom quartile were performing at levels comparable to the average students in their classrooms by the end of the year.

One of the most widely disseminated and researched intervention programs in schools today is Reading Recovery. It is an early literacy, one-to-one intervention designed to help the lowest-achieving first-grade children achieve accelerated progress by developing productive strategies for reading so that they are able to perform at a level commensurate with the average readers in their classrooms and to profit from classroom instruction (Clay, 1993b; Pinnell, 1995; Pinnell, Fried, & Estice, 1990). As an intervention program, it provides daily individual 30-minute lessons for approximately 12–20 weeks. Lessons are taught by specially trained teachers and consist of reading and writing experiences designed to help children develop effective strategies. Attention is paid to phonological awareness and the alphabetic principle in both reading and writing activities. Instruction is provided until the child is reading at or above the average of his or her class and has acquired independent reading and writing strategies. The program is then "discontinued," providing the opportunity for another child to begin the Reading Recovery program.

Reading Recovery was developed by Marie M. Clay, a New Zealand educator and psychologist. During the 1960's, Clay conducted longitudinal research documenting change over time at weekly intervals, enabling her to design techniques for detecting reading difficulties of young children. In the mid-1970's, she developed Reading Recovery procedures with teachers and tested the program in New Zealand (Clay, 1979). The success of the pilot program resulted in the nationwide adoption of Reading Recovery in New Zealand in 1983.

Subsequently, the success of Reading Recovery in New Zealand led to program initiatives in Australia, the United States, Canada, England, Ireland, and Scotland. In the United States, Reading Recovery sites have been established in 49 states and the District of Columbia. Additionally, Descubriendo la Lectura, the redevelopment (not translation) of Reading Recovery in Spanish (see Escamilla, 1994), has been implemented in eight states. Descubriendo la Lectura offers in Spanish the same intensive literacy intervention to eligible first-grade children receiving primary language instruction that Reading Recovery offers to English speakers. (Descubriendo la Lectura will be described in greater detail below.) With all authentic Reading Recovery and

Descubriendo la Lectura programs, data are collected daily and national data are analyzed annually for all children served. (See The Ohio State University and Reading Recovery Council of North America, 1998.) In fact, Reading Recovery has gone further in collecting data on every student involved than any other early intervention program (Pinnell, 1995).

The success of Reading Recovery has been well documented in the United States, New Zealand, Australia, and England (Askew, Fountas, Lyons, Pinnell, & Schmitt, 1998; Clay, 1993b; Frater & Staniland, 1994; Hobsbaum, 1995; Pinnell, 1995; Rowe, 1995). In North America alone, nearly three quarters of a million children have been served by Reading Recovery since it was first introduced in 1985; and, since its inception in North America, 83% of children who had full Reading Recovery programs have become independent readers (The Ohio State University and Reading Recovery Council of North America, 1999). Several longitudinal studies have shown that most Reading Recovery children continue to succeed in reading beyond first grade (Askew et al., 1998; Brown, Denton, Kelly, & Neal, 1999; The Ohio State University and RRCNA, 1999).

Contributing to the success of Reading Recovery is the high-level professional development for teachers (Pinnell, Lyons, DeFord, Bryk, & Seltzer, 1993) whereby they are trained in the practice and theory of literacy acquisition through an intense yearlong graduate course of study. Following their training year, Reading Recovery teachers continue to attend sessions about Reading Recovery theory and practice and receive support from their teacher leaders as they work with the hardest-to-teach first-grade children.

## Bilingual Intervention Programs

Although interventions for bilingual children have been less widely reported, there have been a few reported for children in bilingual classrooms and for English language learners whose first languages are other than English, but who are receiving literacy instruction in English. Goldenberg (1994), though not dealing specifically with early intervention programs, described classroom programs that supported beginning Spanish readers. He concluded that kindergarten children in Spanish bilingual classrooms "learn more about literacy when they are in classrooms that provide additional and direct opportunities for learning about print. They learn more when directly taught" (p. 184). In this case, a strong emphasis on learning letters, sounds, and how they combine to form syllables and words helped Spanish-speaking children become literate. In first-grade Spanish bilingual classrooms, Goldenberg (1994) found that a continuous balance between a code emphasis and reading for meaning and communicative purposes was more effective than an emphasis mostly on learning the code and skills. Additionally, increased pacing of instruction and the systematic inclusion of opportunities for taking books home to read and discuss with parents had positive effects on student learning.

Slavin et al. (1996) reported that in Success For All schools where the bilingual version of the program, Lee Conmigo, was implemented, Spanish-speaking students outperformed control group bilingual students and the differences were significant. The bilingual students scored at or near grade level and more than six months ahead of children in control groups.

Descubriendo la Lectura (a reconstruction of Reading Recovery in Spanish) is an early intervention program for students whose initial literacy instruction is in Spanish. The aim of Descubriendo la Lectura is to help students having difficulties in bilingual first-grade classrooms to read and write within the average band of their peers. Preliminary investigations of Descubriendo la Lectura have shown it to be a successful intervention for Spanish-speaking children who are being taught to read and write in Spanish (Escamilla, 1994; Escamilla, Loera, Ruiz, & Rodriquez, 1998). In a study that examined the initial impact of Descubriendo la Lectura on 23 students who participated in the program during 1991–92, Escamilla (1994) reported that Descubriendo la Lectura intervention students made significant gains in literacy acquisition and surpassed control group students on six reading measures, including text reading. In another study which examined the sustaining effects of Descubriendo la Lectura programs, Escamilla et al. (1998) found that students who had successfully completed the Descubriendo la Lectura intervention program in first grade and were continuing to read in Spanish in second and third grades, sustained their reading achievement as indicated on both informal and standardized measures of reading (text reading and SABE-2 Spanish Reading Achievement Test). Results indicated that 92% of the second-grade former Descubriendo la Lectura students met or exceeded the average band on Spanish Text Reading and 75% met or exceeded the average band on the SABE-2. For third graders, the percentages were 93% and 79%, respectively. The authors concluded that Descubriendo la Lectura had a positive impact on Spanish-speaking children in much the same way that Reading Recovery had on English-speaking children.

## English Language Learner Intervention Programs

The research on the success of early intervention programs for English language learners is limited. Slavin et al. (1996) examined the efficacy of an adaptation of Success For All for "English as a Second Language" (ESL) students and found it to be effective. Asian students in grades 3-5 performed at or above grade level and far better than control students. Many of them had been in the program since kindergarten. Outcomes for non-Asian ESL students were also very positive with statistically significant differences being documented between experimental and control groups.

Reading Recovery has been found to be successful in helping young English language learners become literate. In New Zealand, Clay's (1993b) earlier studies and, more recently, Smith's (1994) research on children for whom English is a second language, confirmed that Reading Recovery was an effective intervention for such learners. In England, Hobsbaum (1995) reported that bilingual children who received Reading Recovery had similar outcomes on An Observation Survey of Early Literacy Achievement (Clay, 1993a) tasks as monolingual English-speaking children. Entry scores for the bilingual children were lower on all subtests of the survey, but by the end of the program, bilingual and monolingual children looked very similar.

In a one-year study of the effects of Reading Recovery on English language learners, Spanish-speaking bilingual children, and monolingual English children, Kelly, Gomez-Valdez, Klein, and Neal (1995) reported that English language learners who received Reading Recovery and Spanish-speaking children who received Descubriendo la Lectura benefited from both interventions. Furthermore, their success was similar to monolingual English children who participated in Reading Recovery.

## The Purpose of the Current Study

The purpose of this study was to extend the work of Kelly et al. (1995) by examining several years of data collected in California between 1993 and 1996 to document longer-term outcomes. The focus of the investigation was the same; that is, to determine if Reading Recovery and Descubriendo la Lectura interventions resulted in reading and writing success for two groups of bilingual children: (a) English language learners receiving Reading Recovery instruction—first-grade children acquiring English as a second language concomitantly with developing literacy in English through instruction provided in English-speaking classrooms; and (b) Spanish-speaking children receiving the Descubriendo la Lectura intervention who were in first-grade bilingual classrooms that provided primary language instruction.

Two important terms used in the sections below are defined here: program children are students who participated in Reading Recovery/Descubriendo la Lectura who received a full program of instruction determined either by successfully completing the program, or by receiving a minimum of 60 lessons of tutoring. Children who have *discontinued* from the intervention programs have met two criteria: (a) they have developed independent strategies in reading and writing; and (b) they have reached the average reading level of children in their classrooms and, therefore, can benefit from classroom literacy instruction without additional assistance. To reiterate, for the purposes of this study, children were designated as program children if they received a minimum of 60 lessons or successfully discontinued from the program at the average level of other first-grade children. (Please note: In the United States currently, the 60-lesson designation is no longer used to identify "program children;" rather, 20 weeks is the recommendation for classifying children as having received a full program.)

In determining whether the Reading Recovery/Descubriendo la Lectura programs were effective literacy interventions, "effective" was defined in terms of three variables. The first variable involved changes in average score levels on the three measures of *An Observation Survey of Early Literacy Achievement* (Clay, 1993a) or *Instrumento de Observacion* (Escamilla, Andrade, Basurto, Ruiz, & Clay, 1996), which are described below. Another variable involved the proportion of children receiving full programs who successfully discontinued from each program. The third variable involved the end-of-year progress of children in Reading Recovery/Descubriendo la Lectura as they compared to random samples of first-grade children. Therefore, the questions that guided the research were:

1. What changes in average scores exist between pre- and post-tests for English language learners in Reading Recovery and children in Descubriendo la Lectura?
2. Do similar proportions of children in these two groups successfully discontinue from the programs as compared to the total population of children in Reading Recovery?

3. How do successfully discontinued Reading Recovery English language learners and Descubriendo la Lectura children compare to a random sample of their peers on average scores of the three selected measures of *An Observation Survey of Early Literacy Achievment* (Clay, 1993a) and *Instrumento de Observacion* (Escamilla et al., 1996) at the end of first grade?

## Method

### Participants and Assessment Instruments

Participants in the study included children who had received Reading Recovery or Descubriendo la Lectura instruction from 1993–1996. They included 2,359 Spanish-speaking children who participated in Descubriendo la Lectura, 3,992 English language learners who participated in Reading Recovery, and a comparison group of 18,787 children who received the Reading Recovery intervention in English.

All children in both Reading Recovery and Descubriendo la Lectura were identified by their classroom teachers as having difficulty learning to read and write. They were selected for intervention based on their teacher's recommendations and the results of their performance on either *An Observation Survey of Early Literacy Achievement* (Clay, 1993a) or *Instrumento de Observacion* (Escamilla et al., 1996). Both of these surveys are administered individually to children in order to determine how well they are developing emergent reading and writing behaviors and understandings. Each survey is comprised of six measures that assess behaviors associated with early reading and writing:

1. *Letter Identification.* The child is asked to identify upper and lowercase letters (54 in English including conventional print for "a" and "g" and 61 letters in Spanish).
2. *Word Test.* The child is asked to read a list of 20 words drawn from words most frequently used in beginning reading texts. Three forms are available.
3. *Concepts About Print.* The child is asked to perform a variety of tasks during a book reading. These tasks check on significant concepts about book handling and printed language, such as directionality and the concepts of letter and word. Two forms are available.
4. *Writing Vocabulary.* The child is asked to write as many words as he or she can in a ten-minute period. The score for this measure is the number of words written accurately.
5. *Hearing and Recording Sounds in Words.* The child is asked to record sounds he/she hears in the words of a sentence that is slowly read aloud. This measure indicates the child's ability both to hear and to record sounds in words. Four forms are available.
6. *Text Reading Level.* Measures of Text Reading Level are obtained by having the child read texts that have been leveled in a gradient of difficulty. The highest level read with an accuracy of 90% or better is considered the child's instructional text level. The leveled texts have been drawn from a series of stories that are not used in Reading Recovery or Descubriendo la Lectura instruction (The Ohio State University and Reading Recovery Council of North America, 1998).

*An Observation Survey of Early Literacy Achievement* (Clay, 1993a) and *Instrumento de Observacion* (Escamilla et al., 1996) provide a means by which a wide range of literacy behaviors can be observed in a systematic way through a set of standard tasks with standard administration, thereby providing a means for educators to track changes over time. All six measures are used in order to assure that multiple indicators are applied in assessing early reading behaviors. According to Clay, "No one technique is reliable on its own. When important decisions are to be made we should increase the range of observations we make in order to decrease the risk that we will make errors in our interpretations" (1993a, p. 7). The tasks on *An Observation Survey of Early Literacy Achievement* (Clay, 1993a) were all developed in research studies and are authentic in that they reflect early literacy behaviors that children need to acquire early in the process of learning to read and write. "All tasks in my observation survey are like screens on which are projected the immaturity or degree of control demonstrated by the young child's tentative responses to print and to books" (Clay, 1998, p. 63).

The children were selected for tutoring from the lowest 20% of children in first-grade classrooms as assessed with these surveys in schools where Reading Recovery and/or Descubriendo la Lectura was being implemented. The lowest-achieving children were selected first. For English language learners, an additional criterion for eligibility for the program was their English language proficiency; that is, their proficiency was sufficient for them to understand the directions and required tasks of the assessment instrument.

## Procedures

Data were collected on every child served in Reading Recovery and Descubriendo la Lectura programs in California for each of the three academic years: 1993–94, 1994–95, and 1995–96. The data analyzed for this study, therefore, represent the total population of children who received Reading Recovery or Descubriendo la Lectura intervention for each academic year. (The data for 1993-94 were reported earlier; see Kelly, et al, 1995.) Pre-program and post-program scores were obtained annually for Reading Recovery and Descubriendo la Lectura children on the three target measures of *Hearing and Recording Sounds in Words, Writing Vocabulary, and Text Reading Level,* in order to determine changes in mean scores for each measure. Scores were analyzed in terms of two sub-groups of children, Spanish-speaking children in bilingual classrooms (Spanish L1) receiving the Descubriendo la Lectura intervention; and, English language learners (English L2) receiving the Reading Recovery intervention. In addition, data were obtained for the total population of children receiving the Reading Recovery intervention. (This included monolingual English-speaking children and English language learners in English instruction classrooms.) Pre-program scores were obtained by school-based trained and in-training Reading Recovery teachers at the beginning of children's programs; post-program scores were obtained when children concluded the program, either as "discontinued," or, "not discontinued with a full program." Table 1 depicts the number of children in each group who received Reading Recovery or Descubriendo la Lectura instruction in California for each of the target years, the discontinuing rates for each group, and the average number of lessons for discontinuing.

**Table 1.** Reading Recovery/Descubriendo La Lectura Data for Three California Populations: 1993–96

| | YEAR | SERVED | PROGRAM | DISCONTINUED | SUCCESS RATE % | AVERAGE NUMBER OF LESSONS |
|---|---|---|---|---|---|---|
| DLL | 93-94 | 243 | 165 | 129 | 78% | 65.34 |
| | 94-95 | 721 | 487 | 386 | 79% | 62.30 |
| | 95-96 | 1395 | 952 | 762 | 80% | 65.31 |
| | 93-96 | 2359 | 1604 | 1277 | 79.6% | 64.40 |
| RR:ELL | 93-94 | 1409 | 885 | 667 | 75% | 66.00 |
| (English | 94-95 | 1474 | 912 | 653 | 72% | 69.12 |
| =L2) | 95-96 | 1109 | 699 | 476 | 68% | 68.12 |
| | 93-96 | 3992 | 2496 | 1796 | 72% | 67.69 |
| RR | 93-94 | 3621 | 2419 | 1789 | 74% | 62.67 |
| (English | 94-95 | 6674 | 4368 | 3268 | 75% | 63.53 |
| =L1) | 95-96 | 8492 | 5658 | 4295 | 76% | 63.33 |
| | 93-96 | 18787 | 12445 | 9352 | 75.2% | 63.27 |
| Totals | 93-94 | 5273 | 3469 | 2585 | 74.5% | |
| | 94-95 | 8869 | 5767 | 4307 | 74.7% | |
| | 95-96 | 10996 | 7309 | 5533 | 75.7% | |
| | 93-96 | 25138 | 16545 | 12425 | 75.1% | |

*Note:* DLL=Descubriendo La Lectura;  ELL=English Language leaner; RR=Reading Recovery

As mentioned earlier, every child selected for Reading Recovery/ Descubriendo la Lectura intervention was administered *An Observation Survey of Early Literacy Achievement* (Clay, 1993a) or *Instrumento de Observacion* (Escamilla et al., 1996) upon entry to the program. However, if they entered within a few weeks of the initial fall testing, the initial test data were used; otherwise, the battery of tasks was re-administered at entry to obtain a current picture of students' strengths. Children received consistent daily tutorial instruction over an average of 17 weeks. Reading Recovery and Descubriendo la Lectura teachers monitored children's progress on the basis of daily observations and successful reading of progressively difficult continuous text.

When the Reading Recovery or Descubriendo la Lectura teachers, in collaboration with the classroom teachers, decided that children's programs could be discontinued, the surveys were re-administered by someone other than the Reading Recovery/ Descubriendo la Lectura teacher. When making decisions to discontinue children's programs, teachers considered whether the children had demonstrated accelerated progress, whether their scores on the surveys fell within the average range for first-grade students in their schools, and whether they exhibited observable behaviors indicative of a self-extending system of literacy learning (Clay, 1979, 1993b). The joint decisions to discontinue children's programs were supervised by a Reading Recovery/ Descubriendo la Lectura teacher leader. The assessments were administered again at the end of first grade for children discontinued prior to April 1st.

To determine the effectiveness of Reading Recovery for English language learners and Descubriendo la Lectura for Spanish-speaking children, we made comparisons between pre- and post-assessment results on three of the measures from *An Observation Survey of Early Literacy Achievement* (Clay, 1993a) for children in Reading Recovery, and *Instrumento de Observacion* (Escamilla et al., 1996) for children in Descubriendo la Lectura: *Writing Vocabulary, Hearing and Recording Sounds in Words,* and *Text Reading Level.* These three measures were selected because they represent authentic reading and writing tasks required for learning to read and are, therefore, valid indicators of children's growth in reading and writing.

Observing children's writing helps us to learn what they understand about print and the features of print to which they are attending. *The Writing Vocabulary* task, a measure of the number of words a child can write in 10 minutes, illustrates how quickly children are building control over a basic writing vocabulary. According to Clay (1998), "The word lists differ from child to child, and so are open products. For a year or two this is a very discriminating indicator of who is becoming a writer; it is a good way of capturing changes occurring at this stage" (p. 106). The *Hearing and Recording Sounds in Words* task is an indication of the specific sounds children hear in words and of how well they are able to record the sounds with appropriate letters (Clay, 1993a). This measure taps into children's phonemic awareness, which has been found to be an excellent predictor of success in reading acquisition (Adams, 1990; Stanovich, 1993/94). The total possible raw score on the task is 37 for the English version and 39 for the Spanish version.

*Text Reading Levels* are obtained by taking samples of children's reading of texts via running records. Running records have shown high reliability (accuracy and error reliability of 0.90) and face and content validity; therefore, they provide teachers with a standardized and reliable way to record reading behaviors that can be analyzed for processing and problem-solving strategies, accuracy, and text difficulty (Clay, 1979, 1993a). In Reading Recovery/Descubriendo la Lectura, children's abilities to read continuous text are assessed on materials not previously seen and which are arranged along a gradient of difficulty from pre-primer levels to a sixth-grade (basal) level of reading. Table 2 displays grade-level equivalents assigned to the *Text Reading Levels* of assessment materials used in Reading Recovery and Descubriendo la Lectura.

The other three tasks from the surveys, *Letter Identification, Word Test,* and *Concepts About Print,* were not used in our pre- post-test analysis because although they have value in discriminating between children who are and are not developing literacy understandings in early stages of reading acquisition, they may not discriminate as well between the groups in later stages. This is because the fixed numbers of answers on the *Letter Identification* and *Word Test* provide a ceiling of possible scores so that frequently even children who are not putting together a reading processing system on continuous text are able to score as well as those who are developing reading skills on

**Table 2.** Grade-Level Equivalents for Text Reading Levels of Reading Recovery and Descubriendo La Lectura Assessment Materials

| TEXT READING LEVEL SCORE | EQUIVALENT BASAL LEVEL |
|---|---|
| 0-2 | Pre-primer A |
| 3-4 | Pre-primer 1 |
| 5-6 | Pre-primer 2 |
| 7-8 | Pre-primer 3 |
| 9-12 | Primer |
| 14-16 | Grade 1 |
| 18-20 | Grade 2 |
| 22-24 | Grade 3 |
| 26 | Grade 4 |
| 28 | Grade 5 |
| 30 | Grade 6 |

**Table 3.** Reading Recovery/Descubriendo La Lectura Data for Three California Populations: 1993-96

| | YEAR | TEST TIME | N | MEAN | SD | T-TEST | P |
|---|---|---|---|---|---|---|---|
| | | | HEARING AND RECORDING SOUNDS IN WORDS | | | | |
| | 93-94 | Entry | 129 | 6.56 | 8.14 | | |
| DLL | | Spring | 126 | 36.87 | 2.51 | 40.06 | < .0001 |
| (Spanish=L1) | 94-95 | Entry | 383 | 7.40 | 9.79 | | |
| Discontinued | | Spring | 352 | 37.06 | 3.05 | 52.38 | < .0001 |
| | 95-96 | Entry | 754 | 8.33 | 10.49 | | |
| | | Spring | 732 | 37.38 | 2.63 | 71.61 | < .0001 |
| | 93-94 | Entry | 36 | 1.08 | 1.63 | | |
| DLI | | Spring | 33 | 25.88 | 9.58 | | |
| (Spanrsh=L1) | 94-95 | Entry | 100 | 2.38 | 3.15 | 10.99 | < .0001 |
| Not Discontinued | | Spring | 91 | 29.23 | 7.69 | | |
| | 95-96 | Entry | 189 | 2.22 | 3.66 | | |
| | | Spring | 172 | 31.24 | 6.42 | 58.72 | < .0001 |
| | 93-94 | Entry | -- | -- | -- | -- | |
| DLL | | Spring | 50 | 33.22 | 7.43 | | |
| (Spanish=L1) | 94-95 | Entry | -- | -- | -- | | |
| Random Sample | | Spring | 56 | 31.14 | 8.81 | -- | |
| | 95-96 | Entry | -- | -- | -- | | |
| | | Spring | 91 | 33.29 | 8.28 | -- | |
| | 93-94 | Entry | 666 | 8.62 | 30.16 | | |
| RR:ELL | | Spring | 647 | 34.43 | 2.86 | 64.35 | < .0001 |
| (English=L2) | 94-95 | Entry | 652 | 7.21 | 9.09 | | |
| Discontinued | | Spring | 630 | 34.40 | 2.67 | 74.30 | < .0001 |
| | 95-96 | Entry | 476 | 7.97 | 10.33 | | |
| | | Spring | 458 | 34.29 | 3.55 | 50.98 | < .0001 |

these tasks of item knowledge. *The Concepts About Print* tasks may not discriminate well with regard to advanced print concepts. Some children who read well may still confuse the concepts of letter and word (Clay, 1998). Additionally, good readers may not notice reversals of text, word, or letters when the tester is reading the text.

## Results

Reading achievement data for three academic years, 1993–94, 1994–95, and 1995–96, are displayed in Tables 3, 4, and 5 for the three populations of children relevant to this study: (a) children for whom Spanish was their first language who were receiving primary language instruction and were served in Descubriendo la Lectura; (b) children for whom English was their second language who received classroom instruction in English and were served in Reading Recovery; and, (c) the total English-speaking population of children served in Reading Recovery. The latter group included the English language learners and these children for whom English was their primary language. This total Reading Recovery group served to establish a standard for comparison of data from the other two groups. For each population represented in Tables 3–5, scores are reported for both "Discontinued" and "Not Discontinued" children.

Table 3. *(Continued)*

|  | YEAR | TEST TIME | N | MEAN | SD | T-TEST | P |
|---|---|---|---|---|---|---|---|
|  | 93-94 | Entry | 218 | 2.23 | 3.64 | 48.18 < .0001 |  |
| RR:ELL |  | Spring | 205 | 27.74 | 7.19 |  |  |
| (English=L2) | 94-95 | Entry | 259 | 1.87 | 3.40 | 51.32 < 0001 |  |
| Not Discontinuert |  | Spring | 231 | 26.68 | 7.23 |  |  |
|  | 95-96 | Entry | 223 | 1.70 | 3.14 | 45.30 < .0001 |  |
|  |  | Spring | 204 | 27.24 | 7.41 |  |  |
|  | 93-94 | Entry | 1773 | 9.99 | 10.91 | 92.10 < .0001 |  |
| RR |  | Spring | 1723 | 34.43 | 2.63 |  |  |
| (English=L1) | 94-95 | Entry | 3251 | 9.67 | 10.78 | 127.77 < .0001 |  |
| Discontinued |  | Spring | 3138 | 34.60 | 2.81 |  |  |
|  | 95-96 | Entry | 4273 | 10.18 | 11.17 | 140.52 < .0001 |  |
|  |  | Spring | 4144 | 34.82 | 2.89 |  |  |
|  | 93-94 | Entry | 624 | 2.18 | 3.13 | 77.44 < .0001 |  |
| RR |  | Spring | 556 | 27.24 | 7.71 |  |  |
| (English=L1) | 94-95 | Entry | 1091 | 2.48 | 3.94 | 98.94 < .0001 |  |
| Not Discontinued |  | Spring | 970 | 27.63 | 7.57 |  |  |
|  | 95-96 | Entry | 1357 | 2.62 | 4.17 | 111.67 < .0001 |  |
|  |  | Spring | 1226 | 27.66 | 7.64 |  |  |
|  | 93-94 | Entry | -- | -- | -- | -- |  |
| RR |  | Spring | 424 | 31.72 | 7.41 |  |  |
| (English=L1 or L2) | 94-95 | Entry | -- | - | -- | -- |  |
| Random Sample |  | Spring | 111 | 31.21 | 7.95 |  |  |
|  | 95-96 | Entry | -- | -- | -- | -- |  |
|  |  | Spring | 177 | 31.01 | 7.57 |  |  |

*Note:* DLL=Descubriendo La Lectura;ELL=English Language leaner; RR=Reading Recovery

In addition, for each academic year, scores are reported for children selected from two random sample populations of two first-grade cohorts. One random sample was from the Spanish-speaking population receiving primary language instruction; this sample served to establish a comparison for scores of Descubriendo la Lectura children. The other random sample was from the English-speaking population consisting of both monolingual children and those children who were learning English-as-a-second language and receiving English literacy instruction. In other words, the sample represents the typical, diverse first-grade population in California. This sample served as a comparison for scores of the English language learners' population as well as the total Reading Recovery population. (Please note: In Tables 3, 4, and 5, "Entry" scores are obtained at the beginning of children's programs; "Spring" scores are obtained at the end of the school year. Totals may differ from table 1 because of missing data from individual subtests.)

Table 3 displays data for all three populations over three academic years on the *Hearing and Recording Sounds in Words* measure (total possible raw score = 37 in English and 39 in Spanish). For each group of Discontinued children, end-of-year mean scores were approaching the maximum scores possible and had changed significantly

**Table 4.** Reading Recovery/Descubriendo La Lectura Data for Three California Populations: 1993-96

| | YEAR | TEST TIME | N | MEAN | SD | T-TEST | P |
|---|---|---|---|---|---|---|---|
| | | **WRITING VOCABULARY** | | | | | |
| | 93-94 | Entry | 129 | 3.83 | 4.43 | | |
| DLL | | Spring | 126 | 38.20 | 11.89 | 31.56 | < .001 |
| (Spanish=L1) | 94-95 | Entry | 383 | 4.63 | 5.96 | | |
| Discontinued | | Spring | 352 | 39.97 | 13.33 | 44.79 | < .0001 |
| | 95-96 | Entry | 755 | 5.59 | 9.05 | | |
| | | Spring | 727 | 43.13 | 12.08 | 71.10 | < .0001 |
| | 93-94 | Entry | 36 | 1.11 | 1.14 | | |
| DLI | | Spring | 33 | 19.55 | 9.38 | 10.99 | < .0001 |
| (Spanish=L1) | 94-95 | Entry | 99 | 1.71 | 1.33 | | |
| Not Discontinued | | Spring | 91 | 26.34 | 11.44 | 20.48 | < .0001 |
| | 95-96 | Entry | 189 | 1.90 | 2.59 | | |
| | | Spring | 172 | 27.47 | 11.08 | 31.35 | < .0001 |
| | 93-94 | Entry | -- | -- | -- | -- | |
| DLL | | Spring | 50 | 29.04 | 12.38 | | |
| (Spanish=L1) | 94-95 | Entry | -- | -- | -- | | |
| Random Sample | | Spring | 55 | 25.91 | 13.32 | -- | |
| | 95-96 | Entry | -- | -- | -- | | |
| | | Spring | 91 | 33.02 | 15.57 | -- | |
| | 93-94 | Entry | 667 | 7.21 | 9.16 | | |
| RR:ELL | | Spring | 647 | 48.61 | 13.52 | 70.66 | < .001 |
| (English=L2) | 94-95 | Entry | 653 | 6.06 | 8.16 | | |
| Discontinued | | Spring | 631 | 48.28 | 12.89 | 77.50 | < .001 |
| | 95-96 | Entry | 476 | 6.78 | 9.81 | | |
| | | Spring | 459 | 48.76 | 13.03 | 61.41 | < .0001 |

from entry scores. Furthermore, the end-of-year scores exceeded end-of-year scores obtained for the random samples of first-grade children.

For Not Discontinued children, mean entry scores for each academic year were lower than entry scores for Discontinued children; end-of-year mean scores were significantly higher than entry scores, though not as high as mean scores for Discontinued children. The end-of year scores for Not Discontinued children in all populations were slightly lower than end-of-year scores obtained each year from the random samples of California first-grade children. Results on *Hearing and Recording Sounds in Words* for each of the three populations of Discontinued and Not Discontinued children were statistically significant at the p < .0001 level.

Table 4 displays data for all three populations over three academic years on the *Writing Vocabulary* measure. This task involves asking children to write as many words as possible in a ten-minute time period. As on the preceding task, all three populations of Discontinued children made remarkable gains in mean scores between entry and end-of-year tests. Additionally, end-of-year mean scores for all Discontinued children were higher than end-of-year scores for the random samples of first-grade English- and Spanish-speaking children.

**Table 4.**  *(Continued)*

|  | YEAR | TEST TIME | N | MEAN | SD | T-TEST | P |
|---|---|---|---|---|---|---|---|
| | 93-94 | Entry | 218 | 2.17 | 1.81 | 32.84 < .0001 | |
| RR:ELL | | Spring | 205 | 30.95 | 12.74 | | |
| (English=L2) | 94-95 | Entry | 259 | 2.27 | 3.38 | 37.50 < 0001 | |
| Not Discontinuert | | Spring | 230 | 29.71 | 11.32 | | |
| | 95-96 | Entry | 223 | 1.89 | 2.07 | 29.22 < .0001 | |
| | | Spring | 260 | 31.28 | 14.58 | | |
| | 93-94 | Entry | 1773 | 8.35 | 10.29 | 107.10 < .0001 | |
| RR | | Spring | 1724 | 47.26 | 12.99 | | |
| (English=L1) | 94-95 | Entry | 3251 | 7.91 | 9.82 | 153.45 < .0001 | |
| Discontinued | | Spring | 3135 | 47.30 | 12.36 | | |
| | 95-96 | Entry | 4274 | 8.60 | 10.85 | 170.67 < .0001 | |
| | | Spring | 4141 | 48.98 | 12.62 | | |
| | 93-94 | Entry | 624 | 20.38 | 2.23 | 54.04 < .0001 | |
| RR | | Spring | 558 | 29.13 | 12.11 | | |
| (English=L1) | 94-95 | Entry | 1092 | 2.32 | 2.31 | 75.39 < .0001 | |
| Not Discontinued | | Spring | 973 | 29.76 | 11.82 | | |
| | 95-96 | Entry | 1357 | 2.42 | 2.55 | 85.52 < .0001 | |
| | | Spring | 1228 | 30.18 | 11.78 | | |
| | 93-94 | Entry | -- | -- | -- | -- | |
| RR | | Spring | 423 | 42.02 | 18.79 | | |
| (English=L1 or L2) | 94-95 | Entry | -- | - | -- | -- | |
| Random Sample | | Spring | 111 | 41.06 | 18.10 | | |
| | 95-96 | Entry | -- | -- | -- | -- | |
| | | Spring | 177 | 37.48 | 16.58 | | |

*Note:* DLL=Descubriendo La Lectura; ELL=English Language leaner; RR=Reading Recovery

Mean scores on the *Writing Vocabulary* task for the Not Discontinued children in all three populations also showed considerable gains between entry and end-of-year testing; however, the means at end-of-year testing did not exceed the means for random sample English- and Spanish-speaking children. Changes in mean scores between entry and end-of-year on Writing Vocabulary for each of the three populations of Discontinued and Not Discontinued children were statistically significant at the $p < .001$ or $p < .0001$ levels.

Table 5 displays data for all three populations over three academic years for the Text Reading Level measure (see Table 1 for a guide to text levels). Discontinued children in each population entered Reading Recovery with mean text level scores below 1; they finished the year with mean scores between 13.29 and 14.79. All mean scores for Discontinued children at end-of-year testing exceeded mean scores for random samples of English and Spanish-speaking children in California for each of the three years.

The Not Discontinued children in all three populations had lower mean Text Reading Level scores upon entry to Reading Recovery than the Discontinued children; at end-of-year testing, they reached text levels between 4.78 and 5.83. These scores

**Table 5.** Reading Recovery/Descubriendo La Lectura Data for Three California Populations: 1993-96

| | YEAR | TEST TIME | N | MEAN | SD | T-TEST | P |
|---|---|---|---|---|---|---|---|
| | | **TEXT READING** | | | | | |
| | 93-94 | Entry | 129 | .043 | 0.73 | | |
| DLL | | Spring | 126 | 14.55 | 4.93 | 31.43 | < .001 |
| (Spanish=L1) | 94-95 | Entry | 383 | 0.62 | 1.26 | | |
| Discontinued | | Spring | 352 | 14.36 | 5.28 | 47.51 | < .0001 |
| | 95-96 | Entry | 754 | 0.61 | 1.06 | | |
| | | Spring | 732 | 14.79 | 5.04 | 73.81 | < .0001 |
| | 93-94 | Entry | 36 | 0.17 | 0.45 | | |
| DLI | | Spring | 33 | 5.03 | 3.11 | 9.34 | < .0001 |
| (Spanish=L1) | 94-95 | Entry | 100 | 0.17 | 0.45 | | |
| Not Discontinued | | Spring | 91 | 4.86 | 3.18 | 14.23 | < .0001 |
| | 95-96 | Entry | 189 | 0.20 | 0.44 | | |
| | | Spring | 172 | 4.78 | 2.65 | 22.32 | < .0001 |
| | 93-94 | Entry | -- | -- | -- | -- | |
| DLL | | Spring | 50 | 10.32 | 8.87 | | |
| (Spanish=L1) | 94-95 | Entry | -- | -- | -- | | |
| Random Sample | | Spring | 56 | 8.86 | 7.76 | -- | |
| | 95-96 | Entry | -- | -- | -- | | |
| | | Spring | 90 | 10.40 | 8.96 | -- | |
| | 93-94 | Entry | 664 | 0.86 | 1.46 | | |
| RR:ELL | | Spring | 648 | 14.31 | 4.48 | 73.51 | < .001 |
| (English=L2) | 94-95 | Entry | 653 | 0.54 | 1.11 | | |
| Discontinued | | Spring | 631 | 13.29 | 4.29 | 73.27 | < .0001 |
| | 95-96 | Entry | 476 | 0.76 | 1.6 | | |
| | | Spring | 460 | 13.90 | 13.95 | 63.93 | < .0001 |

were lower than the mean scores for the random samples of English- and Spanish-speaking children. Results for Text Reading Level for each of the three populations of Discontinued and Not Discontinued children were statistically significant at the p < .001 or p < .0001 levels.

In summary, on all three tasks, children who were successfully discontinued in each of the target populations demonstrated gains that indicated they were operating at levels that exceeded the achievement levels of the random sample population at the conclusion of each school year.

## Discussion

The results of this study serve to address the three research questions posed and will be discussed with reference to each. Our first research question was, "What changes in average scores exist between pre- and post-tests for English language learners in Reading Recovery and children in Descubriendo la Lectura?" For each academic year, 1993–94, 1994–95, 1995–96, the data obtained indicate significant (p < .001 or .0001) progress for discontinued children in both target populations of children on each of three tasks

**Table 5.** *(Continued)*

|  | YEAR | TEST TIME | N | MEAN | SD | T-TEST | P |
|---|---|---|---|---|---|---|---|
|  | 93-94 | Entry | 218 | 0.23 | 0.59 | 29.47 | < .0001 |
| RR:ELL |  | Spring | 205 | 5.43 | 2.52 |  |  |
| (English=L2) | 94-95 | Entry | 259 | 0.23 | 0.60 | 29.30 | < 0001 |
| Not Discontinuert |  | Spring | 228 | 5.52 | 2.66 |  |  |
|  | 95-96 | Entry | 223 | 0.13 | 0.50 | 25.25 | < .0001 |
|  |  | Spring | 204 | 5.34 | 2.96 |  |  |
|  | 93-94 | Entry | 1772 | 1.19 | 1.64 | 123.63 | < .0001 |
| RR |  | Spring | 1726 | 14.16 | 4.16 |  |  |
| (English=L1) | 94-95 | Entry | 3249 | 1.72 | 1.72 | 158.35 | < .0001 |
| Discontinued |  | Spring | 3144 | 4.35 | 4.35 |  |  |
|  | 95-96 | Entry | 4275 | 1.22 | 1.82 | 193.04 | < .0001 |
|  |  | Spring | 4145 | 14.48 | 4.14 |  |  |
|  | 93-94 | Entry | 624 | 0.42 | 0.72 | 46.00 | < .0001 |
| RR |  | Spring | 558 | 5.63 | 2.66 |  |  |
| (English=L1) | 94-95 | Entry | 1092 | 0.34 | 0.71 | 42.99 | < .0001 |
| Not Discontinued |  | Spring | 973 | 5.83 | 3.93 |  |  |
|  | 95-96 | Entry | 1357 | 0.40 | 0.76 | 67.60 | < .0001 |
|  |  | Spring | 1228 | 5.79 | 2.78 |  |  |
|  | 93-94 | Entry | -- | -- | -- | -- |  |
| RR |  | Spring | 423 | 13.79 | 9.12 |  |  |
| (English=L1 or L2) | 94-95 | Entry | -- | -- | -- | -- |  |
| Random Sample |  | Spring | 111 | 12.74 | 8.49 |  |  |
|  | 95-96 | Entry | -- | -- | -- | -- |  |
|  |  | Spring | 177 | 11.54 | 8.72 |  |  |

**Note:** DLL=Descubriendo La Lectura; ELL=English Language leaner; RR=Reading Recovery

related to literacy acquisition: *Hearing and Recording Sounds in Words, Writing Vocabulary and Text Reading Level.* These results demonstrate that the Reading Recovery intervention for English language learners and the Descubriendo la Lectura intervention for Spanish-speaking children consistently enabled initially low-performing children to improve their performance on selected indicators of literacy acquisition.

Our second research question was, "Do similar proportions of children in these two groups successfully discontinue from the programs as compared to the total population of children in Reading Recovery?" The data displayed in Table 1 indicate that 72% of English language learner program children in Reading Recovery discontinued from the program; the mean number of lessons delivered for discontinuing the program was 67.69. This compares favorably with the proportion of total Reading Recovery children discontinued (75.2%) and the average number of lessons (63.27). For Descubriendo la Lectura, 79.6% of program children successfully discontinued; the average number of lessons delivered was 64.4. This proportion was higher than for the English language learner group (72%) and for the total Reading Recovery group (75.2%).

Our third research question was, "How do successfully discontinued Reading Recovery English language learners and Descubriendo la Lectura children compare to a random sample of their peers on average scores of the three selected measures of *An Observation Survey of Early Literacy Achievement* (Clay, 1993a) and *Instrumento de Observacion* (Escamilla et al., 1996) at the end of first grade?" Scores on the three literacy tasks described above for each population for each academic year were compared to scores obtained from annually drawn random samples of the first grade cohort. Results indicate that, for all three years, children in both target populations who received a complete program and achieved end-of-program criteria for discontinuation attained end-of-year mean scores that exceeded mean scores for the random samples of children. This demonstrates that initially low-performing English language learners receiving Reading Recovery intervention and Spanish-speaking children receiving Descubriendo la Lectura were enabled to reach the average level of their peers in approximately 63 to 68 lessons, or 31.5 to 34 hours of instruction.

In addition to results that address the three research questions, we make the following observations from the data presented here. First, the common assumptions that children who are learning English will take much longer to acquire literacy than children whose first language is the language of instruction is not borne out by these data. Over the three years of data collection reported here, the mean number of lessons delivered to discontinue from Reading Recovery for English language learners was 67.69 as compared to 63.27 for the total Reading Recovery population. For Descubriendo la Lectura, the mean number of lessons delivered for discontinuation was 64.40.

We believe the remarkable similarity of total time required for successful acceleration of progress for L1 and L2 students does not eclipse the most desirable practice of providing primary language instruction in both the classroom and intervention programs, as other research has demonstrated (Krashen & Biber, 1988; Ramirez, Yuen, & Ramey, 1991; Snow, Burns, & Griffin, 1998). Rather, the results of this study appear to speak to the power of individual tutoring by specially trained teachers who teach from a theory of teaching and learning that builds on each child's unique strengths. Moreover, the context of one-to-one tutoring is characterized by constant, language-rich interactions between a language learner and an expert user of that language. That children are enabled to accelerate their literacy learning in a daily regimen of authentic reading and writing activities whether they are proficient in the language of instruction or still acquiring academic-level competency in their second language should not be a surprising finding.

Second, the data for three years appear to confirm the validity of the discontinuing assessment that was carried out in regard to determining end-of-program status of children. Since a combination of quantitative and qualitative factors are considered on a case-by-case basis for discontinuing individual children from Reading Recovery and Descubriendo la Lectura, one measure of the quality of the decision process is to observe if there are differential outcomes between Discontinued and Not Discontinued children. Although for all three years, differences between entry and end-of-year scores for these two groups of children in both target populations were statistically significant, differences in means do not reveal if the discontinuing decision-making process was "working" in terms of predicting which children had achieved a measure of independence for no longer requiring individual tuition.

One indicator that confirms discontinuing decisions is the discrepancy in end-of-year scores on *Text Reading Level.* Consistently for each of three academic years for both target populations, the Not Discontinued group scored 8 to 10 levels below the Discontinued group, revealing that Not Discontinued children did not exhibit requisite behaviors that would indicate they had acquired a system for literacy learning on continuous text at an acceptable level for first-grade expectations (see Table 1). Furthermore, the Not Discontinued groups in both populations scored below the mean of the random samples taken for the general first-grade population for each of the tasks. These data indicate that Not Discontinued children did not achieve scores commensurate to their age-mates and, therefore, while the data appear to confirm the discontinuing decision-making process and its veracity in discriminating between children who have and have not developed a system of literacy learning, the larger issue remains of how to better serve the children who do not discontinue from Reading Recovery and Descubriendo la Lectura. A consistent finding of the data is that Not Discontinued children appear to stall in their progress somewhere around level 5 in text reading; also, they take a longer time in the program to achieve this limited record of acceleration. (See Table 1.) Clay, the founder of Reading Recovery, maintains that there are two positive outcomes for children participating in Reading Recovery: (a) successfully discontinuing (having accelerated to the average of their cohort), or (b) referral to longer-term intervention. Therefore, for the small number of children who require longer-term intervention, Reading Recovery or Descubriendo la Lectura has not failed; rather it has served successfully to "recover" those children who are experiencing early confusions about print, while serving as a "screen" for those children whose processing difficulties indicate referral to alternate programs as the appropriate next step. A full examination of this issue is beyond the scope of reporting the results of the present study; however, Reading Recovery and Descubriendo la Lectura personnel are continuing to study the possible obstacles to learning in a short-term intervention that some children experience as we seek to "recover" an ever-greater proportion of children served.

## Conclusions

Early interventions such as Reading Recovery are intended to prevent failure for children who can be identified early as being at high risk for not learning how to read. Metaphors such as "a safety net," "a gift of time," and "an insurance policy against academic failure" describe the various ways in which powerful interventions function in schools to support the most fragile learners in their quest to become literate. The data reported here demonstrate that Reading Recovery is an effective intervention for initially low-scoring children who are acquiring English concomitant with learning how to read and write in English-speaking classrooms, and that Descubriendo la Lectura is an effective intervention for initially low-performing Spanish-speaking children who receive literacy instruction in Spanish.

Sufficient research has been amassed (Askew et al., 1988; The Ohio State University and Reading Recovery Council of North America, 1999; Brown et al., 1999) to conclude that early intervention as a system innovation can work considerably to reduce early reading failure. Reading Recovery/Descubriendo la Lectura, as a specific model of early intervention, achieves its stated goal to enable the lowest-performing children to accelerate their progress in a relatively short period of time, thereby making it possible for them to "catch up" to their peers. This study has served to confirm the effectiveness of Reading Recovery for children acquiring English and for whom literacy instruction in their primary language is not available. It also serves to replicate the success of the Descubriendo la Lectura program, which has been reported elsewhere (Escamilla, 1994; Escamilla et al., 1998).

When considering the resources necessary to mount an intensive intervention like Reading Recovery, school personnel rightfully question the long-term benefits of the intervention: the results of Reading Recovery are impressive, but how do children fare in subsequent years (see Brown et al., 1999)? With regard to long-term sustained effects of an intervention, larger and more complex factors must be considered in an overall implementation effort. Chief among these is the level of commitment by the educational enterprise to place a priority on the prevention of academic failure. The effects of powerful results for intensive interventions such as Reading Recovery are not possible without a determination to invest resources to assure that every child learns how to read, for when access remains unavailable to the full contingent of eligible children, the program cannot be evaluated for its full effectiveness for a school or school system.

Furthermore, gains of children who are recovered in an intervention may remain tenuous as may be appropriately expected when children have just been put on a path of success and continue to have much additional learning to accomplish. Total conditions for success reside within schools and the culture for successful learning that schools foster. As failure in the early grades is almost always related to the failure in learning how to read, responsibility for the eventual success of children served in any literacy intervention must be borne by the total school community. Slavin, Karweit, and Wasik (1992/1993) maintain, "Success in the early grades does not guarantee success throughout the school years and beyond, but failure in the early grades does virtually guarantee failure in later schooling" (p. 11). This quote implies that multiple variables are involved for eventual academic success. Early, intensive interventions such as Reading Recovery and Descubriendo la Lectura provide the best entrée to the world of literacy for the most fragile learners and provide the foundation on which other aspects of schooling can continue to build to assure success for every student.

## References

Adams, M. (1990). *Beginning to read: Thinking and learning about print*. Cambridge, MA: M.I.T. Press.

Allington, R. L. (1995). Literacy lessons in the elementary schools: Yesterday, today, and tomorrow. In R. Allington & S. Walmsley (Eds.), *No quick fix: Rethinking literacy programs in America's elementary schools* (pp. 1–15). New York: Teachers College Press and International Reading Association.

Askew, B., Fountas, I., Lyons, C., Pinnell, G. S., & Schmitt, M. (1998). *Reading Recovery review: Understandings, outcomes, and implications*. Columbus, OH: Reading Recovery Council of North America.

Brown, W., Denton, E., Kelly, P. R., & Neal, J. (1999). Reading Recovery effectiveness: A success story in San Luis Coastal Unified School District. *ERS Spectrum, 17*, 3–12.

California Department of Education. (1995). *Every child a reader/The report of the California reading task force*. Sacramento: California Department of Education.

Clay, M. M. (1998). *By different paths to common outcomes*. York, ME: Stenhouse Publishers.

Clay, M. M. (1993a). *An observation survey of early literacy achievement*. Portsmouth, NH: Heinemann.

Clay, M. M. (1993b). *Reading Recovery: A guidebook for teachers in training*. Portsmouth, NH: Heinemann.

Clay, M. M. (1991). Reading Recovery surprises. In D. E. DeFord, C. A. Lyons, & G. S. Pinnell (Eds.), *Bridges to literacy: Learning from Reading Recovery* (pp. 55–74). Portsmouth, NH: Heinemann.

Clay, M. M. (1979). *The early detection of reading difficulties* (3rd ed.). Portsmouth, NH: Heinemann.

Cunningham, P. M., Hall, D. P., & Defee, M. (1991). Non-ability grouped, multi-level instruction: A year in a first grade classroom. *The Reading Teacher, 44*, 566–571.

DeFord, D., Lyons, C., & Pinnell, G. S. (1991). *Bridges to literacy: Learning from Reading Recovery*. Portsmouth, NH: Heinemann.

Escamilla K. (1994). Descubriendo la Lectura: An early intervention literacy program in Spanish. *Literacy Teaching and Learning: An International Journal of Early Reading and Writing, 1*(1), 57–71.

Escamilla, K., Andrade, A. M., Basurto, A., Ruiz, O., & Clay, M. M. (1996). *Instrumento de observacion: De los logros de la lecto—escritura inicial*. Portsmouth, NH: Heinemann.

Escamilla, K., Loera, M., Ruiz, O., & Rodriquez, Y. (1998). An examination of sustaining effects in Descubriendo la Lectura programs. *Literacy Teaching and Learning: An International Journal of Early Reading and Writing, 3*(2), 59–81.

Frater, G., & Staniland, B. (1994). Reading Recovery in New Zealand: A report from the office of Her Majesty's Chief Inspector of Schools. *Literacy Teaching and Learning: An International Journal of Early Reading and Writing, 1*(1), 143–62.

Goldenberg, C. (1994). Promoting early literacy development among Spanish speaking children: Lessons from two studies. In E. H. Hiebert & B. M. Taylor (Eds.), *Getting reading right from the start* (pp. 171–197). Boston: Allyn and Bacon.

Hall, D. P., Prevatte, C., & Cunningham, P. M. (1995). Eliminating ability grouping and reducing failure in the primary grades. In R. L. Allington & S. A. Walmsley (Eds.), *No quick fix: Rethinking literacy programs in America's elementary schools* (pp. 137–158). New York: Teachers College Press and International Reading Association.

Hiebert, E. H. (1994). A small-group literacy intervention with Chapter 1 students. In E. H. Hiebert & B. M. Taylor (Eds.), *Getting reading right from the start* (pp. 85–106). Boston: Allyn and Bacon.

Hiebert, E. H., & Taylor, B. M. (Eds.). (1994). *Getting reading right from the start.* Boston: Allyn and Bacon.

Hobsbaum, A. (1995). Reading Recovery in England. *Literacy Teaching and Learning: An International Journal of Early Reading and Writing, 2*(1), 21–40.

Kameenui, E. J. (1998). Diverse learners and the tyranny of time: Don't fix blame; fix the leaky roof. In R. Allington (Ed.), *Teaching struggling readers/Articles from The Reading Teacher.* Newark, DE: International Reading Association.

Kelly, P. R., Gomez-Valdez, C., Klein, A., & Neal, J. C. (1995, April). Progress of first and second language learners in an early intervention program. Paper presented to the American Education Research Association, San Francisco. (ERIC Document Reproduction Service, ED 394 296)

Krashen, S., & Biber, D. (1988). *On course: Bilingual education's success in California.* Sacramento, CA: California Association for Bilingual Education.

Lyons, C. A., & Beaver, J. (1995). Reducing retention and learning disability placement through Reading Recovery: An educationally sound, cost-effective choice. In R. L. Allington & S. Walmsley (Eds.), *No quick fix: Rethinking literacy programs in America's elementary schools* (pp. 116–136). New York: Teachers College Press and International Reading Association.

Madden, N. A., Slavin, R. E., Karweit, N. L., Dolan, L. J., & Wasik, B. A. (1991). Success for All: Ending reading failure from the beginning. *Language Arts, 68,* 47–52.

The Ohio State University and Reading Recovery Council of North America. (1998). *Reading Recovery executive summary 1984–1997.* Columbus, OH: The Ohio State University and the Reading Recovery Council of North America.

The Ohio State University and Reading Recovery Council of North America. (1999). *Reading Recovery executive summary 1984–1998.* Columbus, OH: The Ohio State University and the Reading Recovery Council of North America.

Pikulski, J. J. (1994). Preventing reading failure: A review of five effective programs. *The Reading Teacher, 48*(1), 30–39.

Pinnell, G. S. (1995). *Reading Recovery: A review of research.* (Educational Report #23). Martha L. King Language and Literacy Center: The Ohio State University.

Pinnell, G. S. (1989). Reading Recovery: Helping at-risk children learn to read. *The Elementary School Journal, 90,* 161–183.

Pinnell, G. S., Fried, M. D., & Estice, R. M. (1990). Reading Recovery: Learning how to make a difference. *The Reading Teacher, 43,* 282–295.

Pinnell, G. S., Lyons, C. A., DeFord, D. E., Bryk, A. S., & Seltzer, M. (1993). Comparing instructional models for the literacy education of high-risk first graders. *Reading Research Quarterly, 29*(1), 9–38.

Ramirez, J., Yuen, S., & Ramey, D. (1991). Executive summary, final report: Longitudinal study of structured English immersion strategy, early-exit and late-exit transitional bilingual programs for language minority children. San Mateo, CA: Aguirre International.

Rowe, K. (1995). Factors affecting students' progress in reading: Key findings from a longitudinal study. *Literacy Teaching and Learning: An International Journal or Early Reading and Writing, 1*(2), 57–110.

Slavin, R., Karweit, N., L., & Wasik, B. A. (1992/1993, December/January) Preventing early school failure: What works? *Educational Leadership, 50,* 10–19.

Slavin, R. E., Madden, N. A., & Wasik, B. A. (1996). *Success for All/Roots and Wings: Summary of research on achievement outcomes.* Center for Research on the Education of Students Placed at Risk: Johns Hopkins University.

Smith, P. E. (1994). Reading Recovery and children with English as a second language. *New Zealand Journal of Educational Studies, 29,* 141–155.

Snow, C. E., Burns, M. S., & Griffin, P. (1998). *Preventing reading difficulties in young children.* Washington, D. C.: National Academy Press.

Stanovich, K. E. (1986). Matthew effects in reading: Some consequences of individual differences in the acquisition of literacy. *Reading Research Quarterly, 21,* 360–407.

Stanovich, K. E. (1993/94). Romance and reality. *The Reading Teacher, 47*(4), 280–90.

Taylor, B., Short, R., Shearer, B., & Frye, B. (1995). First grade teachers provide early reading intervention in the classroom. In R. L. Allington & S. A. Walmsley (Eds.), *No quick fix: Rethinking literacy programs in America's elementary schools* (pp. 159–176). New York: Teachers College Press and International Reading Association.

# Children's Achievement and Personal and Social Development in a First-Year Reading Recovery Program with Teachers in Training

Lorene C. Quay, *Georgia State University*
Donald C. Steele, *Georgia State University*
Clifford I. Johnson, *Georgia State University*
William Hortman, *Muscogee County School District*

## ABSTRACT

*This paper presents the results of one school district's evaluation of its first year's implementation of Reading Recovery, where the teachers were being trained while they instructed the at-risk children in this early literacy intervention program. At the beginning of the school year, the group of Reading Recovery children and a control group were equivalent on gender, ethnicity, and achievement. At the end of the school year, multivariate and univariate analyses of variance indicated that the Reading Recovery children were significantly superior to the control group children on: (a) the* Iowa Test of Basic Skills *Language Tests; (b) the* Gates-MacGinitie Reading Test; *(c) the six tests of* An Observation Survey of Early Literacy Achievement; *(d) classroom teachers' assessments of achievement in mathematics, oral communication, reading comprehension, and written expression; (e) classroom teachers' ratings of personal and social growth in work habits, following directions, self-confidence, social interaction with adults, and social interaction with peers; and (f) promotion rates.*

## Introduction

Reading Recovery is an intensive one-to-one intervention program for first graders who are at risk of failing to learn to read. New Zealand educator Marie Clay (1993b) designed the program in New Zealand and introduced it to the United States at The Ohio State University, which became the American leader in Reading Recovery training and research (Pinnell, DeFord, & Lyons, 1988). Ohio State established the program in six public schools in Columbus, Ohio in 1984, and since that time programs have proliferated throughout the United States. Ohio State trains university faculty members from all areas of the country to implement Reading Recovery training programs at their own universities. In turn, these faculty members train teachers who are sponsored by the school systems in which they teach.

These teachers become participants in a yearlong program that focuses on helping them develop both theoretical understandings of the reading process and practical applications for teaching at-risk children. At the end of the year, they return to their school systems as "teacher leaders" and train and supervise classroom or specialist teachers who are selected from their schools to become Reading Recovery teachers. Typically, the Reading Recovery teacher tutors in the program for one half of the day and spends the other half of the day teaching in the regular classroom or in small group instruction.

## Research on Reading Recovery

### Program Effectiveness on Children's Achievement

Both the merits and the drawbacks of Reading Recovery programs and evaluations have been described in many published articles and unpublished technical reports. For example, Shanahan and Barr (1995) published an extensive review in which they "... tried to offer a thorough, systematic analysis of all available empirical work on Reading Recovery" (p. 961). They discovered more than 100 journal articles and professional presentations. After an in-depth analysis of five different comparisons of pre- and post-tests of Reading Recovery children, they concluded, "... it appears that the average Reading Recovery child who successfully completes the program makes dramatic progress during first grade" (p. 966). First-grade retentions also appear to decline after schools implement Reading Recovery (Dyer, 1992; Lyons & Beaver, 1995).

Shanahan and Barr (1995) "... found no studies of Reading Recovery that did not suffer from serious methodological flaws" (p.961). They noted that "... the most basic requirement of any instructional program is that it result in learning; not necessarily more learning than would be accomplished by other approaches, but more than would be expected if the intervention did not take place at all" (p. 965). After Shanahan's and Barr's comments, Lyons (1998) provided replication methodology to demonstrate that children who received Reading Recovery instruction from identically trained teachers using the same teaching procedures in very diverse populations achieved remarkably similar gains.

However, the gains achieved by Reading Recovery children could be a result, not of the program, but of any number of factors, including maturation, instruction in the first-grade classroom, and other school-related experiences. One of the most valid ways to determine that the program, and not some other factor or factors, is the cause of gains in reading achievement is to compare Reading Recovery children to a control group of equivalently at-risk children who do not have the Reading Recovery treatment. The majority of Reading Recovery studies are open to criticism because they do not use an experimental method involving a control group. However, the few studies that did so (e.g., Huck & Pinnell, 1986; Iversen & Tunmer, 1993; Pinnell, Huck, & DeFord, 1986; Pinnell, Lyons, DeFord, Bryk, & Seltzer; 1994) produced consistent results indicating that the Reading Recovery children were superior to the control group children on post-test measures of reading achievement.

## Teachers' Level of Experience and Knowledge

The controlled evaluations mentioned above were conducted in mature Reading Recovery settings where the Reading Recovery program had been in operation for some time prior to the evaluation. The Reading Recovery children in these evaluations were taught by experienced, highly skilled teachers. This was one basis of Rasinski's (1995) criticism of the Pinnell et al. (1994) study that found greater gains for Reading Recovery children on several post-test reading measures than for children in other remedial programs, including control children. Rasinski's major criticism was that the Reading Recovery teachers had a higher level of training than the teachers of the other remedial groups and the control group.

Hiebert (1994) indirectly assessed the relationship between Reading Recovery teachers' experience and Reading Recovery children's gains. To do this, she summarized data sent annually to Ohio State from ". . . three sites where teacher leaders have been trained for the most extended period of time" (p. 18) and from the National Diffusion Network Executive Summary, which reports data for all North American Reading Recovery sites. The three seasoned sites were The Ohio State University, the University of Illinois, and Texas Woman's University. Although Hiebert concluded that ". . . a high percentage of Reading Recovery tutees can orally read at least a first-grade text at the end of Grade 1" (p. 21), she found a major source of variation in students' reading levels to be the first year versus subsequent years of Reading Recovery program implementation. During the first two years of implementation at Ohio State, students completing the Reading Recovery program attained a primer level; but during subsequent years, students attained a first to second grade text reading level. Hiebert concluded that ". . . once a program is in place, there appears to be considerable fidelity in the results" (p. 21). This finding suggests that Reading Recovery teachers' effectiveness is related to some level of Reading Recovery experience or program maturity.

In addition, Pinnell et al. (1994) indicate that a major emphasis of Reading Recovery involves the professional development of teachers. They define Reading Recovery as ". . . a systemic innovation that incorporates teacher development as a key element in achieving accelerated progress with at-risk children" (p. 10). Despite the focus on professional development, only one study of the effects of Reading Recovery training on teacher change was found. DeFord (1983) explored teacher change within a year's professional development course, and the results indicated teachers made significant changes in their orientation to reading, moving from a skills orientation toward a whole-language orientation. However, neither the extent to which this change influenced teacher effectiveness nor children's learning was studied. Given all of these questions regarding the level of teacher understandings and competence, research to investigate these relationships to student outcomes is in order.

## Personal and Social Development

Although learning to read is likely to have far-reaching consequences for children, Reading Recovery research typically focuses on its effect on reading achievement and does not assess its influence on social and personal development. Only one study that compared Reading Recovery children to a control group on personal characteristics was found in the literature. Cohen, McDonell, and Osborn (1989), studying feelings of efficacy, found a trend indicating that Reading Recovery children feel more competent to do reading and writing activities than other at-risk children. In another study, where a control group was not included, students responded positively to a self-esteem questionnaire after receiving Reading Recovery instruction (Traynelis-Yurek & Hansell, 1993). There is a need for direct observations of Reading Recovery children's personal and social behaviors.

## Purpose of the Study

The purpose of the present study was to determine whether a group of children who participated at the very beginning of a Reading Recovery program implementation differed from an equivalent control group of children on standardized measures of achievement, teacher ratings of academic progress, promotion rates, and teachers perceptions of personal and social development at the end of the first grade. This study is different from most Reading Recovery evaluations in four ways. First, a control group was included. The Reading Recovery children were compared to an at-risk group that was equivalent to the Reading Recovery group on gender, ethnicity, and initial reading achievement.

Second, the Reading Recovery program in which this evaluation was conducted was in its first year of implementation and, therefore, would not be expected to produce a strong favorable outcome for Reading Recovery. The teachers were being trained as they performed their Reading Recovery tasks, and their training began at the same time that they began instructing children. While this study was not designed to compare results of beginning and mature programs, it did have the goal of ascertaining whether significant gains can occur in a new program with inexperienced teachers.

Third, in addition to standardized achievement tests, teachers' assessments were used to measure the extent to which the Reading Recovery and control children demonstrated their academic progress in the regular classroom. Fourth, an assessment of personal and social development was included to determine whether the Reading Recovery program affected children in areas other than reading achievement.

## Method

### Program Description

A local foundation offered support to a school district for implementation of Reading Recovery at the beginning of the school year. Although the school district had not completed the planning and teacher training for Reading Recovery, it accepted the support and implemented the program while the Reading Recovery teachers were being trained. Thus, teachers began their training at the same time they began instructing children in Reading Recovery. The foundation also required that a concurrent external evaluation be conducted and this paper presents the results of that endeavor.

Because resources were not available for full implementation of the program, the district chose to employ one full-time and two part-time teacher leaders and to select one classroom teacher from each of its 34 elementary schools to become the Reading Recovery teacher for that school. The Reading Recovery teachers-in-training spent one half of the school day working individually with Reading Recovery children and the other half working with other children in small "literacy groups."

## Selection of Subjects

Limited resources and the large size of the school system prevented access to Reading Recovery services for every child in the first-grade cohort who was in need. For this reason, one classroom in each of the 34 schools was randomly designated the classroom from which the Reading Recovery children were chosen, and a different classroom was randomly designated the classroom from which the control group was selected. Children were randomly placed into first-grade classrooms prior to designating the class for the selection of Reading Recovery or control group students.

For the selection of the particular children who would receive Reading Recovery instruction, the classroom teacher ranked all children from highest to lowest on reading ability. Using the six tests of *An Observation Survey of Early Literacy Achievement* (Clay, 1993a), the Reading Recovery teacher individually tested the children who were ranked in the lowest one third of the class and selected the four having the lowest test scores to be tutored individually in the Reading Recovery program. For the selection of the control group, the classroom teacher ranked the six lowest readers in the control class, and the Reading Recovery teacher tested the lowest four using the six tests of *An Observation Survey of Early Literacy Achievement* (Clay, 1993a). If the tests indicated that any child's reading level was higher than acceptable for inclusion in Reading Recovery, the next child on the list was tested.

This procedure resulted in the selection of a Reading Recovery group and a control group, with 107 children in each group. The two groups were equivalent on gender, ethnicity, and scores on all six tests of *An Observation Survey of Early Literacy Achievement* (Clay, 1993a). Approximately 70% of the children in each group were minorities (African-American), and approximately 60% of the children were boys. The Reading Recovery group and the control group in each school lived in the same neighborhood, and an equal number of children in each group (the majority) were in the free or reduced lunch program. The school system administered the *Iowa Test of Basic Skills* (Hoover, Hieronymus, Frisbie, & Dunbar, 1996) in early fall to all first graders.

A multivariate analysis of variance (MANOVA) indicated that the Reading Recovery and control groups did not differ on any of the fall *Iowa Test of Basic Skills* (ITBS) scales, confirming that the groups were equivalent on reading achievement. Some children moved out of the district during the school year, and others were absent when some of the tests were administered in the spring. All Reading Recovery and control children in the original sample who remained in the school were included in the final sample, with the exception of one Reading Recovery child and two control group children who were placed in Special Education classes early in the year. No child was eliminated from the Reading Recovery program or the evaluation for any other reason.

## Procedures

Reading Recovery teachers, using standardized materials and procedures, provided individualized lessons for 30 minutes each day to children in the Reading Recovery group. A student who reached a reading level within the average range of the class was "discontinued" from the program and replaced by another student. Only children from the first wave of students, not the replacements, were studied. The Reading Recovery children were participating in regular first-grade classroom instruction except for the 30 minutes each day during which each child had an individual session with the Reading Recovery teacher. The control group children were participating in the regular classroom program and in any special activities that were available to the other first-grade children, with 66% of them participating in the daily literacy groups conducted by the Reading Recovery teachers.

In April, the school system administered the spring *Iowa Test of Basic Skills* to all first-graders. In May, the *Gates-MacGinitie Reading Test* (MacGinitie & MacGinitie, 1989), a widely used battery that yields four test scores, was administered to the Reading Recovery and the control groups. The six tests of *An Observation Survey of Early Literacy Achievement* (Clay, 1993a) were also administered to both groups.

In May, the classroom teachers of both groups rated the children's growth over the school year in four academic areas and on five personal/social attributes using the *Classroom Teacher Assessment of Student Progress.* This instrument, which is included in the Appendix, consists of two parts. The first requires the teacher to use a 5-point Likert Scale for rating academic progress in each of the following areas: mathematics, reading comprehension, oral communication, and written expression. The second part requires the use of a 5-point Likert Scale for rating growth in the following personal and social attributes: following directions, work habits, self-confidence, social interaction with adults, and social interaction with peers. This instrument, which was developed for and used extensively in large-scale evaluations (Quay & Kaufman-McMurrain, 1995; Quay, Kaufman-McMurrain, Minore, Cook, & Steele, 1996; Quay, Kaufman-McMurrain, Steele, & Minore, 1997), was shown to have high test-retest reliability, yielding correlations ranging from .86 to .92 for the nine scales representing the various characteristics.

The classroom teachers of the Reading Recovery children and the control group children were also queried on retention and promotion status. They indicated on the bottom of the *Classroom Teacher Assessment of Student Progress* form whether each child would be promoted or retained.

## Results

The number of children remaining in the sample for the final testing in May decreased for several reasons. Two children in the control group and one child in the Reading Recovery group were placed in Special Education and did not continue in the regular classroom or the Reading Recovery program. If such a small number had remained in the final sample, the results would either remain the same or show an even larger difference in favor of the Reading Recovery group. Some children moved out of the district during the school year, and others were absent when some of the tests were administered in the spring. For example, the *Gates-MacGinitie Reading Test* was administered to 88 Reading Recovery and 93 control children, but the *Iowa Test of Basic Skills* (ITBS), administered by the district over a period of a week, yielded complete data on 82 Reading Recovery children and 86 control children because some children were absent for one or more days of testing.

Prior to the analysis of each spring measure, the fall data for that measure were reanalyzed comparing only the children included in the spring analysis. The two groups remaining in the sample in the spring had been equivalent on all variables in the fall. That is, even with the attrition, the remaining groups did not differ on any of the variables measured in the fall. The analyses and results of each measurement are described separately below.

## Iowa Test of Basic Skills

Table 1 presents the means and standard deviations for the spring scores of the ITBS. Inspection of the means revealed that the Reading Recovery group had higher scores than the control group on all tests. A MANOVA indicated that the two groups differed significantly on the spring ITBS Language Tests, $F(6, 161) = 4.58$, $p < .001$. ANOVA's indicated that differences occurred on Language Total, $F(1, 166) = 4.98$, $p < .05$; Reading Comprehension, $F(1, 166) = 18.72$, $p < .001$; Reading Total, $F(1, 166) = 3.92$, $p < .05$; and Word Analysis, $F(1, 166) = 6.11$, $p < .05$. The groups did not differ significantly on Vocabulary and Listening subtests.

## Gates-MacGinitie Reading Test

Inspection of the means, listed in Table 2, revealed that the Reading Recovery group had higher scores than the control group on all subtests of the *Gates MacGinitie Reading Test*. A MANOVA indicated that the two groups differed significantly on this

**Table 1.** Means and Standard Deviations for the Iowa Test of Basic Skills Language Tests

| TEST | READING RECOVERY GROUP MEAN (SD) | CONTROL GROUP MEAN (SD) |
|---|---|---|
| Listening | 39.57 (18.04) | 38.67 (17.11) |
| Reading Comprehension* | 48.60 (13.41) | 39.08 (14.40) |
| Vocabulary | 39.64 (16.57) | 38.67 (17.11) |
| Word Analysis* | 36.55 (16.85) | 29.52 (18.66) |
| Reading Total* | 43.88 (14.60) | 39.13 (15.96) |
| Language Total* | 39.34 (14.33) | 33.85 (16.50) |

*$p < .05$; **$p < .01$; ***$p < .001$.

**Table 2.** Means and Standard Deviations for the *Gates-MacGinitie Reading Tests*

| TEST | READING RECOVERY GROUP MEAN (SD) | CONTROL GROUP MEAN (SD) |
|---|---|---|
| Initial Consonant*** | 13.30 (1.80) | 11.59 (2.90) |
| Final Consonant*** | 12.36 (2.34) | 9.80 (2.85) |
| Vowels*** | 12.23 (2.55) | 9.16 (3.61) |
| Context in Sentence*** | 13.07 (2.54) | 9.44 (3.38) |

*$p < .05$; **$p < .01$; ***$p < .001$.

standardized test, $F(4, 176) = 18.48, p < .001$. ANOVA's indicated they differed on all four subtests: Final Consonants, $F(1, 179) = 43.55, p < .001$; Initial Consonants, $F(1, 179) = 22.28, p < .001$; Sentence Context, $F(1, 179) = 65.96, p < .001$; and Vowels, $F(1, 179) = 43.13, p < .001$.

## Classroom Teacher Assessment of Student Progress

The classroom teachers rated the Reading Recovery children significantly higher than the control group children in all areas. Means and standard deviations for the *Classroom Teacher Assessment of Student Progress* are listed in Table 3. A MANOVA computed to compare the groups on teacher ratings of progress on all achievement and personal/social variables was significant for the Reading Recovery group, $F(9, 167) = 10.52, p < .001$. ANOVA's indicated the Reading Recovery group and the control group differed on the ratings in all areas: mathematics, $F(1, 175) = 8.79, p < .01$; oral communication, $F(1, 175) = 30.50, p < .001$; reading comprehension, $F(1, 175) = 67.93, p < .001$; written expression, $F(1, 175) = 46.13, p < .001$; following directions, $F(1, 175) = 24.83, p < .001$; self-confidence, $F(1, 175) = 11.82, p < .001$; social interaction with adults, $F(1, 175) = 19.28, p < .001$; social interaction with peers, $F(1, 175) = 18.61, p < .001$; and work habits, $F(1, 175) = 16.03, p < .001$.

## Promotion Rates

A chi square indicated that a significantly higher percentage of Reading Recovery than control group children were promoted at the end of the year, with 92% of Reading Recovery children and 74% of control children achieving promotion status, $X^2(1) = 9.50, p < .01$.

## An Observation Survey of Early Literacy Achievement

The Reading Recovery children had higher scores than the control children on all of the survey's tests as indicated in Table 4. A MANOVA comparing the scores of the

**Table 3.** Means and Standard Deviations for the *Classroom Teacher Assessment of Student Progress*

| AREA | READING RECOVERY GROUP MEAN (SD) | CONTROL GROUP MEAN (SD) |
|---|---|---|
| Mathematics** | 2.91 (0.84) | 2.56 (0.70) |
| Reading Comp*** | 3.55 (0.95) | 2.31 (0.91) |
| Oral Communication*** | 3.17 (0.83) | 2.52 (0.70) |
| Written Expression*** | 3.16 (0.96) | 2.25 (0.96) |
| Following Directions** | 3.14 (0.98) | 2.46 (0.81) |
| Work Habits*** | 3.02 (1.02) | 2.42 (0.91) |
| Self-Confidence** | 3.39 (1.12) | 2.85 (0.94) |
| Social Interaction with Adults*** | 3.28 (1.01) | 2.67 (0.78) |
| Social Interaction with Peers*** | 3.25 (0.95) | 2.67 (0.77) |

$*p < .05; **p < .01; ***p < .001.$

Reading Recovery and the control group children on the spring administration of *An Observation Survey of Early Literacy Achievement* (Clay, 1993a) was significant in favor of the Reading Recovery group, $F (6, 171) = 24.28, p < .001$. ANOVA's indicated the two groups differed significantly on all six tests: Concepts about Print, $F (1, 176) = 85.32, p < 001$; Dictation, $F (1, 176) = 44.15, p < .001$; Text Reading Level, $F (1, 176) = 125.36, p < .001$; Word Test, $F (1, 176) = 21.41, p < .001$; Writing Vocabulary, $F (1, 176) = 72.95, p < .001$; and Letter Identification, $F (1, 176) = 3.92, p < .05$.

## Summary and Discussion

Reading Recovery has been the subject of innumerable published and unpublished reports regarding the program's effectiveness in raising children's literacy achievement to the average level of their peers. The procedure used in most Reading Recovery research and evaluation is to administer reading achievement pre-tests, to provide the Reading Recovery treatment, and then to administer reading achievement post-tests. In addition, Lyons (1998) reported replication studies of North American children across a decade of instruction. Using these methodologies, researchers have shown that Reading Recovery students make significant gains in reading achievement during this interval of instruction. However, in addition to the Reading Recovery treatment, forces such as maturation, reading instruction in the first-grade classroom, and a variety of other school-related experiences occur during the interval between the pre- and post-tests. Thus, whether Reading Recovery is responsible for the achievement gains cannot be determined conclusively with these methodologies. To assure the gains result from Reading Recovery, and not from other factors, Reading Recovery children must be compared to a control group of equivalent children who do not receive the Reading

**Table 4.** Means and Standard Deviations for *An Observation Survey of Early Literacy Achievement*

| TEST | READING RECOVERY GROUP MEAN (SD) | CONTROL GROUP MEAN (SD) |
|---|---|---|
| Concepts About Print*** | 20.65 (3.04) | 16.03 (3.64) |
| Dictation*** | 33.92 (4.30) | 26.96 (8.84) |
| Letter Identification* | 52.89 (4.85) | 51.10 (6.57) |
| Text Reading Level*** | 16.38 (6.15) | 6.72 (5.55) |
| Word Test*** | 18.20 (3.03) | 13.41 (5.71) |
| Written Vocabulary*** | 46.37 (12.20) | 29.98 (13.40) |

*p < .05; **p < .01; ***p < .001.

Recovery treatment and typically these pre-and post-test comparisons do not do so.

It was the purpose of the present study to evaluate the effects of Reading Recovery with an experimental method that included a control group of children who were initially equivalent to the Reading Recovery group on gender, ethnicity, and pre-test reading achievement as measured by both *An Observation Survey of Early Literacy Achievement* (Clay, 1993a) and the *Iowa Test of Basic Skills*. After attrition, the two groups of children who remained in the study at the end of the first grade continued to be equivalent in all aspects.

The results of the few studies that included comparable control groups are consistent in showing that Reading Recovery children are superior to control children on post-test measures of reading achievement. However, these studies have been conducted in elementary schools that have highly trained teachers in Reading Recovery programs that have been in place for several years. Most local Reading Recovery programs do not have equivalent experience levels to those used in the evaluations. Hiebert (1994), on the basis of data obtained from secondary sources, concluded that Reading Recovery children in more established programs reached higher reading levels than Reading Recovery children in less mature settings. However, controlled studies directly comparing gains in Reading Recovery programs of different maturity levels have not been found. One purpose of the present study was to ascertain whether gains can be achieved at a very early point in Reading Recovery program implementation. The results indicated that, even in this very new program where the teachers were learning Reading Recovery teaching procedures as they were tutoring the first group of children, Reading Recovery had significant effects on all *Gates-MacGinitie Reading Test* subtests and on most of the ITBS language tests at the end of the school year. Thus, it can be concluded that even a very immature Reading Recovery program can produce achievement gains.

Not only did standardized achievement tests indicate Reading Recovery children were superior to the control children at the end of the first grade, but also the classroom teachers perceived them to have made significantly greater academic progress. Using the *Classroom Teacher Assessment of Student Progress*, the Reading Recovery children's classroom teachers indicated a higher level of progress for the Reading Recovery children in reading, mathematics, oral communication, and written expression than the control group children's classroom teachers indicated for them. The validity of these ratings is substantiated by the teachers' higher promotion rates for the Reading Recovery children. Further, these classroom teacher ratings add validity to the standardized test results by showing that, in addition to making gains on standardized tests, the Reading Recovery children could demonstrate their progress in the classroom.

It is reasonable to assume enhanced reading ability and increased academic achievement would positively affect children's personal and social development, particularly their self-confidence. To add to the work of Cohen et al. (1989), which found that children had increased self-efficacy regarding reading and writing, it was the purpose of the present study to determine children's personal and social growth during Reading Recovery instruction. The classroom teachers involved in this investigation rated the Reading Recovery children higher than the control children on their positive development in following directions, self-confidence, social interaction with adults, social interaction with peers, and work habits. This finding strongly supports the notion that Reading Recovery is not simply a program that facilitates learning to read, but also that it has wide-ranging indirect effects on children's development.

## Limitations of the Study and Suggestions for Future Research

One limitation of this study involves the mobility of the population. As with most research involving children from lower socioeconomic strata, attrition was a problematic factor. However, an analysis of the pre-test data on only the children who remained in the study until the end revealed that there were no initial differences between the groups of children in the final analyses.

Another limitation of the current study is that the research design did not permit the control of bias in the teacher ratings. On the *Classroom Teacher Assessment of Student Progress*, the classroom teachers of the Reading Recovery children knew the children they were rating were receiving Reading Recovery instruction. Their ratings may have been positively influenced by this knowledge; that is, they may have expected the children to make progress for that reason. Classroom teachers' ratings are important because they illustrate a different dimension of progress than standardized tests. For future research, it may be possible to eliminate this bias by having external observers, who are unaware of which children are participating in Reading Recovery, sample the children's classroom behavior and record their observations.

The greatest limitation of this study, as well as other Reading Recovery studies and much research conducted in school settings, is that Reading Recovery students and control group students had different classroom teachers. In the real world, this study had to be conducted in this way, but a better design is possible if school personnel could be convinced to accept it. We strongly recommend a future research design that would control for the influence of the classroom teacher. The investigation would be designed so that the children with the lowest reading levels are identified prior to assignment to their first-grade classrooms. All children who are so identified would then be randomly assigned to either a Reading Recovery group or a control group. Finally, an equal number from each group would be randomly assigned to each first-grade classroom.

Finally, additional longitudinal research is needed to ascertain the permanence of the observed early gains attained by Reading Recovery children. Questions of interest include: How long do the gains persist? Do the control group children eventually catch up with the former Reading Recovery children and if so, when? Such information has implications for the cost of early intervention programs. It is a limitation of this study that it spanned only the year of the intervention, precluding an evaluation of the sustainability of the gains achieved by the Reading Recovery children. Although there are studies that support the stability of the gains, others suggest otherwise and unfortunately the present study does not contribute to a clarification of this issue.

For example, Pinnell et al. (1994) found that the gains of Reading Recovery children were sustained at the beginning of the second grade. Statewide follow-up studies in Texas (Askew, Frasier, & Compton, 1995) and Indiana (Schmitt, 1999) have indicated that former Reading Recovery children are performing as well as their classmates on the *Gates MacGinitie Reading Test* in third and fourth grades. On the other hand, DeFord and her colleagues (DeFord, Pinnell, Lyons, & Young, 1988) assessed text reading level and writing vocabulary at the end of second and third grades and found that the gains of the Reading Recovery group exceeded those of the control during the year of the intervention, but the two groups did not differ in the gains they made during the second and third years. And, Center, Wheldall, Freeman, Outhred, & McNaught (1995) found that significant gains occurred mainly during intervention and less so thereafter.

## Implications of the Study

In answer to the question "Does Reading Recovery work?" Shanahan and Barr (1995) respond, with some reservations, in the affirmative. They argue that "...clearer specifications of its success are likely only through additional, more rigorous research than has been conducted up to now" (p. 989). The present study provides a rigorous examination of some very important questions about the immediate effects of Reading Recovery. It permits the conclusion that the early intervention program does indeed "work" as demonstrated by the finding that Reading Recovery children are significantly superior in many characteristics to equally at-risk children who have not participated in Reading Recovery. The results provide further confirmation of previous findings that Reading Recovery children are superior to control group children on standardized reading and language tests and on rates of promotion.

In addition, this study demonstrates that Reading Recovery children's teachers perceive them to be making significant progress, not only academically, but also in personal and social development. Since this enhanced development and performance occurred in a setting where the Reading Recovery teachers were being trained as they were tutoring the very first group of children in a brand new Reading Recovery program, other beginning Reading Recovery programs can be optimistic regarding their potential for benefiting children even at an early stage of program implementation.

The major implication of this study is that schools considering implementing Reading Recovery can feel comfortable that teachers who are concurrently being trained and providing Reading Recovery services to children can be very effective in producing results. Also, since the results of this study with in-training teachers are so robust, it seems likely that as experience increases, Reading Recovery teachers will be even more effective.

This study served to substantiate the results of several other investigations (e.g., Huck & Pinnell, 1986; Iversen & Tunmer, 1993; Pinnell, Huck, & DeFord, 1986; Pinnell, Lyons, DeFord, Bryk, & Seltzer, 1994) in demonstrating that Reading Recovery children are superior to control group children on post-test measures of reading achievement. Since this study used a different methodology than other studies and still produced the same result, the interpretation that Reading Recovery is an effective program for children at risk of failure can be made with a great deal of confidence.

## References

Askew, B. J. Frasier, D., & Compton, C. (1995). *Reading Recovery report: 1988–1995.* Denton, TX: Texas Woman's University.

Center, Y., Wheldall, K., Freeman, L., Outhred, L., & McNaught, M. (1995). An experimental evaluation of Reading Recovery. *Reading Research Quarterly, 30,* 240–263.

Clay, M. M. (1993a). *An observation survey of early literacy achievement.* Auckland, NZ: Heinemann.

Clay, M. M. (1993b). *Reading Recovery: A guidebook for teachers in training.* Portsmouth, NH: Heinemann.

Cohen, S. G., McDonell, G., & Osborn, B. (1989). Self -perceptions of at-risk and high achieving readers: Beyond Reading Recovery achievement data. *National Reading Conference Yearbook,* No. 38: 117–122.

DeFord, D. E., Pinnell, G. S., Lyons, C. A., & Young, P. (1988). *Reading Recovery: Vol. IX, report of the follow-up studies.* Columbus: The Ohio State University.

Dyer, P. C. (1992). Reading Recovery: A cost-effectiveness and educational-outcomes analysis. *ERS Spectrum, 10,* 10–19.

Hiebert, E. H. (1994). Reading Recovery in the United States: What difference does it make to an age cohort? *Educational Researcher, 23,* 15–25.

Hoover, H. D., Hieronymus, A. N., Frisbie, D. A., & Dunbar, S. B. (1996). *Iowa Tests of Basic Skills.* Iowa City, IA: Riverside.

Huck, C. S., & Pinnell, G. S. (1986). *The Reading Recovery project in Columbus, Ohio, Vol. 1, pilot year 1984-85.* Columbus, OH: The Ohio State University.

Iversen, J. A., & Tunmer, W. E. (1993). Phonological processing skills and the Reading Recovery program. *Journal of Educational Psychology, 85,* 112–125.

Lyons, C. A. (1998). Reading Recovery in the United States: More than a decade of data. *Literacy Teaching and Learning: An International Journal of Early Reading and Writing, 3,* 77–92.

Lyons, C. A., & Beaver, J. (1995). Reducing retention and learning disability placement through Reading Recovery: An educationally sound cost-effectiveness choice. In R. L. Allington & S. A. Walmsley (Eds.), *No quick fix:Redesigning literacy programs in America's elementary schools* (pp. 16–36). New York: Teachers College Press.

MacGinitie, W. H., & MacGinitie, R. K. (1989). *Gates-MacGinitie Reading Tests.* Iowa City: Riverside.

Pinnell, G. S., Huck, C. S., & DeFord, D. E. (1986). *The Reading Recovery project in Columbus, Ohio studies, Vol. 3* (Year 1: 1985–86). Columbus: The Ohio State University.

Pinnell, G. S., Lyons, C. A., DeFord, D. E., Bryk, A. S., & Seltzer, M. (1994). Comparing instructional models for the literacy education of high-risk first graders. *Reading Research Quarterly, 29,* 9–39.

Quay, L. C., & Kaufman-McMurrain, M. (1995, April). *The evaluation of Georgia's Pre-kindergarten Program: A broad-based approach to early intervention.* Symposium presented at the meeting of the American Educational Research Association, San Francisco, CA.

Quay, L. C., Kaufman-McMurrain, M., Minore, D., Cook, L., & Steele, D. (1996, April). *The longitudinal evaluation of Georgia's Pre-kindergarten Program: Results from the second year.* Paper presented at the meeting of the American Educational Research Association, New York, N.Y.

Quay, L. C., Kaufman-McMurrain, M., Steele, D., & Minore, D. (1997, April). *The longitudinal evaluation of Georgia's Pre-kindergarten Program.* Paper presented at the meeting of the Society for Research in Child Development, Washington, D. C.

Rasinski, T. V. (1995). On the effects of Reading Recovery: A response to Pinnell, Lyons, DeFord, Bryk, and Seltzer. *Reading Research Quarterly, 30,* 264–270.

Schmitt, M. C. (1999). *An investment in our children: Reading Recovery executive summary, 1993–1998.* West Lafayette, IN: Purdue University.

Shanahan, T., & Barr, R. (1995). Reading Recovery: An independent evaluation of the effects of an early instruction intervention for at-risk learners. *Reading Research Quarterly, 30,* 958–996.

Traynelis-Yurek, E., & Hansell, T. S. (1993). Self-esteem of low achieving first grade readers following instruction intervention. *Reading Improvement, 30,* 140–146.

# Appendix

## Classroom Teacher Assessment of Student Progress

Child's Name: _____

School: _____ Teacher: _____

Place a check in the box that best describes this child's growth in each academic area during this school year.

| ACADEMIC AREA | NO GROWTH | MARGINAL GROWTH | AVERAGE GROWTH | ABOVE AVERAGE GROWTH | EXCEPTIONAL GROWTH |
|---|---|---|---|---|---|
| Reading comprehension | | | | | |
| Written expression | | | | | |
| Oral communication | | | | | |
| Mathematics/Number Concepts | | | | | |

Place a check in the box that best describes this child's growth in each personal characteristic during the school year.

| PERSONAL CHARACTERISTICS | NO GROWTH | MARGINAL GROWTH | AVERAGE GROWTH | ABOVE AVERAGE GROWTH | EXCEPTIONAL GROWTH |
|---|---|---|---|---|---|
| Ability to follow directions | | | | | |
| Work habits | | | | | |
| Social interaction with adults | | | | | |
| Social interaction with peers | | | | | |
| Self-confidence | | | | | |

Please check below to indicate whether this child will be promoted or retained.

This child will be promoted to second grade. _____

This child will be retained in first grade. _____

# Afterword

Marie M. Clay

No authority I consulted could guide me on preparing an "afterword." Publishers end the production of a book with appendices, references, bibliographies, previews of things to come, what goes on the back cover or the dust jacket. The American Psychological Association Publications Manual does not help, and my word processing program's spell checker would not accept the term. I turned to an eight-year-old's poem entitled "It Gets Dark."

> The sunset is fading
> Like my flowery sundress.
> It is not dark yet.
>
> Now a very old blanket
> With starry holes in it
> Is covering the sky.
> The sun on the other side
> Is begging to get through.
>
> The trees are lurking.
> It gets dark.
>
> *Laura Ranger, 1995*

In literacy learning there are lots of old blankets around with starry holes here and there. This publication has focused on some of those stars. In retrospect I am thinking of the weather conditions that might allow us to watch tomorrow's sunrise and study the wildlife in the woods despite the lurking trees.

The papers in this collection focus on an early literacy intervention in which a child who makes "awkward responses" to classroom instruction receives a short series of individually designed lessons. (I use "awkward responses" in this context to refer to the unusual, unexpected, inept, apparently unconnected, or "where did that come from" responses that the lowest achievers produce and that make teachers feel they do not know where to go next.) It is logical for a clinical developmental psychologist like me to work out an individual educational program (IEP) for such a child or to train a special group of teachers to do so. It is also logical to believe that given the wide range of "awkward responses" that can occur, *one child's series of lessons will need to be different from another child's series of lessons.*

Reading Recovery treats the child to the positive opposite of "a double whammy": it leads to good reading progress in the years to come and equally good progress in writing. Most of its critics do not comment on writing because they do not count learning to write as a significant variable in early literacy learning. Yet parents have reported more frequent writing of words and simple sentences at home while their children were in Reading Recovery (Marvin and Gaffney, pp. 231–255). Most critics find it hard to trust teachers to report outcome data in reliable ways, and they search for flaws in the theory, the research, the training of the professionals, and the intervention's delivery.

Reading Recovery produces similar outcomes in three languages, which is surprising considering how much research effort is currently being spent on describing how learning to read differs in different languages. Studies from New York and California reported good results for both the English and the Spanish delivery (Ashdown and Simic, pp. 115–132; Neal and Kelly, pp. 257–295), and there were sustaining effects of Descubriendo la Lectura in grades 2 and 3 (Escamilla et al., pp. 193–214). Normative data for French-speaking children in Canada (Clay 2003) is published in *Le sondage d'observation en lecture-ecriture* (the Observation Survey in French),[1] and it looks to me as though the changes over time in literacy learning in French-speaking Canadian children will be similar to those found elsewhere for English-speaking and Spanish-speaking children. And this is despite some big challenges for French children in the multiplicity of spellings for some of the French phonemes. Data for the total Reading Recovery population for California over the years 1993–1996 showed that speakers of two languages compared favorably with those working in only one language. Educators can celebrate such desirable outcomes.

It is easy in 2003 to believe that a solution to a problem is only an Internet search away. Yet while we do know *what* children learn in Reading Recovery (the outcomes), *how* they achieve a multitude of changes in a short series of thirty-minute lessons has yet to be traced in detail in research studies. Despite our best attempts to capture, analyze, and explain to parents, teachers, politicians, and administrators how Reading Recovery children learn, too much of what is happening remains complex. Fullerton's account of Edward's journey (pp. 43–67) reveals this. How can we capture the idiosyncratic paths to successful progress that are taken by those individual learners who have become confused and defeated by the best practices of classroom teaching? To understand what is effective in these treatments we must use research designs that are sensitive enough to probe how a teacher reduces those "awkward" learning responses and brings quite different children with highly variable response patterns to the point where they can learn from traditional teaching in groups in classrooms.

Carol Lyons's article on the critical role that emotions play in the making of mind (pp. 69–90) combines with Fullerton's article to whet our appetites for the release of a book-length treatment of this topic (Lyons, 2003[2]). The author has experience teaching "awkward learners" and informs her practice with her knowledge of the field of neuroscience. She provides lengthy examples of parent-child or teacher-child interactions in which each shift in instructional emphasis is something like an experiment. Only when the "novice" responds does the "expert" discover whether the teaching interaction has been successful or unsuccessful. Lyons's examples point to new methods of studying how the brain learns to process information in print. With awkward learners it is not a matter of pedaling harder along the same general path that is so easy for successful classroom learners: *it is more a matter of initially changing the route several times in order to get to the same destination. I do not apologize for holding these heretical views of how we need to address some special education issues.*

For ethical reasons it is not easy to obtain permission to run a study in an educational setting with an untreated control group. One risks depriving some children of a good opportunity to learn. The time to do this is during the trials for a new intervention whose effectiveness is not yet established. Once you have a successful intervention, you can only do "real science" by behaving unethically! The Georgia State study (pp. 281–295) is important because the researchers took the opportunity to surmount this problem but also because of the following finding:

> The major implication of this study is that schools considering implementing Reading Recovery can feel comfortable that teachers who are concurrently being trained and providing Reading Recovery services to children can be very effective. . . . Since the results of this study with in-training teachers are so robust, it seems likely that as experience increases, Reading Recovery teachers will be more effective. (p. 293)

Reading Recovery professionals have tended to be cautious about what they expect teachers to achieve while they are "in training," because at that time they are making drastic changes to the ways in which they teach. These good results provide evidence that the "specialists in training" are supported by the professionals supervising their teaching.

If we agree that individuals benefit from the intervention, what are the benefits for an education system? Reading Recovery can only be implemented by education systems: it becomes available only when an education system chooses to adopt the intervention. That is unique. Across the globe Reading Recovery professionals have met the demands of administrators for evidence, and more evidence, to demonstrate at their local site what outcomes are achieved for the money spent. Each country, province, and state annually collects and analyzes data from every child who enters the program, and that data is used to guide adjustments to a district's or school's implementation (Lyons, pp. 69–90). There is sufficient evidence for the efficacy of Reading Recovery when the implementation is strong, and over twenty years reports have replicated the result that high percentages of children can be returned to work successfully in classrooms. Annual monitoring is essential for local quality control checks and for policy planning, but reporting change for every child served and for a random sample of classroom children was only necessary during the years of disbelief. That monitoring could now be done with a rigorous selection of smaller samples by a national data collection center.

Retrospective studies using data collected over the years are also useful, and Reading Recovery is able to access large research samples. The New York research (Ashdown and Simmic, pp. 115–132) used 25,601 Reading Recovery students, plus 18,363 randomly sampled students from first grade classrooms in the same schools and 11,267 other children who needed early intervention treatment but did not receive it. (*This "failure to provide" on the part of education systems deserves more research attention.*) The elegance of this New York study is that when important things like historical changes and environmental effects relating to variations between schools were well controlled by the research design, "the results suggest that Reading Recovery is an effective intervention that narrows the reading achievement gap."

One problem of retrospective analyses must be kept in mind—Reading Recovery's infrastructure was designed to facilitate change, and therefore changes in practice are recommended and occur all the time, passed down through a hierarchy of professionals who are required to attend regular professional development meetings. Reading Recovery is an intervention that is changing each year as we learn from new analyses and new research.

Administrators asked Reading Recovery sites to demonstrate that the outcomes of the program were not limited to a brief spurt in test scores between six and seven years of age, producing an effect that "wore off" with time. In the past decade enough follow-up research has been completed in several countries for us to dismiss the "wearing off" prediction. Favorable outcomes at higher levels in the elementary schools are found (for example, Askew et al., pp. 133–158), and the case for prevention of subsequent failure among the discontinued children has been assessed using the high-stakes benchmark testing established in several different states in the United States and carefully controlled studies in Victoria, Australia. There is even a trend for ex–Reading Recovery children to continue to improve their status over time relative to the average of their peers, a trend that can be explained in theory but that has not been tested in carefully designed research. At a guess it probably has something to do with a self-improving system (whatever future research decides that is). In my opinion the exploration of those issues will require new developmental theory about the shifts over time that bring competent readers aged seven or eight to the competencies of twelve-year-old readers. The discussions around psychological experiments in the fields of "cognitive text processing" and "reciprocal teaching" will probably be linked to such shifts.

The leadership roles of Reading Recovery professionals were highlighted in Bussell's research (pp. 159–192), but the time they can give to leadership activities is seriously reduced when administrators expect them to (a) manage the infrastructure of Reading Recovery, (b) respond to accountability checks (especially in my country), or (c) work with classroom teachers. The professional expertise of early intervention teachers should be turned to *the development of new, startling outcomes in those places in education where individual instruction is clearly indicated.* From the many areas that could be discussed, I select only three as examples: children recommended after Reading Recovery for a longer literacy intervention, children with disabilities and handicaps severe enough that they could be described as making "awkward responses" to traditional classroom instruction, and those children who are confused and defeated when new school subjects are introduced at any level of an education system.

What makes early literacy intervention so effective? What are we doing right? Our critics will want to know why we do this and not that. Piecemeal demonstrations that a specific activity in a program needs to be included are reassuring but not explanatory. We urgently need a better theoretical plot of the paths of change taken by different Reading Recovery children, recording what works for which child and developing a theory about why it works for one child and does not work for another child. Reading Recovery professionals can be very articulate about what happens and why things are working well, but that is not enough. We need research that will distinguish for outsiders what Reading Recovery teachers do to replace "awkward responding" with facilitating responding. Such research will not compare so-called "teaching methods" loosely derived from instruction in classrooms, and its results would not claim to be useful for classroom teachers. I will return to this point.

The positive report by Stahl et al. (pp. 99–114) on phonological awareness and orthographic processing among successful Reading Recovery children weighs up some independent criticisms of Reading Recovery's theory against the findings of these authors. They report that Reading Recovery has effects beyond those it ordinarily claims.

I do not agree with them that my theories do not place weight on explicit instruction, on learning phonological awareness, and on orthographic awareness as in Ehri's theory of word learning. Such interpretations of my theories of early intervention practice have been made by non–Reading Recovery academics trying to fit theories about mainstream instruction for groups of children to a clinical treatment for individuals. I would like to explore these interpretations.

Hearing and recording sounds in words requires that phonemic awareness be linked to orthographic awareness as children analyze speech and find acceptable ways of recording the phonemes heard. In Reading Recovery phonemic awareness is taught with the emphasis on "hearing," using a sliding scale of difficulty in a superbly suitable task, writing. Is this why observers miss the instruction? It occurs every day during the writing segment of the lesson, and (using Elkonin boxes[3]) the teacher moves through a gradient of difficulty from sounds that are easy for a particular child to hear to the hard-to-hear phonemes and combinations, with suitable attention to spelling exceptions. It arose from the work of Charles Read (1975, 1986);[4] the linguistic theories of Mattingly (1981);[5] and from Rebecca Treiman's research (1992).[6] There is no fixed sequence (as in a typical phonics program) because whatever the child already knows is used in his individually designed program to support his new learning. The shaping of phonemic awareness is, in my opinion, expertly developed in each pupil by the teaching interactions that occur daily in the writing segment of the Reading Recovery lesson (and Iversen and Tunmer reported the outcomes of such teaching in phonemic awareness tests they chose to use in 1993[7]). Elkonin (1973) pointed us to a superb tutorial approach for this learning, and Read's Harvard children found their own way to this type of analysis. I have not seen a more effective procedure proposed in the research I have monitored carefully in the last two decades, and I began my monitoring of the literature after reading Bruce's study[8] in the United Kingdom in the 1960s, in which he used a phoneme deletion task that was extraordinarily difficult for his six-year-old subjects.

I suspect that Reading Recovery's success across three languages (English, Spanish, and French) has a lot to do with the possibility that we have theoretically bypassed the limitations of a theory of learning to read based on the particular phonemes of one language. We are struggling with questions about how to help children to use the sounds they speak as they work with the print they see—whatever language system they are using.

The contribution of the writing segment of the lesson does not stop at phonemic awareness. Reading Recovery children learn, daily, how to compose messages of increasing complexity. They construct the words in those messages by finding the letters that record the sounds they can isolate. With the aid of their teachers they accumulate personal writing vocabularies of at least forty very different words by the end of their lesson series. They pay close attention to letters, letter sequences, clusters, and chunks and learn how these "knowns" can be used to get to new words. This is explicit instruction in word making, and the task becomes easier as the repertoire of known words increases. Conceptually, this is orthographic processing of the constructive kind. The child controls the detail of sounds, letters, clusters, words, and word sequences in both reading and writing. At first the teacher prompts from one knowledge base to the other until the child knows without prompting how to search reading for help with writing and vice versa. It cannot be said that Reading Recovery ignores explicit instruction: many observers have failed to notice the expert phonological training and word learning that is being built up through writing and how the child is taught to use this knowledge reciprocally. Critics do not trust this theoretical bypass, and this allowed Elbaum et al. (2001)[9] to declare a huge program effect from the children's scores in writing vocabulary to be an outlier, not able to be interpreted within their theoretical framework of literacy learning.

So it was pleasing to see two studies of writing included in this collection, one attempting to record change over time in progressions in early writing in some classrooms where reading and writing were expected to influence each other (Boocock et al., pp. 25–41) and the other a much needed mapping of some of the outcomes of the writing component of Reading Recovery lessons (Askew et al., pp. 133–158).

When colleagues ask me to write more about "processing" in writing I demur, saying that we are waiting for more evidence of how children work on constructing information while they are reading and writing. Those colleagues protest that much has been written about children's writing, and they ask me what questions I want answered. In fact I do not know what questions to pose, because existing research is about products in both subjects and not about how children use what they learn in writing when they are reading. It is not a question anybody asks! We do not know how children use knowledge gained in one activity in the other. That is a patch of research worthy of cultivation.

Hopefully this volume will do more than merely make the selected papers more accessible: it may also stimulate new investigations, generate new questions, and lead to more effective practices for children who produce unexpectedly awkward responses to the traditional literacy instruction in classrooms.

Reading Recovery is a demonstration of what can be achieved when teaching can be designed to incorporate individual strengths, working one on one. It is in sharp contrast with what can be achieved when instruction is designed for working with a group. Individual instruction and class instruction look extremely different when one looks at them closely. There are many examples of individual teaching that have claimed to achieve unexpected results, from the historical role of the governess in wealthy families to the success of rural schools where one teacher teaches one or two children at several different class levels to home schooling to special coaching in mathematics, languages, and individual sports. We need to ask, for what kinds of learning is individual instruction particularly powerful?

Every major evaluation study of Reading Recovery (including the carefully designed McArthur Foundation study at The Ohio State University) has failed to take into account that an individually designed series of lessons is created for each child: the weighting on various aspects of learning depends on the strengths and weaknesses of each learner, and no child goes through the same sequence of instruction. A teacher does not deliver the same program to any two children: they read different books and achieve very different final writing vocabularies (Askew and Frasier, pp. 1–24). Outside evaluators have found it hard to handle something as simple as the fact that successful children have different numbers of total lessons; and, appalling though it may seem, one oft-quoted critique arrives at some failure rates calculated on the assumption that all children had fifteen weeks in the program! Each Reading Recovery teacher must address the variability in her pupils and design a different series of lessons for each child if he or she is to get the desired results in a short lesson series *because each child begins lessons with a different idiosyncratic pattern of awkward responses.*

Can we design research that will track how the sequence of changes differs (varies) from child to child? Can we demonstrate that there are different paths to common outcomes? Case studies will not do: they will not provide clear and unequivocal evidence of what we need to know. We could learn more from repeated single subject experiments like those published in applied behavioral analysis journals of the 1970s and 1980s (Church, 1996[10]; Clay, 2002[11], pp.196–197, 272–274; Newman and McCormick, 1995[12]) than from the "science" that some Reading Recovery critics have been recommending we adopt. The best research designs for evaluations of classroom or group instruction, or for homogeneous diagnostic groups of subjects in medical research, will not be suitable. The explorations need to demonstrate how children can move to common outcomes despite the diagnostic variety among the subjects. That variability cannot be avoided in a field-based early intervention. Thirty years of rigorous methodological debates in applied behavior analysis research would be a rich resource for discovering a methodology that establishes research control over individual children's progress and captures evidence of changes of direction introduced during a series of lessons. Phillips & Smith (1997) used such an approach with children recommended from Reading Recovery for a third wave of help (first, classroom instruction, second, time-limited individual tutoring, and third, extended treatment).

There is a categorical difference between the kinds of teaching and learning interactions that can occur in individual instruction and the kinds of teaching that can occur in group and class settings. We will have to differentiate our theories rather than treat the two categories as if they were one. It is acceptable to believe that in learning to play golf and learning to play the cello, individual tuition will be more productive than group tuition, and I believe that following surgery, individual intensive care suited to my critical condition will be the treatment of choice for a short period of time even when the level of care provided in the general wards of hospitals is superb! These research papers, while providing us with new insights about this individual tuition intervention, raise provocative questions that can only be addressed through future research.

# Endnotes

1. Clay, M. M. 2003. *Le sondage d'observation en lecture-ecriture*. Toronto: Les Editions de la Cheneliere.

2. Lyons, C. 2003. *Teaching Struggling Readers: Brain-based Research You Need to Know*. Portsmouth NH: Heinemann.

3. Elkonin, D. B. 1973. "USSR." In *Comparative Reading*, edited by J. Downing, 551–580. New York: Macmillan.

4. Read, C. 1975. *Children's Categorization of Speech Sounds in English*. Urbana, Illinois: National Council of Teachers of English. Read, C. 1986. *Children's Creative Spelling*. London: Routledge, Kegan Paul.

5. Mattingly, I. G. 1984. "Reading, Linguistic Awareness, and Language Acquisition." In *Language Awareness and Learning to Read*, edited by J. Downing and R. Valtin, 9–25. New York: Springer-Verlag.

6. Treiman, R. 1993. *Beginning to Spell: A Study of First-Grade Children*. New York: Oxford University Press.

7. Iversen, S., and W. Tunmer. 1993. "Phonological Processing Skills and the Reading Recovery Program." *Journal of Educational Psychology 85*, no 1: 112–126.

8. Bruce, D. J. 1964. "The Analysis of Word Sounds by Young Children." *British Journal of Educational Psychology 34* (June): 158–170.

9. Elbaum, B., S. Vaughn, M. T. Hughes, and S. W. Moody. 2000. "How Effective Are One-to-One Tutoring Programs in Reading for Elementary Students at Risk for Reading Failure? A Meta-analysis of the Intervention Research." *Journal of Educational Psychology 92*: 605–619.

10. Church, I. 1997. "Within-subject Experimental Analysis: A Guide for Students in Education." *State-of-the-Art Monograph 5*. New Zealand Association for Research in Education. Wellington: New Zealand Council for Education Research.

11. Clay, M. M. 2002. *Change over time in children's literacy development*. Portsmouth, NH: Heinemann.

12. Neuman, S. B. and S. McCormick. 1995. *Single-subject experimental research: Applications for literacy*. Newark, DE: International Reading Association.

# About the Authors

**Nancy Anderson** is an Assistant Professor and Reading Recovery trainer of teacher leaders at Texas Woman's University. Her areas of inquiry include early writing development, teacher education, and early intervention.

**Jane Ashdown** is clinical associate professor in New York University's Department of Teaching and Learning in the Steinhardt School of Education. In addition, she chairs the department's committee for the continuing professional education of teachers and directs the Ruth Horowitz Center for Teacher Development. The center brings together several field-based projects that focus on teacher professional development such as Reading Recovery. Her research interests are teacher professional development and decision-making for resource allocation in educational contexts.

**Billie J. Askew** is professor emerita in the Department of Reading at Texas Woman's University. She has worked in the field of literacy as a classroom teacher, reading specialist, special educator, administrator, and teacher educator. Professional interests include early literacy and the prevention of literacy difficulties. Her commitments to comprehensive literacy efforts in schools have been influenced by her work in Reading Recovery and in classroom literacy projects. She is past president of the Reading Recovery Council of North America and the North American Trainers Group.

**Christine Boocock** is a Reading Recovery trainer at the National Reading Recovery Centre, Auckland College of Education, Auckland, New Zealand. She became involved in Reading Recovery in 1983 after several years working as a primary school teacher. Trained first as a teacher, then as a tutor and a trainer, she has worked with Reading Recovery in the United Kingdom, Canada, the United States, Australia, and New Zealand. Christine is the New Zealand representative on the Executive Board of the International Trainers Organization. Research described in this publication was conducted while completing a postgraduate degree at the University of Auckland. She is currently engaged in research on the use of different text types in guided reading in the classroom.

**Jean F. Bussell** served as executive director of the Reading Recovery Council of North America (RRCNA) from 1996 to 2003. Her leadership helped build RRCNA to nearly 11,000 members by her retirement in 2003. Her interest in leadership was reflected in the research study published in this volume on the role of the teacher leader in Reading Recovery. Before coming to RRCNA she served in several leadership positions including Deputy Director of the Ohio Student Aid Commission, Executive Director of the Ohio Council of Community Mental

Health Agencies, founder of the Southwest Community Mental Health Center (now known as Netcare, Inc.), and President of the Junior League of Columbus. She is a life member of the Ohio Wesleyan University Board of Trustees.

**Kathy Escamilla** is a faculty member at University of Colorado at Boulder where she teaches graduate courses in bilingual and multicultural education and is involved in teacher preparation throughout the Southwest. She has taught 30 years in the field of bilingual education from preschool to university levels. Maintaining an active research agenda, she is currently involved in research related to Descubriendo la Lectura (Reading Recovery in Spanish), a first-grade reading intervention designed to assist Spanish-speaking students who are struggling in their acquisition of literacy in classrooms where the primary literacy instruction is delivered in Spanish. Her most recent articles in bilingual education are published in *The Power of Two Languages: Literacy and Biliteracy for Spanish-Speaking Students* and *The Bilingual Research Journal.*

**Dianne Frasier** currently works as a Reading Recovery teacher leader in Fort Bend Independent School District, Sugar Land, Texas. Her teaching experiences include first-grade classroom and Reading Recovery students, teachers, and teacher leaders. She also has worked as an early literacy consultant for Harris County Department of Education in Houston and as a trainer of teacher leaders for Texas Woman's University in Denton, Texas.

**Susan King Fullerton** is a Reading Recovery trainer of teacher leaders at The Ohio State University where she teaches graduate courses in literacy education. Susan is a former Reading Recovery teacher, Title I staff development facilitator, and teacher of the hearing impaired. She has conducted research and published several articles and book chapters in the fields of Reading Recovery, learning and instruction, and education of the Deaf.

**Janet S. Gaffney** is an associate professor of special education at the University of Illinois at Urbana-Champaign. Her research focuses on high-impact interventions for students who are not making adequate progress in reading and writing and on the continued professional development of teachers. She has teaching and administrative experience in Title I and special education and was a Reading Recovery University Trainer for eight years. Recent publications include a chapter in the *Handbook of Reading Research, Vol. III* and two coedited books, *Stirring the Waters: The Influence of Marie Clay* and *Chinese Children's Reading Acquisition: Theoretical And Pedagogical Issues.*

**J. William Hortman** is the associate superintendent for administration, technology, and information for the Muscogee County School District (MCSD) in Columbus, Georgia. He has a strong background in training and experience in measurement, statistics, educational research, and program evaluation. He assisted in the implementation and evaluation of a three-year Reading Recovery project in 34 elementary schools in MCSD.

**Clifford I. Johnson** is a trainer of teacher leaders and the executive director of the Reading Recovery and Literacy Collaborative programs at Georgia State University. His career in early literacy expands over the past 40 years as a classroom teacher and a university professor. He came to Reading Recovery following his post-doctoral training at The Ohio State University during 1990–1991. He served on the Board of Directors since the founding of the Reading Recovery Council of North America through 2002. He has been vice president, president-elect and president of RRCNA. His research and teaching interests include early literacy and the prevention of literacy difficulties in young children.

**Elizabeth Kaye** currently works as a trainer of Reading Recovery teacher leaders and member of the Department of Reading at Texas Woman's University in Denton, Texas. Prior to joining the university, she taught elementary students in special education, Reading Recovery, and the classroom. Her research interests include the exploration of change over time in young students' literacy learning and early intervention.

**Patricia R. Kelly** is a professor in the College of Education at San Diego State University. She is a Reading Recovery trainer of teacher leaders and the director of the Reading Recovery program. Her interests in early literacy began when she worked as an elementary teacher and reading specialist. She has conducted research and published articles on early intervention, reader response, teacher development, effective classroom practices in literacy, and Reading Recovery in numerous journals including *The Reading Teacher, The Journal of Reading, Reading and Writing Quarterly, The Journal of Reading Recovery, The Journal of Reading Behavior,* and *Literacy, Teaching and Learning / An International Journal of Early Literacy.*

**Martha Loera-Olivas** is a doctoral student at the University of Colorado at Boulder. She holds a Master's of Arts degree in Curriculum and Instruction with an emphasis in Secondary Science from the University of Colorado at Denver, and a Bachelor of Arts majoring in Biology from the same institution. She was a bilingual science teacher prior to pursuing her doctoral studies.

**Carol A. Lyons** is professor emerita at The Ohio State University in Columbus, Ohio. She has published numerous articles and book chapters in the fields of reading, learning and reading disability, teacher learning, and the neuropsychology of reading. She is the author of *Teaching Struggling Readers: How to Use Brain-Based Research to Maximize Learning* and the coauthor of three books: *Partners in Learning: Teachers and Children in Reading Recovery, Bridges to Literacy: Learning From Reading Recovery,* and *Systems for Change in Literacy Education: A*

*Guide to Professional Development.* She is the U.S. representative to the International Reading Recovery Trainers Organization and past president of the Reading Recovery Council of North America.

**Chris Marvin** is an associate professor in the Department of Special Education and Communication Disorders at the University of Nebraska-Lincoln. She directs the graduate teacher preparation program in early childhood special education. Her professional training included elementary education and speech-language pathology in addition to early childhood education issues and practices. Her research in literacy issues includes a series of studies that explored the home literacy experiences of children with various disabilities during their preschool years. Her other research interests include the study of home and school contexts on preschool children's talk and the child's use of decontextualized talk in these settings.

**Michael C. McKenna** is Professor of Education at Georgia Southern University where he teaches graduate classes in Reading Diagnosis and Instruction and conducts research. He was a secondary school teacher prior to receiving his doctoral degree from the University of Missouri at Columbia. He has authored or coauthored nine books and more than 70 articles, chapters, and technical reports on a range of literacy topics. His work has been published in journals such as *Reading Research Quarterly, Journal of Educational Psychology*, and *Journal of Literacy Research*. His recent books include *Help for Struggling Readers* (2002) and *Reading Assessment: Strategies and Resources for the Classroom and Clinic* (2003) with Steven Stahl. His research interests include children's attitudes toward reading, comprehension strategies, and word recognition in beginning reading.

**Stuart McNaughton** is a professor of education and director of the Woolf Fisher Research Centre at the University of Auckland in New Zealand. His research and teaching interests are in developmental and educational psychology, focusing on the development of language and literacy, and processes of education, socialization and culture. Publications include books on reading and emergent literacy and papers on aspects of teaching, learning, and development in both family and school settings. Current research involves literacy and language programs and enhancing the transition to school for diverse school populations.

**Mohsen Mobasher** is an assistant professor of anthropology and sociology at University of Houston-Downtown. He has been involved with Reading Recovery at Texas Woman's University since January 2000 as a research associate.

**Judith Chibante Neal** is a professor of literacy and early education at California State University, Fresno. Her areas of specialty are literacy interventions and assessment. During 10 years of service in Reading Recovery, she has served in several capacities including editor of *The Running Record: A Review of Theory and Practice for Reading Recovery Teachers*, founding editor of *The Journal of Reading Recovery*, and president of the Reading Recovery North American Trainers Group. Dr. Neal speaks and writes on topics related to teaching high-risk early readers.

She has published in several journals including *Journal of Reading* (now *Journal of Adolescent and Adult Literacy*), *Reading and Writing Quarterly*, and *Literacy Teaching and Learning: An International Journal of Early Reading and Writing*.

**Judy M. Parr** is a senior lecturer in the Research Centre for Interventions in Teaching and Learning in the School of Education at the University of Auckland, New Zealand. Her research and teaching is focused in cognitive and developmental psychology, including the development of literacy, particularly writing. Recent articles appear in *Language Arts, The Reading Teacher,* and the *International Journal of Educational Research.* Current research projects include designing assessment tools for teaching and learning in writing, examining effective practice in the use of ready-made literacy materials, and evaluating a national literacy leadership initiative in elementary schools.

**Russell Quaglia** is the executive director of the Global Institute for Student Aspirations at Endicott College and a professor of education. He travels extensively presenting research-based information on student aspirations and motivation to audiences throughout the United States and around the world. His opinions and comments on aspirations and controversial educational topics have been published in national media outlets. Quaglia's research has been published in numerous professional journals such as *Research in Rural Education, Educational Administration Quarterly, Journal of Instructional Psychology, American School Board Journal, Adolescence,* and the *Journal of Psychological and Educational Measurement,* as well as in popular family and parent magazines.

**Lorene C. Quay**, professor emerita, continues to work and conduct research in the Department of Early Childhood Education at Georgia State University. Prior to her retirement she was a university research professor. She has published extensively in the areas of child development and early education.

**Anne K. Rhodes-Kline** is the Assistant Director, Applied Research and Methods Team at the United States General Accounting Office, the audit, evaluation, and investigative arm of Congress. She provides research and methodological advice to a variety of GAO products across topics including natural resources and the environment, justice issues, education and social services, and government management and oversight. Prior to joining the GAO in 1997, she directed and conducted research related to early literacy initiatives for the state of Maine, including program evaluation of the Reading Recovery program. She earned her Ph.D. in psychology from Temple University in 1994.

**Yvonne G. Rodríguez** is an assistant professor in the Department of Reading at Texas Woman's University as well as a university trainer for Reading Recovery and Descubriendo la Lectura teacher leaders and trainers. Her teaching experiences encompass special education, bilingual education, and reading. With her bilingual background, she was instrumental in the development of Descubriendo la Lectura, the reconstruction of Reading Recovery for Spanish-speaking children whose initial literacy instruction is being delivered in Spanish. Her research interests involve assessment of bilingual students, Spanish literacy acquisition, oral language as it relates to literacy, and working with the adult learner.

**Olivia Ruiz** retired from the Tucson Unified School District after 27 years as a bilingual classroom teacher, project specialist, and reading teacher. During that time, she participated in the development and implementation of bilingual education materials ranging from assessment and evaluation to content and curriculum. She was trained as a Reading Recovery teacher leader at Texas Woman's University and is one of the original authors of the reconstruction in Spanish of Reading Recovery and the Spanish Observation Survey. Following the development of *Descubriendo la Lectura* and *El Instrumento de Observación*, she trained teachers and teacher leaders nationally in its implementation. With the support of Dr. Marie Clay, she presented the Spanish reconstruction of Reading Recovery at the International World Congress of Reading in Buenos Aires, Argentina.

**Ognjen Simic** is an associate research scientist at the New York University's Reading Recovery Project, where he coordinates program evaluation activities in affiliated school districts and collaborates with project staff on research studies in the field of early literacy intervention. He is working on a doctoral thesis at Fordham University's Psychometric program in the area of multilevel modeling. Current research projects on Reading Recovery include studies of the program's impact on special education referrals and placement, the program's potential to close the achievement gap among students, and the study of long-term effects of Reading Recovery in New York City schools.

**Katherine A.D. Stahl** was a Reading Recovery teacher for four years as part of a 25-year career of teaching in elementary and middle schools. She received her master's and sixth-year degrees from Georgia Southern University and is currently a doctoral candidate at the University of Georgia and teaches undergraduate methods classes at the University of Illinois at Urbana-Champaign. She continues to work privately with children who have reading problems. Her research interests are in teaching comprehension to primary grade students, word study and spelling instruction in the early grades, and fluency development. She can be reached at kaystahl@uiuc.edu.

**Steven A. Stahl** is currently professor in the Department of Curriculum and Instruction at the University of Illinois at Urbana-Champaign. Prior to receiving his doctorate in reading education from Harvard Graduate School of Education, he taught children with reading problems. He directed the reading clinic at the University of Georgia and is in the process of beginning a clinic at Illinois. He is the author of more than 100 journal articles and book chapters and has written or edited a number of books and monographs including *Vocabulary Development* (1999) and *On Reading Stories to Children: Parents and Teachers* (2003). He has a long-standing interest in early reading and vocabulary development. He can be reached at sstahl@uiuc.edu.

# *About RRCNA*

## Literacy Teaching and Learning: An International Journal of Early Reading and Writing

*Literacy Teaching and Learning: An International Journal of Early Reading and Writing* is a scholarly journal that provides an interdisciplinary forum on issues related to language acquisition, literacy development, and instructional theory and practice. The journal publishes original contributions that reflect multiple perspectives and research paradigms from disciplines such as child development, linguistics, literacy education, psychology, public policy, sociology, special education, and teacher education.

Contributions may include:

- reports of empirical research
- theoretical interpretations of research
- reports of program evaluation and effective practice
- critical reviews, responses, and analyses of key conceptual, historical, and research perspectives.

Manuscripts representing diverse methodologies including ethnographic, empirical, and case study research are encouraged.

The Reading Recovery Council of North America (RRCNA) publishes *Literacy Teaching and Learning* but studies need not be related to Reading Recovery to be considered for publication. The journal is published twice annually.

## The Reading Recovery Council of North America

The Reading Recovery Council of North America (RRCNA) is the professional home for the Reading Recovery community. The Council's members work *to achieve a common mission: to ensure access to Reading Recovery for every child who needs its support.* The Council's nearly 11,000 members represent five member categories: teachers, teacher leaders, trainers, site coordinators, and partners.

The Council supports its members by offering information, services, and products including:

**Web site:** www.readingrecovery.org. The RRCNA website is the information hub for Reading Recovery, updated frequently with the latest information about Reading Recovery, its implementation, conference and training opportunities, advocacy and funding news. Contact information for RRCNA board, staff, university trainers, and teacher leaders is also available on the Web site.

**Conferences and Professional Development.** RRCNA provides continuing education opportunities for Reading Recovery trained professionals, schools administrators, and early literacy teachers. Thousands attend one of the regularly scheduled conferences— The Reading Recovery and Early Literacy Conference, the North American Leadership Academy, and the Teacher Leader Institute.

**Products and Publications.** RRCNA offers a variety of publications including two academic journals, *Literacy Teaching and Learning: An International Journal of Early Reading and Writing*, and a practitioner's journal, *The Journal of Reading Recovery*. The RRCNA Web site lists many of the publications and products available.

**Advocacy.** RRCNA promotes government support for Reading Recovery in two ways: advocacy at the federal level and technical assistance to state and local Reading Recovery implementations. By monitoring and working to impact federal legislation, regulations, and research on reading, RRCNA maintains and enhances access to federal funding and support. RRCNA also provides information and professional development opportunities to help supporters become effective advocates at state and local levels.

**Teacher Leader Registry.** RRCNA maintains a current registry of all active Reading Recovery and Descubriendo La Lectura teacher leaders. Registry status is determined by the teacher leader's affiliated university training center and is based on compliance with RRCNA standards for trained teacher leaders. The registry is available through the Web site, www.readingrecovery.org.

**Development and Scholarships.** The Reading Recovery Fund is a charitable program of the Reading Recovery Council of North America. It was created to raise dollars to help advance early literacy through the expansion of Reading Recovery. The Reading Recovery Fund and RRCNA's development activities program have helped to fund over 30 teacher leader training scholarships, nearly 30 conference attendees scholarships, four Reading Recovery trainer training grants, and several small research grants for important research.

**Support for North American Trainers Group.** RRCNA provides staff and financial support for the North American Trainers Group, an organization whose membership includes all Reading Recovery university trainers from the United States and Canada. The group provides leadership and high quality continuous learning for Reading Recovery educators and oversees research, standards, and guidelines that help to ensure consistent quality implementation.

---

**The Reading Recovery Council of North America**

*Vision*

That children will be proficient readers and writers by the end of first grade.

*Mission*

To ensure access to Reading Recovery for every child who needs its support.

*Purpose*

To sustain the integrity of Reading Recovery and expand its implementation by increasing the number of individuals who understand, support, and collaborate to achieve the mission of the Council.

---

For more information about Reading Recovery research, visit the research section of the Web site for the Reading Recovery Council of North America, www.readingrecovery.org

Reading Recovery®Council
of North America